I0086003

DEMOCRATIC MARXISM

DEMOCRATIC MARXISM SERIES

Series Editor: Vishwas Satgar

The crisis of Marxism in the late twentieth century was the crisis of orthodox and vanguardist Marxism associated mainly with hierarchical communist parties, and which was imposed – even as state ideology – as the 'correct' Marxism. The Stalinisation of the Soviet Union and its eventual collapse exposed the inherent weaknesses and authoritarian mould of vanguardist Marxism. More fundamentally, vanguardist Marxism was rendered obsolete but for its residual existence in a few parts of the world, including authoritarian national liberation movements in Africa and in China.

With the deepening crises of capitalism, a new democratic Marxism (or democratic historical materialism) is coming to the fore. Such a democratic Marxism is characterised in the following ways:
- Its sources span non-vanguardist grassroots movements, unions, political fronts, mass parties, radical intellectuals, transnational activist networks and the progressive academy;
- It seeks to ensure that the inherent categories of Marxism are theorised within constantly changing historical conditions to find meaning;
- Marxism is understood as a body of social thought that is unfinished and hence challenged by the need to explain the dynamics of a globalising capitalism and the futures of social change;
- It is open to other forms of anti-capitalist thought and practice, including currents within radical ecology, feminism, emancipatory utopianism and indigenous thought;
- It does not seek to be a monolithic and singular school of thought but engenders contending perspectives;
- Democracy, as part of the heritage of people's struggles, is understood as the basis for articulating alternatives to capitalism and as the primary means for constituting a transformative subject of historical change.

This series seeks to elaborate the social theorising and politics of democratic Marxism.

CAPITALISM'S CRISES

CRISES

CLASS STRUGGLES IN SOUTH AFRICA AND THE WORLD

CAPITALISM'S CRISES

CLASS STRUGGLES IN SOUTH AFRICA AND THE WORLD

Editor: Vishwas Satgar

WITS UNIVERSITY PRESS

Published in South Africa by:

Wits University Press
1 Jan Smuts Avenue
Johannesburg, 2001
www.witspress.co.za

Compilation © Vishwas Satgar 2015
Chapters © Individual contributors 2015
Published edition © Wits University Press 2015

First published 2015

978-1-86814-920-9 (print)
978-1-86814-926-1 (PDF)
978-1-86814-924-7 (EPUB: North America, South America, China)
978-1-86814-925-4 (EPUB: Rest of world)

All rights reserved. No part of this publication may be reproduced, stored in a retrieval system, or transmitted in any form or by any means, electronic, mechanical, photocopying, recording or otherwise, without the written permission of the publisher, except in accordance with the provisions of the Copyright Act, Act 98 of 1978.

Edited by Liz Mackenzie and Mark Ronan
Proofread by Lee Smith
Index by Clifford Perusset
Cover design by Farm Design
Book Design by Hothouse South Africa
Book layout and typesetting by Farm Design

ACKNOWLEDGEMENTS

This volume owes a special debt to the Rosa Luxemburg Foundation. Without their support it would have been impossible to hold a contributors' workshop in South Africa and to ensure that the manuscript was developed sufficiently for publication. We are also grateful to the support given by Athish Satgoor and Andrew Bennie, organisers at the Cooperative and Policy Alternative Centre (COPAC), who played a central role in organising the workshop convened with contributors and activists from various social movements, including worker leaders involved in building the National Union of Metalworkers-led United Front. Special thanks also goes to Kathryn Joynt who assisted with a language and citation edit and Professor Michelle Williams who gave feedback on the manuscript. Finally, special thanks to the team at Wits University Press, particularly Veronica Klipp, Roshan Cader and Corina van der Spoel for supporting this volume and the Democratic Marxism Series.

CONTENTS

ACKNOWLEDGEMENTS   vii

TABLES AND FIGURES   xi

ACRONYMS AND ABBREVIATIONS   xii

INTRODUCTION Vishwas Satgar   1

PART ONE: CONTEMPORARY UNDERSTANDINGS OF CAPITALISM'S
             CRISES AND CLASS STRUGGLE   19

CHAPTER 1:   From Marx to the systemic crises of capitalist civilisation   20
             Vishwas Satgar

CHAPTER 2:   Activist understandings of the crisis   50
             William K Carroll

PART TWO: CAPITALIST CRISIS AND LEFT RESPONSES IN THE
             GLOBAL NORTH   77

CHAPTER 3:   Occupy and the dialectics of the Left in the United States   78
             Leah Hunt-Hendrix and Isham Christie

CHAPTER 4:   Austerity and resistance: The politics of labour in the Eurozone
             crisis   97
             Andreas Bieler and Jamie Jordan

CHAPTER 5:   Beyond social-democratic and communist parties: Left political
             organisation in transition in Western Europe   123
             Hilary Wainwright

PART THREE: CAPITALIST CRISIS AND LEFT RESPONSES IN THE
             GLOBAL SOUTH   165

CHAPTER 6:   Brazil: From neoliberal democracy to the end of the
             'Lula moment'   166
             Alfredo Saad-Filho

CHAPTER 7: The global financial crisis and 'resilience': The case of India   189
            Sumangala Damodaran

CHAPTER 8: Understanding the labour crisis in South Africa: Real wage
            trends and the minerals–energy complex economy   211
            Niall Reddy

CHAPTER 9: Seize power! The role of the constitution in uniting a struggle for
            social justice in South Africa   245
            Mark Heywood

CONCLUSION Vishwas Satgar   277
CONTRIBUTORS   284
INDEX   287

TABLES AND FIGURES

Table 2.1   Groups participating in study of cognitive praxis networks   57
Table 8.1   Real wage growth rates, all workers, 1997–2011 (%)   218
Table 8.2   Union coverage, formal-sector employees, 2001–2012   232
Figure 8.1 Real mean monthly wages, 1997–2011   216
Figure 8.2 Real monthly earnings trends for all workers, 1997–2011   217
Figure 8.3 Per cent change in real monthly earnings, 1997–2011
          (2011 prices)   219
Figure 8.4 Real wage patterns for different skill categories classified
          by occupation   220
Figure 8.5 Distribution of the workforce, 2001–2011   229

ACRONYMS AND ABBREVIATIONS

ANC	African National Congress
ARVs	anti-retrovirals
BJP	Bharatiya Janata Party
BNDES	Brazilian Development Bank
BRICS	Brazil, Russia, India, China and South Africa
CALS	Centre for Applied Legal Studies
COPAC	Cooperative and Policy Alternative Center
Cosatu	Congress of South African Trade Unions
CRID	Research and Information Centre for Development
DAWN	Development Alternatives with Women for a New Era
DGB	Confederation of German Trade Unions
DPD	domestic public debt
ECB	European Central Bank
ECB	external commercial borrowings
ECI	European Citizens' Initiative
EE	Equal Education
EFF	Economic Freedom Fighters
EMF	European Metalworkers' Federation
EMU	Economic and Monetary Union
EPSU	European Federation of Public Service Unions
ETUC	European Trade Union Confederation
EU	European Union
FDI	foreign direct investment
FII	foreign indirect investment
GDP	gross domestic product
GLC	Greater London Council
ICT	information and communications technology
IFG	International Forum on Globalization
IFIs	international financial institutions
IMF	International Monetary Fund
ISI	import substitution industrialisation
LAT	labour aristocracy thesis
LRC	Legal Resources Centre
MEC	minerals–energy complex
MST	The Landless Peasants' Movement
NATO	North Atlantic Treaty Organisation
NCEUS	National Commission for Enterprises in the Unorganised Sector

NDP	National Development Plan
NDR	National Democratic Revolution
NEP	New Economic Policies
NGO	non-governmental organisation
NUM	National Union of Mineworkers
Numsa	National Union of Metalworkers of South Africa
OECD	Organisation for Economic Co-operation and Development
OWS	Occupy Wall Street
PAH	Mortgage Victims Platform
PALMS	Post-Apartheid Labour Market Survey
PASOK	Panhellenic Socialist Movement
PBF	Bolsa Família
PRC	Rifondazione Comunista (Communist Party, Italy)
PRIA	Participatory Research in Asia
PSDB	Partido da Social Democracia Brasileira
PT	Workers' Party
QES	Quarterly Employment Survey
RBI	Reserve Bank of India
RosaLux	Rosa Luxemburg Foundation
SACP	South African Communist Party
SAHRC	South African Human Rights Commission
SBTC	skill-biased technological change
SDS	Students for a Democratic Society
SGP	Stability and Growth Pact
SER	standard employment relationship
SERI	Socio-Economic Rights Institute of South Africa
SOEs	state-owned enterprises
SV	Socialist Left Party
TAC	Treatment Action Campaign
TAPGs	Transnational Alternative Policy Groups
TNI	Transnational Institute
TTIP	Transatlantic Trade and Investment Partnership
UDF	United Democratic Front
UK	United Kingdom
UN	United Nations
US	United States
USSR	Soviet Union
WSF	World Social Forum
WTO	World Trade Organization

INTRODUCTION

Vishwas Satgar

U ntil recently, the Great Depression of the 1930s was considered the worst crisis of capitalism. Today, historians, economists and the business media have confirmed that we are now experiencing the worst crisis of contemporary capitalism. The early-twentieth-century Great Depression seems to pale in comparison to the 'great financial crisis' that occurred at the beginning of the twenty-first century. Despite the massive bailouts given to banks and finance houses, deepening austerity in the heartlands of capitalism and a tenuous continuity in growth rates in countries like China and India, the end of the crisis is not in sight. This, of course, does not mean capitalism is about to collapse – but it is certainly in a state of deepening crisis and will probably reach a historical terminus, like all social systems before it.

However, this volume does not attempt to make catastrophic predictions, but instead sets out to explain and provide an understanding of the unfolding crisis by bringing into view its underlying dynamics.

With such a deep systemic and conjunctural crisis facing neoliberal capitalism, both in South Africa and beyond, one would intuitively expect the Left to be on the rise and gaining ground. Yet there seems to be an unevenness regarding effective left-wing responses to the crisis. In most instances, trade unions, social movements and left-wing parties seem to be advancing responses that are incapable of bridging the gulf between the current realities and popular expectations of progressive transformation, such as employment creation and less inequality. The weaknesses and advances of the Left in response to the current context are critically assessed in this volume.

By applying a rigorous Marxist (and neo-Marxist) political-economic analysis of the contemporary capitalist crisis and the Left's response to it, this volume confronts some of the inherited weaknesses of Marxist theoretical approaches to capitalist crises. The first weakness, according to Lilley (2012: 44), can be referred to as the 'vanguardist' dyad of structural determinism, on the one hand, and voluntarism on the other.[1] Structural-determinist approaches give primacy to the 'laws of history' and the limits of the capitalist system (or the internal weight of its own contradictions). Voluntarist approaches tend to emphasise greater suffering and worsening conditions, and ultimately argue that state repression will reveal the essence of the capitalist crisis. Put differently, neither approach takes account of the connection between capitalist crisis and the challenging task of building democratic, mass-movement-driven politics. The second weakness is how conceptions of capitalist crisis are inserted into struggle. Both of these approaches propagandise capitalist crisis to such an extent that theoretical analysis is used as an instrument to affirm that history is on the side of the working class and therefore an automatic awakening of consciousness is meant to follow. Yet nowhere has this panned out in actual history or struggle.

Furthermore, both of these approaches tend to guide practice in particular ways. A structuralist approach tends to abstain from struggle, whereas a voluntarist approach arrogantly proclaims its need to make history now by accelerating collapse or crisis through adventurist intervention.

In this volume the authors seek to confront these weaknesses of orthodox vanguardist Marxist theory and its practical political conclusions. In the process, the book seeks to go beyond twentieth-century communist and social-democratic understandings of the crisis. Instead, the volume raises democratic Marxist perspectives on the crisis, and looks at contemporary left agency and the need for transformative politics, rather than vanguardist revolutionary or reformist left politics. This volume therefore takes forward themes that are referred to but not fully elaborated in Volume 1 in this series, titled *Marxisms in the 21st Century*. The first volume provided a research agenda and suggested lines of development for democratic Marxism. In this volume, by elaborating on the themes of capitalist crisis and class struggle, the authors affirm the need for open, engaged and living Marxism in relation to contemporary realities of globalising capitalism. At the same time, such perspectives derive from activist scholars, activists engaged in movements and intellectuals from the Left.

None pretend to have all the answers or a monopoly on the truth, but they offer different ways of engaging with the vast historical corpus of Marxism, and provide new analyses of capitalist crisis, situated struggle perspectives and thoughts for strengthening democratic, bottom-up, left agency.

CRISES OF CONTEMPORARY CAPITALISM: SAME AS BEFORE OR UNPRECEDENTED?

Many observers of capitalism, including some on the Left (such as Marxist social democrats, revolutionary socialists or revolutionary nationalists), tend to understand capitalism as a durable social construct – a social system with permanence. In other words, despite cyclical moments of crisis in capitalism – booms and busts that are largely explained by overproduction or underconsumption – in the end, capitalism will adjust by marshalling a set of reforms to get out of the crisis. This view has three pitfalls, however. First, its proponents tend to believe that every crisis is the same. But this is not the case. Some crises of capitalism are cyclical but some are more generalised, which calls into question the accumulation model, state legitimacy and ruling-class strategies of control. Such general or systemic crises of capitalism are driven by their own historical, structural and class-struggle dynamics. In the history of capitalism, there have been three such crises: the first great depression (in the last quarter of the nineteenth century), the Great Depression of the 1930s and the so-called 'stagflation' crisis of the 1970s. According to Panitch and Gindin (2010: 4–5),

> the term 'crisis' is commonly used to refer to interruptions in the process of capital accumulation and growth … Of greater significance is that some such interruptions do not simply come and go, but take on a much larger dimension. So we need to ask not just why crises occur, but why some crises are distinct: why they last so long, are marked by persistent economic uncertainty and produce significant political and social change.

Eight years since the collapse of the US housing market and, subsequently, the US stock market, the global economy has not recovered from the financialised crisis. According to the International Monetary Fund (IMF), Europe is in a state of stagnation, with low inflation and weak credit threatening any attempts of recovery. Greece continues to be the epicentre of the crisis in Europe. Ukraine received a bailout to the sum of 17 billion euros but still requires further assistance. According to IMF Managing Director Christine Lagarde, the Eurozone crisis is far from over and Ukraine could destabilise the world economy (Wearden 2014). In this volume we look at the crisis in the Eurozone in terms of its underlying political-economic dynamics to understand what drives and what is reproducing the crisis. As for the US, modest economic recovery has begun, but the deep-seated inequalities that were foregrounded by the symbolic protest actions of the Occupy movement still haunt American society.

The big hope that economies in the global South would lead recovery in the global economy has also proven to be unfounded. Growth has slowed in the big global-South economies of China, India and Brazil, and in some cases this set in before the 2008 financial crisis. In this volume, the political economies of India and Brazil, and the limits of their versions of globalisation, are analysed. The economies of the global South face challenges from outward flows of finance and from the modest recovery in the US turning that country into a renewed destination for financial flows. In other words, countries in the global South are facing risks from fickle outward movements of finance, and there are strong predictions that financial contagion and turmoil could hit the global South (IMF 2014). Ironically, this is likely to happen despite the coordination and crisis-management role of leading global South economies through the G20.

As well as the long duration of the financial crisis and its widespread global impact, there are two crucial dimensions that accentuate its distinctiveness. First, the economic dimension of the crisis is underpinned by specific dynamics linked to the financialisation of the global economy. For example, the current economic crisis is not the same as the 1987 US stock-market crash as a result of junk bonds or the bursting of the dot.com bubble in 2000/01 because of overinflated values. This crisis, in contrast, has much deeper roots in the financialisation of the global economy. Transnational techno-financialised chaos, grounded in globalised and computer-linked financial markets, is now both endemic and a built-in structural feature of the global economy. Some refer to this as the global casino effect. These dynamics make the current crisis distinctive.

Second, the contemporary financialised crisis is also distinctive because it intersects with and engenders other dimensions of systemic crisis, including climate crisis, peak oil, food-system crisis and the securitisation of democracy.

Contemporary capitalism is experiencing an existential crisis that is historically unprecedented. The total effect of today's crisis of capitalism on civilisation reveals serious challenges and limits to the reproduction of capitalism, to
the extent that a mere reform of the system – in other words, producing more of
the same – will perpetuate a system that will destroy all human and non-human
life forms. Capitalism may not collapse, but it certainly has become the enemy
of planetary existence and it is incapable of resolving these incurable systemic
contradictions without bringing about its end.

In terms of reforming capitalism, the second pitfall is that this imbues the
capitalist class with ingenuity while at the same time reducing capitalism to a
naturalised social system. This largely derives from a veneration of scientific
progress, technological fixes and instrumental rationality. The allure of capitalist modernity looms large in this approach. A simplistic and deterministic
Marxist view converges with such a perspective, and argues that capitalism is
never on its last legs as long as there is room for further accumulation, profits
and technological innovation – in other words, as long as the march of the
forces of production can take place, then capitalism will survive. However,
given the deep systemic and unprecedented character of the contemporary
crises of capitalism, it is necessary to ask, can capital solve every crisis of capitalism so that it ensures the system survives? Whose interests are realised with
these capital-led solutions?

It is revealing that the lessons that capitalism learnt from the Great Depression
are still applied to fashion managerial strategies for the current crisis. According
to the 40th-anniversary edition of Charles P Kindleberger's book *The World in
Depression 1929–1939* ([1973] 2013), it is claimed that Lawrence Summers, a
White House advisor, turned to the writing of Kindleberger and his peers for
guidance in the dark hours of the 2008 crisis.[2] For DeLong and Eichengreen
(2013), who wrote the foreword to the 2013 edition of Kindleberger's classic,
the lessons from the book are informative: 'Three lessons stand out, the first
having to do with panic in financial markets, the second with the power of
contagion, and the third with the importance of hegemony.'[3]

However, even with this advice and the hegemonic stability role prescribed
for the US, the crisis has not abated. This has mainly to do with an intersection of the unprecedented dimensions of a crisis that is systemic, and not just
economic. Even if capital ostensibly asserts solutions, which currently really
means stabilising global capitalism, workers and the 'precariat' are squeezed
and they pay the price in the end. This has become patently clear during the

current crisis.

A third pitfall associated with the reform-of-capitalism perspective is its denial of class struggle to confront capitalism when it is in crisis and vulnerable. This is not just about fear of the unknown, a lack of political consciousness or the weaknesses of the vanguard. More importantly, it is about the failure to connect with and build in a democratic manner a mass-based transformative politics to champion alternatives. This failure is a reflection of the weaknesses of the reformist and vanguardist Left. At the same time, while the civilisational crises of capitalism deepen, mass consciousness veers towards catastrophism or denialism, and, ultimately, abstention from social transformation while capital merely reproduces the status quo of crisis-ridden neoliberal capitalism. With the unfolding of the 2008 crisis, capital has resorted to various strategies of crisis management to ensure it maintains the strategic initiative while rolling back counter-hegemonic agency.

In this regard, the role of passive revolution, a form of class rule that co-opts and incorporates the leadership of progressive social forces (state and non-state, working class and non-working class) is a crucial challenge for the Left (Gramsci [1971] 1998). This prompts the following questions: how do we break out of the trap of this interregnum, in which the old is dying but the new is not yet born? How do we shift the relations of force onto the side of the working class, the poor and landless to advance transformative politics? How should the Left strategically seize the opportunities of what is both an unprecedented but extremely dangerous systemic crisis? Or has the global passive revolution, albeit uneven, succeeded? This volume addresses these questions, rather than the question of how capitalism should be reformed.

CLASS STRUGGLE AND AGENCY OF THE LEFT

A cursory glance at the world today suggests that the Left is in a state of stasis. There is a deepening and intractable number of capitalist crises; the weaknesses of capital are visible; neoliberalism has failed; and there is an urgent need for alternatives. But where is the left agency to bring about transformative change? More importantly, where is the working class and the class struggle? A pessimistic answer to this question would suggest that the working class has been defeated and is exhausted. Ultimately, the Right has won – both the neoliberal and conservative–nationalist Right. This is a world order of only one paradigm, one solution, namely neoliberal capitalism, and there is no alternative. The workers, and the subaltern class more generally, exist in a post-revolutionary age and should succumb to the power of capital. For post-Marxists, this confirms a theoretical and philosophic postulate, namely that the revolutionary subject of history, the working class, is a spent force. Hence there is a need to find a new revolutionary subjectivity in the 'multitude' or in a post-class 'hegemonic construct'.

In this volume, however, there is no obituary or fashionable farewell to the working class or the class struggle. Instead, the authors seek to look closely at the actual pattern and historical manifestation of struggle in the contemporary world to come to terms with the character of the class struggle and left agency. In the twentieth century, three crucial class projects arose to challenge capitalism: Soviet socialism, revolutionary nationalism and social democracy (Amin 1995). Since the 1980s all three of these have been defeated by internal limits, the advance of transnational capital and the onslaught of the imperial neoliberal class project. The defeat of these class projects brought to an end an important cycle of global class struggle and shifted the balance of power to the side of capital. With over three and a half decades of neoliberalisation, a new countermovement of struggle has come to the fore to confront the social engineering of neoliberalism as a class project. This countermovement has entailed a cycle of global struggle against capitalism but it is very different from what has been before.

So, what is this cycle of struggle and what is different about it? The current cycle of resistance is marked by crucial anti-neoliberal struggles that began in Venezuela, with the Caracazo in 1989, a wave of mass protests against increases in the price of transportation and gasoline caused by neoliberalisation. Protests in and around Caracas, Venezuela's capital, lasted for about a week, and hundreds of protestors were killed by the police and military. This was a defining moment for Hugo Chávez, the democratic socialist who rose to become president of Venezuela. The cycle continued with the rise of the Zapatistas and the opposition to the North American Free Trade Agreement in 1994, the opposition to the World Trade Organization in 1999 in Seattle, and various other protests punctuating this cycle against organisations such as the IMF and the World Bank.

At the same time, this cycle of struggle is supported by four other crucial developments. First, transnational activism was strengthened with the formation of the World Social Forum in 2001. The forum has successfully brought together transnational and local civil-society forces that are resisting neoliberalism and attempting to develop post-neoliberal alternatives. It has evoked a democratic left imagination to make another world possible now.

Second, there has been a rise of the anti-neoliberal institutional left in Latin America. This was evident with the elections of Chávez in 1999, Lula in Brazil in 2002 and Evo Morales in Bolivia in 2006. These presidents gave momentum to a leftward shift in Latin America and the emergence of various centre-left and left governments across Latin America (for example, in Uruguay, Ecuador and Argentina). There are advances, contradictions and limits arising from this shift to the Left. Some commentators suggest that these political experiences and left projects are already exhausted, but nonetheless it is important to study and appreciate them as the first attempts at navigating or, in some cases, breaking away from neoliberal capitalism. Interestingly, many of the social movements that drove these institutional political shifts to the Left have not been displaced or disabled.

Third, the emergence of the so-called Arab Spring and the political revolutions in the Arab world have confronted authoritarian and neoliberal class forces. The politics of Egypt's Tahir Square movement gave confidence to a new kind of direct democracy and street politics among unemployed people's movements in Europe and various social forces in the US. For example, the events in Egypt in 2011 provided the international spark for the US Occupy movement and the more recent Hong Kong protests. The historical effect and the ferment of the Arab Spring is far from over, even in the Middle East.

Finally, the emergence of the Climate Justice Movement since 2004 has been crucial in the way it has influenced global awareness about the climate crisis. The movement has spawned key alternatives, such as the rights of nature, socially owned renewables and climate jobs, to the marketised solutions emerging in the UN climate negotiations. This movement is poised to grow as the climate crisis worsens, as indicated by the September 2014 New York climate march, in which over 400 000 people participated.

However, it is important to note that this cycle of global struggle and resistance is different from the twentieth-century cycle of struggle in four crucial respects. In the first instance, the working class is still present in the current cycle of global resistance but has been weakened dramatically in the context of neoliberal restructuring and the shift to globalised accumulation. In Europe the working class has been fighting defensive battles to retain the gains of social democracy. In the US the working class has not succeeded in confronting stagnating wages and deep income inequalities. Across the global South, workers have been squeezed by liberalisation and the push downwards in labour standards as a result of China's low-wage manufacturing economy. Essentially, the Fordist social contract has ended, as greater precariatisation has taken root in labour markets across the world and the institutional power of unions has been weakened. However, the rebuilding of unionism, solidarity and the capacity for struggle among workers' organisations is a major challenge in the current cycle of global resistance. This volume brings this imperative to the fore from various experiences of class and left struggle.

The second difference is that the class structures of most twentieth-century societies were conditioned by Fordist import substitution industrialisation and its attendant international trade relations. However, over the past few decades, neoliberal restructuring has changed the class structure of societies. Class as a social and ideological/political process is being remade from above and below. Traditional forms of monopoly capital are restructuring and deconcentrating in light of global competition, while new fractions of capital linked to financialisation and globalisation are being constituted. Hence, the class forces championing crisis-ridden neoliberalised capitalism and marketised solutions are becoming transnational. Their political positioning and alignments in the context of the crises of capitalism need to be clearly unpacked. Are their interests served by national capitalism or transnational capitalism? Left projects that have tried to win over national capital are showing serious limits in the context of transnationalising capitalism. This is demonstrated in the chapters on Brazil and India in this volume. Class is also being remade from below. Fractions of the working class are coming to the fore, some more precariously than others, and some outside the labour market as a permanent reserve army of labour of the unemployed and the landless. The youth character of the working class is also accentuated in particular national contexts. In some societies the process of 'de-peasantisation' is proceeding through violence and dispossession. This volume brings into view these various class-formation dynamics.

The third difference is that, in the twentieth century, vanguards proliferated: Soviet, social-democratic or revolutionary-nationalist vanguards. Class politics then was about aggregating interests of workers or peasants, or multi-class alliances within such political forms. At the same time, a political line and imagination was diffused from the centres of these ideological projects. In some instances, international movements transmitted mechanistic politics, while in others capital cities loomed large, such as Havana, Moscow and Beijing. In the end, vanguardism capitulated to neoliberalism and workers were betrayed. In contrast to this history of vanguards, today the political forms coming to the fore to champion alternatives to capitalism are diverse and include transnational think tanks, workers' parties, anti-systemic movements, parties of the unemployed, unions and other political entities. No single political group has the monopoly on how the class struggle should be fought and how the Left should advance. This diversity of left agency has also thrown up a challenge for how political instruments are constituted to aggregate different types of social power. Hence we have entered the era of building democratic political forms, such as fronts, alliances, networks, mass party movements and mass movements – all with a transnational dimension and a diversity in their institutional and social forces. This is largely what characterises the new form of political instruments emerging to challenge state power and advance alternatives. This volume brings this phenomenon to the fore in a number of chapters.

Finally, twentieth-century resistance was bedevilled by model thinking, with a strong tendency to copy dominant models, such as centralised planning and the one-party state. In the current cycle of resistance, however, there is a more open way of approaching alternatives to capitalism. This is partly a function of the multifaceted nature of the crises of capitalism. Transnational movements that challenge neoliberalism, whether on food, climate, cyber freedom or the labour front, are all articulating alternatives. Some are more transformative than others, but it nonetheless affirms that the power for change lies with a plurality of left forces. Moreover, every society and context has its own challenges, despite the common reach and presence of the crises of global capitalism. Each context therefore demands different responses from the Left in terms of regionalisation, national development strategies, macro-economic policy and transformation from below. In Latin America, for example, the countries that have moved to the Left are not uniform. Some have tried to add a social dimension to neoliberalism and some have tried to break with it completely. All of these experiences create important strategic lessons. At the same time, such contextual differences caution one against crudely attempting to transplant a 'Lula moment' into, for example, South Africa. This volume underlines this new aspect to left agency in the world today: alternatives for the Left are advanced in their context and translated in a manner that is informed by local realities, political traditions and dynamics of class formation. Of course, this approach does not diminish the importance of learning critically from other experiences and advancing international solidarity.

DEMOCRATIC MARXIST PERSPECTIVES: THE CONJUNCTURE OF CAPITALIST CRISES AND TRANSFORMATIVE RESISTANCE

Part 1 of this volume focuses on contemporary understandings of capitalism's crises.

In Chapter 1, Vishwas Satgar confronts the limitations of classical Marxist theory for understanding the contemporary capitalist crisis. He offers a reading of Marx to understand how Marx thought about the crisis tendencies of capitalism and examines the different conceptions of crisis present in Marx's work. In some of his work before *Capital*, Marx tended to exaggerate the prospects for breakdown or collapse. However, Satgar argues that Marx did not have a single or even a systematic theory of crisis, even at the level of abstract and pure capitalism.

The chapter sets out the limits of Marx's understanding of the tendencies for capitalist crisis. The aim is not to reject Marx, but to find new openings and ways forward for thinking about contemporary capitalist crises. Although Marx abstracted his categories about the workings of the capitalist mode of production, he was grappling with the historical dynamics of a competitive mid-Victorian industrial capitalism, which is different from contemporary transnationalising techno-financial accumulation. Moreover, given that we are dealing with crises in the plural, at a systemic level and on a world scale, which capitalist historical form is in crisis? This poses a challenge for how we think about periodising historical capitalism. This chapter argues for the periodisation of 'capitalist civilisation' not only as the basis to understand its main characteristics, but also to understand the scale at which the systemic crises of capitalism are manifest.

The chapter also looks at how capitalism's tendencies for systemic crisis are rooted structurally, institutionally and ideologically in US imperial power and transnational class-based practices. The chapter concludes with the challenges confronting left agency today by responding to the question: catastrophism or transformative moment? In answering this question, there is an attempt to identify challenges and requirements for a new type of transformative left agency to sustain life.

In Chapter 2, William K Carroll investigates activist understandings of the crises of capitalism through neo-Gramscian political economy. He asks the following questions: how do movement intellectuals and activist researchers associated with the production and mobilisation of counter-hegemonic knowledge view the crisis? And what can we learn from their reflections? This chapter addresses these questions on the basis of interviews with 91 activist intellectuals in 16 transnational alternative policy groups.

Carroll unpacks Gramsci's notion of organic crisis in his engagements with movement intellectuals. Many of the reflections shared by them add substance to a dialectical conception of crisis as objective and subjective, as disintegration and re-formation, as passive revolution and anti-passive revolution. There is a translation of Gramsci at work that recognises that contemporary structural contradictions are 'incurable', thus shifting relations of force away from neoliberal hegemony towards a new conjuncture while rendering the course of history open. Many movement intellectuals show an acute awareness of radical contingency, of various aspects of organic crisis, and of the fierce challenges they face in building a counter-hegemonic bloc in a non-vanguardist manner. This also means organising in ways that reach beyond problematic currents in contemporary activism.

Part 2 of the volume focuses on capitalist crises in the global North and the Left's responses to them.

Three years into the crisis that began in 2008, the world's imagination was suddenly captured by the emergence of Occupy Wall Street (OWS) and the slogan '99 per cent versus 1 per cent'. This represented a rupturing in the neoliberal domination of public discourse and asserted the rage of good common sense. In Chapter 3, Leah Hunt-Hendrix and Isham Christie examine the Left's response to the financial crisis of 2008 in the US, focusing in particular on the emergence of Occupy Wall Street. As participants in the movement, the authors relate their angle on the context and the constraints that shaped the mobilisation. Although not representative of the Left as a whole, Occupy offers insight into some of the dynamics that characterise the Left in the US today, including its antagonism towards the history of dogmatic Marxism, the weakness of current models of organising, and widespread scepticism of the state. By embracing participatory democracy and anti-organisational suspicion, Occupy represents a point in a dialectical movement of left ideology – an orientation that created its own set of conflicts and limitations. In this chapter the authors critically analyse the experience that they were part of, and propose a set of lessons for the Left in the US and more broadly.

Europe is currently haunted by widespread austerity and restructuring. These have been justified in academic and public debates with discussions of 'peripheral' European states having not adequately adjusted to the institutional requirements of the Eurozone's single currency, thereby creating an unsustainable growth of debt and deficits. Chapter 4, by Andreas Bieler and Jamie Jordan, goes beyond the accounts of neo-institutionalism, specifically the Varieties of Capitalism approach, which has various deficiencies, including a reliance on methodological nationalism. Instead, this chapter seeks to explain the onset of the Eurozone debt crisis by analysing the underlying dynamics of uneven and combined capitalist accumulation. Focusing on how the development of production structures and trade and investment patterns created particular political economic hierarchies, the authors provide a more adequate explanation of why a division between core and peripheral European states developed, thereby creating asymmetrical capabilities to deal with the onset of the debt crisis. This also explains the direction Europe is taking in terms of renewing processes of neoliberal restructuring, supported by austerity across public sectors.

In the final section, the chapter looks at the role of labour in the build-up and response to the crisis. The authors reveal that it is not simply Europe's 'peripheral' workers who are under pressure to support particular accumulation strategies, but also those in Europe's 'core'. The chapter focuses on the relationship between capital and labour to better explain developments across Europe's political economy.

Chapter 5, by Hilary Wainwright, explores the question of left agency, in particular the political form, in the context of crisis-ridden Europe. Wainwright argues that the rise of a new Left in the 1960s and 1970s in Europe engendered a transformative approach to power – in other words, a transformative capacity to enable and constitute alternatives from below. This trend has resurfaced with the exhaustion of social-democratic and communist parties in Western Europe, both of which embodied a politics of power as domination, which required state power to assert power over society and citizens. While not rejecting power as domination, Wainwright attempts to find an articulation between both these modes of power and political forms in Western Europe in a way that power as domination is driven by power as transformative capacity.

Wainwright traces moments of experimentation with transformative politics and government in Western Europe. In the context of the current crisis, she highlights the emergence of Syriza in Greece and Podemos in Spain as continuing an experiment with political forms that embraces both logics of power. By reflecting on these experiences, Wainwright poses crucial questions for how a non-formulaic approach to the political instrument can be elaborated by the Left on the terrain of a capitalist crisis. It might just be that transformative politics requires a new way of thinking about the political form, based on political tasks and a political division of labour that is not reducible to a single political instrument or party, but rather a movement or network of organisational forms. At the same time, the author seeks to situate the place of populism in left politics today. She engages critically with a form of left populism that strengthens mass transformative capacities from below to deepen democracy.

Part 3 of the volume looks at manifestations of the crisis in the global South and the Left's responses to it, particularly in Brazil, India and South Africa.

Chapter 6, by Alfredo Saad-Filho, examines the context and implications of two shifts in Brazil: the political transition from a military regime (1964–1985) to democracy (1985 to the present), and the economic transition from import substitution industrialisation (1930–1980) to neoliberalism (1990 to the present). These transitions have shaped the contemporary Brazilian political economy and the policy choices available to recent federal administrations. The chapter also reviews how neoliberal economic policies were implemented under various democratic administrations. Saad-Filho looks at the role and implications of the 'neoliberal policy tripod', namely inflation targeting, large fiscal surpluses and the managed fluctuations of Brazil's currency, the real. At the same time, important policy shifts were introduced during the second Lula administration through heterodox reforms expressing a neo-developmentalism and inaugurating what became known as the 'Lula moment'. However, despite positive distributional effects, the 'Lula moment' has proven to be an inadequate response to a globalised Brazilian economy caught in the tides of the global crisis. Saad-Filho examines the economic and social policies underpinning the 'Lula moment', and the limitations of such policies in the context of the 2008 crisis, the mass street mobilisations in 2013 and the social polarisation exhibited in the 2014 elections. He concludes with a reflection on the challenges facing the Left in Brazil.

In Chapter 7, Sumangala Damodaran debunks the idea of India's resilience since the onset of the 2008 crisis. She critically engages the 'decoupling' hypothesis, which suggests that India's high growth rates, like China's, had an economic capacity to withstand the global turbulence or even provide immunity to it. Moreover, it was generally argued that India and China are likely to be the engine rooms to pull the global economy out of the crisis. Situating her analysis in the historical specificity of this crisis, she shows that the immunity argument fails to appreciate the extent to which India's neoliberal structural reforms since the early 1990s engendered a set of structural features that were implicated in the deceleration of the Indian economy long before the 2008 crisis. At the same time, the impacts of the crisis did not shift the neoliberal consensus but, instead, dominant class and social forces have maintained India's externalised and financialised trajectory even under the right-wing Hindu fundamentalist government. Damodaran concludes with a reflection on alternatives for genuine decoupling of growth from the international economy both at the macro-level and through participatory and decentralised fiscal planning, as is the case in Kerala, India.

In Chapter 8, Niall Reddy foregrounds the crisis of labour in the context of a crisis-ridden neoliberalised South African economy. The position of workers in post-apartheid South Africa remains hotly contested. Powerful, militant unions and strict regulation are said to buttress a 'labour aristocracy', which is blamed for trapping large parts of the population in unemployment and underemployment by driving the price of labour above levels that its productivity justifies. This narrative makes the labour rebellion, which began after the Marikana massacre in 2012, stretching from the peripheries to the heartlands of the economy, very difficult to explain.

Reddy questions the narrative about high wages and the 'labour aristocracy' by tackling its core assumptions. He examines decomposed wage data from a cross-section of South Africa's Labour Force Surveys. The structural roots of the low-wage system in South Africa, grounded in the minerals–energy-complex economy, suggest that a broad political struggle is needed by the working class, in addition to new and more militant forms of shop-floor organisation. Reddy highlights the strategic political defeat of labour, including increasing precariousness in the labour market, as necessary conditions for such a struggle. Realignments among workers in the mining industry, as well as the unravelling of the Tripartite Alliance (led by the African National Congress – ANC) as a result of the metalworkers' union breakaway from the trade-union federation, Cosatu, seem to portend the direction things are likely to take for the working class.

Finally, in Chapter 9, Mark Heywood provides a reading of the South African constitution that challenges simplistic caricatures of the constitution as an obstacle to struggles for social justice. Premised on a recognition that social crises are deepening in South Africa, including through wanton state violence, Heywood places the constitution centre stage in how we should think about unifying struggles for social justice. With experience in the Treatment

Action Campaign, both as an activist and leader, Heywood demonstrates how combining mass mobilisation with human-rights advocacy has been able to secure social justice. He challenges overlapping visions for social change prevalent among various social forces, such as the Economic Freedom Fighters and the newly formed social-movement-driven United Front of the National Union of Metalworkers of South Africa (Numsa). He also highlights four significant constitutional-based strategies that can strengthen democracy and advance transformative politics from below. He emphasises the applicability of the constitution in terms of challenging private power, the importance of socio-economic rights for social justice, the role of South Africa's Chapter 9 constitutional institutions in empowering citizenship, and the constitutional injunctions that commit the state to be responsive and practise 'good governance'. In his argument, he clarifies the real meaning of the property clause in the constitution to help put an end to any confusion arising from the clause and the dogmatic railing against it.

NOTES

1   Anarchism also shares these weaknesses, as Lilley (2012) points out.
2   This claim is made on the back cover of the new release of Kindleberger's (2013) classic book.
3   James DeLong and Barry Eichengreen are based at the University of California, Berkeley. Kindleberger's notion of hegemonic stability has essentially been about a powerful capitalist state having power over others, and serving as a stabilising force by being the consumer and lender of last resort. Eichengreen, influenced by Kindleberger, has built on the idea of 'hegemonic stability'.

REFERENCES

Amin, S. 1995. *Re-reading the Postwar Period: An Intellectual Itinerary*. New York: Monthly Review Press.

DeLong, J.B and Eichengreen, B. 2013. 'Foreword'. In C.P. Kindleberger, *The World in Depression, 1929–1939*. Oakland, CA: University of California Press. Accessed 14 September 2015, www.voxeu.org/article/new-preface-charles-kindleberger-world-depression-1929-1939.

Gramsci, A. (1971) 1998. *Selections from the Prison Notebooks*, edited by Q. Hoare and G. Smith. Hyderabad: Orient Longman.

IMF (International Monetary Fund). 2014. *World Economic Outlook – Recovery Strengthens, Remains Uneven*. Washington, D.C.: International Monetary Fund.

Kindleberger, C.P. (1973) 2013. *The World in Depression, 1929–1939*. Oakland, CA:

University of California Press.

Lilley, S. 2012. 'Great chaos under heaven: Catastrophism and the Left'. In *Catastrophism: The Apocalyptic Politics of Collapse and Rebirth*, edited by S. Lilley, D. McNally, E. Yuen and J. Davis. Oakland: PM Press.

Panitch, L. and Gindin, S. 2010. 'Capitalist crises and the crisis this time'. In *Socialist Register*, edited by L. Panitch, G. Albo and V. Chibber. London: Merlin Press.

Wearden, G. 2014. 'IMF chief Lagarde warns Europe's crisis isn't over'. Accessed 12 May 2014, http://www.theguardian.com/business/2014/may/12/imf-chief-lagarde-warns-europes-financial-crisis-isnt-over-business-live.

CONTEMPORARY UNDERSTANDINGS OF CAPITALISM'S CRISES AND CLASS STRUGGLE

1

FROM MARX TO THE SYSTEMIC CRISES OF CAPITALIST CIVILISATION

Vishwas Satgar

Over the past two centuries, crisis has been endemic to capitalism. Yet classical and neoclassical economics has tended to treat crisis more as an aberration to 'the norm' of a stable self-regulating market. Since the onset of the 2007/08 global crisis, however, this axiomatic truth of capitalist economics has been called into question. The 2007/08 crisis is ongoing and has been compared to the general crisis of the Great Depression (1929–1941). It is now considered one of the worst crises in the history of modern capitalism, having eclipsed the Great Depression. So, how do we characterise the nature of the contemporary capitalist crisis? Are we experiencing a cyclical crisis or a deeper systemic crisis? Are we living through a time of periodic and general crises? Given the scale and depth of the contemporary crisis, which poses major existential threats to planetary life, this chapter argues that we are dealing with an unprecedented civilisational crisis with multiple systemic dimensions: the systemic crises of capitalist civilisation.

I situate the argument in the context of Marx's conceptions of capitalist crisis. Marx's understanding of capitalism, as a body of knowledge and with its valuable contribution to modern social thought, has not been surpassed. However, in engaging Marx it is necessary to appreciate that classical theory on capitalist crisis, originating with Marx, is at an impasse in terms of comprehending the contemporary systemic crises of capitalist civilisation. The critical engagement with Marx is not about refuting his corpus, however, but about seeking new openings and ways of thinking about the contemporary capitalist crisis. It is about finding theoretical space in Marx's understanding of the 'deep structures of capital' for the notion of the 'systemic crisis of capitalist civilisation' and other conjoined concepts, such as 'capital as a geological force'. This is grounded in an appreciation that Marx's work is unfinished and open to development by deploying his own dialectical method of thinking.

Also significant in this search for new openings and ways of thinking about capitalist crisis is the challenge of the level and scale at which we think about this crisis. To merely think about crisis in the abstract, at the level of the 'deep structures of capital', is not very useful in itself. Similarly, to think about the crises of capitalism as merely economic crises is wholly inadequate. Therefore, I argue that abstractions and economic reductionism do not help us come to terms with the level and scale of the crises of contemporary capitalist civilisation. This approach relates directly to the challenge of how we periodise historical capitalism to bring out its historical specificity. This chapter therefore advances a perspective on the historical development of capitalist civilisation and its periodisation at a historical level and as a global social system.

Finally, in this chapter I show how the various systemic dimensions of capitalist crisis can be understood in a non-reductionist way. This brings to the fore the role of the US-led bloc and transnational capital in both constituting and reproducing the systemic dimensions of capitalist civilisational crisis. In this regard, attention is given to the making and operations of the following systemic-crisis tendencies: financialised chaos, the climate crisis, peak oil, the food-system crisis and the securitisation of democracy. These dimensions of the systemic crisis relate to the challenge of left agency today and lead to the crucial question: is left politics about catastrophism or about the politics of a transformative moment?

In summary, the notion of the systemic crises of capitalist civilisation is essentially a thesis, which is tested in this chapter in relation to, firstly, Marx's theoretical understanding of crisis; secondly, the challenge of providing a non-teleological but stages view of capitalism's history, which captures the scale and depth of the crisis; thirdly, the empirical dimensions of the systemic crises of capitalist civilisation; and, finally, the challenges for left agency. The purpose of this approach is to open up new ways of thinking about capitalist crisis, while thinking about how the crises of capitalist civilisation prompt a rethink of left agency. At the same time, this analysis lays the basis for more in-depth theoretical and analytical work.

MARX'S UNDERSTANDING OF CAPITALIST CRISIS

Marx has provided social thought with a simple but powerful understanding of capitalism: it is a system that is prone to crisis and this crisis is internal to capitalism. However, Marx did not develop a systematic or adequate theory of capitalist crisis. His work contains ideas and concepts that suggest the existence of this crisis tendency. In the Preface to *A Contribution to the Critique of Political Economy*, Marx ([1859] 1999: 21) writes:

> At a certain stage of development, the material productive forces of society come into conflict with the existing relations of production or – this merely expresses the same thing in legal terms – with the property relations within the framework of which they have operated hitherto. From forms of development of the productive forces these relations turn into their fetters.

This conception of crisis suggests a technological determinism as the basis of crisis and social change within the capitalist mode of production. The contradiction between forces/relations is also a historical contradiction that leads to the breakdown and then supersession of a mode of production. Yet what constitutes the forces of production is not a conceptually clear issue in Marxism, with some Marxists including, over and above the means of production and labour, science and geography into its definition. At the same time, where does this leave class struggle, particularly if, in the logic of accumulation, the forces of production have primacy? The blind veneration of technology and science associated with this perspective also has implications for the socialist alternative. For Stalin, it meant forced-march modernisation and building gigantic factories as the new basis for socialist relations of production. Yet this did not work and instead produced a tyrannical society. This conception of crisis, and ultimately social change, is a very contentious issue in Marxist thought.

In *Capital*, Marx abstracts to a very high level of generality the dynamics and tendencies that drive capitalism and its mode of production. Generally, the time taken to valorise money into capital, or M–C–M (money–commodity–money), is a simple, and the basic, idea of crisis in *Capital*. In other words, the failure to valorise money into capital produces crisis. In the three volumes of *Capital* there are three more important ideas that point to crisis tendencies in capitalism. This is Marx thinking at an abstract level about the deep structures of capital.

First, there is the notion of disproportionality. This relates to an allocation of resources between department one (means of production) and department two (means of consumption) within the scheme for simple and expanded reproduction. Essentially, given the anarchy of capitalist production, individual capitalists will tend to overinvest in a particular department. Allocation will not happen smoothly or rationally. The excess allocation of investment will lead to excess output, which cannot be sold, and the rate of profit will then decline relative to the narrow market. Furthermore, contraction in the overinvested department will not be matched by an adjustment in the underinvested department. This leads to aggregate demand falling, then to a realisation problem and then to a general crisis that ensues in both departments.

Second, underconsumption refers to a decline in aggregate demand, which ensues when capitalists cannot sell all they produce. Underconsumption points to a gap between supply, and what workers can purchase and consume. With workers not having a large enough proportion of the surplus, or with insufficient incomes, aggregate demand declines. Commodities are not sold and this creates a general crisis.

Third, overproduction refers to high levels of productivity or relative surplus value being produced as part of the generation of surplus output. This output or supply exceeds demand and cannot be sold, thus creating a general crisis.

Despite his recognising these tendencies towards crisis in capitalism, and as expressions of deeper contradictions, Marx did not bring these concepts together into a systematic theory of crisis.[1] Therefore, Marx's rich, complex, inchoate – and, in some instances, contradictory – approach to capitalist crisis laid the basis for further development of crisis theories. This task was left to subsequent generations of Marxists and it is a challenge we still face today. But guiding us in this endeavour is how Marx thought about and approached the study of capitalism (Ollman 2003). Marx abstracted, to different levels, to understand how social change happened in the context of capitalist society and this is presented in different ways, which enabled an appreciation of what is old/new, tendential/non-tendential, contradictory/non-contradictory and essential/non-essential.

This varied approach to understanding change applies to Marx's under-standing of crisis. Without an appreciation of the dialectical method in Marx's thought, his discussion of crisis tendency, which is highly abstracted from capi-talist reality and generalised, can easily be confused with an empirical trend. On the other hand, if crisis tendency is not situated within Marx's method, it can be reduced to mono-causal economic determinism, understood in static terms, without the reader's appreciating its interconnections with larger processes and the necessary conditions that bring it into being. Finally, Marx's approach and method prompts a rigorous and studied approach to capitalist reality. This means that although capitalism is inherently prone to periodic crises, these have to be studied at every moment to understand the historical specificity of each crisis and its connections to larger patterns. This also means that Marxism as a body of knowledge is unfinished.

LIMITS AND CHALLENGES TO MARX'S UNDERSTANDING OF CAPITALIST CRISES

Marx's thought is crucial to help one think about the dynamics and tenden-cies of contemporary global capitalism. The insights he provides from making the 'capitalist mode of production' an object of study are at the heart of how capitalism works in the abstract or pure level. These insights provide us with powerful resources to think about the political economy of global capitalism. However, at the same time, there are limits to how we can use Marx to think about the contemporary crises of global capitalism. This does not mean aban-doning Marx. However, it does mean it is important to think in a Marxist way about our contemporary world. Merely applying Marx's theoretical approach to crisis will not help us think about the nature of the contemporary systemic crises of capitalist civilisation. At most, a modified application of Marx's theory of capitalist crisis will bring into view overproduction or financialised overac-cumulation in our explanatory understanding.[2] This is important, but it is also insufficient. Being aware of the problems and limits of Marx's Marxism in rela-tion to crisis theory helps us renew a Marxist approach to such a theory. Three main shortcomings with Marx's understanding of capitalism and its crisis tendencies have to be considered.

First, although Marx's conception of capitalist crisis and his explication of crisis tendencies in *Capital* are useful, they are economic-reductionist and are not sufficient to explain the nature of the contemporary crises of capitalist civilisation. There are material determinations in contemporary capitalism that go beyond even Marx's conception of pure capitalism, as contained in the three volumes of *Capital*. Although *Capital* is a powerful heuristic device to help us think about the tendencies of capitalism, it is not able to address new concrete historical tendencies of contemporary global capitalism and crisis. For instance, climate change and peak oil are not part of the way pure capitalism is conceptualised in *Capital*, and these are powerful systemic crisis tendencies in today's capitalism, which impose limits on and engender serious contradictions for global accumulation.

This is not to argue that Marx was blind to nature and ecology, or that a green reading of Marx is not valuable. Foster (1999) has done a great job in retrieving the dimension of nature in Marx's conception of historical materialism. Foster's work foregrounds the notion of 'metabolic rift' in Marx – a rift between town and countryside, and between humans and nature. However, the notion of metabolic rift is not a theory of crisis, and although it could be elaborated into such a theory post-Marx, the point here is Marx's understanding of capitalist crisis. In Marx's most elaborated work of capitalist crisis in *Capital*, his theoretical perspective has nothing to do with ecology and how this determines capitalism's systemic crisis tendencies.

Second, Marx believed in general that capital is the all-dominating economic power of bourgeois society. This is a crucial premise for his theoretical understanding of capitalist crisis. In *Capital*, Marx goes further to make capital an object of enquiry as a social relation. Although Marx brilliantly understood capital in a relational sense, and as this applied to labour and capital, the structural power of capital today in the global political economy is shaping and determining not only the logic of capitalist accumulation, but also the future of all living forms – both human and non-human. Capital today is a *geological* force determining the future of planetary life.

Resource extraction, production, consumption and pollution are not just 'technical issues' (in the Marxist sense) but are at the heart of the crisis of civilisational reproduction. Capital, in its organisation of capitalism, has overshot planetary limits, undermined natural cycles and now threatens us with species extinction through climate change. In this context, labour – or the working class – is far from being the gravedigger of capitalism. Labour has been dramatically weakened given the structural and imperial power used to reproduce a globalised capitalist civilisation. This does not suggest the end of class struggle but rather serves to emphasise that capital is dominant and prevailing in a manner that embodies a form of social power that goes beyond just ensuring labour exploitation – it also ensures its supremacy over all forms of life.

Finally, and as a corollary to the previous point, the dialectical logic of capital for Marx was meant to bring both destruction and progress. In its expansion in the world, capital was meant to confront and overcome backward pre-capitalist relations. This was very much a Eurocentric moment in Marx. In *Capital*, Marx foregrounds competition, and how it dynamises and modernises production relations in the drive for expansion. In Marx, capital brings about destruction but also progress at a higher level of accumulation. However, in the contemporary capitalist world the logic of capital is about societal and ecological destruction. Michael Burawoy (2013) makes a very insightful point in this regard, arguing that the current wave of marketisation (i.e. 1973 to the present) is about commodifying nature. But, at the same time, he acknowledges that although exploitation features in the dynamics of accumulation, we have surplus labour populations in which exploitation becomes the privilege of the few. Therefore, more marketisation equals deepening inequality and further commodification of nature.[3] Put more directly, the dialectic of marketisation–destruction (of human beings and nature) is what characterises capital and capitalism in our contemporary world. This raises fundamental challenges to capitalist modernity and its narratives of progress and development. With the current dynamic of marketisation–destruction, capitalist progress and development mean ecocide, or the destruction of conditions that sustain human and all other life forms on the planet.

In short, given the limits of Marx's conceptions of crisis tendencies in helping us gain an understanding of contemporary capitalism, an engagement with his work highlights the need for a theoretical reconstruction of historical materialism and of Marx's own thought. There is a need for an extension and modification of Marx's analysis. There is a need to create theoretical space to bring in the notion of the 'systemic crises of capitalist civilisation' and related concepts, such as capital as a geological force. This needs to be done at the abstract level of the tendencies and structures of the capitalist mode of production, and at the concrete historical level. I now turn to the concrete historical level to further test the thesis of the crises of capitalist civilisation.

PERIODISING THE MAKING OF CAPITALIST CIVILISATION

To argue the existence of the systemic crises of capitalist civilisation presupposes the existence of capitalist civilisation. Such a presupposition takes us into the terrain of concrete history to appreciate the making of capitalist civilisation over time. Moreover, it is important to situate the systemic crises of capitalist civilisation within concrete history to bring into view its constitution and particular features. This means that we have to think in terms of a stages approach to world history to understand the historical specificity of the contemporary systemic crises of capitalist civilisation. Marx was thinking about the capitalist mode of production and, more specifically, competitive capitalism in the mid-Victorian age of the nineteenth century. He did not think in terms of different varieties of capitalism or the specific characteristics of the stages of capitalism. This later became a preoccupation in the classical Marxist tradition, after Marx, and the subsequent revival of Marxist political economy in the 1960s (Callinicos 2001).

Lenin's ([1917] 2011) *Imperialism, the Highest Stage of Capitalism* exemplifies this approach and therefore deserves attention. Lenin draws on Hobson's ([1902] 2006) *Imperialism: A Study*, Hilferding's ([1910] 1981) *Finance Capital* and Bukharin's ([1917] 1929) *Imperialism and World Economy* to periodise capitalism. However, his approach is problematic for various reasons and not very useful in providing an understanding of the contemporary period of capitalism. First, Lenin was fixated on showing how the capitalism of his time differed from the competitive Victorian capitalism of Marx's time. We are living in a different phase of competitive capitalist expansion and restructuring from the one Lenin wrote about. Second, Lenin placed an emphasis on the concentration and centralisation of capital as the basis for inter-imperialist rivalry among colonial empires. In the contemporary world we do not have colonial empires, but instead we have a single US superpower and a bloc of forces it leads at a global level. This also means global rivalry is driven by a new set of accumulation dynamics and conditions. The forms and practices of imperialism have a historical specificity and are distinctive. Third, Lenin's conception of imperialism works with a teleology in which capitalism reaches an end point, or the highest stage of capitalism, after national monopolisation takes root in developed capitalist countries. Yet capitalism has endured for almost a century since Lenin wrote this work, despite various cyclical and general crises. Capitalism has adapted, restructured and is increasingly taking on a transnational character in the contemporary period. Finally, Lenin's conception of capitalism's place in world history fails to recognise that capitalism had origins before Marx's time and therefore imperialism has a longer history. The origins of capitalism and imperialism have to be located in the prototypes of capitalism that emerged in the transitions from pre-capitalist societies. At least in the context of the West, this has to be related to the transition from feudalism to capitalism.[4]

What follows is an attempt to provide a periodisation of capitalist civilisation which draws on but differs from a world-systems perspective. Although world-systems theory provides a reading of world history that allows for variances and continuities by focusing on cycles of accumulation related to hegemonic powers (see Arrighi and Moore 2001), its emphasis on more general historical patterns fails to recognise historical and geographical contingency, or the role of class struggle in shaping capitalism's history. While keeping this in mind, the various keys to periodisation and the technical issues involved are beyond the scope of this chapter (see Jessop 2001), except to say that each of the stages of historical capitalism delineated here can be further delineated into conjunctures and phases based on historical, political, geographic and economic contingencies. For our purposes, the important point is the making and existence of capitalist civilisation and, more specifically, the recognition that this takes place through particular non-teleological historical stages.

Capitalist civilisation, which has been established over the last 500 years, has been marked by three major historical stages, each defined by a particular mode of capital accumulation. In this periodisation there is an emphasis on key features as they relate to forms of capital, imperial power, technological development, ideological shifts and struggles from below:

- *Mercantile accumulation* (1400s–1800s) involved a prototype of capitalism linked to slavery, colonial conquest, trade and exchange. Sea-based expansion took off in this period, supported through merchant capital and empires such as the Spanish, Dutch and British. The Reformation in Europe, which challenged the control of the Roman Catholic Church, the Dutch Revolution (1566–1609), the English Revolution (1637–1660) and the Enlightenment (c.1650–1800) all shaped this stage of expansion.
- *Monopoly industrial accumulation* (c.1750s–1980) involved struggles against land enclosures; technological innovation, such as the steam

engine; the emergence of factories and increasing concentration and centralisation of capital. Colonial expansion continued but was also rolled back by the American Revolution (1775–1783), the Slave Revolution in Haiti (1791–1804) and the so-called Bolivarian revolutions (1810–1830) against Spanish rule in South America. The French Revolution (1789–1794) also shook up the heartlands of capitalism. Mid-Victorian competitive capitalism gave way to national monopolies. The Italian nation state was founded (1859–1870) and Germany was unified (1864–1871). The American Civil War (1861–1865), the Paris Commune (1871), the scramble for Africa (1870–1914) and the first great depression (1873–1896) happened. National monopolies displaced competition, which descended into national rivalries. The period also saw World War I (1914–1918), the Great Depression (1929–1941), World War II (1939–1945), and the end of British hegemony and the Ottoman Empire. The Mexican Revolution (1910–1920) and a wave of socialist revolutions, including those in Russia (1917), China (1949) and Cuba (1959), and various national liberation struggles shaped the peripheries. US-centred hegemony, the cold war (1947–1991), Fordism, the Keynesian welfare state and the end of colonialism also determined the character of this stage.

• *Transnational techno-financial accumulation* (1973 to the present) took root as social democracy reached its limits and stagflation kicked in (1973). There was a wave of struggle (1968–1975) in Western Europe, Prague and the US. The US suffered a defeat in Vietnam, and the Nicaraguan Revolution (1979) took place. There was a shift to containerisation, information-and-communications technology, post-Fordism and global financialised restructuring. Finance was globalised and played a crucial role in transnationalising class structures. The cold war ended, formal political apartheid ended in South Africa (1994), democratisation swept through Africa, parts of Asia, Latin America and the former Soviet Union, while US hegemony was tenuous but increasingly centred on financialised expansion and military power. Power was increasingly diffused with the rise of regional state–society complexes, such as China and Russia, and since 9/11 the War on Terror has expanded. Global rivalries come to the fore as systemic crisis tendencies deepen. Anti-neoliberal and 'anti-globalisation' movements emerged as central to rolling back neoliberalisation and saving planetary life.

In the current stage of transnational techno-financial accumulation, contemporary capitalist civilisation has four crucial dimensions to its global political economy. First, it is underpinned by globalised financial, production and trade structures at the heart of a globalised capitalist system. Second, there is a political system of state and civil-society complexes, intergovernmental organisations and private transnational bodies. Third, there are large and powerful transnational corporations wielding immense structural and direct political power. Fourth, a US-led historical bloc of transnational forces provides strategic leadership and advancing neoliberal ideological concepts of control shaping policy, culture, law, media spheres and consumption. This also means various capitalist class projects come to the fore to advance variants of neoliberal capitalism to deepen globalisation.

THE CRISES OF CAPITALIST CIVILISATION IN THE TWENTY-FIRST CENTURY

We now turn to testing the thesis of the systemic crises of capitalist civilisation empirically. Ahmed (2010) provides a Marxist-inspired account of the current systemic crisis tendencies confronting capitalism. However, there are three crucial shortcomings in his perspective, which this chapter attempts to rectify. First, Ahmed does not provide a historicised premise for his perspective of capitalism and contemporary capitalist civilisation. Second, he does not break with a reductionist account of the systemic dimensions of capitalist crisis. The role of the US superpower and state is not brought into his account of the making of systemic crisis and its dimensions. Third, class practices, including the role of transnational capital and its ideological articulations of neoliberalism, are not linked closely enough to the systemic dimensions he brings into view. Capital as a geological force prevailing over and destroying planetary life is not clearly demonstrated empirically in that work. In contrast, I want to highlight concrete historical and systemic tendencies coming to the fore that are rooted in the institutional structures, ideologies and class-based practices that buttress the destructive logic of capital as a geological force and as part of transnational techno-financial accumulation. These are systemic tendencies that bring down, limit and constrain various dimensions of global capitalism. Moreover, as these systemic tendencies increasingly interlock, they engulf global capitalism in crises of contemporary capitalist civilisation. Such tendencies need to be recognised as part of the dialectic of concrete history and at more abstract levels of understanding contemporary capitalism.

Financialised chaos

Immanuel Wallerstein (2003) has argued that the US has declined as a hegemonic power over the past 50 years. His argument tends to suggest that key defining moments – from the mass resistance of 1968, defeat in Vietnam to, more recently, the War on Terror – have contributed to the decline of the US. Although Wallerstein is alive to contingency, his argument does not take on board a crucial attempt by the US to remake the material basis of its global power, and particularly, to centre this on controlling global finance. While this has been a tenuous coefficient of power, it has increased the complexity, reach and systemic leverage that the US has over the global capitalist system. And, in this regard, Gowan's (1999) analysis of the evolution of the Dollar-Wall Street Regime from the 1970s to the 1990s is crucial. The Dollar-Wall Street Regime has not only remade post-World War II international finance, but has also built up and articulated a complex mix of institutions, financial power, the dollar and US power. These dynamics have been further strengthened by global neoliberal restructuring, which has placed high finance at the centre of the global political economy and with free rein to do as it pleases.

This means that financialisation has ensured that the structural power of finance capital is embedded in three important ways to ensure speculation and short-term profit making. Firstly, financial structures are now part of the systemic dynamics of global accumulation. So, if banks or finance houses fail, this has ramifications on a global scale. In the 2007–2009 financial crisis, banks lost over US$140 billion through sub-prime loans, and the value of credit default swaps was estimated at US$62.2 trillion. The combination of these losses broke confidence in the financial system. Secondly, most state structures, except those that have opted out of the logic of global financialisation, manage their macro-economies to ensure that the risk to financial capital is mitigated. Macro-economic frameworks and regulatory interventions are governed by the imperatives of globalised markets (such as foreign-exchange markets, housing markets, stock exchanges, government debt and commodity markets). Therefore, the state ensures that capital's interests are maintained. Thirdly, the frontiers of financialisation and its crisis-engendering effects span spatial boundaries – extending from households to countries, national and global economic sectors, disaster zones and even war zones.[5]

The global political economy has been driven by the process of financial overaccumulation as a systemic dimension of global capitalism, spreading financialised chaos and instability. Financialised chaos has been registered in the following events: the Latin American debt crisis of 1982; the US stock-market crash because of junk bonds (1987); the 1997 Asian crisis; Russia and Brazil (1990–1999); the bursting of the dot.com bubble because of overinflated values (2000–2001); Argentina and Turkey (2000–2002); and the global financial crisis from 2007/08 until the present, which has engulfed the entire global political economy.

Capital has responded to the crises of 2007/08 with a renewal of the conjunctural project of neoliberalisation. Financial overaccumulation has been rescued through state intervention and austerity, without jettisoning the rationalities, institutional structures or practices of neoliberalisation. Global financial markets are now more deeply integrated and driven by information technology, essentially guaranteeing financialised chaos in the global political economy. Although this historical tendency thrives on its own, it also interlocks with other tendencies through neoliberalisation and commodification, which is evident in relation to the climate crisis, peak oil, food-system crisis and securitisation of democracy.

Climate crisis

Ever since the Industrial Revolution, humans have been emitting large quantities of greenhouse gases into the atmosphere. By the mid twentieth century, human influence had become the dominant cause of observed global warming through greenhouse-gas emissions despite natural variability. The US was for a very long time the leading emitter of carbon emissions in aggregate and per capita terms.[6] At a systemic level of the global capitalist system, this means production, consumption, distribution, exchange and social reproduction are implicated in causing human-induced climate change. More specifically, capital as a geological force has been implicated in emitting greenhouse gases and causing climate change in three respects. First, through the extraction of fossil fuels and their use in economic processes. Second, through ongoing accumulation and growth driven by fossil fuels, greenhouse-gas emission rates are increasing. According to the fifth Intergovernmental Panel on Climate Change report (IPCC 2014), over the past two decades carbon emission rates have not been declining, while planetary temperatures are increasing. Third, with growing income inequality on a planetary scale, the wealthy have a higher carbon footprint and are therefore, as a class, a major contributor to green-house gases and climate change (Hertwich and Peters 2009). In short, the global capitalist system and capital as a geological force are driving the destruction of human and non-human life through human-induced climate change. The climate crisis is systemically driven and caused. Put differently, it is a capitalist-induced crisis, and not a human-induced one.

The US, supported by transnational capital, has failed to address the climate crisis. It did not sign the Kyoto Protocol, which was an attempt to ensure that the rich, carbon-polluting countries took legal responsibility to reduce their emissions. In fact, the Kyoto Protocol has been the harbinger of financialised, green neoliberal solutions, such as carbon trading (Satgar 2014). The protocol does little to address the climate crisis – and yet it was still too much for the US to commit to. Moreover, in 2009 at the UN-led Copenhagen Summit, the US (under Obama's leadership), scuttled any attempt to find binding legal targets to reduce carbon emissions. Instead, a 'pledge-and-review' approach, embodied in an accord without binding targets, was agreed to between the US and other leading emitters, including China, Brazil, India and South Africa. This has become the dominant approach to solving the climate crisis, and more recently a similar agreement was reached between the US and China on the eve of the COP20 UN summit in Lima, in 2014.[7] This is the approach that will be consolidated at the 2015 COP21 UN summit in Paris.

However, despite the global media hype about the US–China deal, both the Kyoto Protocol and the pledge-and-review approach embodied in the US–China deal affirm a corporate-led method of addressing climate change, and embed green neoliberal solutions in the UN multilateral process, such as carbon trading and offsetting. Where they have been adopted, these green neoliberal solutions have thus far failed to address the climate crisis. The window of opportunity to avert catastrophic climate change is closing very quickly (Bond 2011). Since these solutions have been put forward, carbon emissions have still increased over the past two and a half decades. The carbon dioxide concentration in the atmosphere has exceeded the threshold limit of 400 parts per million, which means we are heading for a planetary temperature increase of 2 °C. Continuing on the current trajectory, we will experience the impact of dramatic climate change within the next 20 years.

And crucial climate-change phenomena are already beginning to have an impact (see IPCC 2014). For instance, the western part of the Antarctic is going through irreversible collapse; methane emissions from the receding Arctic ice sheet are on the increase; glaciers are receding dramatically; and sea levels are rising, placing low-lying areas and islands in jeopardy. It is expected that as ocean warming increases, circulation patterns will be affected, aggravating climatic shifts. Moreover, the knock-on effects of climate change are beginning to be expressed in extreme weather activity. As the planetary environment changes, more extreme weather events have been recorded, such as heatwaves, droughts, floods and cyclones.[8] These are becoming increasingly intense and reveal the extreme vulnerability of ecosystems, and many human systems, to climate variability. The poor and working class are likely to be worst affected by the climate crisis and will bear the brunt of capitalism's logic towards species extinction.

Linked to the climate crisis is the historical tendency towards peak oil, which further reveals the destructive logic at the heart of capitalism today.

Peak oil

In the Industrial Revolution, coal became crucial for driving industrialisation by means of steam power. However, by the middle of the nineteenth century, oil had become increasingly important to meet energy needs, particularly to drive the combustion engine. More importantly, oil became a strategic resource for capital accumulation and this necessitated its extraction and geopolitical control to secure supply to Western industrial economies during colonial imperialism. After World War II, during the Pax Americana, the US became central in organising the geopolitics of oil to advance its interests in line with the reproduction of the global capitalist system. With the rise of national independence movements in the Middle East, and the US drive to open markets through decolonisation, the US played a crucial role in the emergence of the Middle Eastern oil-producing sovereign states and ensured its supply through an Anglo-American axis (Van der Pijl 2006).

By the 1970s global oil supply was threatened with the formation of the Organization of Petroleum Exporting Countries (OPEC). Oil-price shocks reverberated through the international economy. The US in this context also had to contend with the economic rise of Europe and Japan since World War II, and this led to the tighter incorporation of these countries into a US-led bloc, including numerous oil-producing states as clients. Countries such as Saudi Arabia and, initially, Iran, were crucial clients for US geo-strategic control of global oil supplies during this period.

By the 1970s the US also faced peak oil in terms of its own domestic production. The notion of peak oil had been advocated by geologist M King Hubbert decades before to determine the output of an oil well (Greer 2008). The bell-shaped Hubbert Curve is one of the basic tools of petroleum geology. Ahmed (2010: 64) sets out Hubbert's basic principles as follows:

> Firstly, production begins at zero. Secondly, production increases until it reaches a peak which cannot be surpassed. This peak tends to occur at or around the point when fifty per cent of total petroleum reserves are depleted. Thirdly, subsequent to this peak, production declines at an increasing rate, until finally the resource is completely exhausted.

The peak-oil model applies to oil wells, oil-producing regions, national output and even global supply. With global capitalism addicted to oil, the rapid depletion of oil reserves and resources poses a major systemic limit on global accumulation. It also causes cost pressures as supply dwindles, which further constrains growth and accumulation.

According to studies conducted by oil corporations, global oil production peaked in the early 2000s, with some reports suggesting as early as 2000 or as late as 2005 (Ahmed 2010). Moreover, the International Energy Agency (IEA 2007) conducted a systematic analysis of the world's leading oil reservoirs in 2007 that contained proven or probable reserves in excess of 500 million barrels. According to Klare (2012), this study affirmed two crucial findings. First, production is declining more than suspected and, secondly, the rate of decline is increasing each year. So, all of the major oil wells that have driven industrialisation and accumulation over the past few decades have now peaked and are rapidly depleting.

This crisis-inducing tendency has two major implications for global accumulation. First, buoyant demand from countries such as China and India has led to a scramble for the last remaining oil resources on the planet, which, in turn, has sparked a shallow resource boom (Klare 2012). At the vanguard of new frontiers of extractivism, oil, coal and gas companies are extracting hydrocarbons from tar sands, shale gas and oil, and from deep-water drilling – all referred to as unconventional hydrocarbons (Yergin 2012). In the US alone there are 800 000 oil and gas fracking wells, with a target of 1 million to be achieved by the end of 2015. Unconventional hydrocarbons are expensive, their extraction has serious environmental impacts, they are increasingly implicated in geopolitical conflicts and are difficult to source. Currently, with overproduction of oil due to fracking in the US, and Saudi Arabia's continued output and reluctance to push up the price of oil, global oil prices are declining. However, this is not sustainable given supply constraints in the medium to long term. Petro-state economies are not only hit badly by declining oil prices in the short term, but the shallow resource boom also means that oil-price volatility is likely to continue, with ramifications through the global economy in the medium to long term. In the end, peak oil and the fact that oil is a finite resource will also limit the future of unconventional hydrocarbons.

The second implication of the hydrocarbons boom is its undermining of efforts to mitigate climate change. The interests at stake are powerful – not only the interests of the top oil-producing countries (such as the US, ranked third by the IEA), but also those of some of the most powerful corporations in the world. These include the world's most valuable company, unlisted state-owned oil producer Saudi Aramco, with annual revenue of at least US$150 billion; the world's top-10 oil companies, ranked by their reserves of oil and gas, which are all state-run corporations; and, ranked by revenue, five of the world's top-six listed companies, which are oil majors – Royal Dutch Shell, ExxonMobil, BP, Sinopec and PetroChina (Hiscock 2012).

To ensure we mitigate the effects of climate change, such as slowing down the rate of the Antarctic's destruction, reducing the rate at which sea levels are rising and generally lowering greenhouse-gas emission levels to prevent runaway global warming, current fossil-fuel extraction and usage has to be abandoned. Yet this solution is not on the agenda (Klein 2014). In short, the close relationship between the oil-peak-driven resource boom and the climate crisis vividly demonstrates the logic of ecocide at work within contemporary capitalism.

Food-system crisis

In the first half of the twentieth century, the US agricultural system underwent a dramatic shift with the adoption of Fordist mass production and consumption systems. This increasingly tended to remake the international division of labour and food systems inherited from colonialism in the peripheries of capitalism (McMichael and Raynolds 1994). After World War II, monoculture production and fossil-fuel-driven, chemical-based, mass-scale agriculture became the norm in the US. This system also became part of the country's international response to the cold war, the end of British hegemony and the need to reconstruct Europe through the Marshall Plan (Friedmann 2004). This model was therefore exported to various parts of the world as part of the Pax Americana, and had implications for family farms in Europe and peasant agriculture in Latin America and Asia as the Green Revolution, as it was known, was rolled out. This process has continued with neoliberal globalisation over the past three decades, through structural-adjustment programmes, through pressure brought to bear by the World Trade Organization to liberalise agriculture and promote the patenting of genetic material, and through alliances of governments and transnational corporations, such as the G7's New Alliance for Food Security and Nutrition in Africa. Today a new global division of labour prevails in the agricultural system, centred on transnational corporations.

Globalised industrial agriculture is controlled by a few transnational corporations at different points in the value chain, from land, seeds and agrochemicals, to biotechnology, trading, retailing and consumer-goods companies. Hilary (2013: 120–121) summarises the global domination of transnational corporations in the food systems as follows:

> Just three transnational corporations – Monsanto, DuPont and Syngenta – control between them over half the world's entire commercial seed market; all three are also ranked in the top ten list of world agro-chemical companies, which Syngenta dominates with close to 20 per cent market share, and all three are major players in the biotechnology industry. The four largest commodity traders – ADM, Bunge, Cargill and Louis Dreyfus – the 'ABCD companies' – enjoy significant power over world trade in grains, oilseeds and palm oil. The top ten food processing corporations control 28 per cent of the global market, with Nestlé far and away the largest single company, followed by PepsiCo and Kraft Foods. In addition, the world's largest ten food retailers have more than doubled their share of the global market over the last decade as the major supermarket chains of Europe and the USA have sought to expand their operations … this intensity of market concentration means that a group of no more than 40 transnational corporations effectively control the global food regime from farm to fork, and have amassed spectacular profits as a result of their market domination.

To understand the food-system crisis we need to concentrate our focus not on single problems in the food system or on the inability of the food system to provide access to certain caloric levels. Such a focus ends up in technocratic problem solving inside the system. To appreciate the systemic nature of the food crisis requires a focus on the systemic logic of the transnational industrial agricultural system and how it engenders systemic food crises. The spread of this systemic dynamic, albeit uneven in the global political economy, is grounded in five contradictions.

First, it creates food injustice, or what Vandana Shiva (2013) terms 'hunger by design'. In 1996 the Food and Agriculture Organization claimed there were about 800 000 hungry people on the planet. Today there are 1.52 billion hungry people and 2.56 billion who are food-stressed (Hilary 2013: 119). The irony of this situation is that farm workers, peasants and rural communities are some of the hungriest in the world, even though they are at the front line of food production. With dramatic increases in global food prices, first in 2006 to 2008 and then in 2010 to 2012, the poor and workers have been hit the hardest. These hikes sparked food rebellions in at least 40 countries, and demands for bread in the case of the Arab Spring revolutions. Yet in 2010 alone the world's largest grain and agrochemical companies made profits between them of US$20 billion (Hilary 2013: 121).

Second, the industrial agricultural food system wastes large quantities of food at several points in the value chain: harvesting, handling, storage, processing, packaging and retail. In South Africa, estimates suggest that thirty-one per cent of annual food production (about 10 million tonnes of 31 million tonnes of food produced) is lost to waste in some form or another. Food waste is highest for fruit and vegetables: over fifty per cent produced is wasted along the value chain.[9] Food wastage is part of a global trend and is tied to the phenomenon of cheap, unhealthy food, which is easily 'disposed of'.

Third, this system increasingly displaces peasant farming and production, with the associated loss of indigenous knowledge systems.[10] This is sometimes referred to as the 'last great dispossession of the peasantry'. It is happening in the context of the economic liberalisation of the farming industry and when farmers are locked into being dependent on industrial fertilisers and genetically modified seeds for cash-crop production (Shiva 2013). In Mexico, South Korea and India, this system has led to widespread dispossession because of debt among farmers. In India alone, over 200 000 suicides among farmers have been reported. Another driver of dispossession is sovereign funds and foreign investors, who are buying prime agricultural land in Africa and other parts of the global South. Increasingly, the trend for land grabbing creates enclaves of export-led agricultural food production and biofuel production.

Fourth, although the transnational industrial agricultural system produces cheap food, it is mainly unhealthy food. This is not to argue a case for expensive food, but to recognise that industrial agriculture and its corollary of fast food have devastating effects on human life. Increasingly, obesity is becoming a worldwide problem along with various attendant health issues, like diabetes and heart disease. In the US obesity increased by seventy-one per cent between 1991 and 2001, and this is mirrored in various parts of the world as national studies and public discourse recognise the urgency of the crisis. However, the media and food corporations tend to claim this crisis is the result of bad choices by individuals, rather than the result of an 'impoverished range of choices' (Patel 2007: 273). With growing income inequality worldwide, obesity correlates with ill health among the working class and the poor.

Fifth, transnational industrial agriculture is considered to be one of the most ecologically destructive sectors in the global economy. There are several reasons for this. Oil is used in the manufacture of various agricultural inputs, such as fertilisers, and as fuel for machinery and transport vehicles. Carbon emissions are released in the value chains and particularly in the shipping of food. Cattle eructation and flatulence release immense amounts of methane into the atmosphere, contributing to global warming. The quantities are significant, considering that there are about 27 billion head of livestock on the planet, which consume 750 million tonnes of fertiliser-intensive grain feed and 200 million tonnes of pesticide-intensive soybeans as feedstock (Roberts 2013: 26). Industrial agriculture is also implicated for the most intensive use of water of all sectors. The chemicals used in industrial farming pollute water systems and oceans. And, most importantly, mono-production of industrial crops kills off biodiversity and limits the capacity for organic plant varieties to adapt to climatic shifts. In short, the system is unsustainable.

Transnational industrial agriculture is destructive to human society and nature. It leads to food crises that tend to be genocidal and ecocidal, and hence it is a key historical expression of the crises of capitalist civilisation. Moreover, it is exacerbated in its links with other systemic crisis tendencies, such as financialised chaos, climate crisis, peak oil and the securitisation of democracy.

The securitisation of democracy

Modern democracy is about a people's history of struggle to limit the power of capital and broaden modern citizenship to embrace non-property holders, women, non-whites and immigrants. It is also the story about the democratisation of the US constitution, particularly after the French Revolution (Wood 2004). In essence, modern democracy, through its advocacy of rights, freedoms and forms (representative, direct, participatory and associative), has embodied an impulse against capitalism as the expression of the will of the people. At the same time, capitalism has generally involved a formal separation between the 'political' and the 'economic'; the state and market are deemed separate and distinct spheres of society, which is specific to a capitalist society. But, in practice, state intervention is crucial to realising the systemic imperatives of the market (Wood 2003). Liberal ideology has further authorised this separation, so that democracy is understood as separate from corporate power and is necessary to protect the individual from the abuse of state power; thus democracy is 'for the people and by the people'. In the US, liberal democracy has been undergoing fundamental changes over the past few decades. In theory and practice, democracy has been reduced to certain basic freedoms: the rule of law, separations of power and basic procedural performance, such as electing representatives by means of periodic elections. Money has also come to play a crucial role in determining representation and the 'people's representatives'.

At the same time, US foreign policy, both during and after the cold war, has trumpeted the virtues of the US liberal model as the standard of democracy for all to follow. This model has become a major export of the US superpower. With the demise of the Soviet Union, a wave of democratisation, including in Latin America, Africa, Asia and former Soviet Bloc countries, entrenched the US liberal model of democracy as the global standard (Robinson 1996). However, the nature of democracy coming to the fore in the US and other parts of the world is prompting serious questions about the character and content of the US democracy standard. Since President Reagan, US democracy has been firmly locked into a path of neoliberalisation, which has conjoined capitalism and democracy as market democracy. This has increased the power of corporations in the political system by allowing greater funding to political parties' (effectively buying lobbying influence), and has reduced electoral politics to a media-driven marketing spectacle requiring large sums of money.[11]

In the meantime, since 9/11, national security concerns have trumped domestic democratic rights and freedoms. The sweeping powers claimed to fight terrorism domestically amounted to secret detentions, suspected American citizens being designated as 'enemy combatants' without any rights, the use of torture in anti-terror police work, scrutinising adherents to the Muslim faith, and the use of assassinations to deal with terrorists (Falk 2004). In this endless War on Terror, privacy has also been a casualty and has been undermined, domestically and internationally. This has been brought to the fore by WikiLeak's revelations, as well as by whistleblowers like Bradley Manning and Edward Snowden (see Harding 2014; Leigh and Harding 2011). Moreover, the War on Terror has violated various international laws and standards, and has purely been driven by the logic that might is right. The illegal invasions of Afghanistan and Iraq, holding prisoners at Abu Ghraib without due process, the interrogation methods used by the Central Intelligence Agency on suspected terrorists, and the use of special killing squads and drone attacks have all raised questions about the nature of US democracy – and how it provides licence for wanton violence, gross abuses of power and violations of international law.

Basically, US democracy is securitised through two tendencies. First, it is narrowed by national-security imperatives, in which freedoms and rights do not matter if you are an enemy or suspected enemy in the endless War on Terror. National security trumps all due process and rights, for both American and non-American citizens. In other words, democracy has become militarised. Second, democracy has become securitised in the economic sense of ensuring that capital, particularly finance capital, prevails over democratic imperatives. Put differently, history has come full circle and so-called free markets are given more power through market democracy – a situation that is similar to the advent of industrial capitalism in Britain, when democracy did not exist. The economic securitisation of democracy ensures that market imperatives come to the fore to secure stability, technocratic forms of governance are strengthened, the power of the media is used to shape public opinion in the interests of markets, and dissent is disciplined through both market and coercive power.

In different parts of the world, the articulation between militarised and economic securitisation of democracy has been evident to different degrees, informed by national conditions and the degree of influence of the US. This democratic project, according to the US standard, has been happening through democratisation, regime change, new constitutionalism, for example in the European Union context,[12] and through good-governance agendas – for example, in Africa. The securitisation of democracy, and its re-articulation as market democracy, has been about hollowing out democracy, reducing it to a formal electoral performance and presenting the undemocratic, hierarchical capitalist corporation as the custodian of democratic freedom. This has created a systemic crisis in which political systems are increasingly discredited and the gap between leaders and the led is widening, creating a legitimacy deficit. True democratic politics, driven by citizens, is being disabled and is in jeopardy. This systemic condition, in its intersection with the other dimensions of civilisational crisis, opens the way for new extreme right-wing nationalist, populist, religious-fundamentalist, authoritarian and even neo-Nazi forces to emerge, as disaffection and political alienation deepen on a global scale.

CATASTROPHISM OR TRANSFORMATIVE MOMENT?

So, where does this leave us? Is the world coming to an end? Is capitalism about to collapse? What are the challenges for left agency?

Without a deep understanding of the systemic tendencies underpinning the crises of capitalist civilisation, many view the civilisational crisis of capitalism as the beginning of the end. This perspective postulates that, if capitalism continues on the path that it is on, it will destroy itself, the human species and other life forms. Human agency is read out of this historical reality and this perspective easily descends into catastrophism with environmental, right-wing and left-wing variants (Lilley et al. 2012). This includes apocalyptic notions of ends and rebirths, millenarian prognoses, ecofascism and various theses on the imminent collapse of capitalist civilisation.

One danger in all this ideological froth is a rejection of humanity: we are condemned as a species and hence we need a post-human perspective of the world and the planet. This is a dangerous perspective in its abandonment of humanity and its resignation to the status quo. Moreover, it is extremely one-sided in its understanding of human beings by failing to recognise the importance of human activity in relation to necessity and contingency in history. Central to this is human agency and almost 10 000 years of human civilisational history, in which human agency and will shaped systemic dynamics, as much as these shaped human beings. This is the normative underpinning of an analysis of the systemic crises of capitalist civilisation. This analysis is not neutral: it is about engendering transformative human agency.

At the same time, an analysis of the systemic crises of capitalist civilisation cannot be uncoupled from the historical conjuncture in which it exists. But, rather than a conjuncture of catastrophism, we need to appreciate that global capitalism, in its stage of transnational techno-financial accumulation, is going through a conjunctural shift: from the conjuncture of neoliberal hegemony to a conjuncture of systemic crises and transformative resistance. Neoliberalism, as a class project and systemic solution, has not worked. As a class project, it is inherently crisis-prone and has systemically transformed global capitalism by embedding the power of finance capital in the logic of global accumulation, which, in turn, has created the tendency for financialised chaos. However, neoliberalism does not have the solutions to financialised chaos, which it needs to ensure financial returns, and neither can it solve what are historically unprecedented systemic crisis tendencies. Even if neoliberalism were abandoned, each of the systemic crisis tendencies identified would persist because these tendencies were not constituted by neoliberalism, except for financialised chaos, but have been exacerbated by it. Each of these tendencies – financialised chaos, climate crisis, oil peak, food-system crisis and securitisation of democracy – is now inherent to contemporary capitalism and part of its accumulation logic. At the same time, each of these systemic tendencies is autonomous and can overlap and interlock in different combinations or cut across each other. In short, we are in a conjuncture of deepening systemic crises and transformative resistance.

However, transformative human agency will not automatically come from an analysis of the systemic crises of capitalist civilisation, nor from a reading of the contemporary conjuncture. At the same time, world history can go in any direction, unless the Left that is immersed in the current cycle of global resistance addresses three crucial and immediate strategic challenges, and grasps the opportunity to transform the current conjuncture.

The first challenge to left agency is to understand the dual political significance of an analysis of the systemic crises of capitalist civilisation and its educative function in political discourse. On the one hand, this provides an antidote to catastrophism and grounds an understanding of the destructive logic of capitalism in a concrete analysis of the dynamics driving this logic. This brings into view the constitution of the systemic tendencies towards crisis and their class character. Put differently, these are not working-class, or more broadly, the people's crises: they are crises of capitalism. This opens up the prospects for resolving these contradictions through left agency. On the other hand, such an analysis implicates the US superpower. It demonstrates how the US is contributing to the crises of capitalist civilisation and strengthening the process of capitalist destruction of life on earth. The US, in the current conjuncture of systemic crises and transformative resistance, is in crisis and incapable of rising to the challenge of resolving the systemic crises coming to the fore. In many ways, the contemporary domination the US imposes on the world, and its current role and place in history, go a long way towards explaining the crises of capitalist civilisation. Moreover, the US is also a major obstacle to resolving the crises of capitalist civilisation. In other words, a systemic analysis of the crisis of capitalism is both an antidote to catastrophism and anti-imperialist.

Although such an analysis will not automatically shift consciousness, it does provide the basis to rethink the challenge of mass-based left politics. This is the second challenge to left agency. An analysis that foregrounds the systemic dimensions of capitalist crises also provides a map for locating left agency within a politics of counter-hegemony or transformative resistance. Although Gramsci ([1971] 1998) argued for a 'war of position' in civil society, this was not grounded in a concrete historical context that unpacked and theorised the nature of resistance in particular historical conjunctures. This means Gramsci's abstractions have to be grounded in the global conjuncture of systemic crises and transformative resistance. Moreover, such a practice of transformative resistance challenges the Left to go beyond a politics of 'reform versus revolution' and to situate its agency within civil society, at the centre of the contradictions that will contribute to the end of capitalism. More practically, this means transformative resistance has to build a politics around the systemic crisis tendencies of capitalist civilisation, so these tendencies are confronted both defensively and offensively. In short, transformative resistance has to be against financialised neoliberalisation and for de-marketised and de-commodified alternatives that expand the commons. It has to be against false solutions to the climate crisis and for legally binding emission-reduction targets for all countries, for resolution of climate debt, rights-based carbon budgets, climate jobs and public transport; against extractivism of fossil fuels and for socially owned renewables and energy sovereignty; against the corporate-controlled industrial food system and for food sovereignty; and against market democracy and for the defence of all democratic rights, freedoms and forms of democracy – that is, more democracy, not less. The Left today has to be clear, consistent and firm on these questions to be able to build transformative mass-based movements and politics.

The third challenge confronting the Left, which is derived from an analysis of the systemic crises of capitalist civilisation and the transformative prospects it creates, is the strategic switch from the momentum of transformative resistance that advances opposition and alternatives, to a hegemonic politics of sustaining life. This means the question of a just transition has to be integral to the politics of contemporary left agency. For such a conception to emerge at the centre of society, it has to be situated in a hegemonic politics that sustains life by realising the following necessary conditions: first, it has to be rooted in mass-based transformative social forces confronting the systemic crisis tendencies of capitalist civilisation, which are accumulating progressive class and social forces into a new state and civil-society historical bloc. Second, it has to be constantly engaged in forms of democratic political pedagogy to raise political consciousness and build self-emancipatory capacities at the grassroots level to help advance alternatives from below. Third, it has to build a deeply democratic and humanised political instrument, anchored in logics of mass power, transformative resistance and international solidarity. And, finally, it has to clarify and develop a transformative conception of the just transition linked to a vision of building democratic eco-feminist socialism in the present as part of realising it in the future.

If the Left rises to these challenges, it would ensure that class and popular struggle are not read out of history or obscured by the current crises of capitalist civilisation. Human civilisations have risen, fallen and regenerated. Contemporary capitalist civilisation is not about to collapse but it is at an impasse, bedevilled by a fundamental question: ecocide or transformation? Class and popular struggle are necessary to ensure the balance of forces and the scales of history tilt towards transformation. The systemic crises of capitalist civilisation add up to the potential for a transformative moment for radical change. Such a moment calls for the creative, ethical and humanised power of the working class and progressive social forces to inaugurate a transition that departs from the marketisation–destruction logic of capitalism. History is still undecided and open. The time for transformative change is now.

CONCLUSION

This chapter tested a thesis about the systemic crises of capitalist civilisation to identify signposts, openings and new ways of thinking. It asked what Marx's thought can offer us, both in its strengths and limitations, to comprehend the contemporary crises of capitalist civilisation. If the empirical world of capitalism is showing morbid signs of civilisational crisis – self-destruction, systemic breakdowns, gridlocks and failures in terms of various dimensions – we need to engage with Marx's way of thinking about capitalism to understand its logic of destruction. This may, however, mean challenging and departing from Marx at the level of our theoretical understanding of the systemic crisis tendencies of capitalism and how we periodise historical capitalism. It also means we have to understand how the systemic crisis tendencies of the capitalist civilisational crisis are constituted by the US-led bloc and transnational class practices. Such an analysis and understanding have to guide us through the millenarian narratives and catastrophic discourses of our time. The crux of the matter is, if the US superpower and capital have produced a crisis-ridden civilisation, then this can be undone with transformative agency.

NOTES

1   Clarke (1994) has done the most extensive and detailed study that confirms this.
2   See Brenner (2002, 2006) for an explication of overproduction and competition, and the centrality of economic-centred explanations for capitalist crisis. Also see Bello's (2013) more recent analysis of the current global crisis, in which overproduction features prominently in his explanation. Also see Lapavitsas (2013), who explicates the notion of financialisation and financial overaccumulation by building on Marx and Hilferding.
3   Harvey (2014) highlights disparities in income and wealth as an important 'moving contradiction', and identifies endless compound growth and capital's relation to nature as 'dangerous contradictions' in his mapping of the 17 contradictions of contemporary capitalism. Also see Piketty (2014) on the state of inequality.
4   In Marxist historiography this is a very contentious issue. Some claim the origins of capitalism lie in mercantile relations, others in agrarian capitalism, others in primitive accumulation and others maintain that capitalism has its origins strictly in industrial capitalism.
5   Sassen (2011) uses the term 'savage sorting', which refers to the spatial spread of systemic financialisation to zones of profit making, such as developing countries and cities.
6   China has eclipsed the US in terms of aggregate emissions, with its share of world carbon emissions estimated at twenty-six per cent while the US is at sixteen per cent.
7   According to *The New York Times* (12 November 2014), China plans to have its CO_2 emissions peak by 2030, while the US plans to cut emissions by twenty-six to twenty-eight per cent from 2005 levels by 2025, which would merely drop US emission output from a high of 6 billion metric tonnes to about 4.5 billion metric tonnes. However, even this is way less than what Obama pledged in the 2009

Copenhagen accord, which was more along the lines of 3.2 billion metric tonnes as a voluntary target, compared with 1.5 billion tonnes in the US–China agreement.

8   The planet has also experienced the hottest years on record over the past decade, with scientists confirming that 2014 was the hottest year in the history of climatology. See http://www.nytimes.com/2015/01/17/science/earth/2014-was-hottest-year-on-record-surpassing-2010.html?emc=edit_th_20150117&nl=todaysheadlin es&nlid=69791458&_r=0.

9   Cock J. 'The political economy of food in South Africa', *Amandla Magazine 37/38*, December 2014.

10   Hilary (2013: 121) suggests 400 million of the 525 million farms that are estimated to exist across the world are classified as small farms (i.e. under two hectares). These farms belong mainly to the global peasantry and provide most food staples required on the planet.

11   Wolin (2008) refers to this as 'managed democracy' and cautions that the American political system and its imperial aspirations are displaying a tendency towards 'inverted totalitarianism'.

12   See Gill (2001) for an elaboration of this concept in relation to the neoliberalisation of the European Union.

REFERENCES

Ahmed, N.M. 2010. *A User's Guide to the Crisis of Civilization*. London: Pluto Press.

Arrighi, G. and Moore, J.W. 2001. 'Capitalist development in world historical perspective'. In *Phases of Capitalist Development: Booms, Crises and Globalizations*, edited by R. Albritton, M. Itoh, R. Westra and A. Zuege. New York: Palgrave.

Bello, W. 2013. *Capitalism's Last Stand? Deglobalisation in the Age of Austerity*. London and New York: Zed Books.

Bond, P. (ed.). 2011. *Durban's Climate Gamble: Trading Carbon, Betting the Earth*. Pretoria: Unisa Press.

Brenner, R. 2002. *The Boom and the Bubble: The US in the World Economy*. London and New York: Verso Press.

Brenner, R. 2006. *The Economics of Global Turbulence*. London and New York: Verso Press.

Bukharin, N. (1917) 1929. *Imperialism and World Economy*. New York: International Publishers.

Burawoy, M. 2013. 'Marxism after Polanyi'. In *Marxisms in the 21st Century: Crisis, Critique and Struggle*, edited by M. Williams and V. Satgar. Johannesburg: Wits University Press.

Callinicos, A. 2001. 'Periodising capitalism and analyzing imperialism: Classical Marxism and capitalist evolution'. In *Phases of Capitalist Development: Booms, Crises and Globalizations*, edited by R. Albritton, M. Itoh, R. Westra and A. Zuege. New York: Palgrave.

Clarke, S. 1994. *Marx's Theory of Crisis*. New York: St Martin's Press.

Falk, R.A. 2004. *The Declining World Order: America's Imperial Geopolitics*. New York and London: Routledge.

Foster, J.B. 1999. *Marx's Ecology*. New York: Monthly Review Press.

Friedmann, H. 2004. 'Feeding the empire: The pathologies of globalized agriculture'. In *Socialist Register 2005: Empire Reloaded*, edited by L. Panitch and C. Leys. London: Merlin Press.

Gill, S. 2001. 'Constitutionalising capital: EMU and disciplinary neo-liberalism'. In *Social Forces in the Making of the New Europe: The Restructuring of European Social Relations in the Global Political Economy*, edited by A. Bieler and A.D. Morton. Basingstoke and New York: Palgrave.

Gowan, P. 1999. *The Global Gamble: Washington's Faustian Bid for World Dominance*. London and New York: Verso.

Gramsci, A. (1971) 1998. *Selections from the Prison Notebooks*, edited by Q. Hoare and G.N. Smith. Hyderabad: Orient Longman.

Greer, J.M. 2008. *The Long Descent: A User's Guide to the End of the Industrial Age*. Gabriola Island, BC: New Society Publishers.

Harding, L. 2014. *The Snowden Files: The Inside Story of the World's Most Wanted Man*. London: Guardian Books.

Harvey, D. 2014. *Seventeen Contradictions and the end of Capitalism*. Oxford and New York: Oxford University Press.

Hertwich, E.G. and Peters, G.P. 2009. 'Carbon footprint of nations: a global, trade-linked analysis', *Environmental Science & Technology*, 43 (16): 6414–6420.

Hilary, J. 2013. *The Poverty of Capitalism: Economic Meltdown and the Struggle for What Comes Next*. London and New York: Pluto Press.

Hilferding, R. (1910) 1981. *Finance Capital: A Study of the Latest Phase of Capitalist Development*. London: Routledge and Kegan Paul.

Hiscock, G. 2012. *Earth Wars: The Battle for Global Resources*. Singapore: John Wiley & Sons.

Hobson, J.A. (1902) 2006. *Imperialism: A Study*. New York: Cosmo.

IEA (International Energy Agency). 2007. *World Energy Outlook*. Paris: IEA.

IPCC (Intergovernmental Panel on Climate Change). 2014. 'Summary for policymakers'. In *Climate Change 2014: Impacts, Adaptation, and Vulnerability. Part A: Global and Sectoral Aspects. Contribution of Working Group II to the Fifth Assessment Report of the Intergovernmental Panel on Climate Change*, edited by C.B. Field, V.R. Barros, D.J. Dokken, K.J. Mach, M.D. Mastrandrea, T.E. Bilir, M. Chatterjee, K.L. Ebi, Y.O. Estrada, R.C. Genova, B. Girma, E.S. Kissel, A.N. Levy, S. MacCracken, P.R. Mastrandrea and L.L. White. Cambridge and New York: Cambridge University Press.

Jessop, B. 2001. 'What follows Fordism? On the periodisation of capitalism and its regulation'. In *Phases of Capitalist Development: Booms, Crises and Globalizations*, edited by R. Albritton, M. Itoh, R. Westra and A. Zuege. New York: Palgrave.

Klare, M.T. 2012. *The Race for What's Left: The Global Scramble for the World's Last Resources*. New York: Metropolitan Books.

Klein, N. 2014. *This Changes Everything: Capitalism Versus the Climate*. London: Allen Lane.

Lapavitsas, C. 2013. *Profiting Without Producing: How Finance Exploits Us All*. London and New York: Verso.

Leigh, D. and Harding, L. 2011. *WikiLeaks: Inside Julian Assange's War on Secrecy*. London: Guardian Books.

Lenin, V.I. (1917) 2011. *Imperialism, the Highest Stage of Capitalism*. Eastford: Martino Publishing.

Lilley, S., McNally, D., Yuen, E. and Davis, J. 2012. *Catastrophism: The Apocalyptic Politics of Collapse and Rebirth*. Oakland: PM Press.

Marx, K. (1859) 1999. *A Contribution to the Critique of Political Economy.* Moscow: Progress Publishers.

McMichael, P. and Raynolds, L.T. 1994. 'Capitalism, agriculture and world economy'. In *Capitalism and Development,* edited by L. Sklairo. London and New York: Routledge.

Ollman, B. 2003. 'Marx's dialectical method is more than a mode of exposition: A critique of systematic dialectics'. In *New Dialectics and Political Economy,* edited by R. Albritton and J. Simoulidis. New York: Palgrave Macmillan.

Patel, R. 2007. *Stuffed and Starved: The Hidden Battle for the World Food System.* New York: Melville House Publishing.

Piketty, T. 2014. *Capital in the Twenty-First Century.* Cambridge, MA and London: The Belknap Press of Harvard University Press.

Roberts, W. 2013. *The No-Nonsense Guide to World Food.* Oxford: New Internationalist.

Robinson, W.I. 1996. *Promoting Polyarchy: Globalisation, US Intervention, and Hegemony.* Cambridge: Cambridge University Press.

Sassen, S. 2011. 'A savage sorting of winners and losers, and beyond'. In *Aftermath: A New Global Economic Order?,* edited by C. Calhoun and G. Derluguian. New York and London: New York University Press.

Satgar, V. 2014. 'South Africa's emergent "green developmental state?"'. In *The End of the Developmental State?,* edited by M. Williams. Scottsville: UKZN Press.

Shiva, V. 2013. *Making Peace with the Earth.* Johannesburg: Jacana Media.

Van der Pijl, K. 2006. *Global Rivalries: From the Cold War to Iraq.* London and Ann Arbor: Pluto Press.

Wallerstein, I. 2003. *The Decline of American Power.* New York: New Press.

Wolin, S.S. 2008. *Managed Democracy and the Spectre of Inverted Totalitarianism.* Princeton and Oxford: Princeton University Press.

Wood, E.M. 2003. *Empire of Capital.* London and New York: Verso.

Wood, N. 2004. *Tyranny in America: Capitalism and National Decay.* London and New York: Verso.

Yergin, D. 2012. *The Quest: Energy, Security, and the Remaking of the Modern World.* London: Penguin.

2

ACTIVIST UNDERSTANDINGS OF THE CRISIS

William K Carroll

Arguably, the financial meltdown of 2008 and its continuing aftermath mark some sort of turning point in global history. As the first capitalist crisis of the twenty-first century, 2008 and its aftermath have been compared to the great depressions of the 1870s and 1930s, and the generalised recession of the early to mid 1970s (Panitch and Gindin 2012). The latter served as an impetus for the transition from Fordist-Keynesian regulation to globalising neoliberalism. But what sort of turning point? Several years on, capitalism seems to be in the deepest, most sustained slump since the 1930s (McNally 2011),[1] and although the crisis has been very uneven in its geographical spread and reach, it is most certainly systemic. This crisis, moreover, is more than just a slowdown or contraction in the rate of capital accumulation, with all that that entails. It is also profoundly ecological. This is most urgently felt in terms of climate change, but also in terms of interrelated issues, such as declining biodiversity through species extinction, rising food insecurity and resource depletion resulting from extractivism.

How do movement intellectuals associated with the production and mobilisation of counter-hegemonic knowledge view the crisis? What can we learn from their reflections? On the basis of in-depth interviews with 91 members of 16 transnational alternative policy groups (TAPGs), this chapter takes up these questions. But first it offers an overall perspective on the crisis, drawing on neo-Gramscian political economy. The chapter concludes with a synthesis of key insights from the research on left responses to the crisis.

A DUAL CRISIS

For more than a century and a half, left intellectuals have analysed capitalist crises within a political-economy framework rooted in Marx's critique of capital. Simple observation of economic history shows capitalism to be a crisis-prone form of society. Yet Marx went further, revealing capital's deep crisis dependence. Capital accumulation follows a familiar boom-bust rhythm. Capital must grow or die; capitalists must reinvest their profits or lose competitiveness – but when aggregated over all capitals, the pursuit of growth in the boom phase creates an expanding volume of capital-seeking profitable outlets, which eventually outstrips the available venues within the 'real economy', threatening to depress profit rates.

As Marx ([1894]1967) noted, the financial system can extend the boom up to a point by funding overextended industrialists and absorbing surplus capital. However, as investment shifts from production to the accumulation of fictitious capital, a speculative bubble emerges. And as the volume of fictitious capital (i.e. paper claims on the future production of surplus value) grows, the prospects for redeeming those claims diminish. Ultimately, 'the financial system heightens instability, by both supporting boom in the productive economy and, as the profit rate falls, increasingly supporting investment of surplus capital in fictitious capital and sending it on other adventurous paths' (Potts 2011: 462).[2]

In the classical Marxist narrative, economic crisis (if not seized politically by an organised working class) becomes the means of restoring conditions for profitability, setting the stage for another boom. On the one hand, surplus capital is destroyed or devalued (including speculative fictitious capital and weaker industrial firms). On the other, wage costs plummet as the ranks of labour's reserve army swell. However, in the crisis of 2008, unprecedented global crisis-management interventions, creating an enormous expansion of credit, opened up a different trajectory, one of 'continual postponement, with low profitability, low growth and high levels of surplus capital seeking adventurous paths and creating new bubbles' (Potts 2011: 465). Indeed, in the aftermath of the 2008 financial meltdown, only a tiny proportion of fictitious capital was depreciated in real terms and thus destroyed. Hence, financial overaccumulation was not significantly mitigated (Candeias 2011). Instead, with the global financial system poised to disintegrate, states effectively socialised capital's bad debts, increasing public debt loads. The provisional result has been a new 'age of austerity', as states attempt to pay down their debts to the financial institutions they bailed out in 2008 (Streeck 2011: 20).

Crises, however, are not merely economic – they are multifaceted, so they activate acute political issues and currents. In their political and psycho-cultural aspects, crises are more than disruptions to capital's expanded reproduction. They are a time for decision. As O'Connor (1987: 3) puts it,

> 'crisis' is not and cannot be merely an 'objective' historical process (such as, for example, the turning point in an illness over which the victim has no control). 'Crisis' is also a 'subjective' historical process – a time when it is not possible to take for granted 'normal' economic, social, and other relationships; a time for decision; a time when what individuals actually do counts for something.

Of particular note are what Gramsci termed 'organic crises' resulting from 'incurable structural contradictions', which shift the terrain of struggle, creating new conjunctures and new combinations of opportunity and danger for the ruling class and for protagonists of radical change (Gramsci 1971: 177). The crisis of 2008 is such a crisis. It matches Gramsci's famous characterisation that crisis 'consists precisely in the fact that the old is dying and the new cannot be born; in this interregnum a great variety of morbid symptoms appear' (1971: 276). The crisis has been more than a 'conjunctural disequilibrium', however. It has posed a persistent set of intractable problems. It is 'a crisis of the entire social formation, both its economic "content" and its political "form"' (Thomas 2009: 145). Organic crisis not only problematises ruling-class visions and strategies, but also deepens the sense of despair. As old ways become untenable and conditions of life deteriorate, popular discontent fuels outbreaks of protest, which, however, stall for lack of organisational infrastructure and radical vision.

In the wake of 2008, neoliberalism, as McNally (2011) holds, may well be incapable of summoning up a compelling vision of the future. But the same can also be said of the Left, at least in its 'Third Way', or neoliberal guise. Yet organic crisis does not necessarily imply a complete breakdown of political legitimacy: 'The problem of political legitimacy for disciplinary neoliberalism has been met by strategies of depoliticization ... as yet we have not seen any of the regimes governing North American or European polities being toppled' (Gill 2012a: 26).

Importantly, the contemporary crisis has an unprecedented dual character: it is both political-economic and political-ecological. In the late twentieth century, as internationalised capitalism scaled up to a system of transnational production and consumption, its ecological externalities also began to reach a global scale. Species extinction, the thinning ozone layer, ocean acidification and global warming are expressions of globalised capitalism in ecological over-shoot. For the Left, this dual economic and ecological character of the crisis creates a host of problems that are not being adequately addressed by ruling elites. These problems constitute 'the *general* political economic structure within which social and environmental movements actually exist' (Clement 2011: 448). They provide these movements with a structure of opportunities not only to resist, but also to pose radical alternatives to an increasingly troubled order.

PASSIVE REVOLUTION AND ANTI-PASSIVE REVOLUTION

The organic crisis has brought with it a dynamic of *passive revolution*, but also one of popular resistance that could converge into '*anti-passive revolution*' (Buci-Glucksmann 1979: 232, emphasis added). Through the latter, subalterns become protagonists of an alternative project. Passive revolution is an elite-engineered 'revolution from above', 'a technique which the bourgeoisie attempts to adopt when its hegemony is weakened in any way' (Showstack-Sassoon 1987: 207). In his time Gramsci saw both Americanism and fascism as passive-revolutionary responses in Northern capitalism to organic crisis (Coutinho 2012). In passive revolution, 'the passive element is to integrate the interests of the subaltern but to keep these groups in a subaltern, powerless position, and to absorb their intellectuals and leaders into the power bloc, while depriving the subaltern of their leadership' (Candeias 2011: 48–49).

Initially, in its Thatcherite form – a 'two-nations' response to the crisis of Northern Fordist-Keynesianism (Jessop et al. 1984) – neoliberalism itself has involved passive revolution. In the global North, it has come to incorporate motifs of New Left libertarianism and liberal feminism into a 'new spirit of capitalism' (Boltanski and Chiapello 2005), in which 'rigid organizational hierarchies would give way to horizontal teams and flexible networks, thereby liberating individual creativity' (Fraser 2013: 220; Gammon 2013). In the South, the passive-revolution dynamic emerged initially in response to the recession-inducing Volcker shock, when tripling of interest rates in the US led to a global debt crisis (announced with Mexico's default in 1982) and to the structural adjustment programmes through which neoliberalism was imposed on debtor states in the ensuing three decades (Morton 2003; Satgar 2008). As Streeck (2013: 19) has argued, in the wake of the 2008 crisis the same debt-driven dynamic has come to the global North, as each state 'reassures its creditors that their claims to public funds will take precedence over the claims of citizens ... [thereby] essentially expropriating social rights and politically created entitlements intended to contain inequality'. In neoliberalism's evolution, elements of transnational passive revolution can also be seen in the rise of global-governance initiatives of hegemonic incorporation, such as the G20 (Wade 2011), and in the project of green capitalism (Goodman and Salleh 2013), which may, as the climate crisis deepens, be conjoined to geo-engineering.

A key resource for passive revolution, well ensconced in the North and exported South in recent decades, is American-style consumerism (Agnew 2005). In the advanced capitalist zone, and particularly the most consumerist neoliberal formations, like the US, the acquisition of commodities functions as 'a social norm, civic duty, display of individual achievement, and a key source of life-satisfaction', rendering resistance beyond the individual level not only hard to materialise, but 'almost impossible to imagine' (Ivanova 2011: 329, 347). Consumerism is a pillar of 'market civilization' whose logic ultimately destroys conceptions of social solidarity, and of social and ecological sustainability (Gill 2012b: 522). Counter-hegemonic responses require us 'to address interdependencies with each other and with nature' (Gill 2012b: 522).

Crucially, passive revolution and anti-passive revolution are antagonistically interdependent. In an organic crisis, 'the failure of the proletariat to exert its alternative hegemony allows the bourgeoisie to continue its rule despite the weakening of its own hegemony' (Showstack-Sassoon 1987: 210). The elite-engineered management of the 2008 crisis – namely, resorting to Keynesian tools only to resume neoliberal austerity once the threat of global depression had lifted, and the failure of the Left to advance a persuasive alternative – offers a textbook example of this interdependence. Looking ahead, movements on the Left need 'to remain attentive to the future tendencies of capitalist development in the form of those passive revolutions still to come, and to how best to organise collective resistances in the struggle against capital in our present situation' (Morton 2010: 333).

TRANSNATIONAL ALTERNATIVE POLICY GROUPS AS MOVEMENT INTELLECTUALS

In these circumstances of organic crisis, marked by a legacy of uneven development and top-down strategies of passive revolution, a key question to ask is how to build a transnational counter-hegemonic bloc of social forces. In part, the challenge is one of dialectically transforming common sense into 'good sense', through new forms of knowledge and praxis. As a dialectical movement, what Gill (2012b: 507) terms the postmodern prince 'not only interprets dominant power as supremacy or "dominance without hegemony", but also, and more constructively, seeks to create new forms of knowledge and culture in an effort to found more just and sustainable forms of state, society and world order ...'

TAPGs offer important sites for such praxis. As collective intellectuals of a fledging 'Global Left' (De Sousa Santos 2006), they create knowledge that challenges existing economic priorities and political policies, and that advocates alternative ways of organising political, economic and cultural life. TAPGs mobilise this knowledge not only through mainstream media, but also through activist networks and alternative media, and they collaborate with movements to implement alternative ideas (Carroll 2014). If, as Gramsci held, counter-hegemonic leaders need to become 'constructors, organizers, and "permanent persuaders"' of alternative practices and worldviews (Gramsci 1971: 10; Reed 2012: 575), TAPGs provide venues for such efforts. This is because they not only challenge 'imperial common sense' (Gill 2012b: 505), but also facilitate what Gramsci termed 'moral and intellectual reformation', which rearticulates and renovates common sense, within an '"interior transformation" [Gramsci 1971: 420] ... making critical the subaltern as part of a process of reconstituting it and generating a revolutionary (counter-hegemonic) politics' (Reed 2012: 568).

This chapter is part of a larger project on the discourses, practices and networks of 16 TAPGs. Although each group pursues its own project, most have participated extensively in World Social Forum (WSF) processes. The groups' worldviews converge on the following ideas and beliefs (Carroll 2014):

- A critical stance on neoliberalism and colonialism;
- Advocacy of global justice and sustainable human development;
- The belief that a better world can be achieved only through grassroots democratic movements;
- An ethical and strategic commitment to North–South solidarity;
- The priority of critical analysis in informing effective and appropriate strategies for change.

Just as mainstream think tanks form part of a well-established transnational historical bloc for neoliberalism, TAPGs are embedded in a global-left network of transnational movement organisations and non-governmental organisations. And, to some extent, TAPGs network with one another (Carroll 2013; Carroll and Sapinski 2013). Elsewhere, I have discussed the class content of this alternative 'nascent historical bloc' and have observed that, as part of a process of transnational class formation, this alternative bloc 'is dramatically overshadowed by the far more extensive and established bloc that sustains capitalist hegemony' (Carroll 2013: 704–705).

It is important to be aware that, as movement intellectuals, TAPGs are not vanguard organisations. Rather, they take up a dialogical relationship in close alliance with popular sectors – learning from the grassroots yet distilling practical and theoretical insights into alternative visions, strategies, policies and practices that challenge the hegemony of capital. As I have explained elsewhere, TAPGs make this contribution via 'modes of cognitive praxis'. These include challenging hegemonic knowledge; engaging critically with dominant institutions, including mainstream media; empowering the grassroots through participation and capacity building; building solidarities through cross-movement dialogue; integrating theory and practice; creating spaces for reflection and political invention; systematising and disseminating alternative knowledge; and prefiguring alternative futures by identifying present practices that have the potential for living otherwise (Carroll 2015). In all these respects, TAPGs differ from hegemonic think tanks (which seek to reproduce advanced capitalism while managing its crisis tendencies in alignment with elite political-economic networks and corporate media), and from vanguard or electoralist parties (which relate to social movements in top-down, instrumental terms, rather than dialogically).

The political insights presented here are gleaned from interviews with activists in TAPGs, which I conducted between May 2012 and June 2013 (see Table 2.1).[3] I first consider participants' analyses of the organic crisis, focusing on their prognoses of its most significant features and the challenges these pose for counter-hegemonic politics. I then take up their readings of the opportunities that the crisis opens up for a global Left committed to transformation.

Table 2.1: Groups participating in study of cognitive praxis networks

Est'd	Name	Acronym	Number of participants
1974	Transnational Institute (Amsterdam)	TNI	11
1975	Third World Forum (Dakar)	TWF	1
1976	Tricontinental Centre (Louvain-la-Neuve, Belgium)	CETRI	1
1976	Centre de Recherche et d'Information pour le Développement (Paris)	CRID	8
1982	Participatory Research in Asia (New Delhi)	PRIA	12
1984	Third World Network (Penang)	TWN	1
1984	Development Alternatives with Women for a New Era (Manila)	DAWN	7
1989	Third World Institute/Social Watch (Montevideo)	ITeM/SW	5
1990	Rosa Luxemburg Foundation (Berlin)	RosaLux	12
1994	International Forum on Globalization (San Francisco)	IFG	7
1995	Focus on the Global South (Bangkok)	Focus	10
1997	Network Institute for Global Democratization (Helsinki)	NIGD	1
1997	People's Plan Study Group (Tokyo)	PPSG	5
2001	Centre for Civil Society (Durban)	CCS	8
2005	Alternatives International (Montreal)	Alter-Inter	1
2005	India Institute for Critical Action: Centre in Movement (New Delhi)	CACIM	1

ACTIVIST INTELLECTUALS REFLECT ON THE CRISIS

The challenges facing TAPGs and the creative responses they have mustered need to be viewed not only in the long-term, structural context of dominant institutions (i.e. state, media, corporate capitalism, and so on), but also with an understanding of the specific time frame of the current conjuncture. That conjuncture has arisen from momentous events and struggles of recent years, including the dual crisis and the intensification of US-led hard-power imperialism after the events of 11 September 2001. The latter saw an escalation of repression and surveillance domestically, and the launch of a War on Terror, all of which chilled what had by the late 1990s become a burgeoning global justice movement. Tony Clarke, an International Forum on Globalization (IFG) board member and executive director of the Polaris Institute, said that the criminalisation of dissent, the politics of fear and other ramifications of this new imperialism led to a 'falling back' from which the global Left as a 'movement of movements' has yet to recover.

In an era of organic crisis, when space opens for a radical imaginary that might posit a clear alternative to neoliberal globalisation, can TAPGs and similar initiatives serve as sites for counter-hegemonic thinking and action? For the purposes of this chapter, the question is, how do movement intellectuals view the organic crisis in terms of the threats and opportunities it throws up for such initiatives?

To probe these issues, I posed these questions: some analysts hold that global capitalism has entered an organic crisis in which 'the old is dying and the new cannot be born', and that this crisis has economic, political, cultural and ecological dimensions. What are your thoughts on the contemporary crisis? How deep and organic is it? What do you see as the key opportunities and threats posed by the crisis for the alter-globalisation movement or global Left?

Samir Amin, founder and director of the Third World Forum (TWF), responded to my query by describing the current era as a civilisational crisis, an implosion of a world capitalism moving into greater chaos. Despite its severity, this crisis has so far inspired 'just the beginning of an awareness of what is needed' as an alternative way of life, and how to bring that about. Amin said:

> If we should have a system based on social justice, okay, but what do you mean – and how? We should have a system respecting human rights, okay, but what are human rights? And how? This is the tragedy of our

time … It is the autumn of capitalism but there is not yet a coincidence between this autumn and the spring.

Amin's perspective forms part of an intellectual project that goes back to his doctoral dissertation, 'Accumulation on a world scale', published in the early 1970s. Activist scholars like Amin have long sought to understand capitalism's crises and to strategise alternatives, and the more political-economy-oriented TAPGs, such as the Transnational Institute (TNI), Rosa Luxemburg Foundation (RosaLux) and Development Alternatives with Women for a New Era (DAWN), have developed some keen insights along the way.

Quite a number of participants offered similar views to Amin's, and some of them ventured into the pressing yet difficult question of how TAPGs might find opportunities in the crisis to help hasten a 'people's spring'. The section that follows includes some of these perspectives.

Prognoses and challenges

Like all crises, the current one has had a spatial dimension. However, in contrast to the 1997 Asian financial crisis, which spread from East Asia to Russia and Argentina in 1998, the 2008 crisis was, in its initial impact, centred on the global North. Even now, with the crisis in its sixth year at the time of writing, severe austerity programmes, the stock-in-trade of neoliberal rule in the global South during the 1980s and 1990s, are being applied in Greece and Spain, but not (yet) in Brazil or India. As Sumona Dasgupta of Participatory Research in Asia (PRIA) observed, 'This is a bit like what the IMF [International Monetary Fund] was doing to a lot of us: unless you do structural adjustments, we won't give you money.' Yet the continuing relative prosperity of the Brazil, Russia, India, China and South Africa grouping (BRICS) has not been shared by other places on capitalism's periphery (for example, in much of Africa). Moreover, recent trends in BRICS are downward.

Meanwhile, as DAWN's Claire Slatter commented, the crisis coincides with 'another round of imperialist pillage and plunder', a 'last grab' by the powerful for whatever resources can be appropriated. DAWN's analysis of the crisis describes a 'fierce new world' in which past gains become insecure and new challenges arise. Nicole Bidegain identified climate change as a core element of the crisis, stemming from an unsustainable production–consumption model based on the financialisation not only of the economy, but also of nature. An important task is to oppose calls for a green economy, which will intensify the commodification of nature as a new investment field, and instead to advocate a re-regulation of capital at the global level. In the South, there is the additional challenge thrown up by governments that say, 'It is our time to pollute.'

But, as mentioned at the outset of this chapter, the crisis is not simply objective (i.e. economic and ecological) – it is also subjective in that it has a psycho-cultural dimension. Michel Lambert of Alternatives International, for example, sees the contemporary predicament as an 'extremely deep' crisis 'of imagination', as policy ideas are retreaded from neoliberalism's 'good old days' to maintain the current system. Roberto Bissio of the Third World Institute/Social Watch pointed to a major political reason for this crisis of imagination, which feeds the passive revolution. In neoliberalism's triumph, he said, 'alternative thinking was destroyed'. The growing stock of neoliberal formulas has, over three decades, displaced contenders within the realm of democratic capitalism (Peck, Theodore and Brenner 2012). This, said Bissio, has placed policymakers in 'a very paradoxical situation, where they know it doesn't work, but they keep applying the same thing because it's the only thing they know how to do'. TAPGs face the challenge, therefore, of creating alternative thinking – that refuses the simple fix of restoring economic growth – a formula that might create jobs and win elections but will exacerbate the ecological crisis. The crisis of imagination is certainly a challenge for those interested in counter-hegemonic alternatives. As Patrick Bond of the Centre for Civil Society suggested,

> Maybe most tragically, we on the Left can't envisage – can't even imagine – how we're going to take advantage of this crisis. We did so badly with the last one – so badly that the ideology behind it – neoliberalism – still is dominant.

Other social-psychological aspects of the crisis of imagination have permeated into everyday life, presenting new challenges. At Focus on the Global South's Bangkok office, Jacques Chai Chomtongdi's ruminations began with a scenario of passive revolution in Europe but extended to the 'global middle class':

> You see how Europeans are moving. They are not moving to a kind of alternative, even though they go deeper and deeper into the crisis. When I was a student, we were saying the poorer you are, the more conservative you are, because you don't want to lose whatever you have left. So

maybe … the global middle class is acting in that way, in which it may even be narrowing the space for alternatives.

Rajesh Tandon, founder of PRIA, offered a parallel insight from contemporary India, focused less on the conservatising impact of fear and more on the growth of a neoliberal form of individualism, goaded on by media, marketing and state policies:

> We are not giving space to the reflection that people need to make about where we are heading in society and the bulk of it is only individualistic reflection. Am I making roads ahead for myself or not? Imagine if 1.2 billion are making roads ahead for themselves, individually – some of us will fall in the ditch because there ain't enough space to make roads for yourself.

How, Tandon asked, at the frenetic pace of rapid capitalist urbanisation and hyperconsumption, juxtaposed in India with a continuing majority of rural subalterns, can one create 'a reflective enabling of people's experience' that recovers the collectivist values and sustainable practices of a spiritual lifestyle in the Indian tradition?

Other participants described a crisis of democracy, bolstering Streeck's (2013) prognosis. Nathalie Pere-Marzano, director-general of the Centre de Recherche et d'Information pour le Développement (CRID), described 'a systemic crisis' extending well beyond 'the economy' to food, energy and other social-ecological issues. The urgency of this crisis may exacerbate the retreat of democracy in contemporary 'democratic' capitalism:

> Even in countries like France, it is not so clear how democracy works … We say 'no' to something and it's still being put in place by our governments. So what does this mean? Greek people say no to the policies their government is implementing, but their government still implements those drastic austerity measures. So, what is democracy when you don't listen to your people?

At PRIA, Kaustuv Bandyopadhyay framed the crisis as one of global governance precipitated by rigid adherence to a paradigm that works for a few, and that accepts a permanent division between rich and poor. 'This paradigm needs to change,' he said. 'And all these decisions [that] resulted in the food crisis or the environmental crisis or economic crisis combined are a governance crisis. It's a global governance crisis.'

A challenge for TAPGs, and the global Left more broadly, is to devise ways of addressing the 'elite capture' of global governance institutions and their undemocratic functioning, which underlie the governance crisis. Nick Buxton of the TNI pointed out that the neoliberal paradigm, as applied to bankrupt countries like Greece, amplifies immiseration and intensifies anger. Some of that anger can be productively channelled into radically democratic politics, and in contemporary Greece, Syriza represents that option. Yet Greek neo-Nazi party Golden Dawn has been aggressively organising communities and enlarging its own base. The challenge for Syriza and its allies, which include the TNI, is to find practical solutions not only at the policy level, but in the everyday realm. As Buxton observed, 'We're going to need to respond to [Golden Dawn] practically and with alternatives, and provide progressive responses, because otherwise any vacuum will be filled by a reactionary one.'

Perhaps the most pessimistic prognosis on the crisis of democracy I heard was voiced by TNI board chair Susan George. Consistent with TNI's published perspective, George sees a convergence of interlinked crises, with the ecological aspect most urgent and the ongoing financial crisis still keeping us 'on the edge'. In all this, George sees 'a huge crisis of democracy'. She said that democracy has become 'too expensive for capitalism'. Capitalists and their allies claim that they can't afford democracy, George said:

> Capital has enriched itself enormously over the past 30 years but they are not satisfied. They have to bring down wages; they have to get rid of the advantages that working people have ... The vast inequalities have also brought about this total disregard for human suffering and human life, and ... I think there will eventually be huge militarisation of it. There's also a food crisis and bad hunger coming ... Frontiers and fortress states, things like that. I believe people will try to resist but if people try to riot, governments and police now have technology they call 'non-lethal weapons' and they will not be allowed to continue. It's going to be bad. I don't see a happy end to all of this and that's why we have to keep working, just in case we can change something.

George's unflinching projection underlines the stakes in the crisis for those committed to global justice and counter-hegemonic praxis.

Others at TNI offered complementary perspectives to Buxton's and George's. Daniel Chavez told me that TNI views the current crisis as different from any previous one, and that it is likely to lead to a radically altered world, but not necessarily 'a progressive kind of alternative'.

Brid Brennan of the Transnational Institute described a 'full-blown crisis of the capitalist system', involving de-industrialisation in places like Europe and North America, and 'the intensification of the redivision of labour at the global level' as capital increasingly needs 'cheap labour without rights', often in the form of migrants. However, the system, Brennan said, 'has a lot of recuperative resources, especially the ideological ones'. Jun Borras also emphasised capitalism's creative capacities to reinvent itself, which have been typically underestimated by the Left. Hilary Wainwright noted as an example neoliberalism's effective appropriation of some of the rhetoric of the Left. In responding to the social disintegration that Thatcherism produced, Wainwright said:

> Neoliberalism has appropriated a lot of our rhetoric around co-ops and big society, searching for social cohesion. So, all these terrains which involve us trying to develop new kinds of collectivity – like participatory democracy in and against the state, forms of economic collaboration that both revive the cooperative movement and renew – potentially change – the trade union movement: these are also areas where neoliberalism is pushing in its own way forms of social organisation that will ameliorate the market.

In view of this, the global justice movement needs to eschew complacency, and build and continuously invent its own forces of struggle.

As political and economic elites learn how to manage the crisis and experiment with new neoliberal approaches that may soften its barbaric tendencies, they create space for not only renewed popular consent but also for renewed accumulation. And even if the crisis has no end in sight, as Focus on the Global South's Pablo Solon emphasised, within it some capitalists can make big profits in the sectors that are expanding and they may prefer the crisis to continue rather than find a resolution, which would weaken their position. For Solon, the crisis is a systemic, structural one, with two new elements: first, we have reached the limits of planet earth and, second, the paper economy has overtaken the productive economy by an order of magnitude. The worrisome implication of these new elements, operating alongside continued inaction on climate, is that the world will overrun a key tipping point.

Participants from RosaLux, including its Institute of Critical Social Analysis, provided further insights on the scope and shape of the organic crisis. The institute's deputy director, Mario Candeias, is of the view that the crisis has been deepening for two decades, with each recovery becoming weaker than the one before. In 2007/08 it reached the critical point, as other crisis tendencies condensed with the immediate economic crisis, including the ecological crisis and the reproductive crisis. The elements cohere in an organic crisis, said Candeias, as the different relations of society no longer fit together: 'Then a small problem can become a big problem when the whole dynamic of crisis develops in that way. Movements start to develop on a different level from before – coming together, not fragmented any more.'

Candeias sees this movement-integrative process as just beginning, and again, as applicable both to the Left and the Right, as the example of Greece clearly shows.

RosaLux's Steffen Kuehn made the useful distinction, developed in Michael Lebowitz's work,[4] between a crisis 'of' and a crisis 'in' capitalism:

> I think it's a very deep crisis, but I think it's a crisis *within* capitalism. It's not a crisis *of* capitalism … I think capitalism would be in crisis if people in the huge majority lose the illusion that this system could work out for them, or could work out for all of us. This has not happened yet. Many people have doubts, many people have criticised, but there is not a movement, there is not an idea of something that is really endangering capitalism itself …

In Kuehn's view, it is wrong to view the ecological crisis as providing impetus for a move beyond capitalism. The creativity of the system can produce 'ways to limit access to natural resources for those who can't pay'. Without an exit from capitalism, the crisis will be resolved on the backs of subalterns. The implication is clear, he said: 'A transformation of the political Left is necessary for anything that transforms capitalism to something nicer or better.' Inasmuch as TAPGs provide practical and theoretical resources for a global Left, the question is, how might they help foster such a transformation?

Other participants from RosaLux also emphasised the great challenges the crisis has posed. For Lutz Brangsch, 'having produced its own class base, neoliberalism is now developing on that base'. This social base has been transformed: the working class has been reshaped into a precariat; capital has been transformed through the financialisation of society, which, in turn, has changed the immediate interests of working people (for instance, through privatisation of their pensions. Once pensions are privatised – converted from a defined benefit to a bundle of financial assets – workers fortunate enough to have a pension come to view it not as a deferred wage but as their own stake in capitalism – as capital, in other words.). Within the affluent strata of the working class, an 'investor aristocracy' arises (Harmes 1998). All this, Brangsch said, has 'stabilized the new phase in the development of capitalism'.

Alex Demirovic also suggested that the crisis may mark a 'breakthrough' for neoliberalism, solidifying its dominance in core capitalist states. In contrast to a scenario of hegemonic crisis, he said that

> all the crisis-management strategies are neoliberal. There is no demoralised ruling class – not in the US, not in Germany, not in Europe. So, you know they feel very strong. They learn how to make use of all the crisis-management tools they developed even in the 1930s. They know exactly how to avoid a deepening of the crisis, such as war, protectionism … I think the problem is … maybe the bourgeoisie – the bourgeois class – can handle it.

In effect, the crisis only becomes truly hegemonic if the Left is able to organise oppositional forces that point persuasively to an alternative beyond capitalism. This is the point of anti-passive revolution. Demirovic went on to consider a second scenario, that of overaccumulation. Given the massive disjuncture, already noted by Solon, between productive capital and speculative financial instruments, the bourgeoisie may succeed in managing the crisis 'for now', but fail to solve the problem of overaccumulation. Ultimately, the ballooning volume of fictitious capital depresses profit rates and necessitates a massive devaluation of assets. In this perspective, the crash of 2008 becomes a dress rehearsal for something much more dramatic. As Demirovic put it,

> the problem is how the destruction of capital is organised – by inflation or by war? Now what is going on … is capital is destroyed in

Europe – Greece, Spain and so on. What Europe is doing [is] to solve the problem in Europe for the euro and what they try is to turn the destruction of capital towards other regions. And this is a serious problem, because for those regions concerned – maybe China, maybe Japan, maybe Latin America – that means a new period of impoverishment, a new period of destruction.

In short, the crisis is organic, and therefore poses great challenges not only for elite management but for any incipient global Left force. It is a crisis of political imagination; it is a crisis of democracy and representation, sharpened by the neoliberal capture of states and intergovernmental organisations, and by the process of hollowing out the capacity of states to intervene on the side of subalterns. At the same time, the incorporation of certain elements of the libertarian Left into a softer neoliberalism poses new challenges, as does the fact that, having produced its own class base in the precariat through, for example, privatised pensions, neoliberalism appears to some as inviolate. Yet the situation is inherently unstable, as continuing financialisation, de-industrialisation of older heartlands, uneven development and ecological overshoot portend more serious problems ahead for global capitalism and for humanity.

Opportunities and openings

Crisis is a time of intense contingency, of both danger and opportunity (O'Connor 1987). Protagonists on the global Left must be alert to the emerging situation and its possibilities. More concretely, Solon offered a prognosis that the beginnings of catastrophic climate change will be felt in the current decade:

This decade, we're going to see severe impacts from the climate crisis in relation to food, to drought, to floods, to water and also in relation to health ... Now are we going to be able to develop strong social movements that in different parts of the world are able to build power and take the power that is in the hands of the transnational corporations, or are we going to be defeated in this attempt? The story is open, but we have to really fight for that.

Crisis is a time of radical contingency. And, by implication, given the dialectical character of crisis – the conjunction of heightened danger and opportunity – some of the challenges noted earlier may also present openings. Lambert of

Alternatives International, who earlier evoked a 'crisis of imagination', detects in the situation 'a lot of opportunities', precisely because the world's problems have become obvious as the crisis deepens. In reference to Quebec, a hotbed of mass politics in the 'Maple Spring' protests of 2012, Lambert said:

> Here we see a lot of people who want to be fed with new ideas. They want to engage on new things because ... they don't see in the newspaper anything that responds to their idea of the world they want to build ... So, that in itself is a huge opportunity and of course, the news is giving us many new opportunities every day. The news is so terrible.

Bad news, in this sense, can be good news if it jolts (or even nudges) people into a political awakening. At TNI, Satoko Kishimoto saw the situation in similar terms: 'undemocracy' has become so blatant, so visible, that its practices are now in question. Although the global justice movement wasted a year and a half with a disorganised, tepid response to the financial crisis of 2008, significant numbers of people have been receptive to reasoned critical responses to creeping authoritarianism.

One instance of using 'bad news' to raise consciousness is IFG's Plutonomy programme,[5] which by showing the connections between far-right plutocrats (such as America's Koch brothers) and ecologically horrendous accumulation projects (such as the Keystone XL pipeline) shines a light on the privatisation of politics and the crisis of democracy. The need for such critical knowledge is acute, and TAPGs are crucial sites for producing and mobilising it. 'People are starting to understand things,' asserted CRID's Nathalie Péré-Marzano, and they are more informed than is often assumed – about tax havens, the ultra-rich, unemployment issues, and so on. This creates an opportunity for groups like CRID, which dialogue extensively with movements to nurture protagonists for change. Paraphrasing WSF intellectual Chico Whitaker, Péré-Marzano explained that if the Occupy movement put the 99 per cent against the 1 per cent, the social forces active in and around the WSF make up only one per cent of that ninety-nine per cent: 'What do we do to take the ninety-eight per cent with us?'

This is the strategic challenge. Within it, the prospects are not bad, according to RosaLux's Rainer Rilling. Crises very often bring defeat for the Left, as we know from the crushing defeats in Germany in 1919 and the 1930s, which in both cases had tragic, world-historical significance. But, in the current crisis, the Left in Germany has not been defeated (though neither has it been reinvigorated, in Rilling's estimation). And, elsewhere, particularly in Latin America, the Left has strengthened.

In the circumstances, TAPGs can be places for dialogue, for raising consciousness and for building solidarities. As PRIA's Kaustuv Bandyopadhyay acknowledged, crisis resolution needs multiple actors to come together in dialogue. This way, he said, 'there will be exchange and better understanding, and that's the way forward. I think PRIA-like organisations have the capacity to stitch together the coalition of these actors and to bring them together and harness this energy.'

Who sits at the table is obviously a big question. It would not be difficult to enumerate all manner of movements committed to social justice and ecological health, but some participants pointed explicitly to certain key constituencies as new social forces that need to be engaged. Just as neoliberal capitalism has created its own class base, a major part of that base – the precariously employed, many of whom are highly qualified yet neither 'middle class' nor 'working class' in any traditional scheme of things – needs to be brought together within the Left, said Brangsch. Related to this, he said, in the global North there is 'a whole new generation of young people', the children of neoliberal capitalism, who have never known anything different. And, as TNI's Fiona Dove observed,

> there's a tiny minority which has been politicised through the Occupy movement, but the vast majority are just ordinary people who want to make money. But they want to be green, they want to be fair ... people want to live sustainable lives, questioning the consumer model, being very concerned about the environment.

Such sensibilities and practices need to be consciously articulated with progressive politics. But, as Dove elaborated, they can also be brought into the project of green capitalism. A softer, greener capitalism appeals to many of neoliberalism's children as the obvious way forward:

> They don't understand why you can't get rich and carry on as usual and be consumers and so forth, *and* save the planet. They don't get it. And we want them on our side, so I think ... that's going to be a big challenge for us.

Indeed, how to bring the localist, lifestyle politics of the global North's middle class into articulation with a counter-hegemonic project that necessarily points beyond localism and ethical consumption is one of the challenges facing TNI and the global Left.

Part of the answer lies in what De Sousa Santos (2006) calls the 'work of translation'. Mary Ann Manahan at Focus on the Global South's Manila office emphasised the need to 'bridge the gap … [between] big ideas and people's ideas', so that the Left's 'isms' resonate with grassroots activists. Said Manahan: 'We have to break down what is really alternative ideas for them, and I think that is really part of the challenge of Focus, while staying true to ourselves and our vision and principles of believing in those "isms".' Left responses to the crisis also need to be formulated through a critique of the 'false solutions' that constitute passive revolution. Focus on the Global South's Joseph Purugganan asserted that in responding creatively to the crisis,

> we have to address the forms by which capital must reconfigure … it is for me a very big challenge of trying to go beyond. I think of the steps to reconfigure [capitalism] as hurdles to trying to address the more funda-mental issues. So, if we are aiming for system change, we have to first remove these obstacles created by capitalism as it reconfigures – false solutions to climate change, things like that.

Elite-engineered so-called solutions, such as carbon markets, present obsta-cles to achieving a 'definite alternative to capitalism', which Gus Massiah of CRID favours as an answer to the crisis. Yet even as technocratic and market-based attempts at passive revolution cloud the issue, the crisis has led to what Brennan called 'an era of real paradigm change', when the ruling paradigm is under question and widely recognised as having failed millions of people. The increased room to manoeuvre is crucial for TAPGs. In Latin America, with US imperial power weakened, groups like DAWN and TNI are pushing hard for basic changes that would usher in sustainable production, public manage-ment of the economy, regional integration and South–South cooperation. In Germany, Candeias recalled that

> before the crisis it was not possible to talk about 'green socialism' or transformation or whatever. It was only possible to say there are so

many injustices – we have to work on these and we don't want the work-fare programme – we want some other kind of organisation of social security … But it was not possible to talk about further transformative perspectives. Now this has opened up.[6]

Even the mainstream media in Germany have begun to sound neoliberalism's death knell, as they tentatively advance such projects as 'de-growth from the right' (as Candeias put it), in which the family is revalorised as the site of care and reproduction. Without doubt, growth, in the sense of private accumulation that degrades ecosystems, is one of the system values that must be challenged, in a way that promotes alternative improvements in human capacities, in the richness of social relations, in social equity and in the vitality of ecosystems. As Jorg Schultz of RosaLux commented:

You have to come out of the growth logic: more and more toys for each and everybody, and the production of things that nobody needs. That is something we have to overcome. But do not ask me how – that still remains to be seen. That's why we are working … to identify very small and basic elements of such an answer. That's what we are trying to do with our international outlook.

The problem that Jerry Mander, founder of IFG, noted is that 'we see the alternative systems over there on the cliff … but there is a river in between'. How to get from here to there? For Mander, that means dismantling the existing power system – 'de-fanging the system' and 'setting a process for moving toward alternative systems'. It is an undertaking that can be summarised in a few words, yet he admits it is 'the hardest thing to do'.

BEYOND CRISIS, TOWARDS A GLOBAL LEFT?

These reflections of activist intellectuals in TAPGs add substance to the dialectical conception of crisis as both objective and subjective, as disintegration and re-formation, as passive revolution and anti-passive revolution. Crisis exists 'when new power centers confront existing structures of domination … when it is generally unknown what can be taken for granted or expected from existing or emerging roles, institutions, and social practices' (O'Connor 1987: 145).

Ultimately, 'the essence of crisis is not social disintegration but social struggle' (O'Connor 1987: 146).

Movement intellectuals show an acute awareness of this radical contingency and of the fierce challenges they face in building a counter-hegemonic bloc. Many of the challenges stem from the structure of class and state power, including the 'de-politicization of power relations through current international security discourses and policies' (Scholl and Freyberg-Inan 2013: 621). Yet some are rooted in activist practices themselves. My interlocutors' comments suggest a need to envision alternatives and to organise in ways that reach beyond some problematic currents within contemporary activism. In the dual crisis, the Left's prospects for waging anti-passive revolution hinge partly on whether these currents can be renovated and rearticulated into a larger counter-hegemonic project that builds South–North and cross-movement solidarities.

One such current, as reflected in Dove's comments on the lifestyle politics that appeal to the desire to live sustainable lives, comprises a cluster of localism, green consumerism and post-capitalism of the sort advocated by Gibson-Graham (2006; Gibson-Graham, Cameron and Healy 2013). Local political and prefigurative initiatives are important to grassroots empowerment, as they create opportunities for alternative learning and new relationships, while bringing new people into the struggle. But if the process goes no further than creating local non-capitalist spaces – community gardens and the like – it can be reincorporated into the hegemonic order, as another lifestyle choice within consumer capitalism (Ivanova 2011). Localism looks past capital's economic power, searching for spaces where that power does not exist. However, 'local spaces and micro-market structures are precisely what neoliberal governments promote' (Sharzer 2012: 136). What is needed, in combination with local initiatives that build grounded solidarities and put people in motion, is forms of collective prefiguration centred in struggles that reach beyond the local. To move beyond the local, conceptually and in practice, is to move from sectional struggle to class struggle, in the broadest sense of the term. As Sharzer (2012: 150) explains,

> class struggle creates a very different kind of prefiguration from radical localism, because it forces activists to think about how power works, how people outside small radical circles relate to power, and how to

build campaigns to appeal to people who, in partial, contradictory ways, are questioning capitalist rule.

A prefigurative alternative that incorporates the virtues of localism while pointing beyond it is the so-called solidarity economy, which the Cooperative and Policy Alternative Center has defined as

> a collective humanist response and democratic alternative from below to the crisis we face. It draws on our common humanity as the basis for solidarity action. More concretely, the solidarity economy is a voluntary process organized through collective struggle and conscious choice to establish a new pattern of democratic production, consumption and living that promotes the realization of human needs and environmental justice. (COPAC 2010: 18)

Thus defined, the solidarity economy incorporates locally centred alternatives into wider grassroots struggles (Satgar 2011). The solidarity economy embodies a left response to the crisis of liberal democracy and to the new austerity, while it builds a social and economic base for a participatory-democratic way of life.

The reflections of the activist intellectuals analysed in this chapter offer complementary ideas for left responses that can help form a counter-hegemonic historical bloc. In conclusion, the following is a summary of some of the key insights from the research:

- The crisis needs to be understood as civilisational in scope. This means that left responses must go beyond episodic protest and the desire to re-establish 'democratic capitalism'. Responses must instead build practical popular bases for a 'people's spring'. The fluidity inherent in the crisis creates opportunities for connecting across what have been siloed domains – from labour to communication, food, social reproduction – to overcome the long-standing problem of movement fragmentation. The challenge is to address the civilisational crisis in ways that construct, from the mosaic Left, a transformative Left.

- Left responses need to vigorously and relentlessly oppose false solutions, such as 'green jobs', and neoliberal schemes such as Big Society in the UK, and Black Economic Empowerment in South Africa. These are passive-revolutionary programmes that divide and rule while creating a class base for further neoliberalisation.

- Left responses need to address the psycho-cultural aspects of the crisis, especially as they pose barriers to building subaltern solidarities and political-economic alternatives. Fatalism, the privatised individualism that neoliberal policies encourage, acceptance of austerity as the new normal, fear of losing whatever one has left – these are commonsensical responses to a situation in which the old is dying but the new cannot be born. Yet far from automatically inducing such dispositions, the seemingly endless stream of 'bad news' provides a resource for the Left to organise itself. Popular outrage at the obscene inequities of the new plutocracy and at the increasingly brutal, armoured state can be amplified and refined through well-informed critiques of capitalism's injustices and irrationalities.[7] The task for movements, parties, alternative policy groups and alternative media is to connect popular outrage to critical analyses that win people to the cause of democratic, green socialism. This involves the dialogical work of translation to bridge the gap between 'big ideas' and 'people's ideas'.

- Left responses need to accentuate the duality of the crisis. As Naomi Klein recently stated, 'Climate change – when its full economic and moral implications are understood – is the most powerful weapon progressives have ever had in the fight for equality and social justice' (in Queally 2014). Klein's *This Changes Everything: Capitalism vs. the Climate* (2014) exemplifies how the two most urgent moments of organic crisis can be articulated in an inspiring political analysis. As ecological conditions deteriorate, the hegemonic bloc will deploy new passive-revolutionary interventions to manage food crises and climate refugees, and new accumulation strategies based on green capitalism and geo-engineering. In response, the global Left needs to press for human development and ecological health as an alternative to the mantra of 'economic growth'. These radical claims can pull the struggles for climate jobs, food sovereignty, agro-ecology, the reclamation of commons and the extension of participatory democracy into a counter-hegemonic project, as they return us to an understanding of the crisis as truly civilisational (see Satgar, Chapter 1 of this volume).

Such a project needs the concerted effort of convergent movements, sustained by democratic political organisations capable of prosecuting a war of position to win space in national and transnational political fields for socially just and ecologically healthy ways of life. Alternative policy groups and related organisations can contribute to these complex processes. However, they are not themselves the strategically key sites for the formation of a counter-hegemonic collective will. Hence, the re-emergence of democratic left parties linked dialogically to grassroots movements – in parts of Europe, Latin America and prospectively in South Africa – marks a crucial step forward for the global Left. Ultimately, left responses to the crisis need to press for the extension (and deepening) of democratic practices to all areas of life by blending such prefigurative initiatives as the solidarity economy with organisational efforts to build a unity in diversity for green socialism.

NOTES

1   According to the Central Intelligence Agency (CIA) World Factbook, global economic growth has been declining since 2010, the peak of a faltering post-2008 'recovery'. By 2012 the estimated world unemployment rate had grown to 9.2 per cent. See https://www.cia.gov/library/publications/the-world-factbook/geos/xx.html, accessed 25 April 2014.

2   As Potts (2011: 462) goes on to note, 'by surplus capital we mean profit/capital that is not invested in the productive economy i.e. it is surplus to the productive economy's investment requirements ... Surplus capital must restlessly seek employment outside of the productive economy, supporting speculation in fictitious capital...'

3   Most interviews took place in person, as part of my intensive fieldwork at 10 of the groups; the others were done via Skype or telephone. Where I name speakers, they have given me permission to do so. See Carroll (2015) for more methodological details.

4   Lebowitz (2013: 346) writes, '...there is a big difference between a crisis *in* capitalism and a crisis *of* capitalism. The latter requires conscious actors prepared to put an end to capitalism, prepared to challenge and defeat the logic of capital. But this requires a vision which can appear to workers as an alternative common sense, as *their* common sense.'

5   See http://kochcash.org/.

6   Candeias (2013) has outlined a counter-hegemonic project of green socialism.

7   See, for instance, the excellent pamphlet on neoliberalism by Albo and Fanelli (2014).

REFERENCES

Agnew, J. 2005. *Hegemony: The New Shape of Global Power*. Philadelphia: Temple University Press.

Albo, G. and Fanelli, C. 2014. 'Austerity against democracy: an authoritarian phase of neoliberalism?' Accessed 5 September 2014, http://www.socialistproject.ca/documents/AusterityAgainstDemocracy.php.

Boltanski, L. and Chiapello, E. 2005. *The New Spirit of Capitalism*. London: Verso.

Buci-Glucksmann, C. 1979. 'State, transition and passive revolution'. In *Gramsci and Marxist Theory*, edited by C. Mouffe. London: Routledge and Kegan Paul.

Candeias, M. 2011. 'Organic crisis and capitalist transformation'. *World Review of Political Economy*, 2 (1): 48–65.

Candeias, M. 2013. 'Green transformation: competing strategic projects'. Accessed 30 August 2013, http://www.rosalux-nyc.org/green-transformation/.

Carroll, W.K. 2013. 'Networks of cognitive praxis: transnational class formation from below?', *Globalizations*, 10: 651–670.

Carroll, W.K. 2014. 'Alternative policy groups and transnational counter-hegemonic struggle'. In *Global Economic Crisis and the Politics of Diversity*, edited by Y. Atasoy. London and New York: Palgrave MacMillan.

Carroll, W.K. 2015. 'Modes of cognitive praxis in transnational alternative policy groups', *Globalizations* 12, published online 19 January, DOI: 10.1080/14747731.2014.1001231.

Carroll, W.K. and Sapinski, J.P. 2013. 'Embedding post-capitalist alternatives? The global network of alternative knowledge production and mobilization', *Journal of World-Systems Research*, 19 (2): 211–240.

Clement, M.T. 2011. '"Let them build sea walls": ecological crisis, economic crisis and the political economic opportunity structure', *Critical Sociology*, 37: 447–463.

COPAC (Cooperative and Policy Alternative Center). 2010. 'Building a solidarity economy movement: A guide for grassroots activism'. Activist Training Guide. Johannesburg: COPAC.

Coutinho, C.N. 2012. *Gramsci's Political Thought*. Leiden: Brill.

De Sousa Santos, B. 2006. *The Rise of a Global Left*. London: Zed Books.

Fraser, N. 2013. *Fortunes of Feminism*. London: Verso.

Gammon, E. 2013. 'The psycho- and sociogenesis of neoliberalism', *Critical Sociology*, 39: 511–528.

Gibson-Graham, J.K. 2006. *A Post-capitalist Politics*. Minneapolis: University of Minnesota Press.

Gibson-Graham, J.K., Cameron, J. and Healy, S. 2013. *Take Back the Economy*. Minneapolis: University of Minnesota Press.

Gill, S. 2012a. 'Leaders and led in an era of global crises'. In *Global Crises and the Crisis of Global Leadership*, edited by S. Gill. Cambridge: Cambridge University Press.

Gill, S. 2012b. 'Towards a radical concept of praxis: imperial "common sense" versus the post-modern prince', *Millennium*, 40: 505–524.

Goodman, J. and Salleh, A. 2013. 'The "Green Economy": class hegemony and counter-hegemony', *Globalizations*, 10: 411–424.

Gramsci, A. 1971. *Selections from the Prison Notebooks of Antonio Gramsci*. New York: International Publishers.

Harmes, A. 1998. 'Institutional investors and the reproduction of neoliberalism', *Review of Radical Political Economics*, 5: 92–121.

Ivanova, M.N. 2011. 'Consumerism and the crisis: wither "the American Dream"?' *Critical Sociology*, 37: 329–350.

Jessop, B., Bonnett K., Bromley, S. and Ling T. 1984. 'Authoritarian populism, two nations, and Thatcherism', *New Left Review*, 147: 32–60.

Klein, N. 2014. *This Changes Everything: Capitalism vs. the Climate*. New York: Simon & Schuster.

Lebowitz, M.A. 2013. 'The state and the future of socialism', *Socialist Register*, 49: 345–367.

Marx, K. (1894) 1967. *Capital: A Critique of Political Economy, Volume Three*. New York: International Publishers.

McNally, D. 2011. *Global Slump*. Oakland, CA: PM Press.

Morton, A.D. 2003. 'Structural change and neoliberalism in Mexico: "Passive revolution" in the global political economy', *Third World Quarterly*, 24: 631–653.

Morton, A.D. 2010. 'The continuum of passive revolution', *Capital & Class*, 34: 315–342.

O'Connor, J. 1987. *The Meaning of Crisis*. Oxford: Basil Blackwell.

Panitch, L. and Gindin, S. 2012. *The Making of Global Capitalism*. London: Verso.

Peck, J., Theodore, N. and Brenner, N. 2012. 'Neoliberalism resurgent? Market rule after the great recession', *South Atlantic Quarterly*, 111(2): 265–288.

Potts, N. 2011. 'Marx and the crisis', *Capital & Class*, 35: 455–473.

Queally, J. 2014. 'Naomi Klein: "Our economic model is at war with life on earth"'. *Common Dreams* 8 (August). Accessed 5 September 2014, http://www.commondreams.org/news/2014/08/08/naomi-klein-our-economic-model-war-life-earth.

Reed, J-P. 2012. 'Theorist of subaltern subjectivity: Antonio Gramsci, popular beliefs, political passion, and reciprocal learning', *Critical Sociology*, 39: 561–590.

Satgar, V. 2008. 'Neoliberalized South Africa: labour and the roots of passive revolution', *Labour, Capital & Society*, 41(2): 38–69.

Satgar, V. 2011. 'Challenging the globalized agro-food complex: farming cooperatives and the emerging solidarity economy alternative in South Africa', *Working USA*, 14 (2): 177–190.

Scholl, C. and Freyberg-Inan, A. 2013. 'Hegemony's dirty tricks: explaining counter-globalization's weakness in times of neoliberal crisis', *Globalizations*, 10: 619–634.

Sharzer, G. 2012. *No Local: Why Small-scale Alternatives Won't Change the World*. Winchester, UK: Zero Books.

Showstack-Sassoon, A. 1987. *Gramsci's Politics* (second edition). London: Hutchinson.

Streeck, W. 2011. 'The crises of democratic capitalism', *New Left Review*, 71: 5–28.

Streeck, W. 2013. *The Politics of Public Debt: Neoliberalism, Capitalist Development, and the Restructuring of the State*. MPIfG Discussion Paper 13/7. Cologne: Max Planck Institute for the Study of Societies.

Thomas, P.D. 2009. *The Gramscian Moment*. Leiden: Brill.

Wade, R.H. 2011. 'Emerging world order? From multipolarity to multilateralism in the G20, the World Bank, and the IMF', *Politics and Society*, 39: 347–377.

CAPITALIST CRISIS AND LEFT RESPONSES IN THE GLOBAL NORTH

3

OCCUPY AND THE DIALECTICS OF THE LEFT IN THE UNITED STATES

Leah Hunt-Hendrix and Isham Christie

The bailout of the banks in 2008 represented a crisis not only in the economic system, but also in the hegemonic political and cultural order in the US. The hundreds of billions of dollars that went to the very banks that crashed the economy represented the extent to which the government had been co-opted by corporate interests. It pointed to the effects of 'too big to fail', and reminded onlookers of the dangers of monopolisation of any sector, but especially finance. The leftist critique of the concentration of wealth in power, in the hands of a few, became as plain as day. For the several decades prior, the financial sector had been slowly deregulated (or regulated so as to allow for great capital accumulation). Prohibitions on interstate banking were removed. Glass Steagall, which separated commercial and investment banking, was repealed. The once-diverse landscape of banks shrank as small banks were acquired by larger ones, leading to the dominance of four mammoths: Citi, Bank of America, Wells Fargo and Chase. Millions of dollars were spent by bank lobbies to influence policy. Meanwhile, millions of Americans were being evicted from their homes, struggling to make ends meet, and graduating from university into an economy that offered a dismal future.

This crisis was experienced differently by different parts of society. While it 'proletarianised' former, largely white, middle-class segments of the population, it had a significantly greater impact on communities of colour. A 2011

Pew Research Center report shows the biggest disparity in family-income ratios since the institution began publishing such data a quarter of a century ago (Kochhar, Fry and Taylor 2011). The median wealth of white households, according to data collected in 2009, was 20 times that of black households and 18 times that of Hispanic households. The report goes on to show that income levels of Hispanic families plummeted by fifty per cent between 2005 and 2009, largely because of the housing bubble. Given evidence that people of colour were being steered into predatory loans, these families bore the brunt of a racialised crisis that was largely caused by bankers seeking to maximise profits.

The other population that was deeply affected was students who were coming of age, graduating from college with heavy loads of debt and few job prospects. In the years between 2007 and 2011, youth unemployment grew significantly across the Organisation for Economic Co-operation and Development, again reaching higher levels than ever before measured. In the US, the unemployment rates for young people aged 16–24 years have been around fifteen to twenty per cent since the economic crisis. The inability to find jobs and the astonishing increase in the cost of education exacerbate the burden of debt, which in 2012 passed the US$1 trillion mark (Chopra 2012). This generation of young people is required to pay exorbitant rates for a university education, saddling them with student debt only for them to graduate into a barren job market. Many students are moving back in with their parents and taking menial jobs to pay off their student loans. For young people, the American Dream of opportunity is hard to square with the harsh economic reality.

As frustration mounted, the American public began to mobilise. Many hopes were placed in Obama, soon to be left unrealised. But rather than sink into apathy, people began to organise outside of electoral politics. Across the US, protests and actions were planned. In Madison, Wisconsin, protests and state capitol sleep-ins connected the labour movement to the general discontent with the economic and political system. Occupations were planned in Washington, DC for October 2011; activists in New York set up Bloombergville, a camp-out reminiscent of the depression-era Hoovervilles, in front of City Hall in the summer of 2011. And in September 2011, Occupy Wall Street (OWS) responded to a global wave of encampments and pushed this momentum even further.

Occupy in no way represents the entirety of left responses to the crisis. It emerged in a much broader context. There have been innumerable analyses of Occupy, so that will not be our primary purpose here. Rather, in this chapter we look at Occupy as a window into some of the aspects and dynamics that characterise the Left in the US today. It represents a point in a dialectical movement of left ideology, and lessons from that time are being absorbed and processed by activists and organisers in a way that seems to signal a departure for left thinking and practice.

ECONOMIC AND POLITICAL CRISIS IN THE US

The economic collapse of 2007/08 and the subsequent bailout of the major financial institutions exposed the intimate relationship between corporations and government in the US and the inability of the public to hold the economic and political elite accountable. Well established in left-wing circles, this analysis spread to the general public but did not immediately lead people onto the streets.

While Occupy Wall Street undoubtedly accrued the attention it did because of the financial crisis that occurred in the US in 2007/08, crises in capitalism by no means necessarily lead to social mobilisation. Indeed, financial crises have a variegated influence on protest and social critique. The Great Depression in the 1930s served as a catalyst for massive labour unrest and wildcat strikes, which helped establish many of the trade unions of the US labour movement (Bernstein 2010). At other times crisis serves as a factor in demobilisation, clipping the wings of leftist movements. After the collapse of many youth organisations in the 1960s New Left in the US, thousands began to build socialist cadre with high hopes that newly politicised white youth and communities of colour could build a radical Left not seen since the second Red Scare of McCarthyism in the early to mid 1950s. However, the 1973 US recession, caused in part by an oil crisis and the breakdown of the Bretton Woods Accord, was a major factor in decimating the hopes and aspirations of the New Communist Movement (Elbaum 2002). Rather than a simple and linear immiseration theory as encapsulated in the phrase 'it must get worse before it gets better', each specific economic crisis can work to dismantle emancipatory social forces, or it can work to inspire social revolt. How this plays out often depends on the current balance of class forces, the nature of the economic crisis, and the ideological context. More concretely, a crisis offers the space for the battle for a right- and left-wing analysis of the causes and solutions. In the US, this was evident in the division between the Tea Party and Occupy Wall Street.

Plenty of attention has been focused on the structural causes of the economic crisis. The contradictions of capital accumulation leading to the financialisation of the economy have been well documented by David Harvey, the *Monthly Review*, Robert Brenner, Costas Lapavistas and, in a longer view, Giovanni Arrighi, among many others. Rather than rehash that analysis, we want to focus on how the economic crisis influenced social mobilisation in the US in the period after 2008.

In the wake of the bailout, two narratives arose simultaneously. One narrative laid the fault of this economic crisis at the feet of the financial institutions, bankers, and Wall Street. This created latent political energy for an emergent left response. However, other voices attempted to lay the blame on working people for taking out mortgages and loans that they could not pay back: people 'living beyond their means'. The old hat of accusing the poor for the vices of the wealthy was an ideological thrust of the post-crisis US discourse. Thus, before Occupy, the Tea Party rose to prominence, leading Slavoj Zizek to claim that the 'primary immediate effect of the crisis will not be the rise of a radical emancipatory politics, but rather the rise of racist populism' (Zizek 2009: 17). It took three years for a left-wing response to develop.

The sub-prime mortgage crisis in 2007 facilitated the collapse of several financial institutions. On 15 September 2008, Lehman Brothers, the fourth largest investment bank in the US, declared bankruptcy. On 3 October 2008, George W Bush signed the Troubled Asset Relief Program authorising US$700 billion (later reduced) to inject liquidity into a collapsing system, and to buy up toxic assets held by financial institutions. While there was, as usual, a chorus that blamed the poor for the collapse, even sections of the right wing began to identify the role of bankers as well. This was because the bailout served as a spectacular and clear reminder that the governing principle of the political and economic policy in the US first serves capital and the agents of capital. Subsequently, nearly every protester knew the chant, 'Banks got bailed out, we got sold out.' However, it took until 17 September 2011 to express and further generate such a position broadly in the US and convert latent outrage into a social movement.

STATE OF THE LEFT AND RESPONSES TO THE CRISIS

Before we look directly at the left response to the crisis, it is useful to take a step back and briefly survey the state of the US Left in the last decade and a half. The US Left suffered a severe setback with the events of 11 September 2001, as everything but the most reactionary patriotism was deemed as siding with the enemy. In the 1990s, an ascendant global justice movement helped cohere a set of forces to challenge the new forms of imperialism and capitalism. This culminated (in the US at least) in the Seattle World Trade Organization protests in 1999. Not only did the Seattle protests shut down the meeting of world leaders through direct action, they also created an unprecedented level of unity among labour unions, environmentalists, liberals, and radicals of various stripes. This atmosphere was chilled by the events of 9/11. But even before that day the global justice movement suffered from tactical/strategic disagreements. While there was agreement about what they were against, demonstrators had less agreement about what they were for. As the police became more brutal in their force and sophisticated in their controlling techniques (using provoca-teurs, militarised tactics, and so on) to prevent another Seattle from occurring, tactical disagreements – about the use of violence, for example – emerged.

With the US war in Iraq looming, historic mass mobilisation occurred in cities throughout the country. Never had the US seen such a strong showing *before* a war had started. However, the US anti-war movement could not use the pre-war momentum to build a sufficient mass movement. The post-9/11 anti-war movement launched inspiring actions on the West Coast's ports, using direct action to stop military shipments, and there were exciting organisational developments with the spread of the new Students for a Democratic Society (SDS) growing to over 120 chapters in a couple of years. But the organisational and tactical kindling could not sustain a fire, leaving many cynical as the war raged on.

The defeat of the anti-war movement led to a period of despair on the Left. And when the economic crisis of 2007/08 occurred, the infrastructure to capture frustration and convert it into action was weak if not non-existent. For many, the crisis of 2008 was a point of personal shame and despair. It is notable that the economic downturn shifted the grammar of resistance in the US from a politics of solidarity (with the Third World or targets of US imperi-alism) to a politics of the first person (lack of jobs, debt, and inequality in the US). Austerity and the economic crisis were affecting a greater majority of the

US. The newly immiserated met with the historically marginalised to create a loose political body soon to be known as the 99 per cent.

The first major manifestation of this new energy occurred in Wisconsin. The Madison protests began to break a leftist stagnation, during which a powerful populist alignment came together to fight against the attempt to strip public-sector workers of the right to collective bargaining. On 26 February 2011 around 100 000 people surrounded and seized the Wisconsin capitol. Many slept there for days.

While Wisconsin can be seen as a forerunner to Occupy, it was certainly not the only influence or inspiration. One cannot begin to understand Occupy Wall Street without zooming out to the international context. While student and consumer debt, the foreclosure crisis – or what should be called the mass seizure of homes – and overall economic conditions supplied the material conditions for unrest in the US, the inspiration of the uprisings in Tunisia and Egypt were catalytic. For the global Left, the resignation of Egyptian president Hosni Mubarak was a point of no return, a time when courage and audacity were being called forth everywhere. Moreover, the tactic of occupation was also spreading. An occupation outside the Ministry of Interior in Tunis in January 2011 helped lay the groundwork for a global cycle of struggle. It then spread most spectacularly to Cairo's Tahrir Square (25 January 2011), to Wisconsin's Capitol Occupation (February 2011), to Puerta del Sol, Madrid (15 May 2011) and to Syntagma Square, Athens (May to June 2011). This set the stage for the first attempt in New York City to pick up the spreading tactic of encampment. New York City activists – some participating in Wisconsin's Occupation and the Spanish 15-M movement in Madrid and Barcelona – were determined to bring the tactic to the heart of capital.

In New York City, 12 May 2011 was set as a day of protest. The city govern-ment was attempting to push an austerity municipal budget through, which would cut funding for education, lay off public-sector workers, defund social services to the needy, and close down homeless shelters. At the same time, Mayor Bloomberg and others were extending tax cuts to corporations and the wealthy. Two groups formed around this struggle: the May 12 Coalition (a broader grouping) and New Yorkers Against Budget Cuts (a militant group). The May 12 Coalition included unions, community organisations, student groups, and socialist's groups. When the day came, around 50 000 people marched on Wall Street. The opening message of the May 12 Coalition was clear: 'The Big Banks crashed our economy, destroying jobs, foreclosing on millions of homes and wrecking city and state budgets across the country'.[1]

The relatively impressive numbers were met with near silence from the mainstream media. Plans for civil disobedience in the form of sit-ins at banks fizzled out when the time came (or, as some say, they were suppressed by the United Federation of Teachers who, as the story went, had cut a deal to decrease the number of teacher layoffs). What was lacking in this mobilisation did not give rise to complacency, but to further resolve to bring the global wave of uprising to the US.

The next attempt to extend the protest against austerity took the shape of a long-term encampment outside of City Hall two weeks before the city budget was voted on. 'Bloombergville' – named after New York City's neoliberal billionaire mayor and referencing the Hooverville shanty towns set up during the Great Depression by the homeless and unemployed – failed to attract public or media attention. However, sleeping on the sidewalk in New York City for two weeks hardened the resolve of most of those involved, and the experience began developing a cadre of radical organisers who later took up the call to occupy Wall Street.

PREFIGURING ANOTHER WORLD

On 1 May 2011, Joseph Stiglitz published an article in *Vanity Fair*, entitled: 'Of the 1%, By the 1%, For the 1%'. The article would launch the meme: 'the 1% vs the 99%'. In July 2011, *Adbusters* magazine sent out a call to 'Occupy Wall Street!' New Yorkers Against Budget Cuts began to mobilise, soon changing its name to the New York City General Assembly. But in the lead-up to 17 September, in addition to hope and inspiration, there was uncertainty and dread among the organisers. The fear of state repression was high and the anxiety around failure was ever-present before the occupation began. There was also hesitation associated with this experiment in a new form of mobilisation. Occupy was endowed with the revolutionary spirit seen in periods of acute social struggle, such as 1848, 1917, 1968, and others. But in the contemporary context, with social media as a new medium and tool, it had a distinctive DNA and faced a new set of opportunities and challenges.

Traditionally, a coalition of groups is built around a demand or set of demands and those groups then turn out their members. Occupy followed a different trajectory, resembling other struggles in 2011, by first spreading on social media and only later leading to a physical meeting. The initial call by *Adbusters* asked occupiers to formulate a single demand, taking a cue from the Arab Spring. In Tunisia the call was: 'Ben Ali Degage!' In Egypt it was: 'The People Want the Downfall of the Regime!' The call to occupy Wall Street, which was accompanied by an image of a ballerina pirouetting atop the charging Wall Street bull, was a provocation to generate a US version of a single demand.

Instead of determining the 'one demand' ahead of time, however, the group that made the call had a sense that the best route would be to focus left-wing energy into a shared set of various actions, in order to generate mass participation. Only once the community formed (arguably) would it assert its demands. Thus, the New York City General Assembly flipped the logic of movement building on its head, deciding not to determine the demand *a priori*, before the occupation. Using images, Facebook, Twitter, Reddit, and a pre-action where a handful were arrested outside the New York Stock Exchange, it simply pushed out the invitation to come occupy.

On 17 September, almost 1 000 people gathered around the iconic Charging Bull. The actual site where the occupation was to take place (Zuccotti Park) was decided by a handful of organisers, and a red herring (the headquarters of Chase Bank) was spread more publicly. Several days before, One Chase Manhattan Plaza was barricaded and surrounded by police. Meanwhile, Zuccotti Park, a concrete platform nestled in between the financial district's skyscrapers, where bankers and office administrators took their lunches on sunny days, became the site of both a protest and an emergent community.

The call to occupy created a focus on the tactic of the encampment. Without a predetermined demand directed to policymakers or the banks, attention was channelled towards how to be together in that shared space. This gave birth to a prefigurative logic, an attempt 'to create the new within the shell of the old'. The concept of prefiguration goes back to the days of the Wobblies and was used extensively during the 1960s in an attempt to break with the characteristic hierarchy of the Old Left, and depict the kind of world that was hoped for. It is a strategy to transform society by bringing together ends and means to enact the future in the present.

Inside the park, one could find almost anything one needed. There was a kitchen that served vegan cuisine, a sanitation crew, a parents' circle, a think tank and regular speeches and music. Working groups were created which tied these issues together with climate change, money in politics, racial justice and women's rights. A facilitation group taught newcomers about meeting procedure and the direct-action group planned ongoing protests around the city. A little village had sprung into being, in which the financial crisis, structural injustice, economic inequality – and the question of human flourishing – were of utmost concern.

After several days, a general assembly was finally held to determine an answer to the long-awaited question: 'What is our one demand?' The public was pressing for an answer: what did the Occupiers want? To break up the banks? To end capitalism? Or was this simply an anarchist stunt? While the movement did display a coherent message about the root cause of a variety of social problems – the dominance of finance that led to the corruption of democracy – a solution was not forthcoming. In Zuccotti Park, disagreements abounded. The assembly began to falter. The facilitators were getting tired and frustrated.

Not only did it become apparent that no single demand would be enough to address the root causes of injustice, but soon the very idea of a 'demand' was put into question. As theorist John Holloway puts it, 'A demand is addressed to someone and asks them to do something on our behalf in the future, whereas in the politics of living now there is no demand. We ask no permission of anyone and we do not wait for the future, but simply break time and assert now another type of doing, another form of social relations' (Holloway 2010: 251). The 'politics of demand,' as Richard Day calls it, assumes that the power to create change lies in the hands of the state (Day 2005). But many individuals involved in the new movements like Occupy and others around the world rejected this theory of power and social change.

In Occupy's theory magazine, *Tidal: Occupy Theory, Occupy Strategy*, Judith Butler attempted to explain this orientation. Butler argued that one way to understand the movement was as a demand for justice. But to demand justice requires asking a profound question about what justice looks like:

> The reason it is said that sometimes there are 'no demands' when bodies assemble under the rubric of 'Occupy Wall Street' is that any list of demands would not exhaust the ideal of justice that is being demanded. We can all imagine just solutions to health care, public education, housing, and the distribution and availability of food – in other words, we could itemize the injustices in the plural and present those as a set of specific demands. But perhaps the demand for justice is present in each of those demands, but *also necessarily exceeds them*. We do not have to

subscribe to Platonic theory of Justice to see other ways in which this demand operates. For when bodies gather as they do to express their indignation and to enact their plural existence in public space, they are also making broader demands. They are demanding to be recognized and to be valued; they are exercising a right to appear and to exercise freedom; they are calling for a livable life. These values are presupposed by particular demands, but *they also demand a more fundamental restructuring of our socio-economic and political order.* (Butler 2011: 12)

Butler suggested that there was a demand: a demand for complete social transformation. This demand went so deep that it could not be captured by practicable requests. Such a demand could not simply be fulfilled by the state. In fact, the most pernicious problems identified by the movement could not be solved through demands, for they had to do with who we have become as people, and what we have come to desire and value. In a certain sense, Occupy was a cultural critique.

If Occupy were to have a demand, therefore, it would need to be a demand of the public to 'occupy!' To occupy meant to be in the place that one was, to claim that space, to be responsible for it, and for the others to join. To occupy – to 'Occupy Love' or 'Occupy the Food Supply' or 'Occupy Homes' – meant to draw attention to specific aspects of our lives in common and take responsibility for them. It meant to focus on what mattered. To care. And to participate in ensuring that love, food, homes, the things we value and hold sacred, were rightly revered.

When, on a fall night in Zuccotti Park, the discussion of demands stalled after several hours of debate, someone suggested that instead of shared demands, the Working Group on Principles of Consolidation could articulate its shared values and principles: the Principles of Solidarity.[2] This list would capture the reasons they had come together and the reasons for which they would stand by one another in their many diverse, but connected, struggles. Reams of paper were produced as small groups worked together to determine their priorities. At last, the list included: 'Engaging in direct and transparent participatory democracy,' 'Exercising personal and collective responsibility,' 'Empowering one another against all forms of oppression,' and 'Redefining how labour is valued.'

Solidarity marked a principle of unity in difference, of coming together across divides, of finding the intersections between issues, the reasons for groups of diverse backgrounds and traditions to band together against a common target: the economic structures which benefit the few to the detriment of the many. But it also involved an attempt to be in community in new ways, ways that modelled a different vision of society. This focus on process rather than goals put the question of demands to rest for the time being and laid the foundation for a principle-based movement, a radical experiment in movement building.

THREE ANTAGONISMS OF OCCUPY

Occupy – and much of the US Left today – can be understood through the lens of three antagonisms: an antagonism with the history of the Old Left, augmented by decades of anti-communist propaganda and the fall of the Soviet Union; an antagonism with the ways in which 'civil society' generally finds expression under current social and legal conditions, which has become a self-perpetuating, disempowered, non-profit industrial complex; and an antagonism to representative democracy, related to an awareness of the thorough corruption of the US government because of the role of money in politics, in elections and lobbying. In conjunction with the historical orientation of US political traditions, which have long emphasised freedom and liberty as core values, these antagonisms have informed a politic that is sceptical of the role of the state and committed to personal autonomy.

There have been right-wing and left-wing incarnations of this orientation. When Occupy began, it was not immediately characterised as 'left'. Milling around Zuccotti, there were libertarians and anarchists, reformists and revolutionaries. For many, the outcry against Wall Street was simply good common sense. But as the days went on, most of the tea partiers took their leave and conversations became more pointed about theories of change. A commitment to participatory democracy and inclusion of all voices emerged as one of the primary characteristics of the nascent community. An increasingly anarchist orientation began to take hold. While some were conscious of the tradition of anarchism and identified it as such, many for whom this was an entry point into activism saw the participatory democracy based on public assemblies as 'the way Occupy did things'. This involved a fierce suspicion of organisational affiliation in regards both to organisations of the traditional Left and of the more moderate, progressive sector.

For many within Occupy, the Old Left signified heated debates between Stalinists and Trotskyists, paper-pushing on street corners, and esoteric revolutionary jargon. Few in the emergent movement had read the works of Marx or knew the content of the debates that they condemned. But many intuitively viewed such ideas as relics of a bygone era. The world had changed, the Old Left had lost; the future was open to be envisioned anew. There were important principled points of opposition to the Old Left. The concept of capitalism's inevitable self-destruction in the face of its own internal contradictions had been put into question long before, as crises had instead become opportunities for its further consolidation. The hierarchical structure of Marxist–Leninism was rejected by a culture that was committed to personal freedom and democracy. And the infighting that was the caricature of leftist parties became a point of disdain for the new generation.

While Marxism offered substance to the contemporary critique of capitalism and inequality, the Occupy Left cannot be understood apart from the history of McCarthyism. Since the 1950s, Marxism has been an object of vehement derision in the US, both culturally and politically. The first Red Scare, which took place almost a century ago, stirred up fear of communism and Bolshevism, equating such movements with violence and chaos. In the 1950s and 1960s, to be a communist was to be considered a traitor. This kind of repression had detrimental effects on the ability to sustain the organisational infrastructure. And with the fall of the Berlin Wall and the demise of the Soviet Union, a narrative of democracy, equated with capitalism, took its place as the global hegemonic discourse.

In conjunction with the rise of the neoliberal doctrine, which made the case for natural supremacy of the free market, McCarthyism played a role in fostering a form of organising that was anti-ideological and limited in vision. The environment of fear that the redbaiting established undermined the Left irreparably. For generations to come, the effects of the propaganda war against communists would continue to inflect radical and progressive organising, essentially closing down the possibility for ambitious visions of systemic alternatives.

In this context, new traditions of advocacy and organising were developed. In the 1960s, Saul Alinsky's Back of the Yards organising in Chicago gained traction, in part as an alternative to the methods of the traditional Left. Alinsky developed a model of organising that was in many ways based on a rejection of ideology. In an interview with *Playboy Magazine* (March 1972), he quips, 'You should never have an ideology more specific than "For the general welfare'". In *Rules for Radicals*, Alinsky (1971) offers a set of guidelines for organising that is rooted in the material needs of a given neighbourhood. The Alinsky model starts with a near-term problem, often rooted in geographic location rather than in workplace conditions. The neighbourhood becomes the locus of power as opposed to the factory floor.

Alinsky himself was not anti-communist. As he notes in the interview with *Playboy Magazine*, 'Anybody who tells you he was active in progressive causes in those days and never worked with the Reds is a goddamn liar. Their platform stood for all the right things, and unlike many liberals, they were willing to put their bodies on the line.' But he did explicitly distance himself from the party. He displayed a distinctly American brand of individualism, which involved autonomy from organised structures: 'I've never joined any organisation – not even the ones I've organised myself. I prize my own independence too much. And philosophically, I could never accept any rigid dogma or ideology, whether it's Christianity or Marxism.' The organisations that he created through the Industrial Areas Foundation (IAF) were thus set on an anti-ideological footing, focused instead on short-term battles, often at the neighbourhood level. His method was practical and pragmatic, a method that would come to influence the next 50 years of organising.

A common critique of the Alinsky model centres on the lack of a deep systemic analysis. Essentially, the goal of short-term change within communities rested on an acceptance of the overarching social structures. While Alinsky spoke out against the consolidation of corporate power, he offered no critique of the internal dynamics of capitalism. Battles were local and immediate. The avoidance of ideology made sense as a rejection of the sectarianism that had come to characterise the Left. However, it created a vacuum. This was then filled by an analysis that was insufficient to counter the larger macro dynamics emerging in the US economic and political landscape, in particular that of a neoliberal dogma of privatisation and the free market.

In this anti-ideological context, a new ideology of pragmatism emerged, as well as new organisational forms. The non-profit replaced the party. Professional staff replaced cadre. In *The Revolution Will Not Be Funded*, a women's collective, INCITE, calls this the development of a 'non-profit industrial complex' (INCITE! 2009). Organisations intending to fight for the rights and wellbeing of the poor and marginalised are dependent on the ability to fundraise from philanthropic entities with divergent interests. This structure is fundamentally fragile. At a basic level, the need to make proposals that appeal to those with wealth requires casting work in more palatable language. This often involves having foundations steer programmatic decision making. The relationship between non-profits and foundations creates dependency where, on the one hand, there is no accountability of funders to their grantees, and, on the other, the grantee organisations rely for their survival on the maintenance of their funder relationships.

But perhaps the most problematic aspect of this sector is the fact that a non-profit tax-exempt status bars these organisations from a variety of political activities. Questions of social and economic justice, which are ultimately political issues, are essentially neutered. Unable to enter into the realm of politics, these organisations often focus instead on delivering services. At a macro level, this has created a widespread conception that issues of flourishing and well-being, issues of distribution of wealth and justice, can be handled outside of the political process. The very structure of advocacy and organising, therefore, is fundamentally limiting and depoliticised.

The third antagonism that characterised Occupy was with the concept of representative democracy. The crisis of 2008 was not only economic but also political. The election of Obama had raised hopes, and while those hopes were already being challenged, the bailout validated the worst of fears. Obama immediately appointed much of the economic team that had flanked Clinton, signalling his alignment with Clintonian neoliberalism. The massive surge of energy that went into his election was quickly undermined as the grass-roots organising initiative, Obama for America, revealed intentions to use the network it had created to support the president, rather than as a vehicle for the president to work in partnership with the communities that had elected him. As the disillusionment set in, much of the Left in the US was reminded that power does not come through an election, but requires much broader-based collective power to hold elected officials accountable.

Other events began to signal the demise of the integrity of American representative democracy. In 2010, in *Citizens United v. the FCC*, the Supreme Court ruled to protect the rights of corporations to make unlimited, undisclosed contributions to political campaigns. The aspirational vision of 'one person, one vote' was cast aside as money flooded the political process. The revolving door of Capitol Hill staffers and lobbyists meant incentives and access into the halls of power for those who could pay.

Representation has long been a questionable concept, challenged from a variety of vantage points. In 'Can the Subaltern Speak?' Gayatri Spivak (1988) addresses the issue of representation in the post-colonial context. The critique applies to the charitable voice, the humanitarian, who benevolently seeks to speak on behalf of others. Spivak challenged the attempt of intellectuals to represent the oppressed in their writings, to take up their positions, arguing that such an attempt resulted in a distortion of those voices. Representation collapses the space for one to speak for oneself. The anarchist critique goes on to reject representation generally, not only in the case of flawed conditions, but on principle. The representative inevitably acts as an interpreter, totalising, essentialising the meaning of the speaker. As Jesse Cohn (2006) explains, there is both a moral critique of representation as reductive, but also a logical critique of the impossibility of any accurate representation. The anarchist tradition has thus turned to direct participation in decision making, direct democracy, as a political alternative.

This, then, was one of the central prefigurative aspects of Occupy. The implementation of participatory democracy in the encampment modelled an alternative to mainstream representative democracy. A consensus process, which emphasises time for deliberation and enables every participant to voice concerns or opposition, has the goal of arriving at a conclusion that is stronger and more appropriate than any individual could achieve on their own. As Marina Sitrin, a frequent commentator on the movement wrote, 'The question for the future is not how to create a plan for what a better country will look like, but how to deepen and broaden the assemblies taking place and how to enhance participatory democracy in the process' (Sitrin 2012: 75). The process, rather than the outcome, becomes the primary focus of concern.

This effort was evident in the organisational structure that emerged at Zuccotti Park. General assemblies were held each night to provide opportunities for shared decision making. Almost all groups were open to anyone who wanted to join. Because meetings were often very large, Occupy Wall Street used a modified consensus process, which included hand signals to indicate agreement, disagreement, or uncertainty. A facilitator would take proposals and then gauge the agreement within the group through the hand signals. Proposals could be modified by amendments but if, after such modifications, some in the group continued to be dissatisfied, they could block the proposal. Blocks could be overridden by supermajorities, which were set at ninety per cent. For example, the arts and culture working group might submit a proposal to use US$500 from the general funds to make signs for a protest. Others in the assembly could weigh in and ultimately approve or block that proposal.

The practice of consensus and horizontalism were not unique to Occupy. Similar practices were used in the movements of the 1960s and more recently in the alter-globalisation movement of the 1990s. And just as the participatory practices of Occupy were not new, neither were its challenges. Jeremy Brecher (2011) writes of attempts at participatory democracy in the SDS, and notes the failure of the SDS to ever resolve many of the complexities of such efforts. As Brecher notes, participatory democracy can resemble mob rule if not paired with structures of accountability. When anyone can enter into a meeting and vote, while others have endured many days and hours of debate and long-time involvement, this can create a sense of unfairness and resentment. Doug Singsen, one of the founders of New Yorkers Against Budget Cuts and organisers of 'September 17th' in Zuccotti Park, noted that while the consensus process was meant to ensure that no part of the group felt alienated, the general assemblies leading up to 'September 17th' were long, acrimonious and often unproductive (Singsen 2012). They continued to be challenging throughout OWS, at times breaking down into shouting and argument.

The anarchist turn among a portion of the American Left, as evidenced here by Occupy, was based on a critique of both capital and the state. It was an acknowledgement of the corporate capture of government, the plutocracy that had come to dominate American politics, and more deeply, it was a recognition of the likelihood of this outcome, not as an aberration but as part of the nature of capitalism. But it also led to a fetishisation of participation that ultimately played a major role in undermining the movement. A significant rift emerged between those who saw the prefigurative practices as the essence of the movement, and those who sought to use the energy of the movement to win political gains that would have benefits for struggling communities, such as homeowners who are 'underwater' on their mortgages or students burdened by debt. While both of these strains had revolutionary intentions, the former saw the latter as reformist, while the latter saw the former as utopian and self-marginalising. The former worried that the latter's engagement in the political process would sap the movement of its energy and compromise its message, while the latter saw the former as confusing tactics with strategy and overly synthesising means with ends.

Ultimately, this conflict signalled an insufficient understanding of a movement ecosystem and of the role of the state. Experiments in solidarity and mutual aid that abandon the political process entirely will remain confined to the margins, the privilege of the few. Such practices do little to address ongoing structural injustices that continue to defeat so much of the American population, such as the incarceration of 1 million black men and women, the ongoing dominance and unaccountability of the financial sector, and the inaccessibility of health care and education. This sceptical orientation was justifiably wary of the ease with which left movements are co-opted by either the Democratic Party or other existing infrastructure.

While the criticisms and concerns that motivated OWS were accurate, the movement was too fractured ideologically, and had too little organisational structure, to sustain itself. Occupy was an action, a moment of protest, that extended beyond what anyone could have imagined. The fact that it had the power it did signified how ripe the conditions were for a challenge from the Left. But ultimately, the movement was torn apart both by internal division and by external repression. The encampments, which provided the main infrastructure of the movement, were evicted by local city governments. Without space to meet, much of the organising fell apart and energy dissipated.

THE PATH AHEAD

Occupy was enormously successful in changing the narrative around wealth and inequality in the US. What began as an economic crisis became an ideological crisis, a fracturing of the hegemonic worldview and an opening for a debate about the dominance of the financial sector, debt as a tool of exploitation and extraction, and the immorality of unaccountable corporate power. Despite its limitations, Occupy opened up new vistas and a new moment in the dialectic of the American Left. OWS can be understood as a justifiable attempt to overcome evident obstacles in left thinking and practice, which now needs to be transcended yet again into a new politics that has integrated these lessons.

Among community organisers and movement organisations, there is a widespread sense of need for a stronger and clearer vision, one that is systemically transformative. There is significant debate under way about ideology, theories of change, and the possibility of new organisational methods and models. Two of the venues for these debates are in the alternative labour movement and in the 'new economy' sector. Alt-labour refers to the organising of non-unionised workers including domestic workers, restaurant workers and freelancers. The National Domestic Workers Alliance, the National Guestworker Alliance, the Writer's Guild and campaigns with fast-food workers and warehouse workers around the country, are paving the way for new forms of thinking about worker power. These efforts are attempting to address the future of work and the future of worker organising. They are examining the problem of precarious and contracted work, and the challenges in obtaining leverage for better wages and more equitable conditions.

Meanwhile, the 'new economy' movement is projecting a vision of a whole-sale economic transformation. Not only is it questioning the motive to maxi-mise profits and to externalise costs; this movement is challenging the very idea of growth as a necessary dictate. Weaving an ecological awareness into our economic thinking requires a re-imagination of what it means to produce, exchange and consume on a finite planet. The movement does not rest on tradi-tional leftist theory, which would see class struggle as the primary driver of social transformation, but instead, it is compelled to urgent action by the threat of climate change, which will most greatly affect the poorest and most margin-alised communities. The ecological and economic imperatives together require a rethinking of ownership and control. They require a deep and thorough re-imagination of the role of finance and compound interest. They require a way of restructuring society so that we produce to meet needs, rather than manufacture needs to absorb what is produced.

Movements like Occupy, which identify a problem and raise popular aware-ness and support, are critical in creating the conditions to alter society. They 'change the weather' and make it possible to achieve outcomes that might have seemed years away if social change were a linear process. As Thomas Kuhn (1996) argued in *The Structure of Scientific Revolutions*, paradigm shifts can occur which make things possible that might previously have been inconceiv-able. But a successful transition towards more equitable conditions will not take place simply by winning popular support. It will require the creation of new structures and institutions that will capture momentum and codify it in progressive wins. Deep thinking about organisational infrastructure and ideology will be necessary as we move into a new era of left political thought and practice. But it will be hard to dispute the claim that Occupy helped pave the way for whatever will come next.

NOTES

1   On May 12 2015. Accessed 14 July 2015, http://www.onmay12.org.
2   Working Group on Principles of Consolidation #Occupy Wall Street: NYC General
    Assembly. Accessed 15 July 2015, http://www.nycga.net/resources/documents/
    principles-of-solidarity/.

REFERENCES

Alinsky, S. 1971. *Rules for Radicals*. New York: Random House.
Bernstein, I. 2010. *The Turbulent Years*. Chicago: Haymarket Books.
Brecher, J. 2011. *Save the Humans? Common Preservation in Action*. Boulder, CO:
    Paradigm Publishers.
Butler, J. 2011. 'For and against precarity', *Tidal: Occupy Theory, Occupy Strategy*, 1:
    12–13.
Chopra, R. 2012. 'Too big to fail: student debt hits a trillion', Consumer Financial
    Protection Bureau. Accessed 15 July 2015, http://www.consumerfinance.gov/blog/
    too-big-to-fail-student-debt-hits-a-trillion/.
Cohn, J. 2006. *Anarchism and the Crisis of Representation*. Cranbury, NJ: Associated
    University Press.
Day, R. 2005. *Gramsci is Dead*. London: Pluto Press.
Elbaum, M. 2002. *Revolution in the Air: Sixties Radicals Turn to Lenin, Mao and Che*.
    London: Verso.
Holloway, J. 2010. *Crack Capitalism*. London: Pluto Press.
INCITE! 2009. *The Revolution Will Not Be Funded*, edited by INCITE! Women of Color
    Against Violence. Boston: South End Press.
Kochhar, R. with Fry, R. and Taylor, P. 2011. 'Wealth gaps rise to record highs
    between whites, blacks and Hispanics'. *Pew Research: Social and Demographic
    Trends*. Accessed 15 July 2015, http://www.pewsocialtrends.org/2011/07/26/
    wealth-gaps-rise-to-record-highs-between-whites-blacks-hispanics/.
Kuhn T.S. 1996. *The Structure of Scientific Revolutions* (Third edition). Chicago:
    University of Chicago Press.
Singsen, D. 2012. 'A balance sheet of occupy Wall Street'. *International Socialist
    Review*, Issue 81. Accessed 15 July 2015, http://isreview.org/issue/81/
    balance-sheet-occupy-wall-street.
Sitrin, M. 2012. 'Horizontalism and the Occupy movements', *Dissent*, 59 (2): 74–75.
    Accessed 20 July 2015, https://www.dissentmagazine.org/article/horizontalism-
    and-the-occupy-movements.
Spivak G. 1988. 'Can the subaltern speak?' In *Marxism and the Interpretation of Culture*
    edited by C. Nelson and L. Grossberg. Campaign, IL: University of Illinois Press.
Stiglitz, J. 2011. 'Of the 1%, By the 1%, For the 1%'. *Vanity Fair*. Accessed 15 July 2015,
    http://www.vanityfair.com/news/2011/05/top-one-percent-201105.
Zizek, S. 2009. *First as Tragedy, Then as Farce*. London: Verso.

4

AUSTERITY AND RESISTANCE:
THE POLITICS OF LABOUR IN THE
EUROZONE CRISIS

Andreas Bieler and Jamie Jordan

Europe is haunted by austerity. Public sectors across the European Union (EU) are being cut back and working-class gains from the post-war period systematically undermined. It is often argued in the media that citizens of richer countries will now have to pay for the 'profligacy' of citizens from indebted countries. Cultural arguments of apparently 'lazy Greek' workers as the cause of the crisis are put forward despite the fact that Greek workers are amongst those who work the most hours in Europe.[1] In any case, it is not the Greek, Portuguese, Irish or Cypriot citizens and their health and education systems that are being rescued. It is banks, that organised the lending of super-profits to peripheral countries, and that were exposed to private and national debt in these countries. For example, German and French banks were heavily exposed to Greek debt, and British banks to Irish debt,[2] with much of this exposure having now been socialised through bond purchases by the European Central Bank (ECB). In this chapter, we will assess the causes of the crisis, its implications for workers and discuss the politics of labour in response to the Eurozone crisis.

Conceptually, assessments of developments in the European political economy have been dominated by institutionalist analyses from within the

Varieties of Capitalism literature. As we will argue in the next section, this literature, which is beset by problems of methodological nationalism, is unable to take into account the underlying social relations of production that link the various political economies closely together, with developments in one affecting the others. Second, development within the EU, especially of countries in the periphery which are now in trouble, such as Greece, Portugal, Spain and Ireland, was generally assessed along the lines of David Ricardo's theory of comparative advantage, with the idea that everybody would benefit from free trade and ultimately reach the same kind of development level. Instead, we will argue that, as borne out in empirical reality, capitalist development and expansion is characterised by processes of uneven and combined development. Importantly, unevenness exists not only between countries in the core and the periphery, but also within countries, be they in the core or periphery.

The conceptual section will be followed by an assessment of the causes of the crisis, highlighting exactly this dimension of uneven and combined development as part of the structuring conditions of capitalism. Then we turn to an analysis of the politics of labour, that is, class agency, in the Eurozone crisis, going right back to the initial response from European trade unions to the establishment of the Economic and Monetary Union (EMU). The conclusion will provide an outlook on the possibilities of labour to resist neoliberal restructuring.

UNEVEN AND COMBINED DEVELOPMENT IN THE EUROPEAN POLITICAL ECONOMY

Comparative European political economy has been dominated for some time by the so-called Varieties of Capitalism literature. It is argued that the way national political economies respond to external pressures is mediated and shaped by their particular sets of national institutions. In Hall and Soskice's (2001) original formulation, this process of analysis led to the development of a dichotomy between ideal types of national political economies: liberal- and market-coordinated economies. Such analysis moved away from arguing that all national political economies would move in the same liberalisation direction in the face of globalisation. Instead, external globalising processes would constrain and mediate various paths of development, with path-dependent institutional complementarities defining the trajectory pursued (Hall and Soskice 2001).

These institutionalist approaches have also been applied to the Eurozone crisis, leading to a new dichotomy of export- and import-led growth models being developed. Bob Hancké, for instance, examines wage formation institutions when explaining the crisis. While wage moderation was enforced in all European countries in the run-up to EMU, once the ECB had replaced independent national banks, wage formation in the Eurozone diverted into two blocs: 'a highly integrated northern block where co-ordinated wage bargaining keeps wage costs under control in all sectors of the economy, and the southern European countries, where labour costs have risen relative to the north' (Hancké 2013: 60). On the one hand, Germany and related countries, thanks to a strong set of wage formation institutions, continued to be able to generate wage moderation and ensure national competitiveness. Countries without such institutions and no longer with an independent central bank, however, fared less well. In the latter, especially public-sector unions used their new freedom and drove up wage increases, ultimately damaging the competitiveness of the whole country (Hancké 2013). A vicious circle ensured that resulting higher levels of inflation led to yet higher wage demands. The ECB, at the same time, was in no position to affect wage formation in individual countries. In short, according to Hancké, public-sector trade unions are responsible for lost competitiveness, having abused a situation in which the necessary institutional constraints were missing. In the final analysis, such conclusions are shared by Peter Hall (2012) in his analysis of the causes of the Eurozone crisis.

These approaches are, however, beset by a number of problems. First, they fall into the trap of 'methodological nationalism', 'an approach that conflates the society with the state and the national territory, and takes it as the unit of analysis' (Pradella 2014: 181). As a result, these approaches not only disregard, but also conceptually inhibit the ability to examine, the underlying social relations of production of the European political economy, with production networks cutting right across national borders. Moreover, these approaches implicitly overlook that not everyone can pursue a low-wage, export-oriented strategy of growth. The manner in which demand has been suffocated in Germany, through downward pressure on wages and growing precariousness of employment (see below), cannot be replicated everywhere. Even if the 'right' wage-setting systems had been in place to keep down unit labour costs, when some countries run large export surpluses, others will inevitably have to manage large import deficits. Finally, at a normative level, Hancké and others do not acknowledge that the downward pressure on unit labour costs results in a falling share of wages as part of the overall creation of wealth. They therefore play directly into the interests of capital. Drawing on Marx, Pradella (2014) puts forward key aspects of an alternative approach and argues that the labour theory of value is relevant for understanding capitalist globalisation. Hence, 'development is not presented only in "economic terms", but as a social and political process that is co-determined by class struggle. Only by bringing labour – or, better, workers – back in, therefore, is it possible to overcome the roots of methodological nationalism and identify the underlying tendencies of the international political economy' (Pradella 2014: 191). Hence, in this chapter we bring labour back into the analysis of the Eurozone crisis and focus on class struggle in our empirical approach.

When Ireland joined the EU in 1973, Greece in 1981 and Spain and Portugal in 1986, their level of economic development was clearly below the EU average at the time. After accession, however, all four countries seemed to develop, rapidly catching up with the other EU countries. This was especially the case in the period of the mid 1980s to early 1990s before convergence criteria for euro accession put pressure on EU member states to pursue austerity policies. For many, this confirmed the liberal understanding of development. As argued by David Ricardo, provided countries focus on their 'comparative advantage' and integrate with others through free trade, everyone involved will benefit with processes of developmental 'catch-up' being attained (Kiely 2007: 13–16). The Eurozone crisis has clearly ripped apart this understanding. As has by now become apparent, peripheral development in Europe occurred on rather weak foundations. Hence, it may be the notion of uneven and combined development which adequately characterises development within the European political economy. At the beginning of the twentieth century, Leon Trotsky pointed out that in order to overcome periodic economic crises, capitalism constantly had to expand outward in the search for new markets. 'In the process of its development, and consequently in the struggle with its internal contradictions, every national capitalism turns in an ever-increasing degree to the reserves of the "external market", that is, the reserves of world economy' (Trotsky [1929] 2007: 137). When analysing the particular location of Russia within the world economy, he argued that this necessary outward expansion led to uneven and combined development. While Russia was economically backward based on a large sector of inefficient agriculture indicating the unevenness of development in relation to advanced Western countries, a number of small pockets of highly developed industries, especially in military-related production, were established as a result of foreign pressure by more developed neighbours in the West (Trotsky [1906] 2007). Hence, capitalist expansion is also 'combined', since peripheral development is closely conditioned by developmental dynamics in the core. Importantly, from a historical materialist perspective, this unevenness is not the result of particular policies, but part of the underlying structuring conditions of capitalism (Bieler 2014). In the words of Ray Kiely (2007: 18), 'capitalist expansion is a dynamic but also an uneven process, and in contrast to the neoliberal (and pro-globalisation) positions, this unevenness is not seen as a result of market imperfections, but is in fact a product of the way competitive markets work in the real world.'

Hence, in this chapter we will pursue a historical-materialist approach, which takes the capitalist social relations of production as a starting point in relation to the structuring conditions of the European political economy around processes of uneven and combined development, as well as social-class forces as key agents. This will also ensure that the different levels of structural power available to social-class forces in class struggle are taken into account, as social-class forces are closely related to their location in the social relations of production.

THE UNDERLYING DYNAMICS OF THE EUROZONE CRISIS

Current problems in the Eurozone crisis go right back to the sub-prime mortgage crisis in the US in 2007, quickly spreading into a global financial crisis, and reaching a first high point with the bankruptcy of Lehman Brothers in 2008. Two major consequences of the crisis can be identified. First, states indebted themselves significantly as a result of bailing out failing banks and propping up the financial system. 'The sudden rise of public debt across the Eurozone in the last couple of years has been purely the result of the crisis of 2007-9' (Lapavitsas 2012: 40). Second, against the background of high levels of uncertainty, financial markets froze. Banks and financial institutions ceased lending to each other as well as to industrial companies. In turn, however, with liquid finance becoming scarce on the global financial markets, the peripheral Eurozone countries in particular have found it increasingly difficult to refinance their debts. Ever higher interest rates had to be offered to the financial markets in order to sell the necessary state bonds.

The global financial crisis, however, only triggered the sovereign debt crisis in Europe. The real cause of the crisis is the underlying imbalances in the European political economy between the core around Germany and the peripheral countries. Rather than resulting in processes of catch-up and convergence, development across the EU has been highly uneven over the last decades. Rather than David Ricardo's notion of comparative advantage in free trade, it is Trotsky's notion of uneven and combined development which characterises best the way development has occurred within the EU. On the one hand, Germany has experienced an export boom in recent years, with almost sixty per cent of its exports going to other European countries (Trading Economics 2013a). Germany's trade surplus is even more heavily focused on Europe. Sixty per cent are with other euro countries and about eighty-five per cent are with all EU members together (De Nardis 2010). However, such a growth strategy cannot be adopted by everybody. Some countries also have to absorb these exports. This is what many of the peripheral countries, now in trouble, such as Greece, Portugal, Spain and Ireland, have done. They, in turn, cannot compete in the free-trade internal market of the EU due to lower productivity rates. 'The net trade in goods between Germany and [Portugal, Ireland, Italy, Greece and Spain] amounted to some 2.24 per cent of gross domestic product (GDP) in 2007, accounting for 27.5 per cent of Germany's trade account surplus' (Laskos and Tsakalotos 2013: 86).

This unevenness is ultimately based on different productivity levels and the related fact that while Germany is mainly involved in high valued-added production sectors, peripheral European countries have historically been strong in low value-added sectors. For example, the Portuguese economy is characterised by low technology, labour-intensive production structures, often poorly organised and based on human resources with low levels of qualification (Rodrigues and Reis 2012). Where production does take place in high value-added industries, the foreign value-added content of the final exports is high. For instance, in Transport Equipment the foreign content of Portugal's exports stood at fifty-nine per cent, with the respective figure for Electrical Equipment at fifty-four per cent (OECD/WTO 2014). This indicates that Portuguese firms are primarily involved in final assembly of imported goods before they are exported, with net value of such exports being low. The figures for Germany are markedly lower (thirty-five and twenty-five per cent, respectively), supporting the distinction made between these states (OECD/WTO 2014). This high foreign value added is unsurprisingly derived from European states. 'Nearly half of the total value of Portugal's exports of *Transport equipment* originated in other European countries', with key states being Spain, Germany, and France (OECD/WTO 2014). In Greece's case, this distinction is only further exacerbated due to an overreliance on exporting primary goods and non-tradable services. Greece's main exports are 'food (19 per cent of total exports), petroleum products (15 per cent), pharmaceuticals (5 per cent) and aluminium (4 per cent). Others include: olive oil, textiles, steel and cement' (Trading Economics 2013b). Greece's domestic value-added content of gross exports stood at seventy-seven per cent in 2009, which is higher than Germany at seventy-three per cent (OECD/WTO 2014). However, the important difference is that much of this domestic content in Germany is exported through high value-added tradable manufacturing goods which are internationally competitive. In Greece 'relatively high domestic value added in Greece's exports in part reflects its specialisation in services exports', for example non-tradables, without any resulting manufacturing base due to lower levels of productivity and competitiveness (OECD/WTO 2014).

The super-profits resulting from German export success, needed new points of investment to generate more profits, and state bonds of peripheral countries seemed to be the ideal investment opportunity with guaranteed profits backed by sovereign states. Thus, 'Germany has been recycling its current account surpluses as FDI (foreign direct investment) and bank lending abroad' (Lapavitsas 2012: 31). In turn, these credits to the periphery were used to purchase more goods in the core. Hence, the recurrent distinction between credit- and export-led economies, frequently employed by Hall and Hancké themselves, is misleading. Firms in core countries would not have been able to pursue export-led growth strategies if global aggregate demand had not been supported by the real-estate and stock-market bubbles that occurred in the periphery. Germany's export successes crucially hinged on the credit-led solutions to neoliberalism's aggregate demand problem, also referred to as financialisation (Bellofiore and Halevi 2011). FDI figures since the establishment of EMU reveal this dynamic in Europe. Before 1999, states such as Portugal and Greece received FDI from quite a diverse set of states, with the US playing a prominent role (OECD 1994a, 1994b). However, since that time, inflows of investment have predominantly come from northern European states, especially Germany, France and Britain, with Spain playing an understandably large role in Portugal (UNCTAD 2012, 2013). This concentration of investments has therefore led to yet more exports from Germany to these countries and yet further super-profits in search of investment opportunities. The introduction of the euro and the related low interest rates in peripheral countries facilitated this financialisation of the European political economy in favour of transnational capital. Peripheral countries, on the other hand, have been unable to compete with German productivity levels and ended up as countries with large account deficits. 'Confronted with the stagnant and export-oriented performance of the dominant country of the Eurozone, peripheral countries have adopted a variety of approaches. Spain and Ireland have had investment booms that were based heavily on real estate speculation and bubbles. Greece and Portugal, meanwhile, have relied on high consumption, driven by household debt' (Lapavitsas 2012: 21). In the long run, such development strategies based on capital inflows were unsustainable. In short, German export success and peripheral countries' inability to compete with Germany are at the heart of the problem.

NEW DEVELOPMENTS IN THE EUROPEAN FORM OF STATE

In the end, Eurozone members were provided with bailout packages by the EU. In May 2010 and March 2012, Greece received financial help, Ireland was bailed out in November 2010, and in May 2011 it was Portugal's turn. Spain and Italy have also been heavily affected. Spanish banks require strong support by their government to stay afloat and Italy has found it increasingly difficult and expensive to secure new loans on international financial markets. Whilst not having to succumb to a formal bailout package, Italy and Spain had to present austerity packages, developed nationally, before the extension of loans from European institutions were made to recapitalise their banks. For those under the 'guidance' of formal agreements, the bailout packages came at a high price, which is visible in their conditionality, making support dependent on austerity policies, including: (i) cuts in funding of essential public services; (ii) cuts in public-sector employment; (iii) a push towards privatisation of state assets; and (iv) the undermining of industrial relations and trade union rights through enforced cuts in minimum wages and a further liberalisation of labour markets.

In more concrete terms, first the EU's peripheral countries were obliged to drastically cut back fiscal spending. For example, the fiscal cuts imposed on Greece amount to 10.5 per cent of GDP for 2010 and 2011, and another 9.9 per cent until 2014. The consequence of this austerity has been a drop in GDP of twenty-five per cent since 2008, the bulk of which came after the memorandum agreement in 2010 (see Crisis Observatory 2015). But imposed austerity also went beyond direct cuts. 'At the same time [Greece] has been forced to introduce new legislation in labour markets and to engage in ambitious privatisation' (Lapavitsas 2012: 120). Labour market deregulation and making wage setting 'more efficient' are clearly directed against trade unions' involvement in social and economic decision making at the national level (Erne 2012). As part of the bailout package for Portugal, the government agreed to stop extending collective agreements automatically to the whole industrial sector in 2011. Unsurprisingly, collective bargaining coverage has fallen drastically. 'In 2010 a total of 116 industry-level agreements ... were extended by government to cover all employees in the industry concerned. However, in 2011 this fell to 17 and in 2012 to 12' (ETUI 2013). Hence, while in 2010, 1 309 300 employees were covered by collective industry-level agreements, in 2012 it was only 291 100 employees (ETUI 2013). There have also been amendments to the Labour Code with the aim of creating greater flexibility for firms, thereby allegedly enhancing competitiveness and wage moderation. These changes have included reduced 'pay for overtime by 50 per cent'; further flexibilisation of fixed-term contracts by extending the 'probationary' period from six months to a maximum of three years; and the relaxing of rules for redundancy and dismissal, especially for reasons revolving around economic circumstances (Clauwaert and Schomann 2012: 9, 11–12; Pine and Abreu 2012: 25). Whilst some reversals on this front have been achieved through legislation having been deemed unconstitutional, officials from the ECB, European Commission, and International Monetary Fund (IMF) (collectively now popularly known as the 'Troika') have taken up the mantle of 'there is no alternative' by calling these 'set backs', with the need to find alternative paths to the same ends. In short, the crisis has been used by Troika officials to undermine the power of trade unions by cutting back their involvement in collective bargaining and industrial relations more generally whilst also creating more flexible labour markets, further enhancing the power of capital. The desire to circumvent Portugal's Constitutional Court rulings in this area also highlights the complete disregard for democratic and politicised processes.

Additional pressure was put on peripheral countries to privatise key national assets in order to improve the balance sheets. This pressure often bypassed democratic procedures. In August 2011 in relation to Italy, Jean-Claude Trichet, the then president of the ECB, and Mario Draghi, who succeeded him in November 2011, urged 'the full liberalisation of local public services ... through large scale privatisations', ignoring the fact that 95.5 per cent of Italian voters had rejected the privatisation of local water services in a valid national referendum less than eight weeks earlier (Erne 2012: 229). This point is further enhanced by the fact that Greece had initially put forward a proposal for only 3 billion euros worth of privatisation. This was eventually, due to the explicit dissatisfaction of Troika officials, raised to 50 billion euros only months later. However, privatisations have stalled in Greece, with projected revenues contin-ually being adjusted to 2020. As the global economy has stagnated, and Greece has been adversely affected, state-owned enterprises (SOEs) have simply been unattractive to international investors, even at deflated market prices. The initial aim of privatisations in Portugal was to raise 5 billion euros. At the time of writing (April 2014), this target has been actively exceeded, reaching almost 9 billion euros, with more still scheduled (European Commission 2013b). This has included various public utilities, with a particularly contentious privati-sation being 'the planned sale of the state water supplier Aguas de Portugal' (Busch et al. 2013: 23). 'The SOEs which remain have been restructured [in other words, redundancies and pay cuts] to bring down costs, and most have reached operational balance by the end of 2012' (European Commission 2013a: 28). Again, the crisis has been used by capital to roll back the state and extend the marketisation of essential public services. The power of capital vis-à-vis labour is strengthened as a result.

Ultimately, these developments continue a policy already laid out in the Treaty of Maastricht and the institutional set-up of EMU. With exchange rates between countries fixed as a result of the common currency and national fiscal policy severely restricted within the Stability and Growth Pact (SGP), the only way to increase competitiveness has been downward pressure on wages and work-related conditions (Bieler 2006). From the very beginning, the institu-tional bias of 'the Eurozone has directed the pressures of economic adjustment to the labour market: competitiveness in the internal market would depend on productivity growth and labour costs in each country, while labour mobility would be in practice relatively limited. As a result, a "race to the bottom" for wages and conditions has emerged in the Eurozone benefiting large industrial capital' (Lapavitsas 2012: 158).

Importantly, austerity in the form of wage cuts in the public sector, and cuts in services, pensions and social benefits has not only been imposed on countries struggling with sovereign debt, but across the whole EU (Erne 2012). At the EU level itself, the bailout packages were thus backed up with a new set of regulations around the so-called 'six pack' on economic governance applicable to all member states. 'According to these six new EU laws that came into force after their publication in the EU's *Official Journal* on 23 November 2011, Eurozone countries that do not comply with the revised EU Stability and Growth Pact or find themselves in a so-called macroeconomic excessive imbalance position, can be sanctioned by a yearly fine equalling 0.2 per cent or 0.1 per cent of GDP respectively' (Erne 2012: 228). The related surveillance procedures are organised in four ever-more intrusive stages: (i) the assessment of countries according to a scoreboard (European Commission 2013b); (ii) in-depth reviews; (iii) corrective action plans; and (iv) surveillance visits (Erne 2012). The new powers of the Commission became visible on 15 November 2013, when the Commission announced its verdict on the planned budget of 16 EU member states, that is, stage 2 in-depth reviews. While no country was asked to revise its budget and thus enter stage 3, it established several cases of substantial criticism, including for Germany's current account surplus. Italy and Spain were identified amongst others as being at risk of breaking the SGP rules.[3]

These mechanisms have been further enhanced by the 'Fiscal Compact', which came into force on 1 January 2013. There are two prominent articles. The first of these regards limiting deficits, called the 'balanced budget rule', requiring the national budgets of participating member states to be in balance or in surplus (European Council 2012). This enhances the fiscal pressure put in place by the SGP by deeming the above goal to have been met if their annual structural deficit does not exceed 0.5 per cent of nominal GDP. This is different to the fiscal deficit in that the structural position is assessed against what output 'would be' if economic performance was at its optimum, as opposed to the fiscal deficit which is simply measured against current output. Needless to say, the economic measurements for this are highly contestable but it represents the social content of such a policy toward ensuring fiscal rectitude. If the balanced budget rule is breached then an 'automatic correction mechanism' should be initiated to bring the 'deviations' in line over a fixed period. It is to be implemented through legislative means, preferably through constitutional amendments (EuroMemo Group 2013: 19). This is all based on recourse to the European Court of Justice if such structural constraints are not observed, with its rulings being legally binding (Degryse 2012).

EUROPEAN LABOUR IN THE EUROZONE CRISIS

Labour losing ground

Workers, and trade unions as their representatives, have come under severe pressure, facing downward pressure on wages and working conditions. From the inception of EMU, European trade unions were not unaware of the dangers implied in an institutional set-up in which wages were the only adjustment mechanism to remain competitive. They recognised that 'the logic of "regime competition" ... has become a main feature and a driving force of current industrial adjustments within the European Union' (Bieling 2001: 94, 103). Nevertheless, it was hoped that economic union would only be a step towards political union including a strong social dimension across the EU. It was the presence of Jacques Delors as president of the European Commission and his emphasis on the necessity of a social counterpart to economic integration, including the participation of trade unions in European politics, which convinced unions to support the internal market. The small gains of the Social Chapter at Maastricht and the relative weakness of trade unions across the EU due to the economic recession in the early 1990s made trade unions accept EMU (Bieling 2001). This support was not uncritical, but followed a 'yes, but' attitude. European integration was supported as such, but additional social-policy measures were demanded. In short, the support for EMU did not imply that European trade unions had accepted the principles of neoliberalism (Bieler 2006).

Nor did support for EMU imply that European trade unions had not tried to counter the negative impact on wage formation. The European Metalworkers' Federation (EMF), which organises workers in one of the most transnationalised sectors in Europe, including many transnational corporations in consumer electronics, car manufacturing and machinery production, became aware of these dangers in the early 1990s. In response to transnationalisation, it was argued that the EMF had to follow and also internationalise its structure and activities. 'Under the influence of the opening-up of the European borders, growing international competition, complete Europeanisation of the economy and massive unemployment in Europe, [the EMF] had noticed a distinct tendency towards a competition-driven collective bargaining policy' (EMF 2001: 1). Plans for EMU further implied the danger of social dumping through the undercutting of wage and working conditions between several national collective-bargaining rounds

(EMF 1998). The EMF realised that wage bargaining was no longer a national issue in its sector, characterised by an increasing transnationalisation of production. In response, the EMF started restructuring itself and began to discuss the potential of coordinating wage bargaining. The EMF coordination strategy had three main pillars (EMF 2001). These were: (i) a sophisticated system for the exchange of information about national collective bargaining rounds, the so-called European Collective Bargaining Information Network (EUCOB@) (Schulten 2001); (ii) the establishment of cross-border collective-bargaining networks including the exchange of observers for collective-bargaining rounds (Schulten 2001); and (iii) the adoption of common minimum standards and guidelines. The coordination of national wage bargaining was approved in 1998 and the EMF tried to ensure that national unions pursued a common strategy of asking for wage increases along the formula of productivity increase plus inflation rate (EMF 1998; Schulten 2001). The main goal of the coordination of collective bargaining was to avoid the downward competition between different national bargaining rounds and to protect workers against the related reduction in wages and working conditions. Thus, 'a co-ordinated European collective bargaining policy will play a major role in intensifying and reinforcing the social dimension of European unity' (EMF 1998: 1). In summer 1999, the European Trade Union Confederation (ETUC) as a whole adopted the coordination of collective bargaining as one of its four main tasks and established an ETUC Collective Bargaining Committee (Schulten 2002). The main goal was to stop the fall of wages as a percentage of GDP based on the understanding that a further fall of workers' real income would damage domestic demand levels across the EU (Mermet 2001).

In short, European trade unions had not been unaware of the dangers built into EMU and the strategy of coordinating national collective bargaining was at the heart of a European-level response by labour. And yet, the coordination strategy failed. In 2006, the ETUC published for the last time data on whether the various national collective-bargaining rounds had been in line with the ETUC guidelines of wage increases along the formula of productivity increase plus inflation. The findings make clear that not only had no country managed to achieve this target except for Finland, but that German trade unions were actually the ones during the cumulative period of 2003 to 2006 which missed it by the largest amount in that the total real-wage increase minus productivity increase was -8.6 per cent in Germany (Erne 2008: 97). Updating the data for Germany until 2012, Steffen Lehndorff demonstrates an even more drastic picture. For the period of 2000 to 2012, the average negotiated salary increase was 5.5 per cent below productivity increase. Even more drastic, the effective average salary increase was a further 9.3 per cent below the negotiated average salary (Lehndorff 2013: 56). Clearly, these wage developments, while ensuring that Germany could emerge with an export boom out of the crisis, have put downward pressure on wages and working conditions elsewhere in Europe and have thus become a problem for other European trade unions. Some observers blame German trade unions for this failure. They argue that German unions cooperated with employers at the expense of workers' interests elsewhere, not only in accepting small wage increases, but also in agreeing on opt-out clauses. These opt-out clauses allowed for lower agreements at company level, and are ultimately responsible for the effective average salary being lower than the negotiated average salary. At the same time, German trade unions have also been significantly weakened over the past 20 to 25 years. Increasing transnationalisation of German production has weakened German unions structurally vis-à-vis employers, and the deregulation of the temporary agency work in 2003 has fragmented the workforce. Taking into account the IG Metall's defeat in a strike in 2003, it is clear that German unions have lost significant levels of power. Perhaps, they have simply been unable to achieve more (Bieler and Erne 2014).

What possibilities for labour to resist restructuring?

In contrast to general assumptions, German workers have not benefited from the current situation. German productivity increases have, to a significant extent, resulted from drastic downward pressure on wages and work-related conditions. 'Germany has been unrelenting in squeezing its own workers throughout this period. During the last two decades, the most powerful economy of the Eurozone has produced the lowest increases in nominal labour costs, while its workers have systematically lost share of output. EMU has been an ordeal for German workers' (Flassbeck and Lapavitsas 2013: 14–16; Lapavitsas 2012: 4). The Agenda 2010, and here especially the so-called Hartz IV reform, implemented in the early 2000s constitutes the largest cut in, and restructuring of, the German welfare system since the end of World War II (Bruff 2010). In other words, Germany was more successful than other Eurozone countries in cutting back labour costs. 'The euro is a "beggar-thy-neighbour" policy for Germany, on condition that it beggars its own workers first' (Lapavitsas 2012: 30). Uneven and combined development, as indicated earlier, takes place not only between countries, but also within individual countries. German export success has been built on increasing inequality within German society. Hence, while the mainstream media regularly portray the crisis as a conflict between Germany and peripheral countries, the real conflict here is between capital and labour. As noted, rather than pursuing a research strategy of methodological nationalism, an analytical focus on class struggle is required for understanding the Eurozone crisis. And this class conflict is taking place across the EU, as employers abuse the crisis to cut back workers' post-war gains. The crisis provides capital with the rationale to justify cuts that they would otherwise be unable to implement.

At the European level, trade unions have been unable to converge around a strong counter-austerity strategy. While southern European trade unions are more supportive of general strikes, Nordic trade unions tend to disfavour doing anything at the European level, as they are confident that they can still contain austerity at the national level. Others, however, would prefer a repetition of the European Citizens' Initiative (ECI) on water as a human right (see below) around an initiative against austerity (Gobin and Erne, forthcoming). In addition to external constraints, Asbjørn Wahl identifies internal political-ideological barriers to successful trade union action in Europe. 'The situation is strongly affected by the crisis on the left, including the fact that social partnership and social dialogue have largely been developed into an overall ideology in dominant parts of the labour movement at both the European and national level' (Wahl 2014: 50). It has been largely forgotten that the post-war class compromise and the related gains by trade unions were the result of harsh confrontations and successful mobilisation. Hence, trade unions continue to focus on talking to employers and governments, while the underlying power balance, as in the case of Germany, has changed and capital no longer needs to make concessions. Moreover, Wahl argues that 'another internal barrier for many trade unions is their attachment to the traditional labor parties' (Wahl 2014: 52). Trade unions continue this historical relationship despite these parties having moved towards neoliberal policies undermining trade unions directly. Nevertheless, although European trade unions have failed to date to mobilise successfully against austerity policies and represent the interests of working people, the potential that they may do otherwise is there:

> The political shift towards the right and the political-ideological crisis
> on the left mean that the trade-union moment itself has to play a more
> central, independent, and more offensive political role – political not in

the party sense, but in the sense that it assumes a broader political perspective in the social struggle. The greater part of the trade-union movement is not prepared to take on such a role today, but it holds the potential. (Wahl 2014: 55)

When thinking about alternative responses to the crisis, short-term measures can be distinguished from more medium- and long-term measures. Immediately, it will be important that German trade unions push for higher salary increases at home so that the German domestic market absorbs more goods, which are currently being exported. Along similar lines is the proposal by the Confederation of German Trade Unions (DGB) for an economic stimulus, investment and development programme for Europe. This new Marshall Plan, published in December 2012, is designed as an investment and development programme over a 10-year period and consists of a mix of institutional measures, direct public-sector investment, investment grants for companies and incentives for consumer spending (DGB 2012). Interestingly, what has emerged from European-level discussions is an ETUC initiative for a European investment programme, adopted at the meeting of the ETUC Executive Committee on 7 November 2013 (ETUC 2013). The ETUC's recommendations, importantly, closely follow the DGB's Marshall Plan for Europe, as they also include the idea that interest-bearing bonds, intended to raise the necessary money for investment, should be partly financed and secured through the receipts from a Financial Transaction Tax and a one-off tax on wealthier people.

Of course, neo-Keynesian measures such as investment programmes will ease the immediate pressure on European economies. However, they will not question the power structures underlying the European political economy. A victorious outcome in the struggle against austerity ultimately depends on a change in the balance of power in society. The establishment of welfare states and fairer societies was based on the capacity of labour to balance the class power of capital (Wahl 2011). Overcoming austerity will therefore require a strengthening of labour vis-à-vis capital. As Lapavitsas notes, 'a radical left strategy should offer a resolution of the crisis that alters the balance of social forces in favour of labour and pushes Europe in a socialist direction' (Lapavitsas 2011: 294). Hence, in the medium to long term, it will be essential to intervene more directly in the financial sector. As part of bailouts, many private banks have been nationalised, such as the Royal Bank of Scotland in the UK. However, they have been allowed to continue operating as if they were private banks. Little state direction has been imposed. It will be important to move beyond nationalisation towards the socialisation of banks to ensure that banks actually operate according to the needs of society. Such a step would contribute directly to changing the balance of power in society in favour of labour.

Another possibility of changing the balance of power in society is alliances of trade unions with other social movements. Class struggle, understood broadly, includes struggles beyond the workplace within the whole 'social factory' of (social) reproduction (Bieler 2014). Out of the European Social Forum process, for example, emerged the Alter Summit movement launched at a meeting in Firenze in November 2012. Here, trade unions and social movements, enlarging the social basis of resistance as a result of their alliance, cooperated in the development of proposals for Another Europe. And while the first Alter Summit in Athens on 7 and 8 June 2013 was only a partial success at best, considering that it was more a gathering of representatives of groups than a mass event, this is, nonetheless, an initiative with the potential for wider, transformative change. As one of the organisers remarked, 'if it proves possible to bring the analyses and proposals developed together in the [Alter Summit] into the participating organisations, anchor them among the members and promote a common consciousness, the bases will have been laid for common action and in so doing the potential for shifting the relation of forces in Europe made more real' (Gauthier 2013).

Such alliances can even be led by established trade unions. The European Federation of Public Service Unions (EPSU) was crucial in launching the first ECI on water as a human right, collecting almost 1.9 million signatures between May 2012 and September 2013. The demands of the ECI were three-fold: '(1) For the EU to recognise the UN right to water and sanitation into EU law; (2) not to liberalise water services in the EU; and (3) to contribute to achieving access to water and sanitation for all across the world'.[4] On the one hand, there is the interest of trade unions in keeping water provision in public hands, as working conditions are generally better in the public than the private sector. On the other, user groups are supportive of universal access to affordable clean water. It is the inclusion of issues beyond the workplace, here the right of access to clean water, which has allowed EPSU to link up with other social movements and, thereby, broaden the social basis for resistance and form bonds of solidarity. It is this kind of initiative, combining alternative proposals with large-scale mobilisation, which may provide the way forward to a different future. Inspired by the successful referendum against water privatisation in

Italy in June 2011 (Fantini 2014), the ECI, in turn, has encouraged citizens in the Greek city of Thessaloniki to hold their own referendum against water privatisation. The referendum was supported by EPSU and the European water movement more generally, which sent monitors on the day of the referendum. This support ultimately led to the withdrawal of the privatisation initiative after ninety-eight per cent of votes had been cast against (Goudriaan 2014). Moreover, these efforts also bore fruit in the broad mobilisation for an independent ECI, launched on 15 July 2014, against the Transatlantic Trade and Investment Partnership,[5] intended to deepen further neoliberal restructuring and also including the infamous investor-state dispute settlement mechanism (Hilary 2014).

Broad alliances require mobilisation of forces. A fairly successful example is the European-wide mobilisation on 14 November 2012, combining strikes in southern European countries with other forms of demonstrations elsewhere. While participation in Greece itself was low, probably due to a large 48-hour strike the week before, 300 000 protested in over 100 cities in Italy where the Italian General Confederation of Labour had organised a four-hour strike. Moreover, there was a huge turnout in Spain, where 'up to 800 000 people were reported marching through the streets of Madrid, and in cities all over the country a total close to two million people participated in "14 November"' (Helle 2015: 230). The purpose of the strikes and demonstrations was clear. They were addressing 'the effects of austerity policies in each eurozone country, with a particular focus on the implementation of the EU, ECB and IMF troika's directives in the debt-ridden countries in southern Europe' (Helle 2015: 237).

There have also been movements whose presence can be directly related to the multiple political and economic crises that have developed over the last six or seven years. These have taken a greater political stance towards the crises, primarily concerned with the undermining, and potential alternatives, of democratic practices. Two interest us here: the 15-M movement (also known as Indignados) in Spain, and the Greek Indignados. From the initial response of occupying space, the various indignados movements have gone on to build important structures of solidarity and direct democracy that reflect national conditions of crisis. A prominent example from Spain is the Plataforma de Afectados por la Hipoteca (PAH) (Mortgage Victims Platform). They have been successfully involved in stopping evictions through direct and legal action, whilst also relocating those who are evicted. When attempting to engage in the legislative process they experienced a gutting of proposed changes to the mortgage law, although they had collected over 1.4 million signatures to initiate the process. In the face of growing pressure, this disappointment has only further exacerbated a feeling that the political class is distant and discredited.[6] Whilst such an initiative operates at the level of a particular issue, the sheer scale of the property boom and crash in Spain has facilitated the potential to tap into a deeper consciousness. This enabled a move from moral accounts of individual deficiencies to a progressive indignation toward the current conjuncture which has become more generalised, encompassing not only the social movements themselves, but engagement with trade unions and, when appropriate, political parties. The Greek Indignados, whilst following a similar strategy of occupation, again had a distinctly national character in their response. An important example has been the growth of Social Solidarity Clinics, which now total a national network of over 50. These clinics offer comprehensive provision of first-level treatment for those who have been excluded from the national health system. Exclusions, prior to the electoral victory of the leftist party, Syriza, in January 2015, included those who had been unable to maintain their social security contributions due to losing their jobs, or through the increase in cost of medicines, and due to being an immigrant without the correct legal status. In Thessaloniki, for example, which has a total population of over one million citizens, the clinic has seen over 50 000 individuals, not including repeat appointments, since it opened over three years ago. In the face of austerity and the dismantling of the already insufficient welfare state in Greece, these clinics have offered a basic safety net.[7] Much like the PAH movement they explicitly bring a political question to the reasons for ordinary citizens not being able to access basic health-care services. Those involved in organising such initiatives are clear that this is not about charity or philanthropy, but solidarity and democracy.

The challenge for both movements is, of course, to move these political struggles into a more generalised push towards a real alternative. Syriza's victory in Greece in January 2015 has opened up new opportunities, where a number of movements have worked autonomously, but nonetheless closely, with the party to create spaces of alternatives in the future development of Greece. In Spain, at the local, sectoral level, it has been possible at times to organise campaigns based on alliances between unions and social movements. In defence of public education, for example, the so-called Green Tide movement, including trade unions, parents' organisations and neighbourhood assemblies, was formed in Madrid from August 2011 onwards (Béroud 2014). Unfortunately, however, at the larger, national level, to date there has been much mistrust between social movements and trade unions, especially in Spain, preventing the emergence of a more permanent and powerful force of resistance. As an editor of the online magazine ROAR told us,

> we are supporting movements such as the PAH, but at the same time we also believe that in some way it is a good thing that the labour unions are not heavily involved with these struggles because, as history has taught us, due to their hierarchical structure they are often easily co-opted by the powers-that-be. By welcoming the trade unions into the anti-auster-ity movements, there is a serious risk that the latter would lose its unique horizontal and autonomous organisational structures, which we believe is the ultimate strength of these movements.[8]

Future developments around the rise of the new political party Podemos will be interesting in this respect.

The above considerations, overall, speak to the fact that in the long run even a change in the power balance between capital and labour in itself will not be enough. It can always only be a starting point. Capitalist exploitation is rooted in the way the social relations of production are set up around wage labour and the private ownership of the means of production. Exploitation, therefore, can only be overcome if the way in which production is organised is changed. First positive signs can be noted in this respect. While trade unions often struggle to identify strategies of transnational solidarity, at times workers take the initia-tive into their own hands, as in the case of factory occupations by workers in Greece, Italy and France. These include the exchange of experiences between workers in the various countries which resulted in the establishment of the South European Occupied Factories' Network in Marseilles, France, in January 2014 (Vogiatzoglou 2015). Trade unions have to be careful to appreciate this new reality if they do not want to run the risk of being pushed aside by more active forces in the wider labour movement.

CONCLUSION

Resistance against austerity and neoliberal restructuring has not been without success. We have already mentioned the successful referendum in Italy in

2011 against water privatisation, the ECI on water as a human right as well as the Thessaloniki referendum against water privatisation. There are a range of successful remunicipalisations of water across the world with Paris being the most prominent European example.[9] Equally, there are a number of interesting experiments of reorganising the delivery of public services in a more democratic way from within the public sector (Wainwright 2014). And yet, European forces against austerity must not be complacent either. The spectre of fascist, xenophobic movements looms large across Europe, partly as both a response to and a part of increasingly authoritarian government and intensified austerity. Electoral successes by the right-wing Greek party, Golden Dawn, which obtained, for example, almost seven per cent in the Greek elections in June 2012 is only one of the most obvious examples in this respect.

Considering that austerity is a European-wide phenomenon, pushed by Brussels but equally by individual national governments, it will remain important that trade unions and the wider labour movement resist neoliberal restructuring at both the European level and the national level. To declare solidarity with Greek workers is a good initiative by German and British unions, for example. Nevertheless, the more concrete support is to resist restructuring at home. Any defeat of austerity in one of the EU member states will assist similar struggles elsewhere. Equally, resistance by labour against austerity in Europe also needs to take into account the global dimension. Transnational solidarity has been undermined at times, when European trade unions in export-oriented sectors supported new free-trade agreements, despite the fact that these were resisted by labour movements in the global South because of job losses and de-industrialisation (Bieler 2013). Clearly, uneven and combined development also remains important in shaping forms of resistance at the European as well as global level.

When Trotsky analysed the way in which Russia had been integrated into the global economy in processes of uneven and combined development at the beginning of the twentieth century, his main interest was not simply an assessment of Russian development. Rather, he wanted to understand the structural preconditions of the Russian situation and in what way they may facilitate revolutionary upheaval. The element of combined development is crucial in this respect, since it brings together the most 'advanced' social relations with 'backward' forms of social relationships, resulting overall in rather unstable social formations (Davidson 2010: 13). Countries in the periphery, therefore, are potentially a more fertile ground for revolutionary uprisings than countries in the core with more coherent social formations. Thinking about the Eurozone crisis, it should be no surprise that class struggle is fought more openly on the streets of Greece, the periphery of Europe, where the exploitation by capital is enforced in a more open, politically direct, authoritarian way, than in the UK, where the cuts are less violent and have less existential effects for people. And indeed, it is in Greece that we can observe wider struggles across the whole of society. 'Especially after 2010, social resistance to austerity included diverse forms of solidarity and initiatives to set up a parallel social economy: from social clinics and pharmacies to social groceries, and from the movement to cut out the intermediaries in agricultural production to various cooperative ventures' (Laskos and Tsakalotos 2013: 143). This included cooperation between trade unions and wider social-class forces. For example, 'the Federation of Hospital Doctors took a number of important initiatives on these lines, climaxing with the establishment of Wednesdays as a day of free access to health care in hospitals for the uninsured' (Laskos and Tsakalotos 2013: 124).

Workers, in the core of both the EU and of individual countries, being in a different location of production due to the overall unevenness of the economy, may initially see their own fortunes in a different light. Nevertheless, as the current crisis in Europe demonstrates, restructuring ultimately affects workers in the periphery and core alike and the situation of workers in the periphery now may simply represent the position of workers in the core in the future. The challenge is to organise this struggle in a way so that it overcomes the initial divisions of interest between workers in the periphery and the core, both between and within countries in Europe.

NOTES

1   McDonald, C. 2012. 'Are Greeks the hardest workers in Europe?', BBC News. Accessed 26 February 2012, http://www.bbc.co.uk/news/magazine-17155304.

2   Rogers, S. 2011. 'Greek debt crisis: how exposed is your bank?', The Guardian. Accessed 17 June 2011, http://www.theguardian.com/news/datablog/2011/jun/17/greece-debt-crisis-bank-exposed#history-link-box.

3   Kelpie, C. 2013. 'Italy, Spain criticised among countries at risk of breaking EU budget rules'. Accessed 16 November 2013, http://www.independent.ie/business/irish/italy-spain-criticised-among-countries-at-risk-of-breaking-eu-budget-rules-29758927.html.

4   Water is a human right. 2013. '"Water is a human right!" will submit certificates for 1.6 million signatories'. Accessed 19 December 2013, http://www.right2water.eu/

news/press-communication-%E2%80%9Cwater-human-right%E2%80%9D-will-submit-certificates-16-million-signatories.

5   Stop-TTIP. 2014. 'ECI "Stop-TTIP" Partner Organisations'. Accessed 22 July 2014, http://stop-ttip.org/wp-content/uploads/2014/07/ECI-Partner-List.pdf.

6   Ainger, K. 2013. 'In Spain they are all *indignados* nowadays'. Accessed 28 April 2013, http://www.theguardian.com/commentisfree/2013/apr/28/spain-indignados-protests-state-of-mind.

7   Data collected from authors' fieldwork interviews, 6 and 8 May 2015.

8   Email communication with the authors, 27 November 2013.

9   Water Remunicipalisation Tracker. 2014. Accessed 9 September 2014, http://www.remunicipalisation.org/.

REFERENCES

Bellofiore, R. and Halevi, J. 2011. '"Could be raining": the European crisis after the Great Recession'. *International Journal of Political Economy*, 39 (4): 5–30.

Béroud, S. 2014. 'Une mobilisation syndicale traversée par le souffle des Indignés? La "marée verte" dans le secteur de l'éducation à Madrid', *Savoir/agir* 27: 52–53.

Bieler, A. 2006. *The Struggle for a Social Europe: Trade unions and EMU in times of global restructuring*. Manchester: Manchester University Press.

Bieler, A. 2013. 'The EU, global Europe and processes of uneven and combined development: the problem of transnational labour solidarity', *Review of International Studies*, 39 (1): 161–183.

Bieler, A. 2014. 'Transnational labour solidarity in (the) crisis', *Global Labour Journal*, 5 (2): 114–133.

Bieler, A. and Erne, R. 2014. 'Transnational solidarity? The European working class in the Eurozone crisis'. In *Socialist Register 2015*, edited by L. Panitch, G. Albo and V. Chibber. Pontypool: The Merlin Press.

Bieling, H.J. 2001. 'European constitutionalism and industrial relations'. In *Social Forces in the Making of the New Europe: The Restructuring of European Social Relations in the Global Political Economy*, edited by A. Bieler and A.D. Morton. Houndmills: Palgrave.

Bruff, I. 2010. 'Germany's Agenda 2010 reforms: passive revolution at the crossroads', *Capital & Class*, 34 (3): 409–428.

Busch, K., Hermann, C., Hinrichs, K. and Schulten, T. 2013. 'Euro crisis, austerity policy and the European social model', *International Policy Analysis*, Friedrich Ebert Stiftung. Accessed 1 June 2013, http://library.fes.de/pdf-files/id/ipa/09656.pdf.

Clauwaert, S. and Schomann, I. 2012. *The crisis and national labour law reforms: a mapping exercise*. ETUI – Working Paper 2012.04, 1–19.

Crisis Observatory. 2015. 'Gross domestic product'. Accessed 10 May 2015, http://crisisobs.gr/wp-content/uploads/2013/03/1.Gross-Domestic-Product1.pdf.

Davidson, N. 2010. 'From deflected permanent revolution to the law of uneven and combined development', *International Socialism*, 128. Accessed 30 March 2014, http://www.isj.org.uk/?id=686.

De Nardis, S. 2010. 'German imbalance and European tensions'. Accessed 2 December 2010, http://www.voxeu.org/article/german-imbalance-and-european-tensions.

Degryse, C. 2012. *The new European economic governance*, ETUI Working Paper 2012.14. Accessed 1 July 2013, http://www.etui.org/Publications2/Working-Papers/The-new-European-economic-governance.

DGB. 2012. 'A Marshall Plan for Europe', Proposal by the DGB for an economic stimulus, investment and development programme for Europe. Accessed 23 March 2014, http://www.fesdc.org/pdf/A-Marshall-Plan-for-Europe_EN.pdf.

EMF (European Metalworkers' Federation). 1998. 'Collective bargaining with the Euro'. 3rd EMF Collective Bargaining Conference, Frankfurt, 9–10 December. Accessed 26 October 2004, http://www.emf-fem.org/index.cfm?target=/default.cfm.

EMF. 2001. 'EMF position on the European industrial relation system'. Adopted by the EMF Executive Committee, Luxembourg, 3–4 December. Accessed 26 October 2004, http://www.emf-fem.org/index.cfm?target=/default.cfm.

Erne, R. 2008. *European Unions: Labour´s Quest for a Transnational Democracy*. Ithaka: Cornell University Press.

Erne, R. 2012. 'European industrial relations after the crisis: a postscript'. In *The European Union and Industrial Relations: New Procedures, New Context*, edited by S. Smismans. Manchester: Manchester University Press.

ETUC (European Trade Union Confederation). 2013. 'A new path for Europe: ETUC plan for investment, sustainable growth and quality jobs. Accessed 7 November 2013, http://www.etuc.org/sites/www.etuc.org/files/EN-A-new-path-for-europe_3.pdf.

ETUI (European Trade Union Institute). 2013. 'Collective bargaining'. Accessed 22 November 2013, http://www.worker-participation.eu/National-Industrial-Relations/Countries/Portugal/Collective-Bargaining.

EuroMemo Group. 2013. 'The deepening crisis in the European Union: the need for a fundamental change'. In *European Economists for an Alternative Economic Policy in Europe*. Accessed 26 June 2013, http://www2.euromemorandum.eu/uploads/euromemorandum_2013.pdf.

European Commission. 2013a. 'MIP scoreboard'. Accessed 22 November 2013, http://ec.europa.eu/economy_finance/economic_governance/macroeconomic_imbalance_procedure/mip_scoreboard/.

European Commission. 2013b. 'The Economic Adjustment Programme for Portugal – Seventh Review – Winter 2012/2013'. European Economy, Occasional Papers 153, June 2013.

European Council. 2012. 'Fiscal Compact enters into force' (21 December). Accessed 2 July 2015, http://www.consilium.europa.eu/uedocs/cms_data/docs/pressdata/en/ecofin/134543.pdf.

Fantini, E. 2014. 'Catholics in the making of the Italian water movement: a moral economy', *Partecipazione e Conflitto*. 7 (1): 35–57.

Flassbeck, H. and Lapavitsas, C. 2013. 'The systemic crisis of the Euro – true causes and effective therapies', *Studien – Rosa Luxemburg Stiftung*: 1–45.

Gauthier, E. 2013. 'Innovation – The Alter-Summit'. *Transform! European network for alternative thinking and political dialogue*, Issue 13. Accessed 27 April 2014, http://transform-network.net/journal/issue-132013/news/detail/Journal/innovation-the-alter-summit.html.

Gobin, C. and Erne, R. (forthcoming) 'Des défis sans précédents mais des réponses faibles. La Confédération européenne des syndicats dans un contexte de crise financière et économique', under submission with *Revue Internationale de Politique Comparée*.

Goudriaan, J.W. 2014. 'Resisting austerity in Greece: the Thessaloniki water referendum', 13 May 2014. Accessed 12 June 2014, http://andreasbieler.blogspot.no/2014/05/resisting-austerity-in-greece.html.

Hall, P.A. 2012. 'The economics and politics of the euro crisis', *German Politics*, 21 (4): 355–371.

Hall, P.A. and Soskice, D. (eds). 2001. *Varieties of Capitalism: The Institutional Foundations of Comparative Advantage*. Oxford: Oxford University Press.

Hancké, B. 2013. *Unions, Central Banks, and EMU: Labour Market Institutions and Monetary Integration in Europe*. Oxford: Oxford University Press.

Helle, I. 2015. 'The 14N and its predecessors: a new European proletariat in the making?', under submission with *Transfer: European Review of Labour and Research*, 21 (2): 229–242.

Hilary, J. 2014. *The Transatlantic Trade and Investment Partnership: A Charter for Deregulation, an Attack on Jobs, and End to Democracy*. Brussels: Rosa Luxemburg Stiftung.

Kiely, R. 2007. *The New Political Economy of Development: Globalization, Imperialism, Hegemony*. London: Palgrave.

Lapavitsas, C. 2011. 'Default and exit from the Eurozone: a radical left strategy'. In *Socialist Register 2012: The Crisis and the Left*, edited by L. Panitch, G. Albo and V. Chibber. Pontypool: The Merlin Press.

Lapavitsas, C. 2012. *Crisis in the Eurozone*. London and New York: Verso.

Laskos, C. and Tsakalotos, E. 2013. *Crucible of Resistance: Greece, the Eurozone and the World Economic Crisis*. London: Pluto Press.

Lehndorff, S. 2013. 'Un géant endormi? Le rôle des syndicats avant et pendant la crise européenne', *Chronique Internationale de l'IRES*, 143 (4): 53–64.

Mermet, E. 2001. *Wage Formation in Europe*. Brussels: ETUI.

OECD (Organisation for Economic Co-operation and Development). 1994a. 'OECD review on foreign direct investment – Greece'. Accessed 2 April 2014, http://www.oecd.org/greece/34383957.pdf.

OECD. 1994b. 'OECD review on foreign direct investment – Portugal'. Accessed 1 July 2013, http://www.oecd.org/portugal/34383696.pdf.

OECD/WTO. 2014. 'Trade in Value-Added (TIVA) indicators'. Accessed 21 March 2014, http://www.oecd.org/industry/ind/measuringtradeinvalue-addedanoecd-wtojointinitiative.htm.

Pine, A. and Abreu, I. 2012. *Portugal: rebalancing the economy and returning to growth through job creation and better capital allocation*, OECD Economics Department Working Papers, No 994. Accessed 27 June 2013, http://dx.doi.org/10.1787/5k918xjjzs9q-en.

Pradella, L. 2014. 'New developmentalism and the origins of methodological nationalism', *Competition & Change*, 18 (2): 180–193.

Rodrigues, J. and Reis, J. 2012. 'The asymmetries of European integration and the crisis of capitalism in Portugal', *Competition and Change*, 16 (3): 188–205.

Schulten, T. 2001. 'The European Metalworkers' Federation's approach to a European coordination of collective bargaining: experiences, problems and prospects'. In *Collective Bargaining under the Euro: Experiences from the European Metal Industry*, edited by T. Schulten and R. Bispinck. Brussels: ETUI.

Schulten, T. 2002. 'Europeanisation of collective bargaining: an overview on trade union initiatives for a transnational coordination of collective bargaining policy', *WSI Discussion Paper*, No.101. Düsseldorf: Wirtschafts- und Sozialwissenschaftliches Institut in der Hans-Böckler-Stiftung.

Trading Economics. 2013a. 'Germany balance of trade'. Accessed 10 May 2013, http://www.tradingeconomics.com/germany/balance-of-trade.

Trading Economics. 2013b. 'Greece exports'. Accessed 30 August 2013, http://www.tradingeconomics.com/greece/exports.

Trotsky, L. [1906] 2007. 'Results and prospects'. In L. Trotsky, *The Permanent Revolution & Results and Prospects*. London: Socialist Resistance.

Trotsky, L. [1929] 2007. 'The permanent revolution'. In L. Trotsky, *The Permanent Revolution & Results and Prospects*. London: Socialist Resistance.

UNCTAD (United Nations Conference on Trade and Development). 2012. 'Investment country profiles: Greece', United Nations Conference on Trade and Development, February 2012. Accessed 3 April 2014, http://unctad.org/en/PublicationsLibrary/webdiaeia2012d9_en.pdf.

UNCTAD. 2013. 'Investment country profiles: Portugal', United Nations Conference on Trade and Development, February 2013. Accessed 15 June 2013, http://unctad.org/en/PublicationsLibrary/webdiaeia2012d16_en.pdf.

Vogiatzoglou, M. 2015. 'Workers' trans-national networks in austerity times: the case of Italy and Greece', *Transfer: European Review of Labour and Research,* 21 (2): 215–228.

Wahl, A. 2011. *The Rise and Fall of the Welfare State*. London: Pluto Press.

Wahl, A. 2014. 'European labor: political and ideological crisis in an increasingly more authoritarian European Union', *Monthly Review,* 65 (8): 36–57.

Wainwright, H. 2014. *The Tragedy of the Private, The Potential of the Public*. Amsterdam: Transnational Institute. Accessed 9 September 2014, http://www.tni.org/sites www.tni.org/files/download/alternatives_to_privatization_en_booklet_web.pdf.

5

BEYOND SOCIAL-DEMOCRATIC AND COMMUNIST PARTIES: LEFT POLITICAL ORGANISATION IN TRANSITION IN WESTERN EUROPE

Hilary Wainwright

Two recent developments stimulate me to rethink the role of the political party in the context of Europe in the twenty-first century. The first is the narrowing of democracy, in contrast to the far-reaching horizons of those who originally fought for it. This narrowing has been a continuing process of containment of democratic pressures since the moments when popular movements eventually won the universal right to vote in different countries at different times. These movements for democracy (in the first instance, the universal franchise) had two features in common: one was an umbilical link between social and economic demands and political power ('social happiness is our goal, political power is the means' [Thompson 1984], as the Chartists put it), and the second was a belief that the franchise was just the beginning of a process of achieving popular self-government, not an end in itself.

The second development is the conservatism and defeat of the nationally organised labour movements of the post-war settlement in Europe which could have been sources of counter-power to the economic and state pressures that were narrowing democracy. This does not mean that organisations of labour cannot be built anew. Indeed, the question of what such a rebuilding involves and what the conditions for its possibility are, will be a theme later in the chapter. Such recreation (because it certainly will not be rebuilding of the old) of organisations of labour is, I will contend, a key aspect of new forms of political organisation. But this will require a radical break from the organisational forms of the past.

THE LASTING POLITICAL LEGACY OF THE REVOLTS OF THE SIXTIES AND SEVENTIES

Exhaustion of the social democratic and communist traditions

Neither the marginalisation of trade unions nor the related narrowing of democracy proceeded without resistance. Indeed, the neoliberal counter-revolution was itself a response to movements to extend the principles of democracy and self-government to every level of society in the late 1960s and early 1970s. These movements were created by a generation whose expectations had been heightened by taking for granted the welfare state and its capacities, which were enhanced by the massive expansion of higher education.

As the social-democratic and communist parties of the post-war decades failed to drive forward the desire for a thorough-going democracy, the new generation came to political maturity in the late 1960s with high expectations of social change and began to search for effective means of achieving it. This search involved experiments beyond electoral politics in forms of direct action and self-organisation, often combining self-change with social change and no longer delegating politics to an increasingly distant and unaccountable 'political class' of professional representatives. The innovations in this new do-it-yourself political organising have been seen more in practice than in theory, and hence have often been ephemeral and unconsolidated. However, it is striking how regularly these innovations have resurfaced, with new elaborations, in every generation of activists since the 'class of '68'.

Two understandings of power

The neoliberal counter-revolution across Europe ensured that the option of radical democracy was generally a suppressed, marginalised option, though like a mountain stream it periodically bubbles up in new forms and contexts. As we shall see throughout this chapter, it does not disappear.

One reason why the repercussions of this moment of revolt keep bubbling up is because it changed the political mentality of a generation. In particular, their processes of struggle and experimentation have produced, again more in practice than in theory, insights into power that can act as a compass to guide us in uncertain but creative times.

On the one hand, there is 'power over'. This is the power of government, for example, or the power of the boss or that of the patriarch. It could also be described as *power-as-domination*, involving an asymmetry between those with power and those over whom power is exercised.

On the other hand is 'power to', 'power to do or transform' or *power-as-transformative-capacity* (Bhaskar 2008). This is the power discovered by social movements as they move beyond protest to practical, prefigurative solutions, from the student movement through the radical workers' movement to the feminist movement. Frustrated by the workings of power-as-domination exercised by political parties of the traditional Left, these movements took power into their own hands, discovering through collective action various capacities to bring about change. This included women changing their relations with men and with each other, workers collectively improving their working conditions and extending control over the purpose of their labours, as well as community movements blocking eviction or land speculation and campaigning for alternative land-use policies for the wellbeing of their communities.

The distinction between the two forms of power will be central to my analysis of the 40-year search for appropriate forms of transformative political organisation in Europe; a search stimulated by the failures of the traditional parties of the Left to bring about the changes in which their supporters had believed and for which they had worked. Moreover, it is a search taking place simultaneously with attempts by the ruling, market-dominated order to appropriate the emancipatory aspirations of social movements. This attempted appropriation produced extensive ambivalence in many spheres – from gender and sexuality through to education and health, between personal freedom through market choice and money and individual self-realisation through collaboration and solidarity in producing a good life for all. The movements of the sixties and seventies involved a rebellion whose dynamic was literally ambivalent, having the potential to develop in two different directions. The question of what the conditions are for individual realisation through mutuality as distinct from through money and the capitalist market is a theme that will recur as the ambivalence of neoliberal politics becomes clear.

Historically, mass social-democratic and communist parties have been built around a benevolent version of the understanding of power-as-domination. Their strategies have been based on winning the power to govern and then using the 'levers' of the state apparatus paternalistically to meet what they identify as the needs of the people. The term 'paternalistically' is used here to highlight the social relations involved in the benevolent exercise of power-as-domination: as with the traditional power of the father over the child, the assumption is the inadequate capacity of the people to govern themselves.

Power-as-transformative-capacity

The emergence of power-as-transformative-capacity had its contemporary origins in the rebellions of the late 1960s and early 1970s. A central and common theme of these rebellions was a challenge to all conventions and institutions based on deference to authority, whether it be children's obedience to their elders; students' acceptance of the authority of those acting *in loco parentis*; women accepting their secondary position to the supposedly superior male; workers acquiescing to management prerogative (Beynon 1975); or citizens deferring to the authority of the state. The other side of the movements' refusal of these forms of authority was a pervasive and self-confident assertion of their own collaborative capacity.

Along with this self-confidence in their transformative abilities went inventiveness about forms of organisation that would build that capacity. The distinctive feature of these movements that I want to highlight, in understanding power-as-transformative-capacity, was their tendency to emphasise the valuing and sharing of different kinds of knowledge: practical and experiential as well as theoretical and historical (Wainwright 1994). In their refusal to defer to authority, they broke the unspoken bond between knowledge and authority – the idea that those in power knew best, including what was best for you. The uncertain, experimental process of democratising knowledge, in practice, usually involved an emphasis on decentralised and networked organisational forms, sharing and developing knowledge horizontally and breaking from models that presumed an expert leadership and a more-or-less ignorant membership (Michels [1911] 2007). A rekindling in new forms of an older socialist and labour movement tradition of self-education, cooperation and self-realisation has also been significant (Yeo 2002).

These radically democratic approaches to knowledge laid the organisational and cultural foundations that have underpinned social movements ever since, from the alter-globalisation movement of the late 1990s through to Occupy and the Indignados. The emphasis on sharing knowledge and decentralisation also helped to create the conditions for the web – born as it was of the Californian counter-culture of the late 1960s – and has created receptivity towards, and creativity with, techno-political tools in the evolution of transformative political organisation (Turner 2006).[1]

Can power-as-domination be a resource for power-as-transformative-capacity?

A central question for political organisation in the future is how far, and under what conditions, power-as-domination (essentially having control over state institutions) can be a resource for power-as-transformative-capacity, essentially in the initiatives civil society, including the economy, has taken to refuse reproducing the status quo, thereby beginning a process of transformation independently of political institutions. In other words, although there is a sharp distinction between these two types of power, they are not necessarily counterposed. Power-as-domination can in theory combine with or be a resource for power-as-transformative-capacity. For example, a change in the balance of power in society – often due in part to the widespread exercise of transformative capacity – can lead to progressive control over the state or progressive shifts within governing parties, which can in turn lead to some form of governmental support for a transformative movement. This can generate deep social changes of which governments on their own, however radical their intent, are incapable.

One example is in the impact of the feminist movement throughout society and how that changed the balance of power to such an extent that governments – for example the 1974 Labour government in the UK – felt obliged, under direct political pressure, to introduce legislation against discrimination on grounds of gender. This in turn legitimated and stimulated women in their own pursuit of self-liberation.

More recently, the decision of the European Parliament in 2013 to award the annual European Citizenship prize to the anti-eviction movement in Spain (Plataforma de Afectados por la Hipoteca [PAH]) gave a significant boost to the grassroots movement as it faced attacks from the Spanish state (and thus domination also has different levels that can contradict each other).[2] There are many examples at municipal level of governmental power being used to support the autonomous exercise of transformative power in the economy or society. A contemporary example is the way that Syriza, the party of the radical and social-movement Left in Greece, decided not to retain the 8 million euros it received as a result of its electoral success for its parliamentary or inner-party activities. Instead, as one of their political organisers, Andreas Kazantzis, reports: 'The biggest part of the new funds should go to what we can do in the neighbourhoods. For example, to employ people to spread initiatives like social medical centres.'[3]

The question of how far the institutions of power-as-domination can support power-as-transformative-capacity remains. It cannot be answered in abstract from the political and social balance of power. The issues involved could be very different, for example, in the context of small left parties in opposition or where social movements have made an important impact, compared to the case of left parties which are on the eve of capturing power under unprecedented conditions of crisis. For this reason, the core of this chapter is a reflection on different examples of attempts to combine the two forms of power, some fairly successfully, some not, and ending with two examples from southern Europe, Syriza and Podemos, that have been electorally successful – though with a changing and often problematic relation with the movements , which in Greece, at least, face their own problems. We need to explore critically their assumptions about the control over institutions that power-as-domination can offer to their struggle for social justice.

The changing historical circumstances of the two sources of power and their relationship

As a background to these examples, it helps to identify significant underlying changes since the 1970s regarding both forms of power, which constrain and shape possibilities for the radical egalitarian change that actors in these examples were working for.

Power-as-transformative-capacity: A decisive weakening of nationally organised labour

A distinctive but short-lived feature of the movements of 1968 and the early 1970s was the active collaboration and cultural cross-fertilisation between radical, mainly young intellectuals and grassroots labour activists. It was not only students who listened to Bob Dylan. And it was not only students and middle-class women who aspired to lives beyond the factory production line and the kitchen sink. A politics of liberation crossed traditional social divides; workers' control and self-management were part of a wide radical consciousness. But it was rarely expressed through national labour movement institutions (union or party). On the contrary, the legacy of the Fordist organisational forms that shaped labour movement organising and dominated production – centralised command, a reduction of the scope for distributed initiative and denial of the capacities of the membership[4] – meant that the leadership of both traditional trade union and party organisations were generally suspicious of the rebellions of the sixties, whose subversive political culture threatened to overturn many of the traditional conventions, boundaries and vested interests in established union organisation. National trade union leaderships generally missed the opportunities of renewal and regeneration that these rebellions potentially offered.

On the other hand was the concerted, politically and ideologically driven defeat of the traditional forms of working-class organisation that had underpinned the class-based social-democratic and communist parties of the Left. A long, drawn-out process of defeat, resisted through some epic struggles, it had multiple driving forces. First, by the late 1960s, employers were facing squeezed profit margins as workers' demands for higher wages as a reward for the tedium and exhaustion of work on the assembly line could no longer, in conditions of intensified international competition, be passed on as price rises. Employers turned instead to reducing the cost of labour, making redundancies, outsourcing and casualising labour, undermining collective bargaining and generally weakening workers' organisations. Employers were looking, too, for a political environment more conducive to their interests than the regulated regimes of post-war social democracy. They found it in the new conservatism that, on both sides of the Atlantic, was translating free-market fundamentalism into a practical programme for dismantling the social-democratic state and its class compromises in the workplace. The political champions of this new creed made the defeat of labour its battle cry and the destruction of the 'nanny state' its regularly repeated mantra.

The end result, internalised and reproduced by 'new social democracy' – whether 'New Labour' in the UK or the Democratic Party in Italy – was a political culture of almost cold war taboos on trade union militancy, state intervention and left-wing politics. The other side of this development was that this new kind of capitalism, unleashed from the macro-economic policy framework and social regulations prescribed by John Maynard Keynes and William Beveridge and reinforced by the institutional innovations brought on by war, involved its own distinctive combination of power-as-domination and power-as-transformative-capacity. To understand this we need to explore further the ambivalence of the rebellions of 1968. Neoliberal political leaders such as Margaret Thatcher and Tony Blair used power-as-domination to dismantle state-based systems of resource allocation, for example in the UK's National Health System, and to give openings to market actors to exercise their own transformative capacities in pursuit of profit. No doubt these entrepreneurs included those whose sensibilities and 'go-getting' entrepreneurial capacities were influenced by the spirit of the sixties but separated from, and uninhibited by, the social critique of that rebellion (Boltanski and Chiapello 2006). In this way we can see the irony of the ambivalence noted earlier: just as the agents of social critique and egalitarian change who gained strength from the revolts of the sixties were facing defeat, the innovative entrepreneurial culture of this period was being appropriated and supported as a force for capitalist renewal.

Power-as-domination: Globalisation, corporate domination, financial and institutional crisis

At the same time as the emergence of significant, economically rooted forms of power-as-transformative-capacity was facing both defeat and appropriation, power-as-domination was being reconfigured, becoming more mobile and flexible and less tied to the nation state and the political institutions of suppos-edly 'representative' democracy. With the beginnings of financial deregulation in the 1970s[5] and the growth of the transnational corporation, the power of national governments to dominate the state and the economy was diminishing, their leverage eroded by corporate capture, the force of deregulated financial flows and the diktats of US-dominated international economic bodies, notably the International Monetary Fund (IMF) and the World Trade Organisation (WTO), as well as the intergovernmental treaties of the European Union. Moreover, by the early seventies, especially with the quadrupling of the oil price in 1973, the world economy entered the first of what developed into a series of severe recessions over the last quarter of the twentieth century. This tendency towards recession combined with a faltering of productivity, an intensification of international competition and the increasing mobility of finance to follow maximum profits. This combination of different levels of economic, industrial and social crisis led to the breakdown of the post-war compromise between labour and capital which had underpinned the welfare state and the rationale of social-democratic parties, and which reinforced, after World War II, the essen-tially national, corporatist institutions of most of the nation states of Europe.

Organisational form according to purpose

A point to bear in mind in drawing lessons from the following narrative is that forms of political organisation should be closely related to collective purpose: we are doomed to impotence if we fetishise a particular form, whether horizontal or hierarchical, regardless of purpose and the level of society and social institutions at which the activity is taking place. The framework of two forms of power that I have suggested helps us to clarify distinct purposes and their associated organisational logics, as long as in applying it we recognise the ambivalences discussed above. For example, the organisational forms appropriate to gain sufficient leverage over power-as-domination to introduce legislation that prohibits evictions – which requires a presence within, and an ability to engage with legislative and electoral institutions – is likely to be very different from the organisational forms necessary, for example, to sustain viable squats in empty buildings. It is important therefore to clarify the strategic issues that shape our purposes so that this can guide our choice of the appropriate forms of organisation and identify what forms of power are most effectively mobilised for what purpose.

TWO HISTORICAL EXPERIENCES OF MOVEMENTS ENGAGING WITH GOVERNMENT

In this section I will develop tools to understand contemporary possibilities and constraints of engaging with political institutions, by analysing critically two earlier phases when transformative movements engaged critically with dominant political institutions. These were periods – the mid-1970s and the 1990s – when power-as-transformative-capacity was developing, experimentally and uncertainly. However, at the same time there remained a legacy of faith in the efficacy of representative democracy, the knowledge of state experts, the power of the nation state and the possibility of closed political systems.

First, I analyse an experience in the UK in the 1970s, of the radical grassroots workers' movement acting in close collaboration with the Left of the Labour Party. Second, I explore experiences of new parties of the Left that emerged after a split either from a social-democratic party in the 1990s, such as the Socialist Left Party (SV) in Norway, or from a communist party, as with Rifondazione Comunista (PRC) in Italy, but were working explicitly as voices of the social movements. I consider both their potential and their tendency to fail, and what can be learnt from this about the need for transformative organisations to tread warily on the treacherous terrain of parliamentary politics.

In and against the state in the UK

First, then, is the 1970s experience of the militant workers' movement engaging with the UK state, mainly through Tony Benn, then minister for industry in a Labour government. The very fact that someone radicalised by a workers' occupation – the Upper Clyde Shipbuilders – could be in such an institutional role was a product of the ambiguous position of the Labour Party as simultaneously a block to, and a means of, political expression for workers' demands.

The British Labour Party: The ambiguities of trade union/party links

The Labour Party's origins in trade union campaigns for political representation led to a dense network of institutional links between workers' organisations at every level of party and union, yet the party's founding leadership gave the parliamentary party an autonomy and overriding power that tended to blunt the possibility of these institutional links becoming a channel for militancy. Moreover, these links were based on deeply rooted conventions dividing politics (understood as strictly the responsibility of the party) and industrial relations as limited to collective bargaining over wages and conditions (the responsibility of the trade unions). These institutional links between party and unions in normal times, in conditions of boom, served to depoliticise trade union militancy. However, in times of crisis they engendered expectations and a consciousness of the political character of the factory struggle that under circumstances of continued trade union strength posed a challenge to the parliamentary custodians of the status quo. The workplace trade union militancy in the manufacturing industry in the 1960s and 1970s produced what was for ruling elites an alarming conjuncture of events with highly confident social and labour organisations putting radically transformative, and hence political, projects into practice and finding support and legitimacy, albeit from a minority, within the political system.

The 1970s was the decade which the Trilateral Commission condemned as producing 'an excess of democracy'. These were circumstances in which, a bit like today, the demand for 'real democracy' could not be easily contained by a highly secretive oligarchic political system. At that point the contradictory structures of the Labour Party sometimes bent under the pressures of a strong political militancy.

Workers enter Whitehall – shock!

The result was that, much to the alarm of UK ruling elites, the occasional radicalised politician spurned the unspoken compromises with the Whitehall/Westminster/City establishment that allowed Labour to govern, and made alliances with activists untamed by the bureaucracies and career ladders of trade union/Labour Party institutions. This was exactly the case with Tony Benn as minister for industry. During the late sixties and early seventies, the worker occupations of factories doomed by corporate management to closure had convinced him that the future of crisis-ridden but complacent British industry lay with workers like those who had organised a 'work in' to keep the Upper Clyde Shipbuilders open in 1969. He consequently insisted on meetings with shop-floor leaders, and not simply national union officials, and encouraged these shop-floor activists to develop their own plans for the future of their companies, which he promised to support using government powers of conditional funding, purchasing and so on (Panitch and Leys 2001).

The most notable example is the 'alternative corporate plan for socially useful production' drawn up by the multi-plant, multi-union joint shop stewards' committee of Lucas Aerospace. A tape recording of the shop stewards' meeting, discussing what the shop stewards' 'combine committee' should do in response to a meeting with Tony Benn, provides evidence of enhanced self-confidence from the knowledge that they had support from a government minister. Out of this sense of new possibilities, an important radical initiative was born: the workers' own plan for their company, based on matching their capacities with unmet social needs. This was a challenge to the logic of private accumulation and an insistence on the logic of use value. The initiative consequently inspired many other examples and helped to strengthen a radical and increasingly political movement of workplace activists.

This movement was defeated, however, not just industrially but also within government (under pressure from corporate business and the financial interests of the City of London) and within the Labour Party (by members of parliament fearing that they would lose their seats if Labour appeared too left wing).

Workers, black activists, gays and lesbians and women enter County Hall – shock!

Before neoliberalism gained a firm grip in Britain – in the mid 1980s with the defeat of the Miners' Strike – there is an example of a part of the state offering support for transformative working-class initiatives and self-organisation. It was again a political initiative that arose from the ambiguous potential of the Labour Party as an institutional channel for popular aspirations and demands. This was the experiment of the Greater London Council (GLC), led by Ken Livingstone.

It was a four-year experience of many extra-parliamentary attempts to achieve social justice and liberation, through a combination of self-organised community, social movement and labour organisations. Their initiatives included community-controlled childcare, community monitoring of the police, support for black self-organisation against racism and for labour and technology strategies influenced by the experience of Lucas Aerospace. Again, the project was about opening up local government to poor and marginalised people to whom in the past it was distant and unresponsive. It was not a revolutionary project but it was radically transformative and challenged many private vested interests that in the past would have had cosy, if not corrupt, relationships with municipal officials and politicians (Mackintosh and Wainwright 1987).

The reaction of the political and economic elites was unanimously hostile. Margaret Thatcher's right-hand man Norman Tebbit summed up the political vitriol of the time when he said, 'this is modern socialism and we will kill it'. Kill it they did: in 1986 parliament passed a law abolishing the GLC. Such are the unwritten rules of the British constitution: that a prime minister can destroy a whole level of democratic government in pursuit of a political vendetta. It was an experience not forgotten.

Perhaps, given the international power and position of the City of London as a financial centre, and the UK's historical imperial and industrial position, this corporate capture and fusion of state and business is particularly notable in the UK. But experiences in Sweden, for example, of the hostile response of business to the proposals of Rudolf Meidner for 'Employee Funds' (which would have gradually given workers majority ownership and control of the companies they worked for), confirm that the opposition of private business to even modest attempts to extend principles of democracy to industry was at that time an international phenomenon. Indeed, such attempts at democratising industry seem to have contributed to employers' determination to install political regimes in the subsequent decade that would put labour back in its place.

Lessons to carry forward

What lessons can be found in these experiences for the discussion of social

BEYOND SOCIAL-DEMOCRATIC AND COMMUNIST PARTIES

movements and political institutions today?

When the balance of power is shifted ...

When the balance of power in society is shifted, albeit briefly, away from capital and towards working people and this is somehow reflected (even in a small, mediated way) within political institutions of power, it is possible for parts of the state – its funds, its contracting powers, its legislative, taxation and owner-ship powers – to be used to support and facilitate the transformative initiatives of working people.

It is important to note that the movements behind this shift in the balance of power were not simply movements of protest or civil-society lobbies; they were transformative organisations of civil society working to bring about radical changes to which radical politicians were committed and for which they had an electoral mandate but which they found impossible to implement through relying on the state apparatus and its expertise. Instead, their ability to bring about change depended on highly practical and productive alliances with knowledgeable, powerful forces for change, outside the political system and based within production and the wider society.

The extent of corporate capture

We can learn from these experiences the extent of the corporate capture of poli-tics and the integration of corporate interests and personnel into the political elite, and the way that this elite mobilise their allies in industry and the media to prevent any shift in state alliances from capital to labour taking place.

The intensity of class war

The shift from the class compromise of 1945–1979 to class war which included the explicit goal of killing 'modern socialism', the politically driven defeat of the National Union of Mineworkers, the abandonment of collective bargaining and the dismantling of the legal infrastructure that sustained it was perhaps most explicitly announced in the UK. However, a similar attack on organised labour and the legal framework of rights that underpinned it occurred in most European countries, undoing the gains of the post-war years. An implication is that policies of class compromise, far from being the orthodoxy they had once been, became the object of vilification and contempt by the political and media elites. Even policies that were purely defensive of wage justice and social provision became, from the late 1990s, policies that could not be won without a militant struggle. Periodic financial crises reinforced this vulnerable position of labour and of social provisions as they were increasingly framed, along with immigration, as scapegoats for the crisis.

The internationalisation of the terrain of conflict

The struggles of the 1970s, especially those that looked to governments or municipalities as a source of support, faced the emerging realities of globalisation. Globalisation pushed the balance of forces further against workplace struggles, at several levels. At one level, the increased mobility of capital meant that threats of investment strikes and general financial instability were more effective at blackmailing national governments to block industrial strategies that challenged management prerogative or shareholder interests. At a company level, the increasingly transnational nature of major corporations meant that international manoeuvres such as double-sourcing and threatened factory closures could undermine local bases of militancy.

Shop-floor trade unions responded by becoming increasingly internationally organised, with the creation of organisations that brought together workplace leaders from across Europe and sometimes across the world. Notable examples were in Ford and Dunlop Pirelli. An organisation, the Transnational Information Exchange (TIE), was created with the support of the World Council of Churches. From a base in Amsterdam, the TIE facilitated international conferences of workplace trade union organisations in different industrial sectors and across chains of production. However, at the same time as international linkages were being created, workplace organisations were being destroyed locally, undermining the foundations of the new international infrastructures. Nevertheless, a consciousness of the importance of international strategies was established that later, in the 1990s, came into its own, as the alter-globalisation movement created a new basis for the confidence and capacity to organise globally. This posed again the problem of where in a globalised world the political leverage is to support extra-parliamentary transformative power.

Mechanisms of marginalisation

We can see how the political system works to isolate and marginalise those whose actions as champions of extra-parliamentary change upset the established order. The systems of patronage available to prime ministers, including Labour prime ministers, meant that anyone wanting a political career kept their distance from Tony Benn. Challenges from the Left are defined as 'divisive' by party leaders and the media alike, and this has implications for public perception.

The exception that proves the rule is Ken Livingstone's radical GLC, which was able to reach the public and win support in spite of a hostile press, so much so that a decade after the GLC was abolished, when Tony Blair's New Labour created the post of mayor of London, Ken Livingstone was able to win the election as an independent candidate despite (or maybe in part because of) Blair's hostility.

The importance of autonomy

Finally, these experiences also point to lessons learnt by the movements that participated, sometimes cautiously, sometimes enthusiastically, in these engagements with political institutions. Above all is that of the importance of movements' developing their autonomous political perspectives and organisational bases so that the relationship with political institutions, which was based on winning power-as-domination could, nevertheless, simultaneously strengthen their transformative capacity. This means that they were able to oppose the state and simultaneously work towards new, more radically democratic, political structures through engaging with the state as a necessary part of a process of transition.

This leads us to what is perhaps the most important insight arising from these early experiences: the idea, drawing on a metaphor from the subversive, transformative movements emerging around the new ITC, of *hacking political institutions*, that is, entering political institutions to understand their logic, then redesigning and subverting them from inside for a radical, oppositional social purpose.

Hacking political institutions?

The authors of the influential book *In and Against the State* (1979) worked mainly as professionals for the state, especially the 'welfare state'.[6] The group of authors addressed the contradiction that 'as "clients" we need the resources the state offers but that in satisfying this need we are necessarily held into the state form of relations' (London Edinburgh Weekend Return Group 1979: 6). They emphasise that the state is not just a set of institutions, but a pervasive form of social relations. The social form that they highlight is the way the state 'treats us as individual citizens, families, communities, consumer groups – all categories which obscure class' (1979: 5). They explore the ways in which it is possible, even from within the state, to resist and subvert this fragmentation and individualisation and resist collectively with alternative solutions. In the context of cuts and privatisation, they insisted on 'ways of fighting back oppositionally, rather than simply defending a state we know to be indefensible'.

One might draw on the hacker phenomenon in computing to explore the potential of this improvised and yet rich concept of 'in and against the state'. Just as hackers know from the inside the rules and contradictions of the system they are hacking, it is similarly so with activists who are in and against the state.[7] And just as hackers use this knowledge to break open a software system and redesign it on the basis of hacker ethics of transparency and collaboration, similarly, radicals working 'in and against the state' used their knowledge of the individualised and fragmented daily lives of state workers, and of the contradictory moments of connection with 'clients' of the state, to turn the paternalistic rules of public provision into a terrain of struggle for popular control and an increase in the social wage.

An example of this was when the New Labour government set up a scheme for 'community-led regeneration' of impoverished estates in the 1990s, mainly intended to bypass left-wing local authorities and facilitate a process of bringing business into local service provision. However, some groups of mainly young people in one of these local estates, on the outskirts of Luton, subverted the policy by 'occupying the rhetoric' of community regeneration and organising local residents to create genuinely community-controlled projects and services (Wainwright 2010).

A theme which will recur later is the possibilities and conditions for hacking political institutions themselves; opening them up and redesigning them to favour movements for radical social and economic transformation.

Party realities: Hopes, traps, blocks and illusions

Against this background, the attraction of a political organisation that gives a public voice to the demands of transformative movements is considerable. An organisation could show during election time – the time of maximum public political intensity – that there *is* an alternative to the marketised politics that frames and constrains political debate in the UK. Such an organisation, which could bring together different movements and campaign on the basis of common principles and work collaboratively to develop a common strategy, is, in other words, a political party.

Looking across to the European continent with such an (albeit simplistic) ideal in mind, the possibilities for parties of the radical Left looked hopeful on first impressions. From our offshore island backwater, many pinned hopes on the New Left parties gaining support across Europe. If only, we thought, we could win proportional representation, we could gain the same kind of breakthroughs. The actual experience of these parties, however, indicates that more fundamental problems arise once such parties break through the hallowed walls of the political system.

Across the continent, from the German Greens through to the SV in Norway to the PRC in Italy, parties of the radical Left faced a contradiction which halted their momentum. The problem was that these parties were campaigning for office within a discredited political system that they opposed. Indeed, they won support on the basis of this opposition. Yet at the same time, in order to win the support of groups of voters beyond their committed supporters, they had to appear governmentally credible as well as radically transformative. This contradiction was especially acute when they entered government. One danger was that in the attempt to be credible and under the pressure of both the privileges and the constraints of government office, they ended up becoming *part of* (or behoven to) the existing political elite, losing credibility with the very movements on which they depended.

I will briefly highlight two of these experiences.

The context of parties of the radical Left in the 1990s

Ever since the rebellions of the late 1960s, parties formed from varying combinations of communist, Trotskyist, Maoist and independent green-left traditions have occasionally, usually fleetingly, acted as a magnet for popular disillusion with mainstream politics. But the constituency for an alternative to neoliberalism was by the late 1990s far greater than any electoral support for the parties of the radical Left.

This constituency was reflected in opinion polls indicating majorities against both the Iraq war and privatisation and most of all in the recurring eruption of resistance on the streets to the global institutions through which the US government and its corporate allies sought to destroy the post-World War II settlement.

A new generation was being radicalised but had no voice in a political system where the main parties had converged, on Margaret Thatcher's insistence that 'there is no alternative'. These young people, supported by older extra-parliamentary leftists, took direct action in many different ways. They organised their own political platforms, media and networks of critical research and education. They also organised their own dramatic ways to attract the attention of the mainstream media and communicate their message, their own means of coordination, alliance-building and deliberation on their demands, and increasingly their own culture and way of illustrating their values in everyday life.

By the 1990s, many of Europe's radical Left parties (formed earlier) were still struggling to develop new projects for social, economic and political change. In the process, many of them became increasingly aware of their own limitations, including the debilitating legacy in their institutions of the traditions of the old communist and social-democratic Lefts from which they had broken. They were seeking therefore, quite explicitly, to refound themselves as new kinds of parties, by working with the radical social movements, organisations and networks that had been gathering momentum transnationally since the 1999 'Battle of Seattle', when labour, environmental and democracy movements converged to oppose (successfully) a decision by the WTO to lift all social and environmental regulations on corporate investment.

'Social movements are the engines of transformation,' said Fausto Bertinotti, leader of Italy's PRC and the Mediterranean maestro of this strategy for outflanking conservative political institutions.[8] He also said that the new kind of party allying itself to social movements was 'one actor amongst many', thereby, rhetorically at least, breaking from the traditionally monopolistic view that social-democratic parties had of their role as the leadership of social change.

Even with the benefit of hindsight, it is not clear how these party leaders understood the distinctive role of social movements. There was an ambiguity about how far they were seen as sources of pressure reinforcing the influence of the parties; as outriders for the party or recruitment grounds for new party members; or as autonomous sources of transformative capacity to be supported and listened to by the party.

The Norwegian Left Party: Influential but invisible

Norway, with its uniquely proportional electoral system, could be seen as a laboratory for the radical Left's experiment with a pluralist[9] approach to power, although its context is distinct, with revenues from oil softening the repercussions of the economic crisis and a geographic context where the small size of the country facilitated public access to politicians, mitigating against a political class distanced from the people.

This was the context of the rise in influence of the Norwegian SV. After an uneven rise to prominence, and riding a wave of labour movement anger over the anti-union measures of a Labour government at the turn of the century, the SV became part of a three-way coalition with the Labour Party and the Agrarian Party in 2005. In 2005, the influence of SV, aided considerably by the pressure of social movements, provided an exemplary case in northern Europe of a positive dialectic between left party and radical extra-parliamentary movement. 'The changes we have achieved would have been impossible without the pressure and initiatives of the movements since Seattle,' commented veteran member of the party's leadership, Dag Seierstad, in 2004.[10] On the other hand, the decline of the SV by 2013, both electorally from 35 seats to 7 and in terms of its credibility with social movements, is indicative of the potential problems of this engagement with parliamentary politics, and especially of participation in government, even in relatively favourable conditions.[11]

The SV's twin-track strategy of working with a global justice movement closely linked to trade unions and campaigning electorally for a coalition of leftist parties, including a reluctant Labour Party, finally bore fruit in 2005. When the left coalition won in 2005, SV – a party committed not only to defending public services and public ownership but also to withdrawal from the North Atlantic Treaty Organisation (NATO) – found itself in government, even though its share of the vote had dropped somewhat from the previous 2001 election when the Labour Party was veering more towards the right. SV's presence in Norway's governing coalition, plus the militant pressure of the unions, stopped in its tracks the privatisation and deregulation programme promoted by the outgoing Conservative government. SV can also claim credit for the reallocation of Norway's oil surplus as development aid, the commitment to withdraw Norwegian troops from Iraq and the withdrawal of Norwegian staff from NATO's Afghanistan operations.

SV remained powerful for a short period because its presence provided a channel into government for movements that have their own social, economic and cultural strength. 'Every day of the three-week-long negotiations, there were demonstrations outside that could be heard as we talked,' remembers Seierstad.[12] The demonstrators symbolised why the government had to listen to SV. Paradoxically though, it was the Labour Party that benefited electorally from the considerable achievements of the government, not SV.

One factor here was that SV complied with parliamentary and state procedure to a point of taking its own beliefs and political identity out of the public picture of politics. It accepted the parliamentary convention whereby neither ministers nor members of parliament express dissent with governmental policies. Moreover, the party remained silent too. On several occasions, the government implemented policies, for example on immigration, contrary to SV's programme and the basis of their relations with campaigning movements, yet SV members of parliament said nothing. In effect they let the imperatives of being 'in' the state overwhelm their commitment to act 'against' the state with the autonomous energies of social movements. As Dag Seierstad said: 'If you cannot express your beliefs, then being in government is useless.'[13]

Many party activists shared Seierstad's assessment. The inability of SV politicians to speak out caused confusion and demoralisation. After initial efforts to retain its autonomy, the party and its elected leaders became increasingly subordinate to the parliamentary party as the media tended to pounce on and highlight the slightest sign of division. The consequence was that although party members did not leave in large numbers, they lost their will to campaign for the party, choosing instead to devote their political energies to social movements and initiatives. Seierstad estimates that of its 10 000 members in 2013 only 3 000 to 4 000 are now active. The party's loss of its ability to speak out clearly and champion campaigning movements also reverberated in the movements, reinforcing a pre-existing wariness toward political parties.

Rifondazione Comunista: Too deeply in the state to be against it

Italy's PRC faced a different political situation, defined most notably by massive distrust of the political system. A survey in 2006 reported that 75.3 per cent of Italians have little or no trust in parliament (reference to come). As one left analyst put it: 'Italy is a country in which the level of corruption is very high and where the political parties are seen as bearing the main responsibility for this' (Ginsborg 2006: 14–16).

As its representatives prepared to enter the Italian parliament, PRC made no clear and strong challenge to this corruption of democracy. It went into the state without making very clear that it was also against it, not just against Silvio Berlusconi's particular brand of corruption. Indeed, the general secretary of PRC, Fausto Bertinotti, accepted and seemed to enjoy the 'insider' position of president of the parliamentary chamber. 'We were implicated in a crisis of legitimacy, representation and of politics generally,' declared PRC MP Paolo Cacciari,[14] a leading urban activist, architect and academic in Venice. One factor encouraging this was no doubt the symbolism of what radical journalist

Marco Berlinguer described as 'the transferring of the party and of its leaders into the state institutions'.

Disillusionment was felt not simply by party activists but by voters too, leading to the collapse of electoral support for PRC in the 2008 elections, followed by a split and effective collapse. The initial euphoria at defeating Berlusconi through the Unione coalition which PRC had helped to put together gave way to dismay as the party made compromises that achieved nothing beyond propping up the government and keeping PRC parliamentarians in their privileged places. The record of the Prodi government was dismal: the withdrawal of Italian troops from Iraq, for example, was not accompanied by an abandonment of the War on Terror or a withdrawal of Italian soldiers from Afghanistan. The government almost fell on this issue in a parliamentary vote, after a huge demonstration against the building of a US military base in Vicenza, near Venice. Radical members of parliament were forced to appeal to the fear of letting Berlusconi get back in to justify their support for the government. Nevertheless, they were ostracised from demonstrations. There were similar problems when it came to taking on the church regarding civil partnerships, low wages and the high cost of living, over which no action was taken.

Nationally, intentions to be 'in and against' the state and make a reality of Bertinotti's claim that the social movements were the engine of social change were effectively overwhelmed by the iron logic and soft embrace of parliamentary politics. This was exacerbated by the narrowness of Unione's majority.

Locally, however, the dynamics were more complex. In many regions, cities and small towns, PRC members were highly creative in building and basing themselves in transformative social movements. In this way, they worked in new ways to shift the balance of power in local politics and achieve changes impossible through either movements or political parties alone. There are many examples of this.[15] Activists involved in continuing well-rooted local experiments in politically supported transformative initiatives will keep experimenting, turning to or helping create whatever political instrument is most fit for the purpose. The failure of PRC was a defeat, but one from which to learn.

Moreover, one should not underestimate the creativity and strength of the Italian Left, constantly reappearing in new and effective forms in what is fundamentally a conservative society.[16] The successful campaign of the National Water Forum in 2009, one year after the Left's electoral debacle, is evidence of this. They campaigned for a million signatures for a referendum on keeping water public, gaining 1.4 million. They spread the arguments for water as a commons so effectively through alliances with local communities, use of social media and various cultural initiatives as well as through alliances with trade unions and traditional political campaigning that there was a turnout of over fifty per cent, gaining a ninety-four per cent *si* to keeping the water public. Thus, hardly a year after the demoralising collapse of the Unione coalition, a powerful campaign defeated Berlusconi's attempt to force municipalities to privatise water. There is no doubt that the erstwhile activists of PRC were on the streets ensuring this victory.

Emerging themes and questions

In the chapter's concluding section, I argue that a challenge now facing any left political organisation (whether it is a party, a movement or a platform) is how to occupy the narrowing open space that remains within the political institutions, through a strategy which changes the balance of forces away from the political caste in favour of transformative popular initiatives without being crushed by the gravitational pull of the state apparatus. Vital to this is for transformative organisations to remain autonomous in both their organisation and their principles as they engage with these political spaces left open by the dominating institutions – including unresolved contradictions that de facto create space for dissent, if cleverly deployed.

Any discussion of the future of transformative politics in the twenty-first century needs to take account of both the destruction of organised and permanent labour and the fact that the precarious and part-time workers struggling to survive in 'flexible' labour markets, are often creating new, temporary but often highly creative organisational forms, which the traditional labour organisations have been slow to recognise, let alone support. Thus, while the left leaders of 1970s social democracy could take militant workplace organisation for granted, the new political forms of the twenty-first century have no such sustained, or homogeneous, organised base. Therefore a shared means of inter-communication – horizontal connection that does not go through a single centre – is increasingly replacing the primacy of centralised organisation, and there are often dense networks of action and solidarity-oriented organisations amongst precarious workers and their communities (Milkman 2004).

Moreover in these circumstances, left populism – the people versus the elites – has tended to become the basis for building a political movement of the Left. Often this involves a broadening of the concept of class – to those who depend on their creativity for the means of livelihood – and a reaching out to struggles and movements challenging oppressive power beyond the traditional workplace, rather than a rejection of class. The question for the future is how these anti-elite movements can be both populist, in appealing directly to the people (e.g. through a charismatic leader), and democratic, in building forms of popular self-government that harness the transforming capacity of each for the benefit of all.

SYRIZA AND PODEMOS: THE POTENTIAL AND LIMITS OF LEFT POPULISM?

Given the chance, different generations create their own politics influenced by their cultural and technological environments. But often an older generation holds on to a great deal of political space and control. By contrast, Synaspismos – the radical Euro-communist coalition that widened and opened up to become Syriza in Greece – did break their habits of control, which proved vital to the emergence of Syriza as a distinctive kind of political organisation. The choice of Alexis Tsipras, then a 32-year-old engineer, to stand as the party's candidate for mayor in Athens in the 2006 municipal elections, is a good example of this new spirit. The success of this initiative (Tsipras won an unprecedented 10.5 per cent of the popular vote) strengthened and stabilised the party's new strategy. Moreover, the president of Synaspismos gave up his position and urged party members to support Tsipras as his replacement. This kind of handing over to a new generation was apparent throughout the party's leading bodies.

One consequence for Syriza was that through its new leaders, it became influential in the student movement, which in Greece has long been highly political and constantly mobilised and has significant influence with the wider Greek public. This proved decisive in Syriza's early years when, between 2006 and 2007, students mobilised against a constitutional amendment that would allow the private sector to establish universities. Syriza was pivotal in changing public opinion to such an extent that the social-democratic Panhellenic Socialist Movement (PASOK) was forced to change its position on the issue. Increasingly, it became evident that Syriza was not just another political organisation treating the movements as instruments for its own party-political electoral purposes but a full participant in the movements and a source of political support. This was a product less of a conscious strategy and more of the instincts and political aspirations of the new generation of activists (Tsakalotos 2013).

The young activists and intellectuals who helped to found Syriza were from the first generation that rejected capitalism after the fall of the Soviet Union, and who came to the Left independently of any 'actually existing' alternative. Their involvement in movements and struggles was itself part of a process of developing an alternative rather than promoting one that had already been worked out.

They knew that governing from above would not work, but they did not know what would. 'We try to find another way,' says Andreas Karitzis, a young colleague of Tsipras in the leadership of Synaspismos and then Syriza. 'I believe you need state political power but what is also decisive is what is you are doing in the movements/society before seizing power. Eighty per cent of social change cannot come through government.'[17]

When, nine years and many movements later, the growing forces of change converged on Syntagma Square, Syriza members were there too. They helped to build the movement, not to recruit to the party, to push a line or take control. They shared principles – for example, not allowing any anti-immigrant slogans – and applied these to find practical solutions through the general discussions. On the first day, for instance, many people came to the demonstration with Greek flags and did not allow party flags. After a few days and much argument the idea emerged of having different flags of other nations, including from the Arab Spring. 'It changed the image of the action,' says Yanis Almpanis, a Syriza member active in the Network of Social and Political Rights, 'This is how to build a radical and political movement.'[18]

It was this principled immersion in the movements, including the uprising in 2008 following the police killing of Alexandros Grigoropoulos, which led many people to decide that Syriza was the instrument they could trust to help them rid Greece of the European Union (EU)/IMF memorandum imposing austerity and privatisation. 'Syriza was always with us,' said Tonia Katerini from the Open City coalition.[19] It was a sentiment repeated again and again.

When in January 2012, Tsipras declared that Syriza was prepared to form a government to stop the memorandum and break the old ruling order, he linked anger with hope. The parliament building stands some distance back from Syntagma Square. Syriza was committing itself to open up a two-way channel of power and energy from the squares and society to parliament and back. But how is this to be done effectively, rather than the road to parliament being a dead end or hidden trap from which few return? This is the key question running through this chapter.

Syriza addressed this question first internally, by strengthening the democratic power of the elected Syriza politician responsible for monitoring and challenging a department of state. Instead of having a single 'shadow minister,' Syriza created an open committee of members of parliament, experts, civil servants and civic organisations whose purpose is to expose to public view the activities of the government minister and propose alternative policies. 'Through Syriza members who are frontline civil servants – and Syriza won over 50 per cent of the vote of these workers – we are mapping the obstacles, knowing who to rely on, how to release the ideas of staff with a commitment to the public good,' said Aristedes Baltaz, coordinator of Syriza's open parliamentary committees.[20] These committees are also intended, through their openness and links with social movements, to counter the tendency of parliamentary procedures to protect the political class rather than open it to public scrutiny.

It is an ambitious strategy for democratising a state that is institutionally deeply corrupt. It is also a direct challenge to the Troika's claim to be modernising the Greek state through privatisation. For each ministry, Syriza committees are preparing to sweep away corruption and open the ministry's work to the stifled capacities of front-line civil servants, encouraging the latent honesty that Baltaz is convinced generally exists amongst public-service professionals.

Alongside these various preparations for government, inside parliament and outside, activists were alert to the dangers of losing their social roots, and becoming 'another PASOK'. In the formation of the new party, a shared priority is to create, as new member of parliament Theano Fotiou put it, 'a structure for the people to always be connected to the party, even if they are not members of the party, to be criticising the party, bringing new experience to the party'.[21]

One factor pulling radical parliamentary representatives in Norway, Italy and Germany away from social struggles has been the resources bestowed on them by the state while the party outside parliament, and often the movement, loses key cadres to the parliamentary routine. I discussed earlier how Syriza will distribute the 8 million euros it will receive as a result of its electoral success, to support and help spread the neighbourhood-based solidarity networks providing medical help, food and so on to those whose lives are being devastated by the government and Troika's austerity measures. Syriza, forged in the heat of the most extreme manifestation of neoliberal austerity, has begun to show that movement-style organising combined with a bold intervention in the political system can win overwhelming popular support.

On 26 January 2015 Syriza won sufficient popular support to form a government, though without an overall majority. They formed an alliance with the right-wing nationalist Independent Greeks, on the basis of a common rejection of the austerity policies of the Troika and its brutally harsh memorandum. Syriza's claims to govern differently, refuse modernisation via the private market and insist on democratisation are now being put to the test. But it is a test in circumstances where the government has a pistol aimed at its head, or at least the politically concerted threat of bankruptcy from the EU finance ministers, the European Central Bank and the IMF.

Democratising the Greek state, eliminating the corruption and clientelism that has been endemic to its state apparatus, is central to Syriza's programme and way of governing. It is not merely an ethical 'add on' to economic and social policies, but integral to their interpretation of democracy. To implement this approach, Syriza has set up a Ministry for Public Service Reform and has appointed strong and radical women to leading positions in the Centre for Public Administration and Local Government, an important public-sector body responsible for training civil servants and local government officials. The Ministry's brief is to prepare legislation to introduce transparent and democratic procedures for the selection of public servants and end corruption, nepotism and clientelism. The Centre's brief is to reinforce this with a process of cultural change in the mentality and training of public servants. Regarding the importance of transformative capacity as a source of power, it is notable that Syriza has not stopped at changes made through the levers of government. It has sought transformative allies in society.

Its first ally has been the networks of the solidarity economy which emerged to meet urgent daily needs created by the Troika's destruction of basic public service. It has created a department in the Ministry of Labour with specific responsibility for working with and providing support for the solidarity economy. But this department also has the brief to facilitate a learning process whereby innovations in the ways that services are delivered – for example in the social health clinics – become a catalyst and possibly a model for transforming the organisation of the state's same services.

Syriza's second potential ally is workers in the public sector and the communities which they serve. Still only a potential, it is limited by the conservatism and clientelist routines of most trade unions. But the strength of resistance to the Troika's attempt to privatise water awoke a consciousness, especially in the region of Thessaloniki, amongst water workers and their trade union organisers of the value of their work in providing a public utility and a common good. They, in turn, alerted and activated the community who depended on this service, to defend it against private take-over (Wainwright 2014). In the process, the flaws of the existing public management became apparent and the successful 'save our water' campaign turned into a movement to improve the quality of water delivery. Both processes of using governmental power to support popular transformative capacity, in public service workers and the solidarity economy are severely constrained by what is, effectively, financial starvation imposed by the Troika.

Podemos and the challenge of left populism

The rise of Podemos in Spain has many parallels with Syriza, though the two organisations have different strategies and organisational forms. They are already collaborating with each other in the European Parliament and their activists are organising together in transcontinental campaigning networks, for example around housing, health and the environment.

Their differences stimulate useful questions for our exploration of political organisation in this era of global politico-corporate elites. Since the search for a single model of radical political organisation is futile, and I certainly have no model in my back pocket, I will end with these questions. But first I introduce Podemos (which translates as 'We Can') to readers unfamiliar with the new bright star that appeared suddenly on Europe's dark sky at the European elections. Podemos, only six months since it was founded, lit up the dull political landscape of the normally low-turnout, low-interest elections for the European Parliament by winning 1.5 million votes, or eight per cent of the overall vote count, and gained five seats. Since then its support has grown further, drawing level with the main parties in opinion polls.

Podemos' spokespeople spurn the language of Left and Right. Indeed, seventeen per cent of its voters previously voted for the conservative Partido Popular. Their slogans echo the anti-elite language of Occupy, 'We are the 99 per cent', and of the anti-austerity movement in Europe: 'The debt is illegitimate.' Anti-elitism drives their strategy. 'All that's left in Europe is a political elite that kneels before the financial powers … some Europeans don't want to be colonies of the Troika,' said Pablo Iglesias, the politics professor and TV star who initiated Podemos and is its current figurehead.[22] Against the elites and the establishment parties, the sworn mission of Podemos is to restore politics to the people.

'We propose a grassroots politics – that is, to do away with the establishment parties and, from there, put in motion a method,' said Iglesias.[23]

Podemos is a method for both change and popular empowerment. Eduardo Maura, another Podemos spokesperson, explained: 'Podemos is not a vanguard of the people: it's the people organising itself, it's the people doing politics, not delegating, not having to choose between one option and the same.'[24] This raises wider questions about the character of such a party.

Combining defensive action with transformative capacity in conditions of economic and political crisis

I raise these questions in a context where the institutions of formal political democracy have been almost entirely corrupted or hollowed out through a process of corporate capture, facilitated by privatisation and deregulation. All that remains in Europe of the democratic gains that followed the defeat of fascism is the formality of the vote: now a vote between elites trying to manage the global corporate market. This process, however, has not been socially neutral. People's lives have been destroyed through the denial of the right to a home and the destruction of the right to employment. Millions are desperate and engaged in a struggle for survival. In social and economic terms, we are back to the problem that faced the Chartists: social misery compounded by political powerlessness. Where they faced the power of aristocratic autocracy, we face the tightening hold of market authoritarianism.

In these circumstances there is a growing popular pressure not only to resist austerity but, positively, to secure conditions of basic security: of a home, a basic income, a pension, preferably a job and fundamental rights. Such basic securities are conditions for developing and asserting power-as-transforma-tive-capacity. Yet, because they involve questions of redistribution and other society-wide, institutional changes, they usually can only be achieved through the exercise of power-as-domination. Today this involves occupying the dimin-ishing spaces of formal democracy, to force them – possibly breaking them in the process – to widen through militant assertions of popular power against all political elites and the institutions that protect them. The memory and asso-ciated expectations of securing formal democracy are still fresh, especially in southern Europe. The rapid rise of Podemos in Spain and the success of Syriza are evidence of this desire to use what formal spaces still exist not as an end in itself, of 'getting into power', but as a resource for deeper, transformative sources of power. This chapter will end by exploring tentatively the possible dynamics of these radical experiments in power-as-transformative-capacity, testing how far the institutions of government using power-as-domination can be remade to provide resources for democracy against the tightening grip of market authoritarianism.

Left populism and its importance now

In an overview of debates on and analyses of populism, Margaret Canovan (1999) suggested that 'Populism in modern democracies is best seen as an appeal to "the people" against both the established structure of power and the dominant ideas and values of society'. It can be based on working-class solidarity and self-organisation. Laclau (2005) argued that such a base in democratic working-class organisations is a condition of ensuring that populism is not hijacked by charismatic but self-seeking individuals and parties. Clearly, there is a considerable variety of populist articulations: populist movements of the Right fuelled by xenophobia or nationalism, as well as egalitarian democratic ones that react to increasingly despotic and oligarchic forms of government with a strong force for democratisation and an inclusive understanding of 'the people'.

Populism becomes relevant in certain conditions. It seems we are in one of those moments now. This can be understood most clearly through a comparison with Chartism, the nineteenth-century English movement of working people for democracy and economic emancipation.

The Chartist tradition

The appeal of populism to 'the people' depends on identifying a 'them': a common enemy of the people. This in turn creates the basis of a discourse that is *popular*, appealing to the mass of people, rather than *sectional*, appealing only to particular groups and interests among the people. Chartist discourse did just this: it identified society's ills as being the product of the abuse of power by parasitic and speculative groups who controlled political power. Chartist discourse divided society into two camps, producers versus 'idlers': the victims of corruption, on one hand, and monopoly power and its beneficiaries, on the other (Stedman Jones 2004).

This brought together not just workers but the many groups affected by enclosures, arbitrary landowner power and an authoritarian state. This created a basis of what Ernesto Laclau, in his classic analysis of populism (Laclau 2005), describes as a logic of *equivalential* demands rather than *differential* ones, that is, demands through which different groups could identify a common cause. In the case of the Chartists this was the universal franchise, recallable members of parliament and annual parliaments. The role of the state in maintaining and participating in the great corruption involved excluding the aspiring middle class as well as working-class people from political power. Economic exploitation and exclusion were seen by all social groups beyond the landed aristocracy and its wealthy industrial cousins as being protected and reproduced through corrupt, closed forms of political power and the laws imposed by this corrupt elite. Rallying to confront this common problem provided the basis of a truly mass movement. The Charter had over 1.3 million signatures when Chartist leaders presented it to parliament. As Dorothy Thompson put it: 'thousands of working people considered that their problems could be solved by a change in the political organisation of the country' (Thompson 1984).

There are many explanations for the disintegration of this massive popular force. But there is one overriding explanation: it is the break-up of the unifying 'enemy' and with it the demise of the conditions that created a common problem and favoured the equivalence of the demands of diverse social groups.

In the 1830s, the confrontational, authoritarian state policy of the period was discontinued and instead more humane legislation was introduced on housing, health and education, thereby responding to some of the needs of the destitute and the working poor. Moreover, the state disengaged from the workings of market forces, placating the concerns of the middle and emerging capitalist class. These changes in the character of political power meant that the interests of the working and the middle or emerging capitalist class began to diverge. The equivalential bonds drawing together the demands of the poor and the demands of those with money but previously deprived of political access were broken. Demands became differential, not automatically convergent. Especially important here was the growing separation of the economy from the state. This withdrawal of the state became a foundation stone of 'liberal democracy', legitimating capitalism with the appearance of political equality, and hiding economic power relationships by which some people have sources of power beyond the vote. The conditions for Chartism as a populist movement, a movement uniting 'the people', collapsed.

I argue that this sheds light on the conditions for a populism of the Left today. My suggestion is that today we are seeing a reversal of the conditions for the disintegration of Chartism: a new concentration of power – this time driven by the logic and power of the global corporate market, rather than of feudal aristocracies – and a return of state intervention in the economy, but this time in the financial rather than industrial markets. A shared political problem is producing a convergence of social protests not simply to found new parties, but to transform political space and its relation to social and economic life.

To apply these thoughts to our analysis of Podemos and Syriza, the two parties born out of the resistance to austerity: Syriza recognised the trend towards an increasing concentration of power, conjoined and reinforced in Greece by PASOK and New Democracy, the two governmental parties of the old regime. It understood that under conditions of impoverishment and the final closure of democracy through the Troika's imposition of the austerity memorandum, people were breaking from old party loyalties in anger and frustration and becoming more fluid in their loyalties. Moreover, the increasingly fragmented labour markets, due to the spread of subcontracting, and the impact of new technology on traditional mass production processes, simultaneously weakened trade union organisation, which was, in addition, closely allied to and dependent on the clientelism of the two main political parties. These conditions of concentration of political power and fragmentation of popular organisation led Syriza's young leadership with their sensitive political antennae toward a populist discourse. Syriza understood that if it was to represent the majority and win their support, it had to move its discourse from talk of 'movements' and 'youth' to 'the people'. This is exactly what it did, as is evident in Tsipras' speeches and in *Avgi*, the only daily newspaper supporting Syriza.[25]

From its origins, Podemos defined its project, as we've seen, as overcoming the separation of the people from politics. It 'systematised the limits of democracy within the bourgeois state' (Zelik 2015). It identified the enemy as the political elite that ran the Spanish state, in close collaboration with the banks and major corporations: 'La Casta', as Podemos labelled them. The new party does not deny its populism but seeks to reframe populism. One of its spokespeople, Eduardo Maura, put it like this: 'Right-wing populism appeals to people's prejudices, we appeal to people's intelligence.' He added,

> 'We appeal to a tired, hard-working, mature, capable people: to the same people that were able to make Spain a democratic open society, to the very same people that have witnessed the dramatic decline of the institutions of the Regime of 78 [the democratic institutions built after the death of Franco]. Democracy is always an open process: it has to be like that. 78 had its moment. Now it's time for change.'[26]

Podemos' populist project has recent foundations in popular support for the Indignados. Surveys in 2011 showed that eighty-five per cent of the population supported the protests that set up camp in the main square of Madrid. Podemos' notion of opening politics to the people, breaking through the self-protective barriers of 'La Casta', was inspired by the experience of these occupations; both their protests against the political system and the direct forms of democracy in the running of the mini-cities that took over the squares of Madrid and Barcelona. Moreover, as a German analyst put it: 'That Podemos is more than a fleeting protest party like the Pirates in Germany has mainly to do with the 15-M movement and the Mareas ("waves" of specific protests and actions in different spheres of society) that followed it.'[27] These movements provided the social roots and radical consciousness that propelled Podemos into prominence. Moreover, inspired by these movements in Spain as well as popular political organisations in Latin America, Podemos is, in its practice, interpreting the idea of popular democracy literally by opening its organisation directly to the participation of the public. The idea is that it is on the basis of what the people decide, through an impressive process of online participation, that they intervene in the political institutions.

The leadership of Podemos opened their first congress, which would decide on their programme, norms and identity, to everyone willing to participate, whether or not they were a member, with around 150 000 people. Similarly, Podemos' local circles are open to anyone. Maura explained: 'We don't think that this should be a process only for people already engaged in politics. We think that this kind of process is a good way of drawing people in and a good way of making people feel that politics is not what they think politics is … Some of them became members, others didn't, but they are willing to participate and we are happy they want to do it.' Their methodology here reflects the influence of hacker thinking, referred to earlier. Maura explained: 'We operated from the very beginning in what we call the logic of proliferation – the hacker logic. You have to be everywhere, you want to be everywhere.'[28]

Thus, the populism of Podemos is not simply discourse but is integral to the way they are building their organisation and their direct forms of democracy. Their populism involves treating the people seriously, in the organisation of the party at least, as knowledgeable, social individuals, active citizens with whom power should be shared. Its vision, evident in the open participatory way that the party has been organised – including limits on Pablo Iglesias' role as leader and the importance of a collaborative leadership with others – is of redefining political representation as a means of opening politics to the direct presence of the public.

A question arises, however, about their perspective on power-as-transformative-capacity from their conscious separation of the role of the party from that of social movements. Podemos recognises the importance of social movements in changing popular consciousness towards seeing supposedly individual problems, such as not being able to pay the rent, as common ones that demand collective action. The social power of the movements prepared the ground for the rapid rise of Podemos whose leadership stresses the autonomy and distinct functions of party and social movements: 'Movements should be autonomous and self-regulating. Parties should appeal to other people,' remarked Mauro when asked about how he understood the relation between Podemos and social movements.[29] This stress on autonomy makes sense and is another lesson to be learnt from the experiences of the 1980s and 1990s in Norway and Italy when the leadership of radical political parties expected social movements to give the party the support it needed on the terms that it laid down. But the open question remains: does a party have any role in at least supporting, facilitating or being a platform for the emerging, transformative power located in social struggles and sometimes gaining their sustainability through becoming a social movement, or is its function to focus on convincing voters to elect it to office? In practice, how far are these different roles in conflict?

It is too early to come to substantial conclusions but I would suggest several lessons can be learnt and also several questions posed to guide our understanding of and engagement with Podemos and Syriza (whatever their ambivalences) as well as the Scottish Radical Independence Campaign.

The first is that populism, normally a term of abuse or contempt for people organised as a collective force, can and should be claimed positively and subverted. Just as the gay and lesbian movement claimed the pejorative 'queer' and proclaimed a queer politics as a refusal of binary sexuality, so we should turn populism (and expressions of contempt for popular mobilisation) against the political caste and extol people's active participation, insisting that populism is a logical implication of democracy; a belief in people's capacities for self-government, valuing people's intelligence rather than pandering to prejudice.

But where does this lead? Through what kinds of organisation and relationships can this capacity be realised and what is the role in this of a political party, and what kind of political party? Here the experiences and prospects of Syriza and Podemos are different. This is partly because of the differing forms that 'La Casta' takes in each country and the differing strategies by which the European 'Casta' imposes its austerity measures. This is also partly because of the differing nature of the movements that preceded and accompanied the parties' formation.

On the one hand, though protests similar to the 15-M movement in Spain converged on Syntagma Square in Athens and the White Tower Square in Thessaloniki, they did not have deep roots in local neighbourhoods or the capacity to produce movements of sustained action in different spheres, like the movement against evictions, PAH, or the many practical neighbourhood assemblies that have grown since 2011 across Spain. Syriza's involvement with the protest movements since 2009, and its position as a clean critic of the discredited regimes of PASOK and New Democracy and of their collaboration with the hated Troika, meant that when Tsipras declared that Syriza was willing to form a government, it was to Syriza that the Greek people, at the end of their tolerance of austerity, turned. Syriza won office on a strong wave of indignation. High hopes were invested in the new champions of the people against the elites. However, beyond the beleaguered networks of the solidarity economy, focused as they were on the struggle to survive, they had few allies actively engaged in social and state transformation, besides occasional groups like the water workers in Thessaloniki. Moreover, the party itself, although ending its programme with a resounding exhortation to mobilise, is currently so preoccupied with government that is has shown itself almost incapable of any deep social mobilisation in the neighbourhoods and workplaces where it matters.[30] In Gramsci's terms, it has been a scenario of winning the war of position without first conquering the foothills; without a war of manoeuvre. Or in this chapter's terms, it has been a case of gaining power-as-domination, without the foundations of deep or extensive transformative capacity. This is now a major challenge but in a context which is exceedingly tight for any expansion or transformation of the public realm. Stimulating transformative change from within government, while lacking appropriate forms of agency to do so, with a noose around its neck, and drip-fed rather than having direct control over public resources, could be an impossible task.

Podemos, by contrast, could benefit from movements whose deep roots produced a continuing momentum following the occupations of the squares in 2011. The millions in the squares created 'waves' (*mareas*), deepening the struggles within different parts of society (health, education, housing, culture and so on), taking direct action such as blockades against evictions, occupations in defence of hospitals, theatres, libraries and other public spaces or using social media to expose tax evaders and bring them to court.

Although these movements have mainly been ones of protest rather than creating alternatives, their experiences are pertinent to the concept running through this chapter of power-as-transformative-capacity. Transformative capacity begins with active, self-confident refusal, refusal to reproduce relations of oppression and subordination that depend on complicity for their sustainability. And successful refusal, as in much of the activity of the Spanish *mareas*, activates actors across the chains of social relations which keep that complicity in place. These acts and chain reactions of refusal build a sense of capacity and power that an alternative could exist, and whether or not it does depends in part on those who are engaged in the acts of refusal. People are searching for the political support, legislation and other exercises of governmental power that could enable them to realise the transformation for which they struggle.

This logic of transformative capacity indicates the importance of a relationship of support and alliance with social movements on the part of a party committed to radical change. 'Regulation' or some other erosion of autonomy is not the only possible relation between a party and social movements. Alliances can and need to respect the autonomy of social movements; their transformative capacities are generated through this autonomy. They depend on it. Therefore, alarm bells sound when I hear Podemos' representatives stress the need for their separation from social movements, which are seen to have a 'different' constituency, as Eduardo Maura has: 'They have different audiences, different targets, a different goal. Once you've developed a party, of course you are going to get a lot of input from the social movements ... in terms of policies ... [however] society is more than activists.'[31]

Clearly, a radical political party aiming to win elections does need to win the support of a wider public, beyond the activists. But electoral politics has its own powerful logic determined by a highly monopolised media closely allied with the political elite, as well as the domination of the electoral field by two main political parties that presume their right to govern and that listen to the preferences of powerful financial and industrial corporations rather than amplifying the voices of the people. Unless a radical party can support, stimulate and amplify an alternative logic rooted amongst the people as organised social forces (rather than as a passive mass to be rhetorically evoked), it becomes a light vessel buffeted this way and that and is often overwhelmed by the waves of the market and the dominant culture.

This has, indeed, begun to happen to Podemos. After reaching an electoral height as a convincing contender for government in January 2015, after a period of stagnation it has suffered from a decline.[32]

Questions for the future of political organisation

Although I must stress that these issues and difficulties facing both Syriza and Podemos, in different ways, will only become clear through the laboratories of experience in the coming year or so, it would be useful to at least explore the implications of our focus on Syriza and Podemos for political organisation. It is clearly insufficient to understand them only through the term of left populism; they have different relations to 'the people' as sources of organised and transformative power. Here, it is interesting to reflect on the differences in organisation and language between Syriza and Podemos, not in order to judge which is 'better' but because the comparison raises important questions.

We have seen a glimpse of how Podemos is emerging, involving a radical break from the organisations of even the radical Left. Whereas the decision-making congress of the parties of the radical Left – PRC and Syriza, for example – are based on delegates from branches, Podemos' congress is open to all, one person one vote. Techno-political tools are used extensively to enable people to contribute online and through mobile phone apps while on the move.

Political debate in Syriza is organised through various ideological tendencies based in part on the political organisations that originally came together to form Syriza. In Podemos, by contrast, proposals come from individual participants on an open, crowd-sourcing basis, some of which gain support and gather momentum, while others do not. This is fed into the physical conference debates.

There are snags with both methodologies: the old, more closed, ideologically based system and the new, open, super-participatory system based on the practical needs and demands of disaffected individuals. Tendency-based discussions, though formally democratic, can become inflexible and dogmatic. Debating political issues through the mediation of tendencies is not always appropriate for learning from new experiments by local circles, issue-based projects or emergent developments outside the political categories and beyond the leading personnel of the tendency debate. This mediation can disempower local assemblies in favour of the struggles between factions. Whether this has been the case in Syriza, I do not know, as there are various pressures at work, including the centralising consequences of government; but it is clear that the neighbourhood branches have become weak since Syriza won the election in early 2015.

The difficulty with the Podemos approach is that it might reinforce rather than challenge the atomistic individualism that underpins a liberal – and ultimately elite – approach to democracy. The problem with liberal democracies has been a narrow form of representation in which citizens are treated as individuals in an entirely abstract way rather than as part of embedded social, and at present unequal, relationships. It is a political process which consequently tends to disguise rather than expose inequalities, and protects rather than challenges private economic power. For the Chartists and many Suffragettes, the vote was the opening of a new phase in this political struggle, not a plateau on which to remain. Political representation meant for them a means of 'making present' in the political system struggles over social and economic inequality. How does Podemos' individual-based approach to participation achieve this? And how does its individual basis of participation avoid reproducing social inequalities in its ranks, or producing the 'tyranny of structurelessness' that became a much-debated problem in the women's liberation movement? It deals with the danger of its founding leadership concentrating power by separating the functions of spokesperson and central decision maker. Does this work in practice? Can the distinction be maintained, given the speed with which spokespeople often have to react in a media-dominated society?

Podemos partially resolves this contradiction between the individualist basis of the franchise and the social nature of struggles over economic inequality by holding to a sharp distinction between the tasks and targets of a party and those of a movement. But since its founding congress in 2014 when it decided to go all out for an electoral victory, with a blitzkrieg-style 'electoral war machine', the party leadership at times counterposed this electoral goal with social-movement activism, including the activism that was at the foundation of the party in the 1 000 citizens' 'circles' that appeared across the country after the decision to stand in the European elections. However, it was not long before, from the point of view of the electoral machine, the circles were flagged by the electorally oriented leadership as 'militant obstacles'. It was said that the considerable weight in the party of these activist circles impeded wider communication with the unmobilised majority.[33]

Syriza would, judging by its practice, take a different view. While sharing Podemos' belief in the autonomy of social movements, their work implies a commitment to act consciously as a resource and support for social movements.

Networked political organisation

This raises the questions: how many of the necessary functions of transformative politics should be combined in a political party? Are these functions in fact best carried out through a single, unified organisation? To return to the two understandings of power introduced at the beginning of this chapter, is it appropriate – politically effective – for a party both to seek to win control over power-as-domination (seek to win elections, including becoming part of government) *and* to act as a resource and support for social movements and power-as-transformative-capacity? Or should political organisation have a more modular character, focused on different tasks, shaping organisational form to the nature of the task? Wouldn't this approach give organisations – both movements and parties – a greater ability to be responsive, creative and flexible?

For example, rather than a party doing everything through a single organisation, one could have different organisational forms for different functions which would all be transparent and loosely networked. Thus, there would be a 'platform', which would be the basis of an electoral intervention – rather like Barcelona en Comú, the electoral platform of movements and parties that successfully campaigned to elect the leader of the anti-eviction movement, Ada Calau , as mayor of Barcelona – with a separate infrastructure of communication available as a resource for the use of social movements, and a separate capacity for popular education. Such a modular approach could also involve collaboration and coordination on the basis of shared values and a common goal. But it is sufficiently spacious to allow for different views, for reflection and for experimentation. Call it a party or a movement – it would be a political organisation of a new type and one in process, not a final static form. It would also be more attuned to making the most of new technology and the collaborative tools and value that it would generate.

CONCLUSION

One main trend seems to span the four decades that this exploration of political organisation examines. It is the recurring formation of radical organisations – whether movements, networks or projects – with transformative goals but independent of political parties, which do however take a pragmatic approach towards electoral parties for particular purposes. I refer to the networks that sprang up around the time of a radical engagement with national and local government in the UK in the 1970s and 1980s, for example, for health and safety at work and other themes of workers' control, promoting social responsibility in science and technology, democratising the health service, promoting local cooperatives and many more. A similar network formed in Italy more recently, with the movements that converged to stop the privatisation of water. We have seen how the ability of political initiatives to win control over power-as-domination has a tendency to be short-lived, whereas organisations that work in society or culture to assert or build power-as-transformative-capacity persist, sometimes lying low but reappearing perhaps in a modified form. At times I have believed that the main challenge is to work for these latter 'fragments' to coalesce or interconnect to be an effective political force. But either this is a very slow process, or maintaining their autonomy is part of the very nature of these organisations (for example, because their energies are so focused on their specific and demanding work that they have little energy left for the equally demanding work of coalescing beyond for practical one-off purposes).

In the meantime, as is evident in Greece and Spain, the pace at which political and economic power is being exercised at the expense of the 99 per cent requires an attempt to win governmental office, initially simply to end the imposition of austerity, far more urgently than these processes of coalescence from below are able to move.

Yet we have also learnt from the experiences described above, especially those of the UK in the 1970s and in Norway and Italy in the 1990s, that the possibilities of winning power-as-domination – government office and so on – to support emerging sources of power-as-transformative-capacity depend crucially on the autonomous political perspectives of these extra-parliamentary organisations. And yet, as the leadership of Podemos shows, this can nonetheless be seen to be in tension with the imperatives of winning elections.

The task of winning political office – with all its secretive, compromising and constraining logics – is more often than not in conflict with the development of transformative capacity in society. This has to be acknowledged as a condition for combining both, preferably in some modular political framework. Such self-conscious acknowledgement of this acute tension can set in motion a process of creating both material and cultural antidotes to the logic of power-as-domination at the same time as protecting and nurturing transformative capacity. This would help to create the conditions where electoral success could open up a dynamic of deeper democratisation, including economic democracy, rather than allowing electoral success to become an overriding end in itself. But the dynamics and conditions of this require deeper interrogation of experience beyond Europe, in Latin America and at this moment in South Africa especially, as well as a permanently reflective and self-conscious engagement with the acute and difficult struggles and organisation building that we now face.

NOTES

1   See for example the importance of collaborative information and communications technology (ICT) tools in the development of the Spanish party Podemos. See also the collaborative discussions since 2006 of the group Networked Politics across generations and left traditions while focused on the significance of new ICTs for political organisation, both practically and in terms of language, metaphor and paradigm.
2   The Spanish government party, the Popular Party, fiercely but unsuccessfully opposed this award in the European Parliament.
3   Wainwright, H. 2015. Greece: Syriza shines a light. Accessed 14 August 2015, http://www.redpepper.org.uk/greece-syriza-shines-a-light/.
4   The term 'rank and file' with its military evocations of those in the ranks following orders from above, says it all.
5   The break of the US dollar from the gold standard, the deregulation of financial flows in the US and then the UK and the eventual breakdown of the post-war financial order institutionalised in the Bretton Woods arrangements.
6   Jeanette Mitchell, Donald Mackenzie, John Holloway, Cynthia Cockburn, Kathy Polanshek, Nicola Murray, Neil McInnes and John McDonald – a collective known as the London Edinburgh Weekend Return Group.
7   'A hacker seeks to learn and build upon pre-existing ideas and systems. He believes that access gives hackers the opportunity to take things apart, fix, or improve upon them and to learn and understand how they work. This gives them the knowledge to create new and even more interesting things' (Levy [1984] 2010).
8   Speech made at the decisive 2006 Congress of Rifondazione Communista.
9   By 'pluralist' I mean a break from the idea that the party has a monopoly on the process of social change, and recognition of a plurality of sources of transformative power.
10   Interview with the author, Oslo, 2004.
11   Including of a relatively strong trade union movement with considerable influence over the Labour Party.
12   Interview with the author, Oslo, 2006.
13   Telephone interview with the author, early 2015.
14   Wainwright, H. 2008. A Red guide to Italian politics. Accessed 14 August 2015,

http://www.redpepper.org.uk/A-red-guide-to-Italian-politics/.

15   See, for example, Wainwright, H. 2004. Local democracy, Italian style. Accessed 15 August 2015, http://www.redpepper.org.uk/Local-Democracy-Italian-style and Wainwright, H. 2006. 'The emerging new Euroleft'. *The Nation*, 10 April.

16   'All Italy's history shows that it is basically a right-wing country, heavily influenced by the Vatican. The composition of the Italian middle classes goes very much in Berlusconi's favour, and dependent workers in small family firms tend to vote the way their bosses vote. But there is also a very strong, though minority, tradition of left-wing action and mobilisation. That is far from dead. It now has to be put in an organisational and intellectual context that is radically new.' (See Wainwright, H. 2008. A Red guide to Italian politics. Accessed 14 August 2015, http://www. redpepper.org.uk/A-red-guide-to-Italian-politics/.)

17   Quoted in Wainwright, H. 2015. Greece: Syriza shines a light. Accessed 14 August 2015, http://www.redpepper.org.uk/greece-syriza-shines-a-light/.

18   Wainwright, H. 2015. Greece: Syriza shines a light. Accessed 14 August 2015, http://www.redpepper.org.uk/greece-syriza-shines-a-light/.

19   Ibid.

20   Ibid.

21   Ibid.

22   Blitzer, J. 2014. 'In Spain, politics via Reddit'. *The New Yorker* 7 October.

23   Ibid.

24   Dolan, A. 2015. Politics by the people. Accessed 17 August 2015, http://www. redpepper.org.uk/podemos-politics-by-the-people/.

25   Characteristic *Avgi* headlines included 'The People and the Left for the new Greece', 'Do not corrupt the mandate of the people'. These had not been typical of *Avgi* in the past. Similarly, Tsipras started, very soon after the election where Syriza won a stunning twenty-seven per cent of the vote, to speak like this: 'Sunday is not just about a simple confrontation between Syriza and the political establishment of the Memorandum. [...] It is about an encounter of the people with their lives. An encounter of the people with their fate. [...] Between the Greece of the oligarchy and the Greece of Democracy. [...] The people unite with Syriza.'

26   Dolan, A. 2015. 'Si se Puede': Interview with Eduardo Maura. *Red Pepper* December/ January 2015.

27   Zelik, R. 2015. 'Theses on Podemos and the "Democratc Revolution" in Spain'. Accessed 16 September 2015, www.socialistproject.ca/bullet/1113.php

28   Dolan, A. 2015. 'Si se Puede': Interview with Eduardo Maura. *Red Pepper* December/ January 2015.

29   Ibid.

30   Though the strength of the 'No' vote on the EU/IMF austerity memorandum indicates that they have the potential for such mobilisation.

31   Dolan, A. 2015. 'Si se Puede': Interview with Eduardo Maura. *Red Pepper* December/ January 2015.

32   Though the electoral alliances in Spain's main cities, of which Podemos was but one part, have been more successful, which partially reinforces my argument here.

33   Lopez, I., Rodriguez, R. and Carmona, P. 2015. The future of Podemos. Accessed June 2015, https://www.jacobinmag.com/author/lopez-rodriguez-carmona/.

REFERENCES

Beynon, H. (1975) *Working for Ford*. London: Penguin

Bhaskar, R. [1993] 2008. *Dialectic: The Pulse of Freedom*. London: Routledge.

Boltanski, L. and Chiapello, E. 2006. *The New Spirit of Capitalism*. London: Verso.

Canovan, M. 1999. 'Trust the people! Populism and the two faces of democracy', *Political Studies* 47 (1): 3.

Ginsborg, P. 2006. 'Is Berlusconi finished?' *London Review of Books* 28 (7): 14–16.

Laclau, E. 2005. *Populist Reason*. London: Verso.

Levy, S. (1984) 2010. *Hackers: Heroes of the Computer Revolution*. Sebastopol, CA: O'Reilly Media.

London Edinburgh Weekend Return Group. 1979. *In and Against the State*. London: Pluto.

Mackintosh, M. and Wainwright, H. 1987. 'A Taste of Power': The Politics of Local Economics*. London: Verso.

Michels, R. (1911) 2007. *Political Parties: A Sociological Study of the Oligarchical Tendencies of Modern Democracy*. New Brunswick, NJ: Transaction Press.

Milkman, R. 2004. *Rebuilding Labour: Organisers and Organisers in the New Union Movement*. New York: Cornell University Press.

Panitch, L. and Leys, C. 2001. *The End of Parliamentary Socialism*. London: Verso.

Stedman Jones, G. 2004. *An End to Poverty?* London: Profile Books.

Thompson, D. 1984. *Chartists: Popular Politics in the Industrial Revolution*. New York: Pantheon.

Tsakalotos, E. 2013. *Crucible of Resistance: Greece, the Eurozone and the World Economic Crisis*. London: Pluto Press.

Turner, F. 2006. *From Cyberculture to Counterculture*. Chicago: University of Chicago Press.

Wainwright, H. 1994. *Arguments for a New Left: Answering the Free Market Right*. London: Blackwell.

Wainwright, H. 2010. *Reclaim the State: Experiments in Popular Democracy*. London: Seagull Books.

Wainwright, H. 2014. *The Tragedy of the Private; the Potential of the Public*. Geneva and Amsterdam: Public Service International and Transnational Institute.

Yeo, S. 2002. *Co-operative and Mutual Enterprises in Britain: Ideas from a Usable Past for a Modern Future*. London: Centre for Civil Society, London School of Economics.

Zelik, R. 2015. 'Theses on Podemos and the "Democratic Revolution" in Spain'. Toronto: Socialist Project. Accessed 16 September 2015, www. socialistproject.ca/bullet/1113.php.

CAPITALIST CRISIS
AND LEFT RESPONSES
IN THE GLOBAL SOUTH

6

BRAZIL: FROM NEOLIBERAL DEMOCRACY TO THE END OF THE 'LULA MOMENT'

Alfredo Saad-Filho

This chapter examines the context and implications of two transitions in Brazil: the political transition from a military regime (1964–1985) to democracy (1985 to the present), and the economic transition from import substitution industrialisation (ISI) (1930–1980) to neoliberalism (1990 to the present). These transitions have shaped the contemporary Brazilian political economy and the policy choices available to recent federal administrations. The chapter also reviews how neoliberal economic policies were implemented in a democracy, first under the centre-right administrations led by Fernando Henrique Cardoso (1995–1998, 1998–2002) and then under the centre-left presidencies of Luís Inácio Lula da Silva (2003–2006, 2007–2010) and Dilma Rousseff (2011–2014, 2015 to the present).

In this context, it is especially important to examine the policy shifts introduced during the second Lula administration. These shifts did not signal a decisive break with neoliberalism, but they inaugurated what became known as the 'Lula moment': a decade of significantly higher growth rates than had been achieved previously, and remarkable advances in employment, distribution and poverty alleviation. The chapter examines the economic and social policies underpinning the 'Lula moment', and reflects on the limitations of their policies, and those of neoliberal democracy, which have emerged through the political crisis of the Rousseff administration.

Following are eight sections. The first outlines the process of ISI and its limitations. The second describes the transitions from the military regime to democracy, and from ISI to neoliberalism. The next three review the first and second Lula administrations and the Rousseff administration. The sixth examines the distributional achievements under these administrations. The seventh considers the challenges now posed for the Brazilian Left, after the exhaustion of the 'Lula moment'. The eighth section presents the main conclusions.

IMPORT SUBSTITUTION INDUSTRIALISATION

ISI is a system of accumulation based on the sequenced expansion of manufacturing industry, with the primary objective of replacing imports.[1] Manufacturing expansion usually departs from the internalisation of the production of non-durable consumer goods (textiles, processed foods, beverages, tobacco products and so on). It later deepens to include the production of durable consumer goods (especially household appliances and automobile assembly), simple chemical and pharmaceutical products and non-metallic minerals (especially cement).

In the larger countries, including Brazil, ISI can reach a third stage, when the manufacturing structure includes the production of steel, capital goods (for example, industrial machinery and electric motors) and technologically complex goods, such as electronic machines, shipbuilding and aircraft design and assembly. This 'deepening' of the manufacturing base is accompanied by backward, forward and horizontal linkages between the established firms. As a result of these processes, in the 1950s, primary exports were no longer the driving force of the Brazilian economy. Brazil offers a particularly striking example of these processes: agriculture declined from thirty-six per cent of gross domestic product (GDP) in 1910 to only ten per cent in 1980, while manufacturing increased from fourteeen to forty-one per cent of GDP (Abreu, Bevilacqua and Pinho 2000: 162). Although ISI often starts spontaneously, international experience shows that its success requires activist industrial, financial and trade policies, and state provision (or incentives for the private provision) of finance and infrastructure.

At the political level, Brazilian ISI was associated with the uneasy coexistence of populism, nationalism, corporatism and statism, and by conflicts of interest within the elite, especially between agrarian and urban interests and between manufacturing capital and finance, as well as between the elite and other social groups, especially the urban workers and the emerging urban middle classes. Stripped of their rich complexity, these conflicts essentially centred around the extent to which resources should be transferred away from the primary export sector and where they should be allocated. Conflicting demands were played out in the media, in educational and research institutions, in state institutions and on the streets, with outcomes contingent on timing, circumstances and the constellation of forces mobilised on each side. These conflicts were displaced by the 1964 military coup.

Despite its important economic achievements, Brazilian ISI was severely limited. The six most important limitations were the balance of payments constraint, the fragility and inefficiency of the domestic financial system, fiscal fragility, high inflation, high inequality, and lack of policy coordination (see further Saad-Filho, Iannini and Molinari 2007). These limitations were varied but they can be attributed, in general terms, to the fact that the Brazilian state was interventionist but it was also institutionally disarticulated and unable to impose consistent priorities over conflicting interests, especially among the dominant economic power blocs. In turn, those groups generally found detailed planning and large-scale state intervention unacceptable because it upset the political balance within the elite, and it sometimes promoted the interests of the poor majority at the expense of those of the established social powers.

The structural constraints and fragilities of ISI and the strongly negative impact of the external shocks of the 1970s and early 1980s made macroeconomic management extremely difficult, culminating on a slide towards hyperinflation which peaked only in the mid 1990s, when inflation rates exceeded forty per cent per month. The social conflicts intensified, political instability became endemic, and policy choices were limited by institutional weaknesses and creeping political paralysis. The military government lost the capacity to manage the economy. In the early 1980s, it became widely agreed that political changes were imperative.

THE TRANSITIONS TO DEMOCRACY AND TO NEOLIBERALISM

The military regime disintegrated gradually after 1974 due to the political exhaustion of naked repression, and the economic exhaustion of the regime's growth strategy. Political contestation encompassed critiques of the regime's corruption and lack of accountability, trade union militancy, the ballot box, and mass mobilisations for democratic reforms. Yet, Brazilian democracy did not emerge through the destruction of the dictatorship (as was the case, for example, in Argentina). Instead, the military and the traditional elites eventually reached a pact to secure political freedoms, in exchange for the preservation of elite privileges. Under these limited conditions, the democratic transition, achieved in 1985, established the most open and stable regime in the history of the republic.

The political transition to democracy was rapidly followed by an economic transition to neoliberalism. This transition followed from the slow convergence of the Brazilian elite, between the late 1970s and the late 1980s, to the view that ISI faced three insurmountable problems: the inefficiency of the financial sector, continuing industrial backwardness, and the difficulty of creating a dynamic national system of innovation. It was increasingly accepted that these obstacles could be overcome only if the state was 'rolled back' through expenditure cuts; the reform of the fiscal, tax and social security systems; and the privatisation of most state-owned enterprises (SOEs). It was expected that fiscal reforms would reduce inflation, while financial liberalisation would increase domestic savings and investment. Finally, it was hoped that the liberalisation of foreign trade and capital inflows and the resolution of the external debt crisis would bring direct and portfolio investment flows and facilitate industrial restructuring. Productivity would rise, followed by a structural improvement in the balance of payments. In sum, the strategic vision was that the integration of Brazilian productive and financial capital into transnational conglomerates would drive a virtuous circle of growth which would turn Brazil into a developed economy.

These policy prescriptions were implemented gradually and increasingly consistently by successive governments. In 1988, during the Sarney administration, the domestic financial system was reformed and, starting in 1989, international capital flows were liberalised. The exchange rate regime was made increasingly flexible in the following years. From 1990, during the Collor administration, Brazil reduced import restrictions incrementally. The Collor and Franco administrations adopted strongly contractionary monetary policies in order to control inflation, attract foreign capital and generate exportable surpluses. The Cardoso government fully implemented a neoliberal economic strategy, especially through the Real Plan of inflation stabilisation, and the first Lula administration pursued essentially the same policies as its predecessor (see below).

However, the neoliberal reforms did not resolve the shortcomings of ISI, and they destabilised the balance of payments and the country's productive system. The reforms hollowed out the industrial chains built during ISI and reduced the local content of manufacturing production. Wages and profits declined because of competing imports, the rising share of interest in the national income (due to the financial reforms and higher real interest rates), and the difficulty of developing new competitive industries. Structural unemployment mounted. Neoliberalism discarded import substitution and promoted, instead, 'production substitution' financed by foreign capital.

The Brazilian experience shows that the neoliberal reforms can secure macro-economic stability and growth in the short term. This is for two main reasons. First, they are part of the conventional wisdom of our age, and are embedded in the belief systems of most domestic and international institutions. Therefore, they are 'credible' by definition. Second, if international liquidity is high and interest rates are low, as was the case in the mid 1970s, in the early 1990s, and between the recovery from the 2000/01 slump and the end of the global boom in 2007, trade and capital account liberalisation seem to abolish the balance of payments constraint. They can bring capital inflows to finance a large trade deficit, allowing consumption, investment and growth rates to increase rapidly, in a virtuous circle that may last several years. However, if these foreign capital flows decline, as they did in the early 1980s, in the mid 1990s, in 2000/01 and in periods after the 2007 global crisis, countries following neoliberal policies can find themselves in a vulnerable position. The balance of payments constraint can reappear suddenly, either because of the scarcity of foreign exchange or because higher international interest rates push up the domestic interest rates, squeezing the economy both internally and externally at the same time.

In Brazil, the crisis of the Real Plan, in 1998 and 1999, led to the introduction of a new macro-economic policy regime including inflation targeting, large fiscal surpluses and the managed fluctuation of Brazilian currency, the real (the 'neoliberal policy tripod') (Morais, Saad-Filho and Coelho 1999). The main goal of the policy tripod was to preserve low inflation, stabilise the domestic public debt (DPD) and the exchange rate, and eliminate the current account deficit.

Permanently high real interest rates during the period of the real had perverse macro-economic implications which help to explain the country's slow economic growth rates in the late 1990s and early 2000s. GDP growth rates picked up only after the trade balance shifted into a surplus in 2001 (the current account moved into a surplus two years later). A large part of this uplift was due to the global commodity boom of the early and mid 2000s, which was associated with an increase in the share of primary commodities in Brazilian exports from forty to sixty per cent. However, this renewed modality of primary export-led growth is not easily compatible with the creation of quality employment and the improvement of social welfare in a large urbanised economy with a considerable manufacturing base.

The neoliberal reforms transferred state capacity to allocate resources inter-temporally (the balance between investment and consumption), intersectorally (the distribution of investment, employment and output) and internationally to an increasingly integrated and US-led financial sector. With the completion of these reforms, the Brazilian economy has become structurally more dependent on foreign trade, investment and technology. Brazil's productive base has, then, shifted away from the long-term requirements of national accumulation and towards the short-term imperatives of global accumulation. By the same token, the Brazilian state became depleted in the areas of economic planning, control and policy implementation. In contrast, state capacity in monetary policy implementation and regulation of finance increased significantly. The financial reforms embedded private-sector interests into the policymaking process through the decisive role of finance in the pricing of government securities, the determination of interest rates and the financing of the public sector. The reforms also increased the role of the private financial institutions in the foreign exchange market and, therefore, in the country's relationship with the rest of the world.

At a further remove, the neoliberal transition contributed to the disorganisation of the workforce and to a significant shift in power away from the majority regardless of (and, to some extent, because of) the stabilisation of political democracy. Rather than relying on military force, the neoliberal consensus disciplined the working class through 'economic' policies, institutions and processes.[2] They include contractionary fiscal and monetary policies, higher unemployment and labour turnover, personal debt, and the continuing threat of inflationary or balance of payments crises, should the distributive conflicts get out of hand. These limitations of democracy are sufficiently strong and pervasive to overwhelm marginal local initiatives initiated by the Brazilian Left, including, for example, participatory budgeting.[3]

In sum, democracy has become established as the political form of neoliberalism in Brazil. In this country, the neoliberal transition and the democratic transition were mutually reinforcing and, eventually, they became mutually constituting. They were associated with a shift in the mechanisms of social domination towards a combination of democracy and neoliberalism, which has fostered social fragmentation and the dismantling of the resistance movements that had emerged during the dictatorship. The symbiosis between neoliberalism and procedural democracy operates at three key levels (see Ayers and Saad-Filho 2014; Saad-Filho and Morais 2014). First, the neoliberal economic transition was achieved through, and validated by, democratic means. Second, neoliberal policies support the democratic regime because they fragment the workers through higher unemployment, faster labour turnover, the repression of trade union activity and the rise of economic insecurity. Under neoliberalism, the repression of working-class activity relies primarily on 'economic' rather than 'political' structures, as was the case under the dictatorship. Third, democracy is the best political regime for neoliberalism because it guarantees the stability and predictability of the 'rules of the game', making it more reliably managed by the moneyed interests.

THE FIRST LULA ADMINISTRATION

Lula was elected president in 2002 by an 'alliance of losers': a coalition of heterogeneous social groups that had in common only the experience of losses under neoliberalism (Morais and Saad-Filho 2005). These groups included the organised working class, the domestic bourgeoisie, large sections of the traditional oligarchy and sections of the middle class and the informal proletariat (see Boito 2012 for a description of the Brazilian class structure). This collection of disparate supporters had few objectives in common beyond more expansionary macro-economic policies and some redistribution of income, and it could not be relied upon to support radical policies leading, for example, to a serious break with neoliberalism. In this sense, the common complaint among the Left that Lula 'betrayed' his supporters is misplaced: in 2002, Lula neither sought nor received a mandate to introduce radical policy changes. In order to bring together the 'losers' and avoid a fourth consecutive defeat in the presidential elections, after his previous attempts in 1989, 1994 and 1998, Lula's discourse emphasised a diffuse spirit of 'change', but he studiously avoided making specific commitments. The only exception is Lula's 'Letter to the Brazilian People', issued under duress in June 2002, in the midst of a severe currency crisis. In this document, Lula declared that his government would respect contracts (in other words, service the domestic and foreign debts on schedule) and enforce the policies agreed between the Cardoso administration and the International Monetary Fund.

Lula's administration maintained the neoliberal policy tripod introduced in 1999 by his predecessor, the Marxist sociologist-turned-neoliberal, Fernando Henrique Cardoso. In order to secure further his credibility with 'the markets', Lula appointed a prominent member of Cardoso's right-wing social democratic party (Partido da Social Democracia Brasileira, PSDB) president of the country's independent Central Bank, with carte blanche to raise interest rates to the level required to secure low inflation. The government also raised the primary fiscal surplus target from 3.75 per cent of GDP to 4.25 per cent, and cut fiscal spending by almost one per cent of GDP. The minimum wage was virtually frozen for two years, and the government pushed through Congress a harsh reform of social security that had eluded Cardoso for years, partly because of the opposition from the Workers' Party (PT) and its left-wing allies.

The conservative credentials of Lula's administration were tempered, first, by a significant expansion of the federal programmes of social assistance. In late 2003, the government consolidated four existing programmes into the *Bolsa Família* (PBF, or Family Grant) which, initially, reached 3.6 million households. The programme was scaled up rapidly, reaching 11 million families in 2006 and 14 million in 2014, with 50 million beneficiaries (one-quarter of the country's population).

Second, the Lula administration appointed a large number of progressive political, trade union and non-governmental organisation (NGO) cadres to the federal administration, not always from the trade union arm of the PT. The president, a former metal worker, appointed five working-class cadres to ministerial-level posts; more than 100 trade unionists took other high-level posts in the public administration and in SOEs; in turn, they appointed hundreds of lower-level colleagues (Boito 2003; Singer 2010). Their elevation opened the floodgates to the election of an unprecedented number of poor candidates by parties across the political spectrum to all manner of posts since 2004. While these changes aligned the material interests of the leaders of many social movements (with the exception of the landless peasants' movement, Movimento dos Trabalhadores Rurais Sem Terra, MST) with the government's agenda and the interests of the state bureaucracy and effectively 'nationalised' them, they also changed the social composition of the Brazilian state. For the first time, poor citizens could recognise themselves in the bureaucracy and relate to friends and comrades who had become 'important' in Brasília. This change in the social composition of the state greatly increased its legitimacy, and it supported from inside the government's distributive policy agenda.

In mid 2005, Lula's first administration was paralysed by a furious right-wing and media offensive triggered by the *mensalão* corruption scandal, involving allegations that government officials paid deputies and senators a monthly stipend in exchange for votes. Although no firm evidence was ever provided, the *mensalão* led to the resignation of the president's chief of staff, the president of the PT, and several high-ranking federal officials; years later many of them were imprisoned under various charges relating to the scandal.

This scandal triggered a catastrophic loss of support for the PT. After 25 years of growth, the PT had reached twenty-five per cent of voter preferences in early 2005; after the *mensalão*, these rates fell by half, and Lula's bid for re-election seemed close to collapse. Yet, Lula's share of first-round votes reached forty-nine per cent in October 2006 (up from forty-six per cent in 2002), and he maintained his second-round share at sixty-one per cent.

This surprising feat was due to the dissolution of the 'losers' alliance' and the transformation of Lula's support base. He lost the middle class after the *mensalão*, but conquered the unorganised poor because of the distributive programmes introduced in his first administration: PBF, university admission quotas, the formalisation of the labour market, mass connections to the electricity grid (the Light for All programme, or *Luz Para Todos*), and a forty-eight per cent real increase in minimum wages since mid 2005, which triggered automatic increases to most pensions and benefits.

For the first time since the PT was founded in 1980, support for the party became inversely correlated with income (Singer 2014). In households earning more than 10 times the minimum wage (roughly, the 'middle class'), PT support fell from thirty-two per cent in 2002 to seventeen per cent in 2006. Lula's rejection among voters with university education jumped from twenty-four per cent to forty per cent between August and October 2005; sixty-five per cent of these voters chose the opposition candidate in 2006. In 1997, the PT had 5.5 million 'high-income' and 3.1 million 'low-income' supporters, and only seventeen per cent of PT supporters earned less than twice the minimum wage. In 2006, the PT had only 3.3 million 'high-income' supporters but 17.6 million 'low-income' ones, and forty-seven per cent of its supporters earned less than twice the minimum wage (Singer 2010: 96–97).

Lula won in 2006 because of his massive majority among first-time voters, beneficiaries of transfer programmes, poor women (the main recipients of PBF) and low earners. Correspondingly, Lula lost in most rich states, but he received more than three-quarters of the votes in several poor states. In contrast, the PT elected only 83 Federal Deputies in 2006 (down from 91 in 2002), showing that the support of the poor was tightly focused on the president. Voting patterns between 1982 (just after the PT was founded) and 2006 suggest that the Brazilian poor have traditionally voted for the right, and they shifted to Lula only *after* he had been elected by other social groups, and had delivered to the poor higher incomes, benefits and considerable improvements to their living conditions.

The transformation in Lula's base of support was part of a structural realignment of Brazilian politics. On the side of the government, we now find the domestic bourgeoisie, the organised working class and the informal proletariat, including most landless peasants (see below). The opposition is based on the alliance between the neoliberal bourgeoisie and the middle class, bound together by a rabid mainstream media.

THE SECOND LULA ADMINISTRATION

In Lula's second administration, a number of elements of neo-developmentalist economic heterodoxy diluted the neoliberal policy tripod (Morais and Saad-Filho 2011, 2012).[4] This inflection – the policy core of the 'Lula moment' – and the favourable global economic environment in the mid 2000s, led to a marked uplift in macro-economic performance and in employment creation, and supported an unprecedented reduction of inequality in the country.

Brazil's growth surge in the mid- and late 2000s was driven by consumption and state-led investment. The latter is easily justifiable. The fiscal and financial stresses experienced after the international debt crisis in the early 1980s, and during the neoliberal transition in the 1990s, followed by successive rounds of public spending cuts aimed at stabilising the DPD-to-GDP ratio contributed to a severe degradation of the country's infrastructure. In order to release funds for investment without overtly confronting the neoliberal lobby, the second Lula administration changed the form of calculation of the primary fiscal surplus in order to exclude the SOEs (especially the oil and electricity conglomerates, Petrobras and Eletrobrás). This allowed SOE investment to quadruple in nominal terms, rising from 1.8 per cent of GDP in the mid 2000s, to 2.2 per cent of GDP in 2010.

This investment spree was supplemented by private investment, mostly directly funded or at least guaranteed by the state-owned banks (especially BNDES, the Brazilian Development Bank, which became the largest development bank in the world). The government also launched a 'growth acceleration programme' in early 2007, focusing on energy, transport and infrastructure. This was followed by a large housing programme ('My Home My Life', or *Minha Casa Minha Vida*), increased funding for education, health and other public services, and the expansion of the civil service, together with significant pay increases, in order to recover policymaking capacity and reduce the number of subcontracted workers in the state sector. The government also supported diplomatically and through BNDES the transnationalisation of selected domestic firms ('national champions'). They include Itaú and Bradesco (banking), Embraer (aviation), Odebrecht (construction), Vale (mining), Inbev (beverages), Gerdau (steel) and Friboi and Brazil Foods (processed foods) (Boito 2012).

In turn, consumption rose because of the rapid rise in the minimum wage; the increase in federal transfers to pensioners, the unemployed and the disabled from R$135 billion (US$50 billion) to R$305 billion (US$113 billion) between 2002 and 2009; and the quadrupling of personal credit, which rose from twenty-four per cent of GDP to forty-five per cent; while mortgage lending expanded from R$26 billion (US$10 billion) in 2004 to R$80 billion (US$30 billion) in 2009 (Pochmann 2011: 25–27).

Even with these aggressive spending initiatives, the fiscal deficit remained stable and the domestic public debt declined from fifty-five per cent of GDP in mid 2002 to forty per cent in 2010, because of the rapid growth of GDP, the increase in fiscal revenues due to economic growth and the programme of formalisation of the labour market, which brought in new social security contributions. The average rate of growth of real per capita GDP rose from 0.75 per cent per annum between 1995 and 2002, in the Cardoso administration, to 2.4 per cent between 2003 and 2006, and to 3.5 per cent between 2007 and 2010, in Lula's second administration, despite the adverse impact of the global crisis.

DILMA ROUSSEFF'S ADMINISTRATIONS

Lula's approval rate touched on ninety per cent towards the end of his second term. He hand-picked and secured the election of his successor, former Chief of Staff Dilma Rousseff, who won fifty-six per cent of the ballots in the second round. Rousseff was a technocrat; she had never fought an election before, and had no support base. Having been anointed by Lula, she inherited both his voters and his detractors and, unsurprisingly, the voting pattern in 2010 closely mirrored that of the 2006 elections: Dilma won in the poorer states of the north and northeast and in most of the southeast, except São Paulo state. In each state, her vote was concentrated in the poorer areas and among the least educated voters. Her main rival, from the nominally social-democratic PSDB, won in São Paulo and in the richer states in the 'arch of agribusiness' across the south and the centre-west and, nationally, among higher-income and more educated voters.

After Dilma's inauguration in January 2011, the government expanded further its social programmes, aiming to eliminate absolute poverty which still impinges on 17 million people, and tilted economic policy a bit further toward neo-developmentalism, but without formally abandoning the neoliberal tripod. Monetary and exchange rate policies were aligned more closely with the government's industrial policy, in order to limit the current account deficit and support the internalisation of strategic production chains. Real interest rates fell to their lowest levels in 20 years (from an average of twenty-two per cent in Cardoso's first administration, to less than three per cent), and the Central Bank started extending the maturity and lowering the costs of the domestic public debt. The government introduced successive rounds of tax rebates in order to incentivise production and control inflation (in a significant departure from the single-minded focus on the manipulation of interest rates under neoliberalism), and strong-armed the private operators into reducing the price of electricity. Finally, the government sought to attract private investment into infrastructure and transport through concessions, public-private partnerships and regulatory changes, in order to bypass budgetary constraints and legal limitations to state funding, and to commit the domestic bourgeoisie to the government's investment programme.

Despite these policy changes, the Brazilian economy has slowed down significantly, with GDP growth rates tumbling towards two per cent per annum. It has become clear that the government has failed to kick-start a virtuous circle of growth driven by private investment, despite the increase in fiscal spending, SOE investment, loans by state-owned banks and the profusion of incentives and tax rebates. The country has also experienced a deteriorating balance of payments due to the slowdown in Brazil's main markets (China, the European Union and the US), sluggish commodity prices and the aggressive devaluations and export-led recovery strategies in several large economies. Moreover, low interest rates and quantitative easing in the advanced economies triggered capital flows to Brazil in the early years of the global crisis. They led to the appreciation of the real, and worsened the country's competitive position. The country's current account deficit rose from 2.1 per cent of GDP in 2011 to 2.7 per cent in 2012, 3.7 per cent in 2013 and 4.2 per cent in 2014.

This worrying trend was tempered by the reversal of capital flows, anticipating the unwinding of quantitative easing in most advanced economies. This outflow sucked the life out of the São Paulo stock exchange, which tumbled from 62 000 points in January 2013 to 46 000 in July, and triggered a rapid devaluation of the real between May and June. For this reason, and because of poor food crops, inflation edged up in the first half of 2013.

Under severe pressure from the media, the financial markets, its parliamentary base, the middle class and most economists, and given the apparent failure of its attempt to kick-start growth through domestic investment, the government changed course: it reaffirmed the commitment to the inflation targets and signalled to the Central Bank that it was time to start raising interest rates. At the same time, the Ministry of Finance announced cuts in public spending. Inevitably, wage income and the level of employment started a gradual decline despite the exceptional spending associated with the 2014 FIFA World Cup and the 2016 Olympic Games. These policy adjustments do not necessarily signal the return of naked neoliberalism, but they illustrate the limits of governmental power in a globally integrated middle-income capitalist economy.

In the first months of 2013, the opposition media was trumpeting the 'failure' of every aspect of government policy, and the 'imminent threat' of runaway inflation. Their negative campaign shifted the popular mood, and Dilma's popularity fell by 8 to 10 percentage points, although starting from an extraordinary level of seventy per cent, which had never been achieved by any Brazilian president at that stage in their administration.

The government's economic difficulties were compounded by political limitations. Lula was a charismatic leader, and he excelled at the conciliation of differences. Dilma lacks these virtues. Although she is an accomplished manager, she is said to be abrasive and intimidating, and her government has deliberately turned away the trade unions, left-wing NGOs and the MST in order to pursue a progressive technocratic agenda, which has created a sense of despondency even among her strongest supporters.[5] On top of it all, the entire – badly divided – Left controls less than one-third of the seats in Congress, of which only half (around fifteen per cent of the seats in the Chamber of Deputies and in the Senate together) are held by the PT. This makes it impossible to govern without volatile alliances with undisciplined parties and grubby individuals, which have to be managed under the gaze of a hostile press and the scrutiny of a right-wing judicial system. After 10 years in federal office, the PT seems to have political hegemony without the substance of power; at the same time, it seems to engage in the same dirty political games as everyone else, belying its historical claim to hold the moral high ground.

These limitations came to light in early 2015, after Dilma's tight re-election against the PSDB candidate, Aécio Neves. Despite the essential role of left mobilisation in this victory, the government immediately shifted economic policy further towards the neoliberal policy tripod, leading to a sense of abandonment among Dilma's supporters. At the same time, the media, finance and the upper middle class have risen in strong opposition against the PT and the administration through a series of mass demonstrations and a relentless campaign online and on mainstream media demanding Dilma's impeachment or her removal from office.[6]

DISTRIBUTIONAL SHIFTS UNDER LULA AND DILMA

The pattern of growth under Lula and Dilma was unquestionably pro-poor (Saad-Filho 2007; Saad-Filho and Morais 2014). It has led to the reduction of poverty and inequality in Brazil across a broad spectrum of measures.

In the 2000s, 21 million jobs were created, in contrast with 11 million during the 1990s. Around eighty per cent of them were in the formal sector, which expanded from forty-five to fifty-one per cent of the workforce (Pomar 2013: 42).[7] Significantly, around ninety per cent of those jobs paid less than 1.5 times the minimum wage (in contrast with fifty-one per cent in the 1990s). Unemployment fell steadily, especially in the lower segments of the labour markets, reaching, in 2014, less than six per cent of the workforce for the first time in decades.

After a decade-long stagnation, average real wages grew 4.2 per cent per year between 2003 and 2012, and real per capita household incomes grew 4.6 per cent per year. The real minimum wage rose seventy-two per cent between 2005 and 2012 (8.6 per cent per year), while real GDP per capita increased by a more modest thirty per cent. Rising minimum wages lifted the floor of the labour market and triggered simultaneous increases in federal transfers and pensions. Between 2001 and 2011 the income of the poorest ten per cent rose, on average, 6.3 per cent annually, in contrast with 1.4 per cent per annum for the richest ten per cent (Paes de Barros, Grosner and Mascarenhas 2012: 15). These gains have been concentrated in the poorer regions, with average real wages in the northeast rising at twice the national rate (see Morais and Saad-Filho 2011). Incomes rose faster in the periphery than in the centre of São Paulo, and more in rural than in urban areas. Female income rose by thirty-eight per cent against sixteen per cent for men (sixty per cent of the jobs created in the 2000s employed women), and the income of blacks rose forty-three per cent against twenty per cent for whites (Bastos 2012; Pochmann 2010: 640, 648; 2011: 38; 2012: 32; Tible 2013: 68).

Poverty has fallen rapidly. The country had 60 million poor people in 1993 (41 per cent of the population) and the same number again in 2003 (thirty-five per cent).[8] Poverty subsequently fell rapidly, to under 30 million (fifteen per cent of the population) in 2012. The number of extremely poor individuals touched 29 million in 1993 (nineteen per cent of the population), and 26 million in 2003 (fifteen per cent), but fell under 10 million in 2012 (five per cent). The proportion of poor households fell from thirty-five per cent in 1993 to twenty-eight per cent in 2003, and twelve per cent in 2012.

Federal social spending increased 172 per cent in real terms (125 per cent per capita) between 1995 and 2010, rising from 11.0 per cent of GDP to 15.5 per cent (16.2 per cent in 2011) (Castro et al. 2012: 29; Chaves and Ribeiro 2012: 11). These growth rates were especially rapid after 2003. Higher spending permitted the expansion of existing programmes, the creation of new ones, such as PBF, higher payments (two-thirds of which are fixed at one minimum wage, and rose in real terms by 130 per cent), and an increase in the number of beneficiaries from 14.5 million to 24.4 million (seventy-seven per cent of citizens above the age of 60 now receive benefits). However, the informal workers remain largely excluded from social security coverage, including maternity pay, illness cover and pensions in case of retirement, illness or death (Castro et al. 2012).

The outcome of these processes has been a significant improvement in the distribution of income. The Gini coefficient fell from around 0.60 at the turn of the century to 0.53 in 2012, while the income ratio between the top ten per cent and the bottom forty per cent fell from 23 to 15.

The improvements outlined above have not been driven primarily by changes in social policy or public transfers, but by the labour markets: higher labour income (due to labour market shifts, greater labour demand and rising minimum wages) was responsible for sixty-five per cent of the decline of the Gini coefficient between 2001 and 2008, while the social benefits paid by the government were responsible for only 34 per cent (Hall 2008: 812; Mattei 2012: 167–168). It follows that the main drivers of poverty and exclusion in Brazil are the lack of secure and well-paid employment, and the insufficient provision and quality of public services. In order to break these structures of reproduction of poverty, government policy should clearly focus on labour markets and the expansion of public services. These can be supported, but not replaced, by the further expansion of social transfers.

Higher wages, the distribution of income, the expansion of social programmes and the growing availability of consumer credit have benefited tens of millions of people. For the first time, many poor people can visit shopping centres, fly across the country and buy a small car. Nevertheless, rising incomes at the bottom of the pyramid have not been accompanied by improvements in infrastructure, leading to a generalised perception of deterioration in the quality of urban life.[9] The ensuing tensions may have contributed to the social explosion in the country during June and July 2013, and they have influenced significantly the outcome of the 2014 elections, in which Rousseff won by a very narrow margin.[10] They were also in the background of some of the 2015 protests, even though the latter were mostly driven by the right-wing upper middle class.

In summary, the improvements in poverty and distribution during the last decade are due to several mutually reinforcing drivers. They include the creation of large numbers of jobs at the low-paid end of the labour markets, the formalisation of employment, the increase of the minimum wage, and the expansion of federal income transfer programmes. However, subcontracting continues to rise in services, in large private companies and even in SOEs. These workers earn forty to sixty per cent less than their peers in formal employment performing similar tasks. This might help to explain the extremely high proportion of very low-paid jobs created during the 2000s and the slow recovery of the wage share of national income, which rose only from thirty-eight per cent in 2000 to less than fifty per cent today (the same level it had been 30 years ago, at the end of ISI and still under the military dictatorship) (Pomar 2013: 42). Further non-marginal gains in poverty and distribution will require a change of approach.

CHALLENGES FOR THE LEFT

The emergence of mass protests in mid 2013 and again in early 2015, and the challenging outcome of the 2014 elections have posed difficult challenges for the Brazilian Left. Most radical left parties, trade unions and mass organisations were disabled long ago by the neoliberal reforms; the mass base of the Left has been extensively decomposed, collective action has become harder, and the Left has been both supported and tainted by association with the PT federal administrations. The cultural identifiers and political expectations of the formal and informal working class and the middle class have been transformed, and the internet has changed radically the modalities of social interaction among the youth. For many workers and students, the military dictatorship is ancient history, and the PT is the only party they have ever seen in office in Brasília. The demands and expectations of the formal and informal working class have shot up in the last decade, while the upper middle class, stuck in opposition for years, has become embittered, leading to the emergence of a 'New Right' in the country. The press devalues the political system and harasses the Left relentlessly, and the economy has been slowing down since 2010. Suddenly, the streets seemed to explode: every social group paraded its own frustrations, unprecedented rioting took place, and the government – already disconnected from the organised Left and the middle classes – was clearly bewildered. Then came the narrow victory in the presidential elections in October 2014, accompanied by a significant shift of Congress to the Right. This was rapidly followed by a shift of economic policies towards neoliberalism, and by a new wave of bitter demonstrations against the government. What now?

The first challenge for the Brazilian Left is to appreciate what has been achieved in the last decade. The second challenge, inseparable from the first, is to recognise the shortcomings of the PT administrations and identify where progress is most urgent.

The economic, social and political achievements of the administrations led by Lula and Dilma are in no way revolutionary, but they are real enough, both for the workers and for the national economy. The fragilities of Dilma's administration are due, in part, to her personal style, the increasing fragility of her parliamentary base, her isolation from the organised workers and the middle class, the dysfunctionalities of the political system, widely held perceptions that politics is inherently corrupt, the legal straitjacket that makes it painfully difficult to spend public money, the growing activism of a conservative judiciary, media hostility, and the depth and extent of the remaining inequalities in the country. Dilma's fragilities are also due to the *achievements* of the PT administrations, which have raised the expectations of the workers and the poor much faster than their income or the state's capacity to deliver public goods. The economic slowdown has also created the impression – likely well founded – that the cycle of prosperity which started with Lula has become exhausted, leading to a pervasive sense of dissatisfaction.

It follows, in summary, that the new wave of social protests is the outcome of three distinct processes. First, it results from a confluence of dissatisfactions. The upper middle class has lost much through the recent improvements in income distribution and the democratisation of the state, and finance has lost because of the policy inflection towards neo-developmentalism. Finance is clear about its own losses, and it seeks to rebalance the books through the perpetuation of a 'fear of inflation' leading to fiscal contraction, higher real interest rates and better returns on its assets. In contrast, the upper middle class has no clear understanding of its predicament, and it has projected its discontent onto the state and the political system ('corruption', 'inefficiency', and the 'domination of politics by the PT'), and the threat posed by inflation to its standard of living. These are purely negative platforms. In contrast, the formal and informal workers want to protect what they have achieved, and they also demand more *right now*. This confluence of frustrations is a recipe for social and political volatility.

Second, the PT has been unable to manage the demands emerging through the success of its own policies, and it is, in this sense, a victim of its own success. For example, economic growth, income distribution and the wider availability of credit and tax breaks to domestic industry have led to an explosion in automobile sales (see above), while woefully insufficient investment in infrastructure and in public transport has created traffic gridlocks in many large cities. Rapid urbanisation has overwhelmed the electricity, water and sanitation systems, leading to power cuts and repeated disasters in the rainy season. Public health and education have expanded, but they are widely perceived to offer poor-quality services. There has been virtually no progress on land reform, condemning millions to a life of marginality while agribusiness prospers. The press remains heavily concentrated, and it attacks the government insistently. In this sense, the protests in 2013 and 2015 were *not* primarily due to perceptions of losses, except by the upper middle class (which poured into the streets en masse). Instead, the 2013 protests were sparked by popular demands for the improvement of services that are already available but that have become completely unsatisfactory in the light of the growing expectations of the workers and the poor, while the 2015 protests have been ideologically driven by the emerging New Right. As the economy has stagnated and social and distributive conflicts have picked up, the government has found it increasingly difficult to juggle these contradictory pressures, and it shows signs of running out of steam.

It is impossible to address these challenges purely institutionally, without the aggressive deployment of public resources for strategic ends and the mobilisation of the working class to confront the traditional elites. However, these destabilising options were never considered by the PT administrations, and the scope for their deployment has narrowed down significantly since the 2014 elections. Instead, the PT has systematically chosen a gradualist strategy including minimal legislative and regulatory changes and, until recently, as little involvement by the popular organisations as possible. The recent protests suggest that this strategy may be exhausted, and it may even help to paralyse the government.

Third, the protests have revealed a deep disconnect between most social classes and fractions and their political structures of representation. The demonstrations were, generally, against politics as a whole, rather than focusing on specific administrations or political leaders. It is also sobering for the radical Left to realise that there were no mass demands for socialism: discontent is high, but revolution remains off the working-class agenda, and the recent waves of demonstrations have done little to bring the idea of radical changes to the table.

CONCLUSION

This chapter has reviewed the economic and political transitions in Brazil, and traced their macro-economic implications during the 'Lula moment'. The two transitions have largely dismantled the production systems established during ISI and the corresponding social structures and patterns of employment. The Brazilian economy has become structurally more dependent on foreign trade, investment and technology, and the country's productive base has shifted away from the long-term requirements of national accumulation, and towards the short-term imperatives of global accumulation. These outcomes were tempered but not fully reversed by the federal administrations led by the Workers' Party and, in this important sense, the 'Lula moment' has been limited and it may be exhausted.

Despite their limitations, the Lula and Dilma administrations have achieved significant gains for the workers and the poor. Such progress has been important, but it remains insufficient to satisfy the distributive and democratic aims of the Brazilian workers and the Left. Brazil remains one of the most unequal countries in the world and, clearly, more could have been achieved since 2003. However, the severe obstacles faced by Lula's and Dilma's administrations suggest that a more ambitious agenda would have been feasible only through the mobilisation of the working class to confront the traditional elites and the aggressive deployment of public resources to fund faster welfare gains and deliver strategic investments. These transformative options were never considered by these administrations, which have chosen, instead, a gradualist strategy supported by minimal legislative and regulatory changes. The scope for continuing along this path has narrowed down significantly since the 2014 elections, and it remains unclear how the second Dilma administration will respond to this constraint.

A new policy agenda for the Left can be based on the government's recognition that it has failed to improve living conditions in urban areas sufficiently rapidly, and that further improvements in these areas, and in growth and distribution more generally, require not only technocratic solutions with a progressive character, but the integration of left social movements into the policymaking process. This could help to strengthen and radicalise the political agenda, increase the legitimacy of the administration's policies, and expand the mass base of the government. This would also incorporate the most significant lesson of the recent protests for the Left: that the careful choice of targets, organisation, and dedication to the struggle and persistence can bring important successes. The mass demands for the reduction of transport fares have put public services at the top of the political agenda. This is a massively popular area of struggle, directly affecting tens of millions of people. However, and beyond that, the demonstrations have been a political school for a new generation of workers, with potentially far-reaching consequences.

NOTES

1   The system of accumulation is determined by the economic structures and institutional arrangements that typify the process of capital accumulation in a specific region, in a certain period of time. This is a relatively concrete concept, with no direct relationship with relatively abstract concepts such as mode of regulation (Aglietta 1979; Boyer 1990).

2   For an overview of the ways in which neoliberalism imposes a particular modality of social discipline, see Brown (2003) and Dardot and Laval (2013).

3   For a critical review of participatory budgeting and its limitations, see Santos (1998) and Souza (2001).

4   Neo-developmentalism draws upon several heterodox traditions, especially the evolutionary, post-Keynesian and structuralist schools. It suggests that economic policies should aim beyond the neoliberal goal of monetary stability and focus, instead, on a broader concept of macro-economic stability supported by growth-promoting monetary, fiscal, financial, exchange rate and wage policies (Morais and Saad-Filho 2011, 2012).

5   The case of the MST is especially significant, because this is the most important radical left-wing mass organisation in Brazil. In contrast, the far-left parties are relatively small, and they have been largely ineffective in terms of their own programmatic ambitions. The MST has been frustrated and alienated by the administrations led by Lula and Dilma, which have made very little progress toward land reform. Nevertheless, the MST maintains its critical support to the PT because of the political spaces opened at the federal level by these governments, and because of the threats posed by the return to power of the PSDB and its allies.

6   For a detailed analysis, see Saad-Filho and Boito (forthcoming 2016).

7   See monthly employment survey, www.ibge.gov.br.

8   These are people in households with per capita income below the poverty line, which is defined as twice the line of extreme poverty. The latter is determined by the cost of a food basket including the minimum calories recommended by the UN Food and Agriculture Organization (FAO) and the World Health Organization (WHO) (see www.ipeadata.gov.br). Note that '[i]f Brazil were to implement a poverty line at the level currently used in the European Union – 50 per cent of median per capita income – the current poverty rate would soar to 40 per cent … In 2011, median per capita income in Brazil amounted to only 466 reais a month, around $240; this … means that two-fifths of the … population lives with a per capita

monthly income of less than $120' (Lavinas 2013: 31).

9   Former president Lula has famously insisted that, during the last decade, much has changed in the homes of the poor in terms of access to consumer goods. However, once they step outside, they find that nothing has changed in terms of public goods and services; see Saad-Filho (2013).

10   For contrasting left-wing analyses of the elections, see the interview by Maria Orlanda Pinassi at http://www.correiocidadania.com.br/index.php?option=com_content&view=article&id=10128:manchete081014&catid=25:politica&Ite mid=47, and Emir Sader's analysis at http://www.cartamaior.com.br/?/Blog/Blog-do-Emir/Por-que-a-Dilma-quase-perdeu-E-o-que-fazer-para-nao-correr-mais-esse-risco-/2/32201. The Brazilian Left generally agrees that the government suffered the consequences of 12 years in power and the adverse turn of the global economy, and it was penalised for having failed to push through more radical reforms of the economy and the media. It is not clear how these challenges can be overcome, especially given the right-wing shift in the composition of Congress in 2014.

REFERENCES

Abreu, M., Bevilacqua, A. and Pinho, D. 2000. 'Import substitution and growth in Brazil, 1890s–1970s'. In *An Economic History of Latin America (Vol.3)*, edited by E. Cárdenas, J. Ocampo and R. Thorp. London: Palgrave.

Aglietta, M. 1979. *The Theory of Capitalist Regulation: The US Experience*. London: Verso.

Ayers, A. and Saad-Filho, A. 2014. 'Democracy against neoliberalism: paradoxes, limitations, transcendence', *Critical Sociology*, 41 (4/5): 597–618.

Bastos, E.K.X. 2012. *Distribuição Funcional da Renda no Brasil: Estimativas Anuais e Construção de Uma Série Trimestral*, Texto para Discussão IPEA, No. 1702. Brasília: IPEA.

Boito, A. 2003. 'A hegemonia neoliberal no governo Lula', *Crítica Marxista*, 17: 1–16.

Boito, A. 2012. 'Governos Lula: a Nova Burguesia Nacional no Poder'. In *Política e Classes Sociais no Brasil dos Anos 2000*, edited by A. Boito and A. Galvão. São Paulo: Alameda.

Boyer, R. 1990. *A Teoria da Regulação: Uma Análise Crítica*. São Paulo: Nobel.

Brown, W. 2003. 'Neo-liberalism and the end of liberal democracy', *Theory & Event* 7 (1). Accessed 16 July 2015, https://muse.jhu.edu/login?auth=0&type=summary&url=/journals/theory_and_event/v007/7.1brown.html.

Castro, J.A., Ribeiro, J.A.C., Chaves, J.V. and Duarte, B.C. 2012. 'Gasto Social Federal: Prioridade Macroeconômica no Período 1995–2010', *IPEA Nota Técnica* No. 9.

Chaves, J.V. and Ribeiro, J.A.C. 2012. 'Gasto Social Federal: Uma Análise da Execução Orçamentária de 2011', *IPEA Nota Técnica* No. 13.

Dardot, P. and Laval, C. 2013. *The New Way of the World: On Neoliberal Society*. London: Verso.

Hall, A. 2008. 'Brazil's Bolsa Família: a double-edged sword?', *Development and Change*, 39 (5): 799–822.

Lavinas, L. 2013. '21st century welfare', *New Left Review*, 84: 5–40.

Mattei, L. 2012. 'Políticas Públicas de Combate à Pobreza no Brasil: O Caso do Programa Bolsa Família', *Revista da Sociedade Brasileira de Economia Política*, 33: 147–176.

Morais, L. and Saad-Filho, A. 2005. 'Lula and the continuity of neoliberalism in Brazil: strategic choice, economic imperative or political schizophrenia?', *Historical Materialism*, 13 (1): 3–31.

Morais, L. and Saad-Filho, A. 2011. 'Brazil beyond Lula: forging ahead or pausing for breath?', *Latin American Perspectives*, 38 (2): 31–44.

Morais, L. and Saad-Filho, A. 2012. 'Neo-developmentalism and the challenges of economic policy-making under Dilma Rousseff', *Critical Sociology*, 38 (6): 789–798.

Morais, L., Saad-Filho, A. and Coelho, W. 1999. 'Financial liberalisation, currency instability and crisis in Brazil: another plan bites the dust', *Capital & Class*, 68: 9–14.

Paes de Barros, R., Grosner, D. and Mascarenhas, A. 2012. *Vozes da Classe Média: Caderno 2 – Desigualdade, Heterogeneidade e Diversidade*. Brasília: Presidência da República.

Pochmann, M. 2010. 'Estrutura Social no Brasil: Mudanças Recentes', *Serviço Social & Sociedade* ,104: 637–649.

Pochmann, M. 2011. 'Políticas Sociais e Padrão de Mudanças no Brasil durante o Governo Lula', *SER Social*, 13 (28): 12–40.

Pochmann, M. 2012. *Nova Classe Média?* São Paulo: Boitempo.

Pomar, W. 2013. 'Debatendo Classes e Luta de Classes no Brasil'. Accessed 15 July 2015, novo.fpabramo.org.br/sites/default/files/fpa-discute-01.pdf.

Saad-Filho, A. 2007. 'There is life beyond the Washington Consensus: an introduction to pro-poor macroeconomic policies', *Review of Political Economy*, 19 (4): 513–537.

Saad-Filho, A. 2013. 'Mass protests under "Left Neoliberalism": Brazil, June-July 2013', *Critical Sociology*, 39 (5): 657–669.

Saad-Filho, A. and Boito, A. (forthcoming 2016). 'Brazil: The débâcle of the PT and the rise of the "New Right"', in *Socialist Register*, edited by L. Panitch and G. Albo. London: Merlin Press.

Saad-Filho, A., Iannini, F. and Molinari, E. 2007. 'Neoliberalism and democracy in Argentina and Brazil'. In *Political Economy of Latin America: Recent Issues and Performance*, edited by P. Arestis and M. Sawyer. London: Palgrave.

Saad-Filho, A. and Morais, L. 2014. 'Mass protests: Brazilian spring or Brazilian malaise?' In *Socialist Register*, edited by L. Panitch, G. Albo and V. Chibber. London: Merlin Press.

Santos, B.S. 1998. 'Participatory budgeting in Porto Alegre: towards a redistributive democracy', *Politics & Society*, 26 (4): 461–510.

Singer, A. 2010. 'A Segunda Alma do Partido dos Trabalhadores', *Novos Estudos Cebrap*, 88: 101–127.

Singer, A. 2014. 'Rebellion in Brazil: social and political complexion of the June events', *New Left Review*, 85: 19–37.

Souza, C. 2001. 'Participatory budgeting in Brazilian cities: limits and possibilities in building democratic institutions', *Environment & Urbanization*, 13 (1): 159–184.

Tible, J. 2013. 'O Fenômeno Político do Lulismo e a Construção de uma Nova Classe Social'. Accessed 15 July 2015, novo.fpabramo.org.br/sites/default/files/ed01-fpa-discute.pdf.

7

THE GLOBAL FINANCIAL CRISIS AND 'RESILIENCE': THE CASE OF INDIA

Sumangala Damodaran

The global financial and economic crisis that unfolded from 2008 onwards in the epicentre of capitalism appeared to have affected large 'emerging' economies such as India and China less in its initial phase. This was explained by some experts using a 'decoupling' hypothesis, where it was hypothesised that the high growth rates of these economies did not seem to be affected by turbulence in the international economy, particularly the crisis in the US economy. While the idea of decoupling had its origins in the explanations for India's and China's supposed relative immunity, it was also used to explain the cases of Brazil and other Latin American countries regarding the independence of their growth rates from the growth rate of the US (Wyrobek and Stanczyk 2013).[1] In fact, for over a year from when the crisis unfolded, it appeared that many emerging Asian economies, especially India and China, would not only remain relatively insulated from the crisis, but would also play a major role in moderating the global downturn and paving the way for a worldwide recovery.

Several features distinguished the recent crisis from the various financial crises that affected mostly emerging economies in different parts of the world in the phase of globalisation. Firstly, the origin of the crisis was at the core of capitalism, in the US economy, rather than in emerging markets that were typically perceived as more vulnerable. The rapid spread of the crises' contagion to the entire global economy differed from previous crises that were usually confined to one region or a small number of countries. Indeed, the intensity of the crisis was revealed as a complex financial entanglement exposing the fragility of even supposedly healthy institutions and countries. This global crisis spread rapidly and extensively to economic agents, sectors and economies that were previously perceived to be relatively immune. The fact that the crisis could not be blamed on faulty domestic policies of 'errant' governments in emerging economies, as had happened previously with crises in Asia, Latin America and Russia, called into serious question the rationale for full openness and complete reliance on market signals in economic activity under neoliberal economic regimes.

In such a scenario, when large parts of the globe were reeling from the impact of the crisis by the latter half of 2008, the idea and supposed evidence for decoupling in some parts of the world, particularly India and China, also allowed for the argument that these emerging economies had offered a new model of successful and sustainable growth based on economic reforms. Particularly in the case of India and China, the new model that was being referred to increasingly consisted of being able to break out of the stagnation of pre-reform economic regimes on the one hand, while maintaining prudence with regard to financial deregulation on the other.

India's 'success' in withstanding the crisis thus drew attention to the monetary and financial management methods adopted by its central bank, the Reserve Bank of India (RBI). Joseph Stiglitz stated:

> ... your policy makers, particularly the Reserve Bank of India, are already doing a great job. I wish the US Federal Reserve displayed the same understanding of the role of regulation that the RBI has done, at least so far ... India was one of the countries that resisted the wholesale deregulation movement that the United States had been exporting ... They [India] did it against political pressure ... and now I think the financial markets are thankful that they did resist those pressures. The result is that India's financial markets are in better shape than they would have been if they had engaged in the kind of wholesale deregulation that the United States engaged in.[2]

Further, by 2011, advocates of the Indian success story focused again on the recovery of the growth rate from 2009/10 onwards. One leading academic noted:

From all accounts, except for the agricultural sector initially … economic recovery seems to be well underway. Economic growth stood at 8.6 percent during fiscal year 2010/11 per the advance estimates of CSO [the Central Statistics Office] released on February 7, 2011. GDP (gross domestic product) growth for 2009/10 per quick estimates of January 31, 2011 was placed at 8 percent. The recovery in GDP growth for 2009/10, as indicated in the estimates, was broad based. Seven out of eight sectors/sub-sectors show a growth rate of 6.5 percent or higher. The exception, as anticipated, is agriculture and allied sectors where the growth rate needs to be higher and sustainable over time. Sectors including mining and quarrying; manufacturing; and electricity, gas and water supply have significantly improved their growth rates at over 8 percent in comparison with 2008/09. When compared to countries across the world, India stands out as one of the best performing economies. Although there was a clear moderation in growth from 9 percent levels to 7+ percent soon after the crisis hit, in 2010/11, at 8.6 percent, GDP growth is nearing the pre-crisis levels and this pace makes India the fastest growing major economy after China. (Bajpai 2011: 11)

The nature of India's financial deregulation and the stability of its growth process is the evidence that is cited above as being indicative of India's relative immunity on the one hand and its bounce-back after some turbulence experienced on the other. Even if the decoupling hypothesis were seen to be irrelevant, orthodox evaluations observe the 2008 financial crisis as a mere interruption in a highly successful growth path because of the interconnectedness of countries under globalised regimes, and not as something that calls into question the features of India's growth process or the economic reforms regime.

This chapter attempts an evaluation of the 2008 financial crisis on the Indian economy, locating it in the trajectory of Indian capitalist development and the dynamics of the accumulation process, particularly from the time when neoliberal reforms were initiated in the 1980s. The chapter argues the following. First, the growth rate of the Indian economy from the 1980s, while sustained over a long period of time, has also been characterised by, for example, structural features such as high inequality, low levels of (mostly poor-quality) employment growth as well as rising and unsustainable current account deficits. Second, the fragility as well as the built-in inequity of the Indian growth process was apparent even before the world crisis broke out and its manifestations began to be seen in terms of economic slowdown, slow growth in consumption demand and in the numbers of people who could be classified as 'poor and vulnerable' in the high-growth phase. Third, even if the 'decoupling' hypothesis may have appeared to be true for a certain period, the Indian economy was affected through trade, finance and export channels, calling into question the degree of supposed immunity, and reflecting the vulnerability induced by the overall economic reform process as well as its class dynamics. Fourth, the structural constraints inherent to the globalisation and growth process are far from being addressed by the policy interventions that followed the crisis, while even partially sustainable or mitigating alternatives are not being implemented.

ECONOMIC REFORMS AND STRUCTURAL FEATURES OF INDIA'S GROWTH PROCESS

The Indian economy has experienced high growth rates over more than three decades. This growth experience has been lauded, first for being able to break out of what was termed the 'Hindu rate of growth' of 3.5 per cent per annum that characterised the period until the early 1980s,[3] and second, along with China, for setting an example for emerging economies to reap the advantages of globalisation. Between 1980 and 1990 and in the decade 1990–2000, the decadal growth rate rose from 5.38 per cent to 5.58 per cent, and then jumped to 5.99 per cent by the period 2000–2005. In fact, annual growth rates remained above eight per cent for several years between 1999 and 2000, and 2004 and 2005 (Dutt and Rao 2000; Government of India 2000–2009).

The so-called break in the growth trajectory occurred in the 1980s. India broke away from a policy regime that was characterised by relatively dirigiste policies and initiated partial economic reforms in the foreign trade and industrial sectors, under what came to be known as the New Economic Policies (NEP). It was argued, in radical analyses of the growth process from the 1980s, that a very serious demand constraint was previously generated by the low purchasing power of the vast majority of the people, engaged particularly in the agrarian economy. This was counteracted to some extent, from the 1980s onwards, by purchasing power in the hands of a middle class constituted by the wealthier agriculturists, employees in public enterprises and in the service sector, which had started contributing to more than half of the GDP by then.

Patnaik (1985) argued that a persistently slower rate of industrial growth, generated by the demand constraint and by slowing down public investment,

> put a damper on the investment outlook of the big bourgeoisie ... it has attempted to break out of the shackles of the constricted home market by setting up projects abroad, by entering the international market from its home base and by entering new avenues, eg., certain luxury consumption goods, for which a pent-up demand has built up in the economy over the years. For many of these options however it needs to collaborate with metropolitan capital, and it also needs the lifting of a number of controls in the economy. Just as controls in a growing market can be an instrument for preempting rivals and building up monopoly positions, likewise decontrol in a sluggish market with entrenched monopoly positions can be a means for the monopolists to oust others. (Patnaik 1985: 12–13)

In this set of partial reforms which focused primarily on increasing trade openness and industrial delicensing under the NEP, policies were rolled out that provided high incentives to 'sunrise' industries and services that would be consumed by a burgeoning middle class. These 'sunrise' industries, such as consumer durables and automobiles, were in contrast to basic industries under import substitution industrialisation (ISI). Kohli (2006) termed this the pro-business policy shift by the Indian state, referring to the Indian state's changing role since 1980, especially the prioritising of economic growth and a slow but steady embrace of Indian capital as the main factor ruling all. This stood in contrast to a supposedly socialist or pro-poor policy. Thus, there was an attempt to mitigate the large demand constraint that had put brakes on the growth process by the late 1970s by the demand from a burgeoning middle class. The public-sector bureaucracy was a significant part of this middle class. The class also included groups of 'intermediate classes' (constituted by self-employed groups, small- and medium-enterprise owners, traders in urban areas and middle peasants in the rural areas), as well as a whole range of traditionally dominant classes, in other words, the rich peasantry and the big bourgeoisie. The state, which had functioned ambivalently with respect to often conflicting dominant-class interests while also appearing to take on a broadly developmentalist role in the dirigiste phase, thus began to gradually abandon the pro-poor agenda from the mid eighties.

The major economic regime shift took place in 1991, when India introduced market-oriented economic reforms in most of its sectors and increased its openness to the global economy. The reform package, implemented in steps, consisted of what are known as 'first generation reforms' in the literature. These reforms involved extensive trade reforms, domestic financial-sector reforms, agricultural opening up, almost complete industrial delicensing, liberalisation of foreign investment, both direct and indirect, and disinvestment of public-sector enterprises. In analysing the class forces that pushed for major reforms, implemented under standard Stabilisation and Structural Adjustment Programmes initiated by the World Bank and International Monetary Fund, Patnaik (1985) argued that even domestic monopoly capital would be averse to blanket reforms and might in fact resist policies such as complete import liberalisation. However, a so-called consensus was beginning to be forced on the economy. In this, the groups that pushed for the reforms were new business houses which were on the rise, aspiring to break existing monopoly positions in the domestic market with the help of metropolitan capital, an 'upstart' group of Indian capitalists (many non-resident and many resident with large assets abroad) and international financial institutions.

> The essential point about liberalisation is that it represents a move towards greater accommodation with metropolitan capital in a situation of economic crisis. This move, spearheaded by certain sections of upstart big bourgeoisie, draws qualified support from the entrenched big bourgeoisie in the context of the crisis, and seriously threatens not only the economic position of the working people, but also that of large sections of petty bourgeoisie and non-monopoly bourgeoisie. Greater penetration of the domestic market by metropolitan capital which such liberalisation entails and which even domestic monopoly capital is worried about, must lead to the going under of large sections of non-monopoly capital whose staying power is necessarily limited. This would be the case not only in industries where metropolitan capital and products directly enter, eg., electronics, auto-ancillaries, etc., but also in other industries, from which demand shifts away in favour of the new and sophisticated products turned out under the aegis of metropolitan capital. (Patnaik 1985: 13)

Indeed, this came true, with the whole package of reforms being initiated in response to a foreign exchange and balance of payments crisis in 1991.

The structural break in India's growth trajectory, therefore, came before the formal initiation of comprehensive economic reforms in 1991. The break came with several structural features. First, in a primarily agrarian country, where over half the population still earns its livelihood from agriculture and allied activities, the growth rate of agriculture remained meagre, even as the break-through was made in overall growth in the economy. Between 1991 and 1992 and 2006 and 2007, during the economic reform phase, the compound annual growth rate of agriculture was a mere 1.3 per cent (Vakulabharanam, Zhong and Jinjun 2010), implying that the high overall growth of the economy may have been quite independent of the largest segment of the population. However, while the economy may have grown irrespective of conditions in the agricultural sector, India also faced a serious food crisis as production fell and food inflation hit high levels. More than 271 000 farmer suicides occurred between 1995 and 2011, according to the official National Crime Records Bureau, with an aggravation in the yearly figures from 2001 onwards.[4] Economic reforms resulted in a reduction in public investment in agriculture, as well as partial withdrawal of state support to various small farming groups. Especially before 2004/05, the cutback in subsidies and the slow growth of subsidised agricultural credit on the one hand, and the introduction of trade liberalisation on the other, which caused agricultural output prices to fall for some key agricultural commodities, caused a 'double squeeze' of the farming community (Vakulabharanam, Zhong and Jinjun 2010).[5]

Second, in the phase of very high growth, particularly from 1999/2000 to 2003/04, the proportion of people who were found to be 'poor and vulnerable' was as high as seventy-seven per cent of the population. In a highly publicised 2007 report by the National Commission for Enterprises in the Unorganised Sector (NCEUS), it was shown that in 2004/05, a large proportion of the population was consuming less than half a dollar a day per capita, less than half of the US$1 norm fixed by the World Bank for the poorest countries of the world (Government of India 2007). In fact, India did not enter such a category by the reckoning of the World Bank, with its absolute poverty level being determined at US$2 a day. Indeed, official poverty estimates of the government projected a fall in numbers of people in absolute poverty based on income, but in consumption terms more than three-quarters of the population had abysmal consumption levels. This was also reflected in a significant change in the propensity to consume, which has an important bearing on GDP growth. Between 2005/06 and 2006/07, growth of private consumption declined by as much as 1.6 per cent even though there was a 0.5 per cent rise in GDP growth. The slowdown of consumption in relation to aggregate income was also due to the decline in personal disposable income as a ratio of GDP, apart from the high numbers of poor and vulnerable people. Additionally, there was an almost four per cent increase in the Gini coefficient between 1993/94 and 2004/05 (Vakulabharanam, Zhong and Jinjun 2010).

The coupling of poor agricultural performance and low levels of consumption may have established the conditions for a classic underconsumption crisis characterised by low effective demand from large segments of the population. However, the factors that mitigated the possible adverse effects of low mass consumption were also seen as structural features of the growth process, in turn generating potential constraints that were expressed with the outbreak of the financial crisis.

Indeed, the so-called independence of the growth rate from conditions in the agricultural sector, even as the majority of people continued to be dependent on it, was based on the argument that India had acquired lucrative export markets, especially in services, which sustained high growth rates for long periods of time. It was also argued that the existence and consumption pattern of the large Indian middle class, consisting to a large extent of salaried people in the government and the public sector, delayed the potential dampening effects of low consumption by the large agrarian majority on the growth rate. Both of these factors, although initiated through partial industrial and trade reforms from the second half of the 1980s, as mentioned earlier, became structural features with the onset of the formal economic reform package.

Thus, third, India experienced substantial opening up in response to economic reforms that were formally initiated in 1991. This, for one, was reflected in very high trade ratios as well as external financial liberalisation as its economy opened up, with the combined ratio of exports and imports to GDP increasing to more than fifty per cent even as the economy began to slow down. Another reflection of this was seen in extremely high import elasticities and a consequently high current account deficit over the reform period, creating a foreign exchange constraint from trading activity.

Financial opening brought an end to a policy regime which was characterised by segregated banking, with preferential credit availability for agriculture, small businesses and other 'priority' sectors, and restrictions on the flows of overseas capital. However, banking per se, in comparison to the extent of liberalisation in other parts of the world, was subjected to greater prudential norms. For example, due to the high degree of exposure of the banking system to the real estate sector, banks were advised to establish a proper risk management system to contain the risks involved, to formulate specific policies around limits to exposure, collaterals and margins. Similarly, with the strong growth of consumer credit and the volatility in the capital markets, the Reserve Bank of India increased the risk weight for consumer credit and capital market exposures.

However, the changes in the financial sector were substantial, even though the banking sector had not been as exposed to financial fragility as elsewhere. Successive reforms that were implemented over the next decade and a half introduced several changes in India's financial sector. For example, foreign institutional investors were allowed free access to stock markets, bans on derivative trading were lifted and they were treated an a par with securities in stock markets, thus ending the restrictions imposed earlier in terms of the Securities Contract and Regulation Act. Traded derivative markets were simultaneously opened where options, futures and swaps on interest rates and currencies could be traded, and the ban on commodity futures was also lifted. India's balance of payments subsequently saw extremely favourable portfolio investment flows, rendering the overall foreign exchange position comfortable, but highly volatile and susceptible to disturbances in international financial markets. As was the case with other emerging economies in the globalisation period, cross-border flows of capital, especially those with short-term duration, have today gained a large presence in India's capital market. Short-term capital flows, highly incentivised under the liberalised policy regime, have also caused a lot of problems for Indian monetary authorities, especially in achieving the twin goals of managing a competitive real exchange rate along with some degree of autonomy in catering to the goals set for the real domestic economy (Sen 2010).

Further, since financialisation of markets, an offshoot of financial deregulation, does not remain confined to financial assets alone, the systemic potential for fragility and spillover effects to the real economy also existed in India. As channels of speculation are opened up for short-term capital, it spills over across markets which include financial assets, real estate and commodity exchanges and this became evident in India's case as well, even if the much talked about sub-prime loan crisis kind of situation that was seen in the housing markets of the US was not seen in India. As Sen (2010: 9) points out:

On the whole, official policies in India to manage the surges in speculative short term capital inflows in the money market have not been able to arrest its spillover to the commodity market, which continues to provide profits to financiers on futures and forward trading. The end result has been the unrelenting inflation as at present, in food prices which affects the survival for large sections of the population in India ... The benefits of financial deregulation remain confined to those who can speculate in markets, while the costs are borne by those who are affected by speculation on commodity prices and cuts in social sector spending by the government.

Fourth, the growth process was characterised by rising capital intensity and slow growth in employment, as emphasised by the NCEUS. It was seen that in the liberalised environment, the product composition of exports was in favour of higher capital and skill intensity (Chandrasekhar 2009; Goldar 2009). Further, it was also seen, in a situation where mass demand was constrained, that the expansion in domestic demand was in favour of products demanded by high-income groups, such as automobiles and white goods, whose consumption grew at a much higher rate due to rising incomes and credit-induced expansion in demand. These product groups on average tend to be more capital intensive and generate less employment. For example, Bhaduri (2008) notes:

> Jamshedpur steel plant of the Tatas employed 85,000 workers in 1991 to produce one million tonnes of steel worth $ 0.8 million. In 2005, the production rose to five million tonnes, worth about $ five million, while employment fell to 44,000. In short, output increased approximately by a factor of five, employment dropped by a factor of half, implying an increase in labour productivity by a factor of 10. Similarly, Tata Motors in Pune reduced the number of workers from 35,000 to 21,000 but increased the production of vehicles from 1,29,000 [129 000 in the international numbering system] to 3,11,500 [311 500] between 1999 and 2004, implying a labour productivity increase by a factor of four. Stephen Roach, chief economist of Morgan Stanley, reports similar cases of Bajaj motor cycle factory in Pune. In the mid-1990s the factory employed 24,000 workers to produce one million units of two-wheelers. Aided by Japanese robotics and Indian information technology, in 2004,

10,500 workers turned out 2.4 million units – more than double the output with less than half the labour force.

Fifth, the high growth period saw the share of wages in value added consistently declining and real wages of workers being virtually stagnant. Also, with the worsening distribution of income between those engaged in what came to be referred to as 'sunrise sectors' and the vast and growing majority of the populace working in unorganised, informal enterprises, as well as the rise in prices of articles entering the consumption basket of workers, the impact on consumption demand was significant, as noted.

What these structural features meant, in combination, was that the fragility of the growth process was beginning to be felt even before the actual crisis broke out in the advanced countries. The Indian economy was already in a highly demand-constrained situation, reflected in the low levels of consumption of the majority of the population, and dependent on sources of demand from the external sector and on capital flows that are inherently volatile, which were affected by the financial crisis.

Macro-economist Mihir Rakshit (2010) outlined the domestic as well as the external features of the Indian economy before and during the crisis. India's GDP growth, he argued, had started decelerating in the first quarter of 2007/08, nearly six months before the outbreak of the US financial turbulence and considerably ahead of the surge of recessionary tendencies in all developed countries from August to September 2008. The slowdown, which occurred in industrial and service sector growth, was not compensated enough by agricultural growth, which picked up by 2007/08, lending greater credence to the argument that the Indian economy's growth rate has been quite independent of the agricultural sector's performance.[6]

IMPACT OF THE CRISIS

After the outbreak of the crisis it was concluded that the Indian banking sector was unaffected to a large extent because of prudent regulations, a proactive regulator, and its very limited operations outside India or exposure to subprime lending by foreign investment banks. A higher provisioning requirement on commercial bank lending to the real estate sector, imposed by the

RBI, helped to curb the growth of a real estate price bubble. This, it is argued, has been one of the few global examples of a counter-cyclical capital provisioning requirement by any central bank. Further, Indian banks were not overly exposed to sub-prime lending, allowing them greater protection.

The decoupling hypothesis, however, appeared to be flawed as India began to experience the impact of the crisis soon enough. The direct impact was seen in the capital account of the balance of payments, in remittances and exports within the current account and in the exchange rate, all significant variables from the point of view of the neoliberal policy regime. Further, even if banks were not affected in the same way as elsewhere, in India the real economy was affected through various channels and banks were impacted by the slowing down of the economy. Rakshit (2010: 100) notes:

> ... despite the resilience of Indian banks, the global financial meltdown has had some adverse consequences for credit-financed economic activities. Widespread banking troubles created a serious credit crunch for traders. Instances of banks delaying or not honouring guarantees extended to traders became more frequent. Domestic exporters were also finding it increasingly difficult to secure credit ... The difficulty of importing components or raw materials directly required for producing exportables also has had a negative impact on domestic demand. Again, with the globalisation of the supply chain in the production process, a disruption anywhere in the cross-border flow of intermediate inputs tends to create a disproportionately large effect on output and employment in both the domestic and the international economy.

The capital account, whose net balances reflect capital inflows and outflows for a country, saw a decline in three crucial inflows – foreign direct investment (FDI), foreign indirect (or portfolio) investment (FII) and external commercial borrowings (ECB) – which were adversely affected by the turmoil in the financial markets in advanced economies. Between September 2008 and 2009, the capital that Indian corporates managed to raise in international markets fell by over a half. Portfolio investment was extremely volatile and largely negative (indicating net outflows) from the beginning of 2008, and this dominated the overall foreign investment trend. Likewise, FDI inflows witnessed negative growth in 2008/09. The sluggishness of the inflows of FDI and ECBs, combined with the massive outflow of FII, resulted in a significant deterioration of India's capital account following the crisis, eroding the capital account surplus.

With the capital account of India's balance of payments turning negative after a long period, it brought forth an important vulnerability in the economy that arose from the deregulatory processes that had taken place in the period of economic reforms. Large inflows of short-term capital in the form of portfolio investments, which are also volatile and unpredictable, have been encouraged as part of financial deregulation. However, monetary authorities in India had also been active to arrest what they considered untoward effects of these flows on money supply or exchange rates. Their role in creating a capital account surplus and keeping India's foreign exchange position comfortable thus also carries the downside of rendering the capital account vulnerable to shocks in international financial markets. One of the most critical aspects that came out of the crisis has been the demonstration of the fact that, as Jayadev and Kapadia (2009) note, importers of capital, especially importers who do not have the reserve currency or are not hegemonic, are always at substantially more risk than is easily seen because of the network effects of the global financial system. They argue that,

> as a result, east Asia broadly took the route of a 'neo-mercantilism'. The countries moved from being importers of capital to undervaluing their exchange rate (already low after the crisis) and earning export revenues. As export revenues soared, several developing countries became exporters of capital, especially to the US. Large developing and emerging economies, such as India, Brazil, Russia and China, as well as other countries gathered an enormous stockpile of reserves as self-insurance, although, especially in the case of Russia, such insurance appears to be rapidly being run through ... As many have noted, these self-insurance policies are enormously costly, but the cost of insurance is weighed against the benefits of security, export-driven growth, and technological development. (Jayadev and Kapadia 2009: 167)

On the current account, the main variables that were affected were remittances and exports. Remittances, an important source of inward foreign capital flows that in the past have helped to balance India's large trade account deficit and keep the current account deficit at a reasonable level, were affected from late

2008 onwards. Further, there was a steep decline in demand for India's exports in its major markets. One of India's top export categories, gems and jewellery, which was the first sector to feel pressure at the very beginning of the global meltdown, saw a sharp decline in export orders from the US and Europe, resulting in direct retrenchment of over 300 000 workers. Following this, other export-oriented sectors such as garments and textiles, leather, handicrafts, marine products, and auto components were also strongly affected (Kumar and Vashisht 2009). Exports of services, which constituted one of the main drivers of economic growth in India, also saw a steep decline, from a thirty-four per cent growth rate to less than six per cent during 2008/09.

The impact of sharply declining exports was seen in employment. The government of India's Labour Bureau stated that 500 000 jobs were lost during October–December 2008 and 1 million jobs were lost during January 2009 alone (Government of India 2013). In the agricultural sector, those producing export crops confronted collapsed prices, aggravating the abysmal conditions in the agrarian economy. Small-scale producers in all sectors were faced with the 'pincer movement' of falling demand and severe credit crunch, with actual investment being limited due to conditions in which banks are willing to lend only to the most secure borrowers, who in turn are unwilling to invest because of greater uncertainty.

These aspects, which point to ways in which a highly demand-constrained situation can lead into a seriously recessionary one, with strong multiplier effects that aggravate the dismal real conditions of the majority of the population, have been underplayed in most conventional assessments of the impact of the global crisis on India. In fact, the government has paid hardly any attention to these real conditions its response to the crisis. In turn, the so-called turnaround in terms of the growth rate and of capital flows has obfuscated the nature and extent of the impact of the crisis.

INDIA'S RESPONSE TO THE CRISIS

How did India respond to the different aspects of the crisis? The contrast with China is interesting here, with differences in the political economic understandings of the crisis, the nature of their tradable sectors, and the relative openness of their capital accounts. Thus, in contrast to China, with an export-led economy and a highly managed capital account, India, with a porous, de facto open capital account, has been faced with flows that are generated, as mentioned above, by portfolio inflows and external commercial borrowings, making the current account deficit precarious due to falling export earnings with the crisis. There has been no significant move to question the logic of financial deregulation that allows for large-scale, short-term international capital flows (Sen 2010).

As far as the domestic economy is concerned, the initial responses of the government focused on the financial rather than the fiscal side of the crisis, with the understanding that the economy was constrained by a shortage of liquidity. Thus, there were confidence-building measures to infuse liquidity into a banking system that had become very constrained, to reduce interest rates, and to provide some relief to non-bank financial institutions, particularly insurance companies. These were measures that became necessary, as Ghosh (2010) points out, not because the international contagion was spreading to the banking system but because the Indian banking system had (in a less extreme form) several of the fragilities that undermined the US banks. However, in reality, credit conditions did not ease in any significant way, because in the absence of a serious fiscal stimulus, banks' actual willingness to lend as well as borrowing by enterprises to stimulate production were constrained by stringent demand conditions.

There was a great delay in employing an expansionary fiscal stance to create more economic activity, boost demand, and thereby lift the economy from slump, in contrast, for example, to China. The government of India took an inordinately long time to announce the required fiscal stimulus and, when the much awaited fiscal package was finally announced, it turned out to be relatively small. It was less than 0.5 per cent of GDP, a tiny fiscal input where some of the most critical areas of spending that were creating serious constraints were neglected or ignored and which was, in any case, too small to have much effect. This reflected, again, an understanding that the effects of the crisis were temporary or a mere interruption in a growth process that could be sustained (Ghosh 2010). Additionally, there was little or no resource allocation to state governments, direct investment to ensure mass and middle-class housing, interventions to improve the livelihood conditions of farmers and enlargement of employment schemes to provide relief to working people as well as a macro-economic model case.

CLASS DYNAMICS AND THE HINDU FUNDAMENTALIST RIGHT-WING GOVERNMENT

With the formal adoption of wholesale economic reforms from 1991, it has been suggested that there was a consolidation of a new class structure in India (Chatterjee 2008), with the rising inequality being reflected by winners and losers in class terms. Vakulabharanam, Zhong and Jinjun (2010), in a careful study of consumption-based inequality, show that from 1993 onwards, the urban–rural divide widened considerably, with urban classes gaining over rural ones taken as a whole, even as intra-urban and intra-rural inequality also worsened. In the rural areas, marginal farmers, tenants and agricultural workers saw worsening conditions, especially in the context of the severe agrarian crisis. Urban professionals, capitalists and managers gained substantially in relative terms, making the urban areas crucial centres of worsening inequalities, even as the urban–rural divide worsened. The study notes:

> The rural intermediate classes are not quite as important in this new scheme, although their interests are usually protected, directly or indirectly. Members of this class have also unevenly moved on to urban occupations to become constituents of urban capitalist classes. The working groups (the rural poor – small and marginal farmers, agricultural workers; as well as the urban poor – unskilled urban workers) are no longer among the main foci of the state but their interests have continued to be addressed mainly through a populist mode in order to enlist their support during elections. The owners and managers in the informal sector in urban areas are quite heterogeneous and certain groups (e.g. wholesale and retail) have probably benefited (even this may not last long once liberalisation takes deep roots in these occupations) while a large section (petty vendors) has probably not. However, the employment numbers suggest that the informal sector as stated above plays the key role of absorbing employment in the face of insufficient employment opportunities in the formal sector, although this does not apparently improve the consumption levels of the informal workers. (Vakulabharanam, Zhong and Jinjun 2010: 19)

With the consolidation of entrenched dominant-class interests as well as the creation of newer groups that sustain their ideologies, the Indian state's response to the crisis, as noted, has been to view it as a temporary interruption in a successful growth strategy and a resilient developmental model.

Six years after the financial crisis broke out at the global level, what are the challenges that are faced by the broad public due to the persistence of neoliberal policies as a new right-wing Bharatiya Janata Party (BJP) government has been voted to power in India?

In May 2014, the right-wing Hindu fundamentalist government of the BJP was voted to power in India under the leadership of Prime Minister Narendra Modi, a rabid reformer and 'moderniser' with the track record of having presided over one of the worst genocides in post-independence history as chief minister of the western state of Gujarat in 2002. The BJP's rise on the electoral scene in India happened in substantial terms from 1989 and it emerged as the single largest party from the second half of the 1990s. After this rise, it was argued (for example, by Sridharan 2004; Yadav, Kumar and Heath 1999) that a new social bloc had come into existence, consisting of groups that were united by relative economic and social privilege, and was forming the support base of the BJP. Consisting of urban rich and middle classes, upper castes and rising landed peasant castes, the picture of 'shining India' consolidated these groups into the main support base of the party, which translated into a massive mandate in the 2014 elections.

The economic policies that were outlined in the BJP's election manifesto and that have unfolded under the new regime, while rhetorically enveloped in ideas of restoring 'national dignity', show equal commitment to deepening economic reforms as the previous governments, euphemistically referred to as 'minimising government' and 'maximising governance'. Specifically, this has involved enhancing the degree of privatisation of the economy, fiscal consolidation and discipline by bringing down the fiscal deficit (like under the previous governments), hikes in railway fares and freight rates, cutting down allocations to public programmes and liberalising foreign investment norms. More importantly, the commitment to deepening reforms is seen in a clear agenda for labour law reform that aims to provide incentives to private capital and further flexibilise an already flexible and vulnerable workforce. Indirect tax structure modifications aimed at improving private profitability and direct tax changes aimed at increasing the disposable incomes of the middle classes (and within them the better-off segments) have been effected in the new government's first Union Budget, which clearly indicates a continuity with previous neoliberal policies. It is unlikely, therefore, that the economic crisis and its impact on the largest segment of the population will abate and that the serious demand constraint will be eased.

ALTERNATIVES FOR GENUINE DECOUPLING

The alternative policies that have been discussed, or seem necessary in the context of the serious economic crisis, fall into two categories. First, there are those that can mitigate the effects and make them relatively manageable within the contours of the existing development strategy. Second, there are those that can point towards alternative production and consumption systems rooted in local economies and domestic markets. The policies suggested as ones that could mitigate the crisis have involved the following measures: (i) to begin with, as mentioned above, a standard Keynesian device of using an expansionary fiscal stance to create more economic activity and demand, and thereby lift the economy from slump; (ii) a shift in the focus of spending towards those that have hitherto been ignored under neoliberal policies, such as resource allocation to provincial governments, direct investment in mass and middle-class housing, employment schemes in sectors like construction; (iii) the expansion of rural employment guarantee schemes and revival of credit availability for the farming sector; (iv) the allocation of significantly increased resources towards expanding, universalising and improving the functioning of the public distribution system for essential commodities; and (v) the reversal of financial-sector liberalisation, given the huge imperfections in such markets and the ability of unregulated finance to destabilise real economies.

It is important to underscore that such policies that aim to boost demand and create purchasing power among larger segments of the population to counteract the tendencies towards underconsumption will do little to address fundamental structural inequities in the economy. It is true that public spending will be more economically effective and more welfare-improving if it is directed predominantly toward employment schemes, social spending and rural and urban infrastructure that is used by large numbers of people. However, they neglect some essential elements for moving towards a new economic paradigm that could address the structural inequities, including land reform as well as the creation of democratically accountable systems that also aim to alter consumption and production patterns in more sustainable directions.

An example of such a participatory and accountable system was seen in the south Indian state of Kerala in the 1990s under a left government led by the Communist Party of India (Marxist) (CPI[M]) where, as a unique experiment in participatory democracy, the state devolved forty per cent of its finances to local government institutions that came to be in charge of drafting local development plans along with local communities. This became possible because land reform as well as participatory politics initiated under a left government in the late 1950s and successive mobilisations created a culture of devolving developmental outcomes in response to demands from below, which in turn translated into decentralised planning involving collective mobilisation. As Williams (2008) noted, a substantial proportion of the funds allocated were for local economic development projects, mostly through cooperatives. The methods used were participatory, with local communities involved in visualising, developing and implementing these projects.

While the devolution appeared, on the face of it, as a financial decentralisation initiative, its objectives were multifaceted: to use state funds to respond to the demands from below that came from a culture of social mobilisation; to stimulate productive investments and expand a stagnant and low-growth economy in sustainable ways and at appropriate scales suited to local needs; and to combine state-based financial devolution with organisation of subordinate groups in civil society into small-scale cooperative production units. Organisationally, this involved the decentralisation of decision making to neighbourhood groups and locally elected representatives at village level through publicly visible forms of mobilisations. The planning process, decentralised up to the local level, was converted into an exercise in social mobilisation as well as decentralisation to overcome economic stagnation and deterioration in the quality of social-services delivery in the state. In an assessment of the programme's impact, Isaac and Franke (2000) argued that the process, involving collective action in decisions as well as implementation at the lowest levels, allowed for the priorities of those with poor asset positions, as well as poor skill and income positions, to become recognised and integrated into developmental priorities.

The linking of state-controlled finances with devolution rooted in participatory politics made it necessary for the state to be responsive to needs from below. It also pointed out the possibilities from redistributive development that combined allocations from above with local needs which were essential for effective service delivery as well as local development. In other words, what was attempted was the sowing of the seeds of an alternative logic of accumulation to achieve broad-based economic development.

However, these kinds of alternatives go against the grain of a standard development paradigm, particularly a neoliberal one, and do not find any voice in the existing scenario in India.

In a country where the majority of the people earn their incomes from the agrarian sector and small-scale activities, including in the manufacturing sector, it is essential to develop decentralised development models, with the Kerala experiment as one possible example, as alternatives to the neoliberal paradigm, which targets growth even as it bypasses the largest number of people in the country, as the Indian evidence clearly shows.

CONCLUSION

The Indian economy, which is supposed to have offered, as with China, an alternative model of capitalist development in recent times and which is publicised as having been impacted relatively little by the global economic crisis, is far from being so, as this chapter has attempted to demonstrate.

Apart from the low levels of consumption of more than three-fourths of the population, India is faced with an acute food crisis and food insecurity is widespread, particularly given the significant food inflation over the past few years, which continues despite large food grain stocks. In December 2013, Bloomberg tracked consumer prices in 17 Asia–Pacific economies, of which the growth rate of consumer prices was highest in India, at 9.87 per cent.[7] Growth rates of the sales of consumer goods had started declining by December 2012, but from September 2013, sales by volume started contracting. Policies of neoliberalism, which aggravated fundamental structural inequalities in the Indian accumulation process, have been continued and intensified, even after the global financial crisis is seen to have had a substantial impact. It remains to be seen whether the demand-constrained situation that should have rung alarm bells in policymakers' minds long ago will finally have a serious impact on the actual growth rate and bring some of the structural features outlined in this chapter into focus, in turn asking serious questions about the viability of the much publicised 'India growth path'.

NOTES

1   Decoupling can mean different things, as Dervis (2012) suggests. Firstly, it can refer to the divergence of the gross domestic product long-term path of emerging economies and advanced economies, which need not mean an actual divergence, but may only indicate a higher growth rate required for catch-up. Secondly, decoupling can refer to the growing differences between business cycles, or a delinking of cyclical movements especially with regard to global shocks, which can be interpreted as different stimuli and response structures in the two types of countries.

2   See Stiglitz, J. 'India is well placed to take on round 2 of recession', *The Times of India*, 10 May 2010.

3   The immediate post-independence period of 1950 to 1980, often disparagingly referred to as the years of the 'Hindu' rate of growth, had an average rate of growth of 3.56 per cent for the entire period. Although this was three times the rate of growth of the last 30 years of colonial rule, the fact remains that during the first 30 years after India's independence, the improvement in the per capita income was hardly between 1 and 1.95 per cent (Kannan and Raveendran 2009).

4   See Sainath, P. 'Farmers' suicide rates soar above the rest', *The Hindu*, 18 May 2013. Sainath, an eminent journalist, notes that even such a high figure is an underestimate due to under-reporting by some states.

5   In an agrarian sector where small farmers depend on credit from informal moneylenders in interlinked credit and output markets, farmers have had to pay much higher interest rates, compared to the rates available in financial institutions. In this process farmers also sometimes lose control over production and cropping-pattern decisions.

6   There was a significant increase in agricultural (GDP) growth, from 3.8 per cent in 2006/07 to 5.1 per cent in 2007/08. In sharp contrast, the growth in the secondary and the tertiary sectors declined from 10.6 per cent and 11.2 per cent in 2006/07 to 7.5 per cent and 11.1 per cent, respectively, in 2007/08.

7   Goyal, K. 'Rajan won't raise India rate if prices soften'. Accessed 21 March 2014, http://bloomberg.com/news/articles/2014-01-01/rajan-won-t-boost-india-rate-if-inflation-eases-adviser-says.

REFERENCES

Bajpai, N. 2011. *Global financial crisis, its impact on India and the policy response.* Working Paper No. 5, July, Columbia Global Centers, South Asia, Columbia University.

Bhaduri, A. 2008. 'Predatory growth', Development Dialogues Blog, 23 February. Accessed 17 June 2014, http://development-dialogues.blogspot.in/2008/02/amit-bhaduri-predatory-growth.html.

Chandrasekhar, C.P. 2009. 'Must banks be publicly owned?', *Economic and Political Weekly*, 44 (13): 64–71.

Chatterjee, P. 2008. 'Democracy and economic transformation in India', *Economic and Political Weekly*, 43 (16): 53–62.

Dervis, K. 2012. 'Convergence, interdependence, and divergence', *Finance and Development*, 49 (3): 10–14.

Dutt, A.K. and Rao, J.M. 2000. *Globalization and its social discontents: the case of*

India, SCEPA Working Paper series. Schwartz Center for Economic Policy Analysis (SCEPA), The New School of Social Research, New York.

Ghosh, J. 2010. 'The global financial crisis, developing countries and India'. Accessed 12 June 2014, www.networkideas.org.

Goldar, B. 2009. *Impact of trade on employment generation in manufacturing in India*. Working Paper No.E/297/2009, Institute of Economic Growth, Delhi.

Government of India. 2000–2009. Economic Survey, Department of Economic Affairs, Ministry of Finance.

Government of India. 2007. *Report on Conditions of Work and Livelihoods in the Informal Sector,* National Commission for Enterprises in the Unorganised Sector, New Delhi.

Government of India. 2013. *Indian Labour Journal*, 54 (10), Ministry of Labour and Employment, Shimla/Chandigarh.

Isaac, T. and Franke, R. 2000. *Local Democracy and Development: People's Plan Campaign for Decentralised Planning for Kerala*. New Delhi: LeftWord.

Jayadev, A. and Kapadia, A. 2009. 'When the facts change: how can the financial crisis change minds?' *Economic & Political Weekly*, 44 (13): 165–170.

Kannan, K.P. and Raveendran, G. 2009. 'Growth sans employment: a quarter century of jobless growth in India's organised manufacturing'. *Economic and Political Weekly*, 44 (10): 80–91.

Kohli, A. 2006. 'The politics of economic growth in India: 1980–2005, Part II', *Economic and Political Weekly*, 41 (14): 1361–1370.

Kumar, R. and Vashisht, P. 2009. *The global economic crisis: impact on India and policy responses*. ADB Institute Working Paper No. 164.

Patnaik, P. 1985. 'On the political economy of economic liberalisation', *Social Scientist*, 13 (7/8): 3–17.

Rakshit, M. 2010. 'India amidst the global crisis', *Economic and Political Weekly*, 44 (13): 94–106.

Sen, S. 2010. *Managing finance in emerging economies: the case of India*. Working Paper No. 2010/06. New Delhi: Institute for Studies in Industrial Development.

Sridharan, E. 2004. 'The growth and sectoral composition of India's middle class: its impact on the politics of economic liberalisation', *India Review*, 3 (4): 405–428.

Vakulabharanam, V., Zhong,W. and Jinjun, X. 2010. 'Does class count? Class structure and worsening inequality in China and India'. Paper prepared for the 31st General Conference of The International Association for Research in Income and Wealth, St. Gallen, Switzerland.

Williams, M. 2008. *The Roots of Participatory Democracy: Democratic Communists in South Africa and Kerala*. India: Palgrave Macmillan.

Wyrobek, J. and Stanczyk, Z. 2013. *Global financial crisis and decoupling hypothesis*. Working Paper Series / Social Science Research Network (SSRN). Accessed 25 May 2014, http://papers.ssrn.com/sol3/papers.cfm.

Yadav, Y., Kumar, S. and Heath, O. 1999. 'The BJP's new social bloc', *Frontline*, 16 (23): 6–19.

8

UNDERSTANDING THE LABOUR CRISIS IN SOUTH AFRICA: REAL WAGE TRENDS AND THE MINERALS–ENERGY COMPLEX ECONOMY

Niall Reddy

Three years after the massacre of mineworkers by police at Marikana, which led to waves of wildcat strikes across the economy, South Africa's labour regime remains enthralled in crisis. June 2014 saw the conclusion of the longest-ever strike in the history of South Africa's mines, involving 70 000 platinum workers over five months. It was followed immediately by 220 000 workers in the manufacturing sector, led by the country's largest and most militant union, the National Union of Metalworkers of South Africa (Numsa). At the time of writing, a special congress of the Congress of South African Trade Unions (Cosatu) had just confirmed the removal of Numsa and left-leaning former general secretary, Zwelinzima Vavi, who look set to form an alternative federation, along with eight allied unions, which is likely to be more responsive to the radical mood sweeping South African workers.

Employer groups have responded to the crisis with intensified lobbying for diluted regulation and controls on unions, rather than accommodating worker demands. For its part the government appears sympathetic to this, as we argue below, but is prevented from decisive action by the danger of losing further support at its base. Unrest in the labour market, combined with deep popular resentment over poverty, lack of delivery and corruption, is already spurring major political realignments. At the end of 2013, Numsa formally ended its participation in the African National Congress (ANC)/South African Communist Party (SACP)/Cosatu Tripartite Alliance and took the initiative to launch a united front of social movements and more radically oriented unions, which is likely to feed into a party formation at some stage. Expelled ANC dissident Julius Malema launched his party, the Economic Freedom Fighters (EFF), at Marikana in 2013, garnering more than 1.1 million votes in elections the next year on a radical platform of nationalisation and redistribution.

However, according to a dominant narrative of post-apartheid political economy, these events should be difficult to understand. Whilst some uptick in social unrest, as a result of intractable poverty and inequality has been widely predicted, the agent of this is generally presumed to be the massive 'underclass' that has been barred from participation in the formal labour market. Next to this largely youthful mass, formal-sector workers are regularly depicted as a privileged constituency of the post-apartheid dispensation, whose high wages and rigid legal protections are themselves to blame for the declining circumstances of the unemployed. What we may term the 'labour aristocracy thesis' (LAT) has various roots in state discourses, the media and academia, which we unpack below, and hence commands both scholarly and popular traction. This chapter offers a critique of the LAT, and in turn a very different understanding of major features of post-apartheid political economy and the crisis which they have produced. Using new data we show that increases in average real wages have been driven by the top of the distribution while most workers experienced wage stagnation. We sketch the political economy of these wage trends by showing how the ANC's economic policies only exacerbated extremely uneven development based on a highly financialised minerals–energy complex (MEC). The union movement, caught in fruitless corporatism, has failed to resist the effects of systemic unemployment and massive casualisation. In the last section we examine the class contours of the ruling bloc that were exposed in the Marikana massacre, and their implications for labour struggles.

THE LABOUR ARISTOCRACY THESIS

Although the apartheid system of labour control no longer matched the interests of the dominant sections of capital by the 1980s, the system of cheap labour was far from dismantled, as we show in detail below, and the more recent internationalisation and export orientation of capital renewed efforts to compete on the basis of globalised standards of wage repression. South African employers therefore remain militantly hostile to the existing labour regime, often claiming that unions constitute an existential threat to the democratic project. In the World Economic Forum's Global Competitiveness Index, based on business surveys, South Africa has featured at the bottom of 144 countries in the field of labour relations in recent years. The bellicose anti-labour attitude of capital, unjustified by the actual tempo of industrial conflict for most the democratic period, is the first pillar of the LAT.

It secures greater public reach through the role of a highly corporatised media establishment. Whatever the relative plurality in the political debate, economics and business journalism is overwhelmingly dominated by conservative theories and reflexive anti-labour attitudes.[1] It has a major function in linking economic crisis to the 'unfair demands' of workers in the public imagination and in cohering unity and class consciousness amongst South African businesspeople and elites. A major role is played by business-affiliated think tanks, which honed the skills of public and policy manipulation in the period of South Africa's 'elite transition', and more recently by private-sector 'economic hit-men' (Wittenberg and Kerr 2012).[2]

Employer propagandists have a solid backing in academia, particularly in the economics departments of South African universities which are dominated by neoclassical thought. Mainstream economic theory, nuances notwithstanding, remains overwhelmingly exercised by the belief that markets left to themselves will result in a general equilibrium and the optimum allocation of scarce resources. Methodologically, it offers no means for an understanding of the unemployment crisis rooted in the specificities of South African industrialisation and global integration. The crisis appears therefore as simply a 'market failure' on a colossal scale, the natural remedy of which is a reassertion of 'flexibility' by removing distorting regulations and union influences, and allowing the downward adjustment of wages (see Fedderke 2012 for a recent example). The same conclusion remains a constant in the reports of most international financial institutions (IFIs) and Western-dominated multilateral bodies which have a significant influence on policy (see Klein 2012).

Elsewhere, perhaps the pre-eminent theorisation of the LAT is the seminal *Class, Race, and Inequality* by Seekings and Nattrass (2008), which develops the category of a 'distributional regime' to describe the institutional configuration in which the state, capital and labour interact to determine the allocation of the economic product; not simply directly though taxes and government spending, but including 'policies affecting education and the labour market and, more generally, the rate and path of economic growth' (2008: 4). The main argument of their book is that a post-apartheid distributional regime has shown strong continuity with its predecessor, but that the composition of the 'insiders' who are its beneficiaries has changed. Formal-sector workers have replaced white workers and a black capitalist layer has been included, shifting the conditions of privilege from race to class.

However, this regime continues to exclude and marginalise 'outsiders' – the unemployed masses in the contemporary setting. Like other versions of the LAT, the institutional privilege of formal workers is based on a generously regulated labour market and strong unions with control over a powerful corporatist apparatus. By no means endemic to the Right – a range of sociologists and activists have perceived a process of class stratification involving the emergence of a new 'precariat' or 'underlass' with diverging political interests from the traditional proletariat. These views have been used to explain the apparent conservatism, until recently, of much of the workers' movement and its disjuncture from wider community and social struggles, generally concomitant with some disillusionment in the historical agency of the industrial working class.

Underlying this has been the discourse and practice of the ANC-controlled state, which has been keen to propound formal employment as the basis of a disciplined citizenship in South Africa. This has been most clearly demonstrated by the work of Franco Barchiesi, chiefly in *Precarious Liberation* (2011). Barchiesi carefully traces the roots and evolution of the imaginative emancipatory project of the ANC, in which waged labour is redeemed from its associations with apartheid exploitation and sub-citizenship, and made the vehicle for material liberation and equal inclusion in the new society. This vision reaches its theoretical apogee in the 'two economies' thesis of former president Thabo Mbeki in which South Africa is rigidly divided into a modern formal sector of secure employment and advanced industries, and a separate hinterland of informality and survival economies. Government strategies of building ladders from the second to the first economy rely on extending the boundaries of the latter by enhancing its competitiveness, chiefly by exhorting labour to recognise its relative privilege and exercise restraint in wage demands. This has formed the basis for the social-contract style corporatism in which the national project of the ANC was severed from the Freedom Charter and wedged into a framework of neoliberal globalisation.

The intertwining of the work/wage question together with the national question helps to explain some of the intensity and polarity in the debate. For workers, the continuing disjuncture between notions of decent work and the reality of precariousness and poverty wages under historically continuous patterns of ownership undermines the fundamental promises of liberation. For South African capital, hegemonised by metropolitan-oriented fractions dependent on cheap labour, the failure of the wage to adjust downwards in order to clear the labour market jeopardises the whole virtuous capitalism that the social contract was to guarantee. It opens the door to uprisings by the real 'dangerous class' in the elite imagination: the unemployed masses who seem to be politically coalescing in Julius Malema's EFF. The 'meaning of Marikana' for South African capital, therefore, is that unions must be restrained before a delicate political compromise comes unstuck.

While the ruling ideas are again those of the ruling class, there have been important exceptions. A range of unionists, scholars and activists have been raising the flag on a long-standing crisis of labour of which Marikana was the crystallisation. This narrative has tended to focus on the undermining of decent work through the rise in precariousness and atypical employment and the ways in which co-option and bureaucratisation have stripped the ability of the union movement to represent the interests of all workers, formal and informal (McKinley 2015). Barchiesi's (2011) *Precarious Liberation* goes on to enumerate how the reality of precarious labour has undermined the promises of secure and decent employment propounded by the victorious liberation movement. However, the scholarly and public debate has been impoverished by a dearth of detailed, time series-based statistics on real wages, opening the door for spurious data from private-sector-linked economists.[3]

Amongst more rigorous interlocutors, wage data from employer-based Quarterly Employment Surveys (QES) is popular. However, as the QES only reports averages it allows for limited investigation of South Africa's highly segmented, unequal labour market. Here we add a crucial element to the understanding of labour in the post-apartheid period through a presentation of real wage trends based on the Post-Apartheid Labour Market Surveys (PALMS). We show that the South African labour market has experienced a massive increase in inequality, with fanning out at the top twentieth and tenth percentiles, and stagnation of real wages for the bottom half of workers.

REAL WAGES IN POST-APARTHEID SOUTH AFRICA

This section analyses and decomposes real earnings trends in South Africa since the end of apartheid.[4] Figure 8.1 shows mean real monthly wage trends between 1997 and 2011. For most of the economy, average wages declined slightly in the first period, before turning up after 2003 although, for the public sector, increases began earlier.

Figure 8.1: Real mean monthly wages, 1997–2011

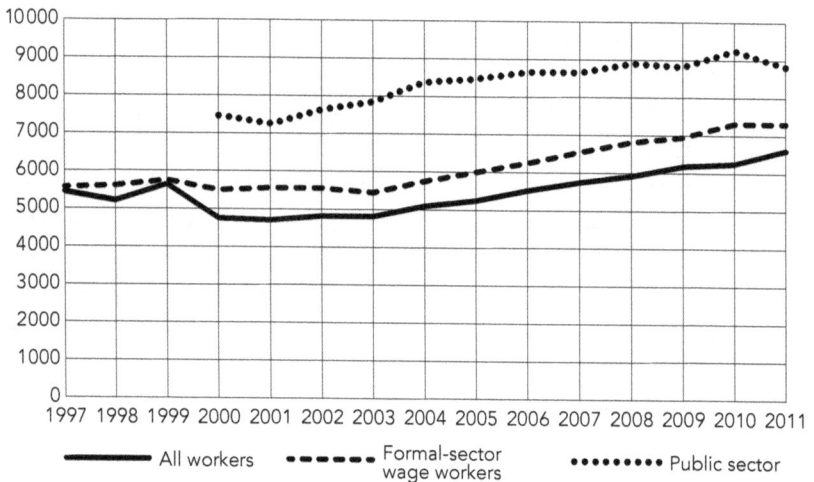

Source: PALMS, author's calculations

Note: Constant 2011 ZAR

The average wage across the economy declined between 1997 and 2003 from R5 550 (US$478) to R4 765 (US$410) per month in 2011 prices. For formal-sector employees, decreases were smaller, ranging from R5 531 (US$476) to R5 415 (US$466). Thereafter, mean wages in the economy grew steadily, by thirty-seven per cent and thirty-five per cent between 2003 and 2011 for all workers and formal-sector employees respectively, to R6 564 (US$565) and R7 316 (US$630) in 2011. Data for the public sector separately begins later, showing a slight decline in 2000 to R7 244 (US$623) in 2001, thereafter increasing by twenty-two per cent to R8 838 (US$761) in 2011. There is thus evidence of fairly substantial wage increases, particularly in the second half of the 2000s, leaving the average 2011 pay package roughly R1 000 (US$86) greater than it was eight years prior. But in the context of a highly divided, unequal labour market, such aggregates need further decomposition to be meaningful.

Figure 8.2: Real monthly earnings trends for all workers, 1997–2011

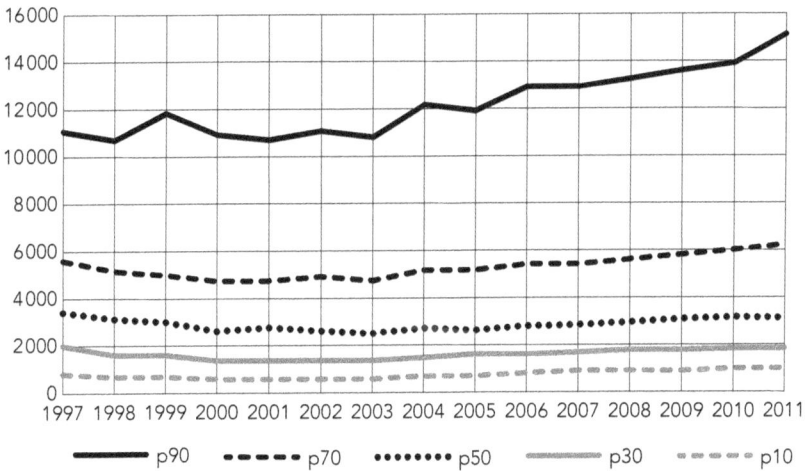

Source: PALMS, author's calculations

Note: Constant 2011 ZAR; p = percentile

Figure 8.2 shows real monthly earnings trends for all workers by percentile (see also Wittenberg and Pirouz 2013). A rise in wage inequality, with fanning out at the top half of the distribution and relative stagnation at the bottom, is evident. The median wage in the economy actually declined from 1997 to a low of R2 451 (US$211) in 2003 before recovering to R3 038 (US$261) in 2011. The thirtieth percentile wage also dropped over the 15 years by just over R200 (US$17) to R1 724 (US$148) per month in 2011. The poorest workers saw a slight convergence with those immediately above them, with the tenth percentile wage rising from R654 (US$56) to R851 (US$73) per month, but still remaining firmly in the region of poverty wages. The graph demonstrates that the average increases described above were entirely driven by increases for higher earners. The seventieth percentile wage also declined notably in the six years after 1997 from R5 457 (US$470) to R4 597 (US$396), thereafter recovering fairly strongly to R6 084 (US$524) per month in 2011. By far the largest gains, however, were for the top ten per cent of workers, whose wages increased by R4 115 (US$354) between 1997 and 2011 to R15 028 (US$1 293). Table 8.1 shows the growth rates for different percentiles over the period.

Table 8.1: Real wage growth rates, all workers, 1997–2011 (%)

Percentile	1997–2001	2002–2006	2007–2011	1997–2011
p90	-2.82	16.30	16.97	37.70
p70	-15.78	11.02	15.68	11.5
p50	-19.02	7.80	9.24	-7.19
p30	-35.75	19.64	6.53	-12.25
p10	-19.02	39.42	10.47	30.05

Source: PALMS, author's calculations

All percentile groups depicted saw substantial percentage declines in the four-year period after 1997, except the ninetieth percentile for which the drop was only 2.82 per cent. Wages across the spectrum turned upwards over the next four years, but were slowest at the median, with substantial gains at the top end and the bottom, in percentage terms. Growth continued for all groups in the 2007–2011 period but was again considerably higher at the top, fairly constant at the median and slower than the previous four years for the thirtieth and tenth percentiles. For the period as a whole, the highest growth in percentage terms was at the top and bottom ends of the distribution at 37.7 per cent for the ninetieth percentile and 30.05 per cent for the tenth. The thirtieth percentile workers were the biggest losers with 12.25 per cent declines in real earnings, and 7.19 per cent declines for median workers. Workers in the upper middle did better with earnings growing by 11.5 per cent over the period.

Figure 8.3 depicts the distorted u-shape distribution pattern over the period for 10 percentiles, with gains for the poorest workers, bottoming out at the lower middle part of the distribution and significant fanning out at the top end.

Figure 8.3: Per cent change in real monthly earnings, 1997–2011 (2011 prices)

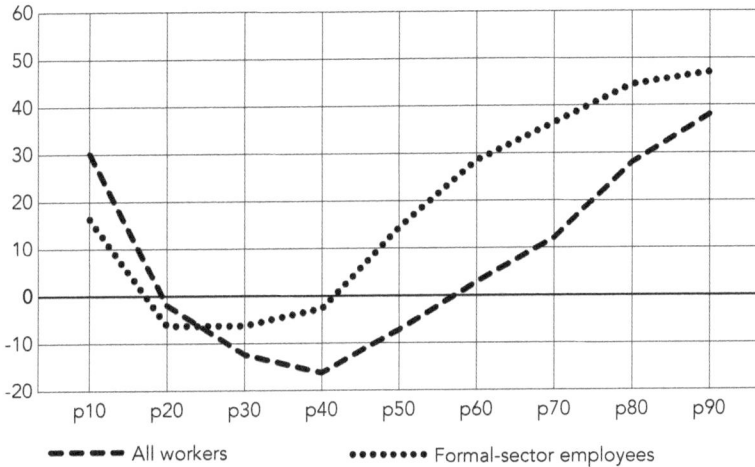

Source: PALMS, author's calculations

Catch-up at the bottom was restricted to the poorest ten per cent of formal-sector employees, with even twentieth percentile workers seeing negative earnings growth between 1997 and 2011. From the graph, wage trends for the economy as a whole mimicked those of formal-sector wage earners, although earnings growth was lower for all groups except the bottom two deciles. For the top half of the distribution the differences were fairly substantial. The median and sixtieth percentile wage of formal-sector employees grew by 13.9 per cent and twenty-eight per cent respectively between 1997 and 2011. However, over a *15-year period* these increases translate into a mere 0.087 per cent compound per annum for median workers and 1.65 per cent for the sixtieth percentile group.

Figure 8.4 shows average real wage patterns for different skill categories classified by occupation. Similar patterns to previous graphs are discernible. Elementary occupations and domestic workers (low-skilled) received a similar mean wage in 2011 as in 1997, around R2 200 (US$189). Semi-skilled workers saw wage declines at the beginning of the period before a slow increase to R4 924 (US$424) per month in 2011. Skilled workers saw moderate gains from R7 647 (US$658) to R9 126 (US$785) over the 15-year period. However, again it was only highly skilled workers at the top of the income distribution that had significant earnings increases. Wages for this group, mostly managers and other professionals, increased by 71.3 per cent to R18 661 (US$1 606), almost twice that of the next skill category.

Figure 8.4: Real wage patterns for different skill categories classified by occupation

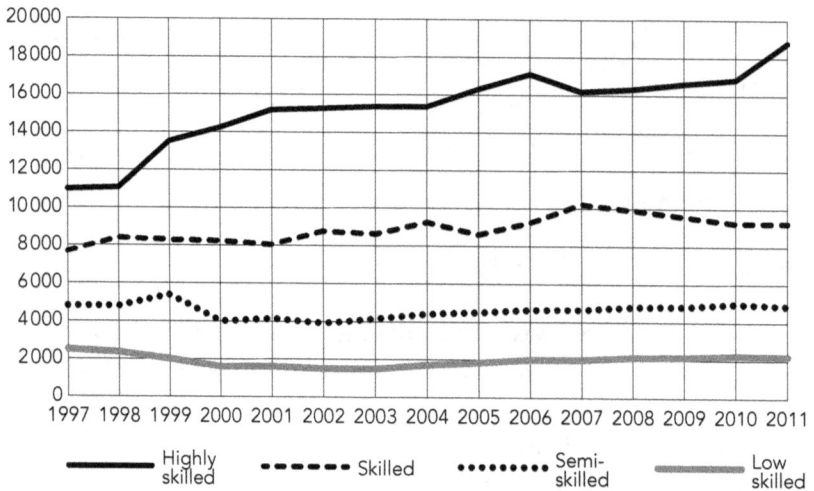

Source: PALMS, author's calculations
Note: Constant 2011 ZAR

These findings are corroborated by various firm-level studies. Based on comparative studies of the automotive industry, Black and Hasson (2012: 7) note that 'the most striking feature about the labour market in South Africa is not so much that wages of production workers are higher than competitors (although in many cases they are), but the exorbitant costs of managers and skilled staff'. A major 2007 report for the World Bank (Clarke et al. 2007) found that the median monthly wage for a manager in South Africa (about US$1 850) was over twice that of Poland and three times that of Brazil. Moreover, managers in South Africa were found to earn nine times as much as unskilled workers in South Africa, whereas in Brazil and Poland managers earned only three times as much as unskilled workers. Similar patterns were found for other skilled and professional workers. Their study concurred with our finding that 'high wages in South Africa appear to be mainly due to high wages for managers and professionals and not to high wages at the bottom of the income distribution' (Clarke et al. 2007: xviii).

Thus average real wage trends show decent improvement across the economy, although decomposing these trends shows that only a minority of the best-off workers were driving these changes. Economy-wide productivity increased by around seventy per cent between 1994 and 2011; much faster than average wages, meaning a decline in the adjusted wage share of gross domestic product (GDP) by around eight per cent (Onaran and Galanis 2012). The vast majority of workers, including in the formal-sector, have not benefited from these advances, thus if there is a 'distributional regime' in this setting it is neoliberal. If there is labour aristocracy in this market, it is an aristocracy of a more traditional sort consisting of a professional, managerial petite bourgeoisie ('highly skilled' in official statistics) and not a privileged fragment of the proletariat or the formal-sector as a whole. The figures here demonstrate the cardinal failures of the post-apartheid economic system, not only its inability to provide formal employment to a growing quotient of South Africans, but the failure of employment itself to act as a means out of poverty or of redressing inequality.

ROBOTS OR CLASS WAR? THE ECONOMIC DEBATE ON WAGE INEQUALITY

The wage trends described above more or less conform to patterns familiar over the last three decades in nations that have adopted Washington Consensus economics. The pre-eminent response of mainstream economics to these trends is a theory of skill-biased technological change (SBTC) rooted in the neoclassical theory that in normal circumstances with properly functioning markets, factors of production (capital and labour) exchange at their 'marginal productivities' (Autor, Katz and Krueger. 1997). It is argued that recent technological revolutions, primarily in information and communications technology, have increased the productivity of higher-skilled forms of labour relative to those in the middle (although in some cases low-skilled, basic work has also benefited). In a cross-sectional macro investigation the International Monetary Fund (IMF 2007: 153) argued that '... the main factor driving the recent increase in inequality across countries has been technological progress', largely exonerating 'globalisation' in the process.

In South Africa, SBTC has not been widely applied in academic literature other than to explain the specific failures of lower-skilled wages to rise with liberalisation, which was predicted to attend the shift towards relatively abundant labour in accordance with classical trade theory (Edwards 2001; Fedderke, Shin and Vaze 2003). A recent attempt is (Bhorat, Goga and Stanwix 2013), although they are more modest with their conclusions, only pointing out that specific occupations associated with technological change appear to have experienced wage effects and not proposing it as a general theory of wage inequality. In any case, their own figures on the occupational composition of employment do not seem to suggest any strong trends in the technological reorganisation of production domestically. However, neoliberal ideas on skills and educational failure, rooted in human capital theory, hold an extremely important place in debates on the South African labour market and its pathologies, with toxic implications for education policy (Vally and Motala 2014).

These are positions built on theoretical sand as they reprise all the central fallacies of the Cambridge Capital Controversies and marginal productivity theories. Mishel, Shierholz and Schmitt (2013) pick apart the empirical case for the US, showing the SBTC fails to explain wage trends post-1990 and that the 'job polarisation' thesis meant to correct this explains even less, since it has been ongoing since the 1950s and during periods when wage and income trends were markedly different. Stockhammer (2012) shows that broadening the set of variables in macro-economic inequality regressions yields quite different results; collapsing wage shares in the developing world are mainly explained by 'financialisation', 'globalisation' and 'welfare state retrenchment', with technological change actually associated with slight gains for labour.

Investigations of distribution in most strands of political economy take their point of departure as the recognition that the labour market is not just another market involving the neutral exchange of commodities. The commodity in this case has the exceptional quality of being able to talk and to bargain, and of not being produced in a capitalist process. Wage formation and the distribution of the social product in general is thus irreducibly political and historical. In the abstract schema of *Capital*, Marx (1992) assumes that the value of labour power will equal the value of the bundle of goods needed to reproduce the working class at a given level of culturally, 'morally' and historically determined subsistence and that this value will, as always, act as a centre of gravity for the actual price of a working day. He argues that wages are inversely related to the size of the reserve army of labour, the unemployed workforce. No one has yet succeeded in developing a theory from these first principles that may be applied to a concrete historical investigation of wage trends within a social formation, let alone one with the complex, segmented labour markets of advanced capitalist states. In practice, the moral and historical determinants of consumption norms have been left in the black boxes in which Marx put them, and most applied studies of wage trends in heterodox political economy have focused on diachronic accounts of the bargaining power of labour or, more expansively, the class struggle. Our focus here, therefore, will be the class struggle dynamics behind the continuation of the cheap labour system in South Africa, both on the shop floor and in relation to the state and wider terrain of capitalist development.

EXPLAINING LABOUR'S DEFEAT: THE MINERALS–ENERGY COMPLEX AND THE UNEMPLOYMENT CRISIS

The above wage trends indeed demand serious explanation. Apartheid-era wage data are notoriously sketchy and incomplete, but the best estimates suggest that wages for black workers began to rise in the eighties, from an extremely low base, with the re-emergence of the union movement (Standing, Sender and Weeks 1996: 185). Working poverty of some definition was still extremely widespread at the time of the transition. Although the negotiated economic policy was stripped of any radical commitments, a reasonable expectation would have been that full freedom of organisation, a sympathetic state with labour leaders in influential positions, and significant amendments to labour regulations, would have fostered a continual rise in wages, at least in the early years. Thus, although there are important exceptions, perhaps the dominant view is that the post-apartheid dispensation has been at least partially favourable to workers, allowing them some institutional influence and decent representation.

Marikana and the issues it has thrown into relief are starting to shift the debate. Here we question each of the above points and argue that the record after 20 years has been overwhelmingly one of defeat and setback for workers in light of what could have been expected from political liberalisation. In the first place this stems from the failure to contest the economic trajectory sanctioned by the new ANC government, which allowed an evolving MEC to lead to extensive globalisation and financialisation of the South African economy. These trends have empowered capital at the point of production, as well as produced an unemployment crisis and general economic environment hostile to labour. Secondly, a bureaucratising workers' movement has offered no response to precariousness, severely undermining the protections afforded by the labour law.

Ben Fine and Zavareh Rustomjee (1996) coined the term 'minerals–energy complex' to refer to the historical nexus of mega-conglomerates rooted in mining and downstream interests but eventually covering wide areas of the South African economy, including finance, and interpenetrating the state and public sector. More than simply a weighty set of industries, the authors characterise the MEC as a 'system of accumulation' which, through its linkages with other industries and close relation with the state, imparts a particular dynamic on the accumulation path of the entire economy. The term entered popular discourse after the proceedings of the Farlam Commission of Inquiry into the killings at Marikana revealed the networks of power connecting state elites and mining capital. As a tool of political economic analysis it has gained increasing currency for the explanatory power it brings to bear on key trends and patterns in the post-apartheid economy and the ongoing dominance of extractive and related industries. In more recent work on the MEC, scholars see themselves as engaged in an attempt to construct a 'middle-range' theory that examines the dialectical mediations between capitalism's universal tendencies and the historical articulation of capitalist relations in actual social formations (Ashman, Fine and Newman 2013).

With the end of apartheid, the central imperatives of MEC were to align with global trends from which they had been barred by apartheid's isolation, by internationalising and financialising operations (Ashman, Fine and Newman 2013). This also reflected a desire to minimise exposure to a country with potential ongoing political instability. In the first place this process involved extensive corporate restructuring along traditional neoliberal lines, including core-functions focus, shareholder-value maximisation and greater involvement in financial markets by 'non-financial' businesses. The traditional MEC core, centred on several conglomerates, dispersed itself in a flurry of mergers, acquisitions and unbundlings, peaking at 630 mergers and acquisitions in 1998 (Mohamed 2010). Global mobility and openness was achieved with an agreement by the former minister of finance, Trevor Manuel, to allow key firms to relist to international financial centres and the accelerated dismantling of exchange controls.

With an open capital account, the ANC government hoped to disincentivise illicit flight and encourage short-term flows to balance out appreciative inflows and long-term leakages. Nothing of the sort occurred. The income section of the current account fluctuated between negative two and three per cent of GDP in the democratic period, but far more worrying has been the systemic looting of national wealth through illicit expatriation. Illegal capital flight has been a cardinal feature of the post-apartheid economy. Wits researchers estimate that it averaged twelve per cent of GDP between 2000 and 2007, much of it due to transfer pricing in the mining sector (Ashman, Fine and Newman 2011). This is roughly enough to plug the deficit in investment levels needed to match ambitious official employment targets, yet all major economic policy statements are virtually silent on the issue. These large systemic outflows are also behind the instability of the rand, which fell victim to speculators and experienced six major crashes over the last two decades, providing a major deterrent to productive investment and rubbishing claims of having achieved a 'stable environment for business' through price (inflation) stability. Excessively high nominal interest rates did little to stem the instability in asset prices and simply contributed to collapsing investment.

Extensive financialisation in the South African economy is also associated with the historical influence of the MEC, which developed sophisticated financial infrastructure in the 1980s whilst capital was trapped by strict exchange controls (Fine and Rustomjee 1996). Deregulation and external opening allowed the financial system to evolve rapidly along lines similar to the parasitic US model, which is overwhelmingly disposed to consumer and mortgage lending to supplement declining labour incomes, and not to financing productive investment which is generally covered by retained earnings. Finance was the second fastest growing sector post-apartheid, ballooning from 17.3 per cent to 24.3 per cent of gross value added between 1994 and 2013, along with the massive acquisition of financial assets by firms and households.

As well as globalising, South African non-financial corporations have become highly financialised and undergone extensive restructuring to align with the principles of the so-called shareholder-value revolution. This has its origins in the 1980s in America, as shareholders sought a means of aligning the interests of managers with their own. The emergence of large institutional investors with huge capital ensured that managers put the short-term aims of shareholders above all else and those who didn't comply were subject to hostile take-overs, which could only be avoided by driving up the share price through large buybacks or 'rationalisation' (Lazonick 1992). Shareholder-value maximisation encourages corporate managers to focus on short-term profits and capital gains. Aspects that fall outside of the 'core functions' of the business are disgorged and outsourced, and capital that cannot guarantee high returns quickly diverted back to shareholders.

The result is a shift from 'retain and reinvest' to 'downsize and distribute', a decline in long-term investment and a squeeze on workers. Financialisation also opens greater avenues of non-productive investment to capital, increasing its effective 'mobility' in the same way that globalisation grants it a regional freedom of movement. Labour is now forced to offer a price that makes domestic investment favourable not only compared to cheaper labour regimes abroad, but compared to what financial markets can offer in short-term takings. Financialisation is also associated with greater control of financial institutions over economic and social policy, which tends to entrench the neoliberal orientation of state action.

The ANC inherited an economy with systemic unemployment, likely around thirty per cent, but a 'shock doctrine' style trade liberalisation rapidly exacerbated the situation. Key labour-intensive industries, such as textiles, collapsed under cheap imports whilst others such as agriculture mechanised and restructured towards exports, slashing hundreds of thousands of jobs. Cutbacks under state austerity and massive layoffs in gold mining following the depletion of cheap reserves compounded the situation. Over the 1990s employment creation fell behind new entrants to the labour market, leading (broad) unemployment to top forty per cent by 2003. Strong industrial policy was urgently needed to guide diversification and develop the linkages that were historically missing from an extraction-oriented MEC. But Roberts (2008) blames the failure for this to materialise on the ongoing influence of the MEC, not simply as an industrial structure but as a political-economic 'complex' impacting accumulation across the economy and impelling state policy. According to Ashman, Fine and Newman (2013), the MEC continues to comprise around twenty-one per cent of GDP and almost sixty per cent of export revenues. Elsewhere, growth has been overwhelmingly concentrated in retail, transport, communication and 'finance' (in fact, mostly outsourced work). Many of the jobs created in these sectors are low-paid and insecure. Official broad unemployment hovers at around thirty-six per cent following the loss of more than 1 million jobs in the global crisis, but this is based on revisions to the definition of discouragement that were made in 2008, meaning actual unemployment may be higher.

The dialectic of massive capital flight, currency instability, financialisation and laggard domestic demand ensured that the collapse in investment, which started in the 1980s, did not alleviate. Investment averaged just 15.6 per cent of GDP for 1994 to 2003 and 19.2 per cent between 2004 and 2013 compared to 26.4 per cent in the 1970s (SARB 1994). Consequently, growth has been, and remains, far short of promises, and woefully inadequate to seriously tackle unemployment at the present rates of capital intensity.

The presence of Cosatu and the SACP in the Alliance and in corporatist institutions appears to have provided no counterweight to the hegemonic bloc which has led the neoliberal policy direction in South Africa, a situation which we discuss further in the next section. Ultimately, it is the persisting unemployment crisis – forcing the employed into vicious competition with a swelling 'reserve army' of over a third of the workforce – that has likely constituted the primary barrier to a successful struggle against the cheap labour system. Conservative economists often claim that unemployment ceases to have its usual depressing effect on wages due to regulative inflexibility and skills shortages, points which we rebut below. Nevertheless, it does become interesting to ask whether the inverse relationship between unemployment and wages generally observed at 'normal' rates of unemployment (two to nine per cent) continues to hold in the case of excessive labour market failure, when the labour supply is virtually elastic, as far as employers are concerned. If unemployment tops forty per cent again are wages likely to fall further?

Anecdotal evidence, such as regular newspaper reports on a handful of job openings receiving tens of thousands of applications, suggests not. More rigorously, however, Kingdon and Knight (2006) econometrically tested the sensitivity of wages to local unemployment and found an elasticity comparable to markets with 'normal' unemployment rates, suggesting that the standard inverse relationship still holds (although this was based on old data). Further evidence for this comes from the ongoing hostility from employers and their allies to the social grant system, which is blamed for creating a 'culture of dependency' and weakening the inducement to sell labour-power (a narrative that has also been crucial in the state's efforts to underpin the interrelation between work and citizenship described by Barchiesi). However, it requires a comfortable distance from the reality of South African communities to believe that the meagre amounts offered by social grants, which are commonly divided by large dependency networks, offer any credible means of mitigating dependence on the labour market (Surender et al. 2010). In short, strategies for fully transcending the cheap labour system in South Africa are unlikely to succeed as long as the unemployment crisis remains in place.

EXPLAINING LABOUR'S DEFEAT: THE MYTHS OF OVERREGULATION AND UNION MILITANCY

The 'evidence' for putatively 'excessive regulation' almost always comes from the employer surveys, that is, perceptions of business leaders themselves. In fact, most attempts to construct international comparisons have demonstrated South African labour law to be relatively liberal. South Africa's latest score on the Organisation for Economic Co-operation and Development (OECD) employment protection legislation index was 1.25 (for 2008), the lowest of all the Group of Twenty (G-20) emerging markets and well below the OECD average (cited in Klein 2012). Benjamin, Bhorat and Cheadle (2010: 87) find, using World Bank data, 'that in most measures of labour regulation ... South Africa is not an extraordinarily over-regulated (or indeed under-regulated) labour market'. Moreover there is significant evidence that actual compliance with labour regulation is episodic (Webster et al. 2008). Bhorat, Kanbur and Mayet (2011), for example, find systemic violation of minimum wage legislation. Indeed, the IMF noted that the fact that South Africa lost more than 1 million jobs in just over a year after the onset of the great recession was very surprising given a putatively rigid market (Klein 2012).

In any case, these reviews are constrained by a very formalistic methodology that prevents them giving any adequate consideration to the far more pressing limitations of the post-apartheid amendments, specifically the failure to provide serious protections in the face of massive shifts to informalisation. The extent of informalisation is difficult to measure, due in equal part to definitional issues and the lack of effective data, but extensive trade union and sociological studies firmly establish that variant alterations to the standard employment relationship (SER) have been the primary means through which capital has ensured that formal protections do not translate to a stronger bargaining position for workers (Hinks 2004). As Figure 8.5 shows, although the unemployed portion of the workforce may have come down to thirty-three per cent from the start of the decade, new jobs that were created were not likely to have met common standards of decency and security. The proportion of the workforce in formal, permanent work actually dropped from thirty-four to thirty-three per cent over the same period, whilst non-permanent and informal work grew by around five per cent each.

Figure 8.5: Distribution of the workforce, 2001–2011

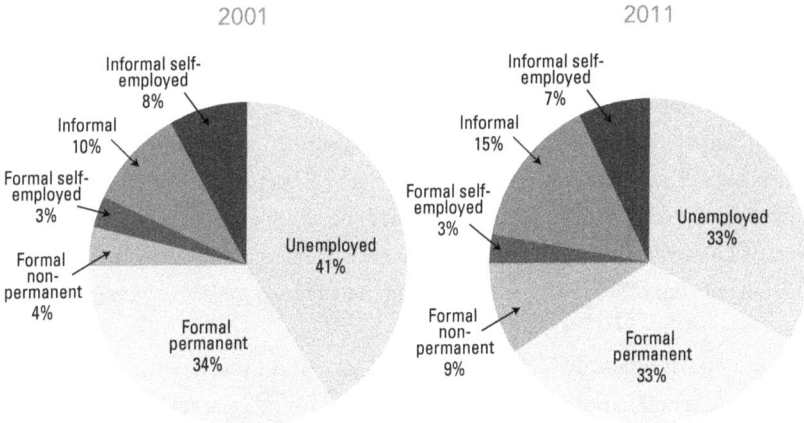

Source: PALMS, author's calculations

For Barchiesi (2011), it is through the unhindered spread of precariousness coupled with the government's unflinching commitment to macro-economic 'prudence' that the promise of wage labour to deliver security and material upliftment has been so severely undermined. He cites Cosatu's own recognition of this, a few years into the transition:

> The sub-contracting, casualising and division of workers is an attempt to deny workers the very citizenship rights that democracy promises them: the right to organize and to engage in collective bargaining and the right to work in fair and decent conditions. It is the re-emergence of a new form of apartheid employment strategies. It undermines Cosatu's project of extending democracy and the rights of citizenship into the economy and working life. (cited in Barchiesi 2011: 76–77)

Perhaps the pre-eminent form of informalisation in South Africa has been labour broking or triangular employment. The 1995 Labour Relations Act reaffirmed the legality of a practice that has its roots in agents working for mines and farms dependent on migrant labour, and grew concomitantly with the strength of unions and labour reforms of the 1980s. The explosion of labour broking after the post-apartheid amendments was incentivised by greater formal protection for SER workers and space for organising (Theron, Lewis and Godfrey 2005). The Labour Force Surveys (LFS) fail to adequately capture triangular employment, but a possible proxy suggests that there are over 1 million labour-brokered workers in the economy, representing an enormous portion of new job creation over the last decade (Bhorat, Goga and Stanwix 2013). Labour brokers themselves and bargaining councils provide similar estimates, although some experts give figures of over 2 million workers.[5] The efficacy of brokers for employers turns on generating confusion in the application of labour law through the triangular relationship, and on segmenting the workplace, a practice which Cosatu has gone as far as to term a 'modern form of slavery'.

Other parts of South Africa's labour market institutions have similarly failed to provide an effective springboard to progressive wage increases or improved conditions. The bargaining council system (renovated from the old apartheid industrial councils), voluntary associations between employers and registered unions with provisions to extend agreements to non-parties, has been a consistent target for those lamenting the lack of flexibility in South African labour markets. But bargaining councils have atrophied over the decades as part of a marked trend away from centralised bargaining. Veteran trade unionist Neil Coleman argues:

> While centralised bargaining is critical for the labour movement ... it is not in its current voluntaristic form, able to drive the transformation demanded by the South African situation. Indeed the fragility of collective bargaining institutions can be used by employers to attack wage levels. (cited in Di Paola and Pons-Vignon 2013: 633)

Over eighty per cent of applications for exemption from bargaining council extensions are granted, suggesting that employers have little reason to be threatened by agreements that cannot be forced by their own workforce (Di Paola and Pons-Vignon 2013). The sectoral determinations instituted where bargaining councils are lacking may have had some successes in raising wages but have hardly been sufficient to provide a real challenge to poverty wages. As Di Paola and Pons-Vignon (2013: 635) conclude from a macro review of South Africa's labour market institutions:

> The pervasive increase in atypical employment has eroded trade union ability to protect workers and take advantage of many of the provisions of the new legal framework. In South Africa, labour market restructuring, in a context of economic liberalization, has benefited capital … This lies at the heart of the broader failure, for instance visible in macro-economic policy, of trade unions to advance the interests of labour as a class.

The same corporatist orientation that prevented the labour movement from posing a political alternative to the ANC's neoliberalism, has also deeply compromised its ability to respond to pro-capital restructuring on the shop floor. In the immediate post-apartheid period, labour leaders were at the forefront of efforts to put the brakes on labour demands as part of the generalised demobilisation called by the ANC in the name of the national project described at the beginning of this chapter. The rewards for compliance with the desires of state and party have been considerable and most visibly reflected in the personal trajectories of heavyweights such as Cyril Ramaphosa, Gwede Mantashe and Kgalema Motlanthe, whose road to the top echelons of the ANC was through the union movement. But the use of union positions as a 'transmission belt' to better things has not been confined to executives, or to the state sector. In the latest Cosatu survey, fifty-two per cent of workers said they had seen a shop steward promoted to a managerial position, often in human resource departments. Of course, the story of the National Union of Mineworkers in the platinum sector is the most dramatic and tragic illustration of union co-option.[6]

The result, by all accounts, has been the dilution of the strong traditions of workers' control and workers' democracy forged during the adversity of the 1980s, as the main axis of organising has shifted from the factory floor to the boardroom (McKinley 2015). As the focus of organising work has shifted to boardroom negotiations and state lobbying, union officials and other experts have become dominant and participation by the rank and file has declined. According to the 2012 Cosatu survey, around forty-two per cent of workers said they had not attended a union meeting in the last year and around thirty-five per cent said they had not had shop-steward elections in the last four years. Although a majority of workers say they continue to directly elect shop stewards instead of having them appointed, they exercise less direct control over their immediate representatives. In 1994, seventy-two per cent of respondents said that shop stewards should do only what membership told them to do. By 2008, this had decreased to only forty-six per cent. At the same time, these processes have stifled the organic creativity that may have ensured a more flexible response to the challenges thrown up by the rapidly changing world of work (Cosatu 2012).

As it were, an entrenched and privileged bureaucracy has shown little interest in risking new endeavours, meaning the continuing dominance of a mode of industrial unionism that has been highly ineffective at organising precarious workers. The 2012 Cosatu survey found that ninety-three per cent of members held permanent contracts, in contrast to 64.25 per cent for the workforce as a whole (Cosatu 2012: 35; PALMS 2014).

Unionisation rates in the formal private sector slipped from 29.2 to 25.86 per cent between 2001 and 2012 (Table 8.2). For public-sector workers the trend was the opposite, with union density climbing from 68.62 to 71.58 per cent in 2012.

Table 8.2: Union coverage, formal-sector employees, 2001–2012

Year	Private sector		Public sector		All	Union workers in public sector (%)
	Union members	Coverage (%)	Union members	Coverage (%)	Coverage (%)	
2001	1 641 941	29.20	1 332 338	68.62	39.42	44.80
2003	1 701 619	28.18	1 288 333	67.05	37.54	43.09
2005	1 904 679	29.22	1 315 332	66.99	37.96	40.85
2007	2 097 997	28.53	1 535 315	69.55	37.86	42.26
2010	1 794 838	28.58	1 551 831	74.24	39.97	46.37
2012	1 763 832	25.86	1 674 247	71.58	37.51	48.70

Source: PALMS, author's calculations

Noting that the 2005 average union density for OECD countries was thirty per cent, Bhorat, Naidoo and Yu (2014: 6) argue that 'the ... evidence at least initially suggests that the level of union membership in South Africa does not reflect an unusually highly unionized labour market'. They note that figures from the early 2000s suggest that Brazil had a union density as high at seventy-one per cent. PALMS also shows that in 2011 blue-collar workers made up sixty-six per cent of unionised workers, which is five per cent less than 15 years earlier (PALMS, author's calculations). These figures reflect significant changes in the composition of unions away from a traditional industrial blue-collar base in favour of public-sector workers and higher skill grades.

If this is an accurate description of the evolution of the South African unions in the last decades, it should be difficult to explain the extreme militancy that is imputed to the workers' movement by the business press and other prominent voices. In fact, however, the latest serious interrogation of South African strike data by economists came to the conclusion 'that strike action in South Africa is not remarkably different from similar activity in other similar emerging economies' (Bhorat, Naidoo and Yu (2014: 14).

Bhorat, Naidoo and Yu (2014) note that only 2.8 per cent of South African workers were involved in strike action over the period 1999 to 2008, which is comparable to Australia and far less than Spain (7.3 per cent) and Argentina (30.7 per cent). Moreover, the authors note that only 0.05, 0.45 and 0.13 per cent of working days were lost due to strike action in 2003, 2007 and 2011 respectively. Assessing the 'depth' of strikes by the percentage of strikers' work days lost per year, they found that South Africa's rating of 3.77 is less than 12 times that of Brazil, less than 5 times that of Turkey and less than 3 times that of Nigeria. South African workers, it seems, are not particularly quick to down tools, nor are the results particularly dramatic when they do. With the recent crisis we should of course expect some change to these figures. However, the general perception of acrimonious labour relations and a strike-prone workforce amongst business leaders long predates the Marikana massacre. The disjuncture between these perceptions and the reality is symptomatic of the entrenchment of the cheap labour system in South Africa and the need for radical strategies to overcome it.

Fully casualised, labour brokered or externalised jobs may be the most extreme manifestation of precariousness and the focus of most studies, but the restructuring of production over the last decades has likely affected all forms of employment. Even where the formal stipulations of a SER exist, the increasingly financialised, short-termist and 'just-in-time' orientation of business has empowered capital to impose new forms of insecurity across employment grades. Even for those workers where the experience of precarity is not direct, its effects are felt in the division of workplaces, the corroding effect on organisation and the general weakening of workers' bargaining positions. Undoubtedly, employers have in many places succeeded in using degrees of flexibility to deliberately Balkanise workplaces, creating an apparent divergence of interests which has not been overcome by organisation, reflected in the massive underrepresentation of casualised workers within unions.

But the segmentation of employment in this way, important as it is, does not amount to any fundamental *class* fragmentation, or the birth of a new precariat with substantively different conditions of existence and objective forms of action to a formal 'labour aristocracy'. The common experience of stagnating wages for the vast majority of workers, formal and informal, is the greatest evidence of this. Theories of the precariat, as a new phenomenon, in any case bear a distinctly northern bias in treating the experience of one section of mostly white, mostly male workers during one stage of capitalism in the metropoles as somehow the norm. In the history of the global proletariat, precariousness has been the default state, and South Africa is no exception, with atypical employment really emerging as a response to relatively recent legislative amendments. Theories of permanent class stratification are even less convincing when we step out of the factory and into the sphere of reproduction, as Ceruti (2010) and others show. Finally, the idea that there are rigidly separate categories of workers in South Africa is undermined by the evidence of massive 'churning' in the labour market, involving the rapid movement of workers through different states of employment and security. Valodia and Devey (2012: 142) show that fifty-three per cent of respondents in the panel portion of the LFSs changed status between informality and employment between 2002 and 2004, which is further evidence of entrenched flexibility.

A great deal of further research needs to be done at a micro and intermediate level to decompose and describe wage trends amongst other sub-groups and categories, for example, describing wages by gender, education level, precariousness and so on. This work could shed further light on the particular aspects of labour market reconstruction in South Africa, capital's structuring of the workforce and the differential ways in which particular groups have suffered or benefited from these changes. The background narrative is sketched above. Most workers (both the lower skill grades) saw virtually no improvement in real wages in the decade and a half for which there is data. This is due to the weakening of worker organisation under informalisation and bureaucratisation, and to the continuing dominance of the MEC, which was the dynamic centre of the kind of economic restructuring that Stockhammer (2012) found most associated with collapsing wage shares: globalisation and financialisation. In the last sections we discuss the insights offered by Marikana into the nature of the post-apartheid state and the ruling party, and their implications for strategy.

MARIKANA AND THE UNPATRIOTIC BOURGEOISIE

The essence of the ANC/Cosatu/SACP Alliance's programme for rebuilding the South African nation has always been one of classical national bourgeois development, loosely articulated in the National Democratic Revolution (NDR). In a sentence, the programme envisages the cultivation of a patriotic black capitalist class which, in a historic bloc with workers organised through the ANC and its partners, will drive the deracialisation of the South African economy and a new inclusive growth trajectory. White monopoly capital, to the extent that its influence remains, will be cajoled into cooperation with the national programme. In later years, the state's ideological register has shifted closer to notions of a relatively autonomous 'developmental state' inspired by the Asian Tigers. Although Alliance manifestos, and the government policy they ostensibly inspire, are always dissonant and conflicted with the difficulties of 'talking left and walking right', the spirit of the NDR continues to animate debate at least within the ANC. Thus the discussion document on the Second Transition at the ANC's 2012 Congress still invokes hope in the creation of a 'patriotic bourgeoisie' which will act along its 'objective interest' in deracialising the economy, along with promoting industrialisation, massive job growth and improvements in skills and productivity (African National Congress 2012: 21). However, the document goes on to sound a telling warning, that 'dependence of this stratum on white and multinational capital and the state, makes some susceptible to pursue narrow interests, which may not always be in the interest of economic transformation' (African National Congress 2012: 21).

Circulated for the 53rd annual congress that took place in the aftermath of the Marikana massacre, one wonders whether the author was not inspired by those events. However, the decision of that congress to elect Cyril Ramaphosa, the most exemplary figure of revolving-door capitalism, to its deputy presidency, shows that the warnings have not been taken seriously. In a 2010 lecture Neville Alexander (2010: 8) famously predicted that the 'final disillusionment' will come when the new state of the ANC turns its guns on struggling workers. But more than just revealing the contours of an 'ordinary' capitalist state, structurally ordained to ensure the normal reproduction of the wage form and compound accumulation, Marikana was educative in a political way precisely for its exposure of the specific class allegiances constituting the ruling bloc. Ramaphosa appeared in the course of events to act as the direct functionary of 'multinational capital', commanding the repressive apparatus of the state in the 'narrow interest' of his own accumulation. Indeed, the whole tragedy seems to perfectly distil the central motifs of post-apartheid political economy sketched above: the ongoing dominance of an internationalised and politically reconstituted MEC, the financialisation of which acted against any more inclusive form of management; the co-option of the very founder of the mineworkers' union through his ANC involvement; the ongoing struggle of migratory workers whose conditions have seen little change; and the inability of their union to represent those struggles due to its own incorporation with mining capital.

The national bourgeois development of the ANC failed because the Alliance never succeeded in mobilising the class forces capable of transforming the South African state or diminishing the leadership of MEC capital. Despite the continued insistence in Alliance theory that the working class remains the primary 'motive force' within the movement, this has plainly never been the case. In fact, it is a state-capitalist bourgeoisie that has been the hegemonic formation within the Alliance, leading a wider small- and petit-bourgeois layer of state functionaries and middle businessmen connected to state activities. The toothless corporatism to which Cosatu submitted, which encouraged union leaders to leverage their positions for personal advancement and pacified workers to institutional strategies, prevented the development of any counterweight to pro-capital elements within the ANC's 'broad church'. Despite the assertive, developmentalist rhetoric of the ANC leadership, the only real concessions wrested from capital have been participation in elite formation through Black Economic Empowerment (BEE), which in reality was warmly embraced as the most cost-effective means of re-legitimating existing property relations and developing new terms of access to the state, as Marikana demonstrated.

The neoliberal state has been incapable of cultivating the conditions for new sites of accumulation outside the core MEC that might have under-pinned national-bourgeois development premised on subverting the structural demand deficiencies inherited from apartheid through rising wages. Instead, the small black capitalist class that has been created, and it is small indeed if ownership figures are to be believed, forms a dependent fragment, enmeshed or reliant upon the forms of accumulation of multinational, MEC-led capital. Mining and finance have been the primary sites of elite formation (Southall 2007: 73). As indicated above, the orientation of those sectors has been funda-mentally de-nationialising, concerned to secure the globalisation of capital and retain competitiveness through a rate of exploitation based on low wages rather than productivity increases.

Far from taking hold of the state to institute a national democratic project based on breaking apartheid patterns of growth and distribution, the existing capitalist state has taken hold of the ANC. Southall (2012) gives the most complete account of the ANC's transformation into a classic post-liberation 'party machine' geared to the capture and distribution of rents accruing from its hold over the state. Southall identifies the 'state-bourgeoisie' that has been the primary beneficiary of this, consisting of four layers: a higher-level cohort of 'state managers' and a 'corporate bourgeoisie' occupying the top echelons of public and private sectors, and below them a broader 'civil petite bourgeoisie' and 'black business and trading bourgeoisie' centred in middle management and small, medium and micro-sized enterprises (SMMEs). Occupational and income data, of course, cannot map directly onto class, but Southall's statistics nonetheless suggest that the latter groups have seen prodigious growth, with the numbers of black professionals increasing significantly. This is in large part linked to state-directed accumulation and the expansion of the public sector. Since this group has proved incapable of articulating a strategy for inclusive development outside of dependence on the MEC, contestation remains within the ANC of 1.2 million members. But the recent series of defeats for the Alliance Left, stretching from Zuma's backsliding after his victory against Mbeki to his overwhelming re-election, and including the expulsion or secession of Malema and major trade union opponents, effectively signifies the final entrenchment of bourgeois components in the ANC and the defeat of any force capable of challenging them.

This is mostly amply demonstrated by the election of Ramaphosa but also by the adoption of the National Development Plan (NDP), a document with which, as deputy of the National Planning Commission, he is strongly associated. The 494-page NDP is a catch-all manifesto meant to inform and synchronise all areas of government into a long-term 'vision 2030', but is too thin on policy detail and overall coherence to be of much use. Its heart appears to be the economic section which, beneath sometimes murky phraseology, reasserts the economic programme of the National Treasury, which was the former fiefdom of Planning Chair Trevor Manuel and which reportedly had a strong hand in re-editing the NDP document prior to publication (Coleman 2013). Segatti and Pons-Vignon (2013) have demonstrated the critical role of the Treasury as the nerve centre of the neoliberal project in South Africa, staffed by well-trained, internally cultivated technocrats who exert fiscal control over other departments, thus ensuring overall fidelity to macro-economic 'prudence' and shielding policymaking from the normal democratic pressures of the liberal state. Within the state, the significance of the NDP may well be in reasserting Treasury control over economic policy against elements disposed to more dirigist approaches, such as the Economic Development Department, created as a reward for leftist allies after Zuma's initial victory. The NDP is likely unpopular with the ANC's base and certainly with Alliance partners, who demanded the reworking of the economic provisions, leading only to the creation of a defunct commission, and it has become the target of the emerging left opposition led by Numsa. But it is hugely popular with business and vital in maintaining 'confidence' in the post-Marikana climate of instability by acting as a guarantee on behalf of the ANC against any pressure to tack leftwards in response to popular pressures, which helps to explain the ANC leaderships' commitment to it despite obvious political risks.

CONCLUSION: SOCIAL CONTRACTS, 'LULA MOMENTS' AND THE WAY FORWARD

The NDP may prove to be important as a cohering factor in light of the pressures that are likely to arise from the inability of the current ruling bloc to pose any manageable solution to the crisis. The hegemonic fractions of capital retain a completely outward orientation in which any increase in the risk profile of the country or a threat of a decline in competitiveness is met with capital strike. Profitability returned quickly after the global crisis, with returns on the Johannesburg Stock Exchange hitting world-beating levels and various studies claiming that large South African corporates have been among the most valuable for shareholders in the world. But capital retains a sense of political disenfranchisement and no confidence in the long-term growth prospects of the economy given demand deficiency and other structural limitations and political uncertainties.

Within the ruling bloc there is therefore no purview of measured redistribution to meet the labour crisis; no force capable of leading a 'passive revolution' that may set new terms for the inclusion of labour in a new growth regime. Capital's response to the crisis has been overwhelmingly aggressive, pushing the ANC to complete its social-liberalisation and evolution into a hard-nosed party of business prepared to take a firmer stand against unions and to roll back labour legislation.[7] Ramaphosa, it is hoped, will be the agent of this. Growing calls for a 'new social contract' from sections of business and the state are frankly risible; simply a repackaging of the incumbent crisis-ridden system with nothing material offered to undergird a new consensus. The NDP itself outlines such a social contract by calling for labour to accept wage demands 'lower than what productivity would dictate' (in other words, further declines of the wage share of GDP) in return for promises that capital will reinvest boosted profits.

Those seeking to infuse a more progressive spirit in the search for a new compromise have clustered on the notion of a 'Lula moment'. This refers to the left, neo-developmentalist turn undertaken by Brazil's President Lula in his second term, described in this volume by Alfredo Saad-Filho (chapter six), and connotes either a specific strategy of pushing the second Zuma administration in a similar direction, or more broadly the prospects for post-neoliberalism in South Africa. Unfortunately, the calls for a Lula moment have not generally been accompanied by the same careful class analysis that Saad-Filho provides here. Indeed, the thumbnail review of South African class constellations above suggests rather dim prospects for a local rendition of the process described in chapter six.

Far from corruption scandals undermining middle-class support and forcing the ruling bloc to form new allegiances with workers and the urban poor, Zuma's re-election appears to derive from a consolidation of the state-bourgeois formations described above. These groups are fully committed to the alliance with MEC capital, which is not prepared for any compromise on the cheap labour system. Moreover, as already argued, the 'domestic', manufacturing-based bourgeoisie, another important pillar of Lula's reconstituted support base which was responsive to wage-based demand growth and stronger planning led by the Brazilian Development Bank, does not appear to exist in the South African context. Instead, what South Africa has developed is closer to what Nicos Poulantzas (1975: 73) in a different context named an 'internal bourgeoisie'; one 'implicated by multiple ties of dependence in the international division of labour and in the international concentration of capital under the domination of American capital...' and hence lacking the certain political and ideological autonomy from metropolitan sections of capital that the term 'national bourgeoisie' usually signified.

The progressive achievements of the so-called 'Pink Tide', which have seen a reversal of the usual neoliberal indexes of distribution, with falling Gini coefficients and rising labour shares and employments rates, naturally exert a large influence on left debates in South Africa. Ultimately, it is not impossible that the domestic crisis reaches the intensity of those that preceded neo-developmentalism in Brazil or Argentina, giving rise to a bloc of forces either within the ANC or from one of its new competitors, which may be willing to attempt Keynesian macro-economics and more interventionist industrial policy.

In general, as Desai (2004) shows, national bourgeois development from the low level of industrialisation that South Africa currently experiences has only been possible given a very specific historical balance of forces and organisation of global power, which receded along with the threat of social revolution and re-composition of US imperial power around the 1980s. The ongoing transnationalisation of states, capital and value chains raises further issues for the prospects of such programmes. In any case, national bourgeois development has tended to curtail far short of any serious convergence with advanced capitalist nations, and to have a self-liquidating character as capital that develops under state protection grows to resist efforts at state planning and control (Chibber 2004). Growing signs of a crisis in many of the Latin American neo-developmentalist projects may reveal new evidence of the limitations of these programmes. Ultimately, in South Africa the challenges of formulating and articulating an accumulation path that diverges out of the MEC form of industrialisation may require a more radical programme involving greater confrontations with capital and more direct state and worker control over the economy.

NOTES

1   Duncan, J., Bond, P. and Vally, S. 2014. 'The myopia of economics journalism'. *The Con*. Accessed 11 September 2014, http://www.theconmag.co.za/2014/09/10/the-myopia-of-economics-journalism/.
2   Forslund, D. and Reddy, N. 2013. 'When Adcorp's folly reaches presidency, it is time to worry'. *Independent Online*. Accessed 18 May 2015, http://www.iol.co.za/business/opinion/when-adcorp-s-folly-reaches-presidency-it-is-time-to-worry-1.1520313#.VVmFxzqXK2w.
3   Makgetla, N.S. 2012. Schussler report is 'pay in the sky'. *The M&G Online*. Accessed 1 October 2014, http://mg.co.za/article/2012-06-01-schussler-report-is-pay-in-the-sky/.
4   The author would like to thank Ilan Strauss for contributions to data work in this section.
5   Schroeder, I. 2012. 'Labour brokers bad for SA workers, but trade unions not much better'. Accessed 26 March 2014, http://sacsis.org.za/site/article/1230.
6   Hartford, G. 2012. 'The mining industry strike wave: what are the causes and what are the solutions?' Accessed 15 May 2014, http://us-cdn.creamermedia.co.za/assets/articles/attachments/41878_2012_10_03_mining_strike_wave_analysis.pdf.
7   See T. Cohen, 'In the shadow of Marikana, a welcome change in direction', *Business Day* 28 February 2013; T. Motoshi, 'ANC needs to be Liberated from alliance ties that bind it', *Business Day* 31 July 2014 and *Business Day* editorials 25 October 2013 and 16 May 2014 for exemplary statements of this from business ideologues.

REFERENCES

African National Congress. 2012. 'The second transition: building a national democratic society and the balance of forces in 2012'. Accessed 15 April 2015, http://www.anc.org.za/docs/discus/2012/transition.pdf.

Alexander, N. 2010. 'South Africa: An unfinished revolution?' Address at the Fourth Strini Moodley Annual Memorial Lecture, University of KwaZulu–Natal. Accessed 6 October 2014, http://www.marxistsfr.org/archive/alexander/2010-unfinished-revolution.pdf.

Ashman, S., Fine, B. and Newman, S. 2011. 'Amnesty International? The nature, scale and impact of capital flight from South Africa', *Journal of Southern African Studies*, 37 (1): 7–25.

Ashman, S., Fine, B. and Newman, S.A. 2013. 'Systems of accumulation and the evolving MEC'. In *Beyond the Developmental State: Industrial Policy into the 21st Century*, edited by B. Fine, J Saraswati and D. Tavasci. London: Pluto Press.

Autor, D.H., Katz, L.F. and Krueger, A.B. 1997. 'Computing Inequality: Have Computers Changed the Labor Market?', National Bureau of Economic Research. Accessed 28 September 2014, http://www.nber.org/papers/w5956.

Barchiesi, F. 2011. *Precarious Liberation: Workers, the State, and Contested Social Citizenship in Postapartheid South Africa*. Albany: State University of New York Press.

Benjamin, P., Bhorat, H. and Cheadle, H. 2010. 'The cost of "doing business" and labour regulation: the case of South Africa', *International Labour Review*, 149 (1): 73–91.

Bhorat, H., Goga, S. and Stanwix, B. 2013. *Changing dynamics in the global labour market: evidence from South Africa.* DPRU Working Paper, Development Policy Research Unit. Accessed 27 March 2014, http://staging2.ilo.org/public/english/dialogue/actemp/downloads/events/2013/symp/changing_dynamics_sa.pdf.

Bhorat, H., Kanbur, R. and Mayet, N. 2011. *Minimum Wage Violation in South Africa.* Cape Town: Development Policy Research Unit, University of Cape Town.

Bhorat, H., Naidoo, K. and Yu, D. 2014. 'Trade unions in an emerging economy', United Nations University. Accessed 4 April 2014, http://www.wider.unu.edu/publications/working-papers/2014/en_GB/wp2014-055/_files/91363608585311303/default/wp2014-055.pdf.

Black, A. and Hasson, R 2012. 'Capital intensive industrialisation and comparative advantage: Can South Africa do better in labour demanding manufacturing?' Paper presented at Strategies to Overcome Poverty and Inequality: Towards Carnegie III Conference. University of Cape Town, 3–7 September. Accessed 30 November 2013, http://carnegie3.org.za/docs/papers/29_Black_Capital%20intensive%20industrialisation%20and%20comparative%20advantage%20-%20can%20SA%20do%20better.pdf.

Ceruti, C. 2010. 'One class or two? the labour reserve and "surplus population" in Marx and contemporary Soweto', *South African Review of Sociology*, 41 (2): 77–103.

Chibber, V. 2004. 'Reviving the developmental state? The myth of the national bourgeoisie'. Accessed 8 January 2014, http://escholarship.org/uc/item/2bq2753n.pdf.

Clarke, G.R. 2007. *An Assessment of the Investment Climate in South Africa.* New York: World Bank Publications.

Cosatu, 2012. *Findings of the Cosatu Workers Survey 2012.* Johannesburg, South Africa: Cosatu. Accessed 12 June 2014, http://www.cosatu.org.za/docs/reports/2012/final%20workers%20surveys%20results%20August%202012.pdf.

Desai, R. 2004. 'From national bourgeoisie to rogues, failures and bullies: 21st century imperialism and the unravelling of the Third World', *Third World Quarterly*, 25 (1): 169–185.

Di Paola, M. and Pons-Vignon, N. 2013. 'Labour market restructuring in South Africa: low wages, high insecurity', *Review of African Political Economy*, 40 (138): 628–638.

Edwards, L. 2001. 'Globalisation and the skills bias of occupational employment in South Africa', *South African Journal of Economics*, 69 (1): 40–71.

Fedderke, J. 2012. 'The Cost of Rigidity: The Case of the South African Labor Market'. *Comparative Economic Studies*, 54(4): 809–842.

Fedderke, J., Shin, Y. and Vaze, P. 2003. Trade, *Technology and the Labor Market in the South African Manufacturing Sectors*, Econometric Research Southern Africa Working Paper 15. Accessed 27 March 2014, http://www.econrsa.org/system/files/publications/working_papers_interest/wp15_interest.pdf.

Fine, B. and Rustomjee, Z. 1996. *The Political Economy of South Africa: From Minerals–Energy Complex to Industrialization.* Boulder: Westview Press.

Hinks, T. 2004. 'Changing nature of work and "atypical" forms of employment in South Africa: prevalence/magnitude of casualisation and externalisation in South Africa.' Commissioned Research Project for the Department of Labour. Johannesburg, South Africa: National Institute for Economic Policy. Accessed 10 August 2015, http://www.workinfo.com/sub/ir/ir/atypical.htm.

IMF (International Monetary Fund). 2007. *World Economic Outlook: Globalization and Inequality.* Washington, DC: International Monetary Fund.

Kingdon, G.G. and Knight, J. 2006. 'How flexible are wages in response to local unemployment in South Africa?', *Industrial and Labor Relations Review*, 59 (3): 471–495.

Klein, N. 2012. *Real wage, labor productivity, and employment trends in South Africa: a closer look*. Working Paper No. 12/92, IMF Publications. Accessed 25 April 2014, https://www.imf.org/external/pubs/cat/longres.aspx?sk=25825.0.

Lazonick, W. 1992. 'Controlling the market for corporate control: the historical significance of managerial capitalism', *Industrial and Corporate Change*, 1 (3): 445–488.

Marx, K. 1992 *Capital: A Critique of Political Economy (Vol 1)*. London: Penguin.

McKinley, D.T. 2015. 'Labor–community alliances in South Africa: reclaiming (some of) the past, inventing the future?', *South Atlantic Quarterly*, 114 (2): 457–466.

Mishel, L., Shierholz, H. and Schmitt, J. 2013. *Don't blame the robots*. Working Paper, 19 November 2013, Economic Policy Institute (EPI) and Centre for Economic and Policy Research (CEPR). Accessed 27 March 2014, http://mercury.ethz.ch/serviceengine/Files/ISN/173732/ipublicationdocument_singledocument/addd55e0-c679-4c1b-b9a0-87f301a25389/en/technology-inequality-dont-blame-the-robots.pdf.

Mohamed, S. 2010. 'The state of the South African economy'. In *New South African Review 1*, edited by J. Daniel, R. Southall, P. Naidoo and D. Pillay. Johannesburg: Wits University Press.

Onaran, O. and Galanis, G. 2012. *Is Aggregate Demand Wage-led or Profit-led?* Conditions of Worth and Employment Series No.40. Geneva: ILO.

PALMS (Post-Apartheid Labour Market Survey). 2014. Datafirst, University of Cape Town. Accessed 20 May 2014, https://www.datafirst.uct.ac.za/dataportal/index.php/catalog/434.

Poulantzas, N. 1975. *Classes in Contemporary Capitalism*. London: NLB.

Roberts, S. 2008. 'Patterns of industrial performance in South Africa in the first decade of democracy: the continued influence of minerals-based activities', *Transformation: Critical Perspectives on Southern Africa*, 65 (1): 4–35.

SARB (South African Reserve Bank). 1994. Quarterly bulletin, statistical tables. Accessed 10 February 2015, https://www.resbank.co.za/Publications/QuarterlyBulletins/Pages/QuarterlyBulletins-Home.aspx.

Seekings, J. and Nattrass, N. 2008. *Class, Race, and Inequality in South Africa*. New Haven: Yale University Press.

Segatti, A. and Pons-Vignon, N. 2013. 'Stuck in stabilisation? South Africa's post-apartheid macro-economic policy between ideological conversion and technocratic capture', *Review of African Political Economy*, 40 (138): 537–555.

Southall, R. 2007. 'Ten propositions about black economic empowerment in South Africa', *Review of African Political Economy*, 34 (111): 67–84.

Southall, R. 2012. 'The ANC: party vanguard of the black middle class?' In *One Hundred Years of the ANC*, edited by A. Lissoni, J. Soske, N. Erlank, N. Nieftagodien and O. Badsha. Johannesburg: Wits University Press.

Standing, G., Sender, J. and Weeks, J. 1996. *Restructuring the Labour Market: The South African Challenge*. Geneva, Switzerland: International Labour Organization.

Stockhammer, E. 2012. 'Why have wage shares fallen? A panel analysis of the determinants of functional income distribution'. *Conditions of Work and Employment Series* (15). Accessed 17 June 2014, http://www.pepov.org/sites/default/files/wlg_stockhammer_ilo_wp_wo_no.pdf.

Surender, R., Michael, N., Gemma, W. and Ntshongwana, P. 2010. 'Social assistance and dependency in South Africa: an analysis of attitudes to paid work and social grants', *Journal of Social Policy*, 39 (02): 203.

Theron, J., Lewis, P. and Godfrey, S. 2005. 'The rise of labour broking and its policy implications'. *Development and Labour Monograph Series*, 2005/1. Accessed 26 March 2014, http://blogs.uct.ac.za/gallery/679/The%20Rise%20of%20Labour%20 Broking%20and%20its%20Policy%20Implications%201-2005%2004-03-08%20S. pdf.

Vally, S. and Motala, E. 2014. '"No one to blame but themselves": rethinking the relationship between education, skills and employment'. In *The Economy, Education and Society*, edited by S. Vally and E. Motala. Pretoria: Unisa Press.

Valodia, I. and Devey, R. 2012. 'The informal economy in South Africa: debates, issues and policies', *Margin: The Journal of Applied Economic Research*, 6 (2): 133–157.

Webster, E. et al. 2008. 'Making visible the invisible: confronting South Africa's decent work deficit'. Report commissioned by the Department of Labour, Pretoria. Accessed 26 March 2014, http://www.skillsportal.co.za/download_files/skills-development/Making-visible-Webster.pdf.

Wittenberg, M. and Kerr, A. 2012. 'Science and nonsense: further criticisms of Adcorp'. *Politicsweb*. Accessed 1 April 2014, http://www.politicsweb.co.za/politicsweb/view/ politicsweb/en/page71619?oid=285837&sn=Detail&pid=71616.

Wittenberg, M. and Pirouz, F. 2013. 'The measurement of earnings in the post-apartheid period: an overview'. Accessed 29 November 2013, http://www.opensaldru.uct. ac.za/handle/11090/638.

9

SEIZE POWER! THE ROLE OF THE CONSTITUTION IN UNITING A STRUGGLE FOR SOCIAL JUSTICE IN SOUTH AFRICA

Mark Heywood

*Our constitutional design is emphatically transformative.
It is meant to migrate us from a murky and brutish past to an
inclusive future animated by values of human decency and solidarity.
It contains a binding consensus on, or a blueprint of, what a fully
transformed society should look like.*

Deputy chief justice, Dikgang Moseneke, 2014

*All mass formations have faced fundamental political questions of
how to relate to both the opportunities and challenges of the 1994
democratic breakthrough, especially the implications of direct access
to, and participation in, the democratic state and all its institutions.*

Axed Cosatu general secretary, Zwelinzima Vavi, 2014

ANTI-IDEOLOGY AND THE POLITICS OF RIGHTS

In April 2014, in an editorial in the *Daily Maverick* titled 'Building Unity to Restore Democratic Rule', Raymond Suttner, former African National Congress (ANC) and South African Communist Party (SACP) leader, appealed:

> Those who cherish South African democracy need to draw in people from a range of sectors and organisations that may never have acted together in the past. While retaining their autonomous identities, such groups should develop a unifying vision, which binds them. That does not exclude members of the ANC or any other organisation who identify with these goals. It includes trade unions, social movements and NGOs (non-governmental organisations), a range of community organisations, based in urban and rural areas, as well as business, big and small because there can be no wishing away of capital for the foreseeable future.[1]

In the context of South Africa's deepening social crisis, growing levels of inequality, private and public violence, there can be no doubting the importance of Suttner's appeal. Suttner's article was written before the May 2014 election in which the ANC was able to claim a sixty-two per cent majority, albeit less than forty per cent of the total number of people eligible to vote. But predictably the ANC's overwhelming victory did nothing to staunch the political impasse that pervades our society, with the ongoing controversy over the financing of the president's private homestead at Nkandla, and strikes and service-delivery protests commencing again barely before the ink was dry on the election results. Judging by the levels of protest, South Africa is a country in revolt against the status quo. There is enormous criticism and growing dissent. What is missing in this is an answer to the question about what could be a 'unifying vision' for those 'who cherish South African democracy'. Is it possible to construct and implement a vision that could unify the polyglot classes and movements that Suttner suggests?

This chapter attempts to suggest an outline for an answer to this question. At the outset it points to the ferment in party politics and notes three competing but overlapping visions that have emerged amongst activists on the Left. These are: (i) the political demand for 'economic freedom' associated with Julius Malema's political party, the Economic Freedom Fighters (EFF);

(ii) the demand for socialist alternatives driven by South Africa's largest trade union, the National Union of Metalworkers of South Africa (Numsa); and (iii) an increasing number of campaigns for 'social justice', now the mantra of a growing number of civil-society organisations and social movements.

What unites these movements is the conviction that 21 years of successive ANC governments have failed to narrow inequality. Whilst there have been very important social and democratic reforms (the 17 million people on social grants being the most commonly cited example), these reforms have failed to lift tens of millions out of dire poverty, unemployment and dependence on health and education services that many say are worse than those that existed under apartheid. Fewer and fewer people believe the promises and rhetoric of the ANC leadership to change this situation.

Yet equally significant are the ideological divides between these movements. Therefore, to try to find Suttner's elusive vision, I begin by looking at the distinguishing features of the EFF, Numsa and the social justice movements; their strengths, shortcomings and contradictions. However, drawing on the experience of the social movement, the Treatment Action Campaign (TAC), I make no bones about my belief that it is the combination of mass mobilisation together with campaigns to realise the human rights in our constitution which holds the best prospect for achieving far-reaching social reform in the short to medium term.

I therefore argue for making the quest for social justice the unifying vision of the Left and for organising militant struggles to win the fundamental rights already enshrined in the bill of rights of the constitution of the Republic of South Africa, 1996. In this context, I question the self-defeating scepticism from the Left about the constitution. I ask what has been the price of the Left having adopted a purist and ideological aloofness from the constitution instead of using it to invigorate and animate struggle. Finally, in this regard I try to draw attention to some of its far-reaching transformative powers and argue that at this watershed point in South African politics the greatest potential for Numsa's initiative, the United Front, to emerge as a mass movement lies in its leading campaigns for social and political reforms already envisaged in the constitution.

Three visions of radical transformation: Economic freedom, socialism and social justice

In three short years since the massacre of mineworkers at Marikana in August 2012, South Africa's post-apartheid consensus that the ANC-led Alliance would lead social transformation in South Africa has exploded.

The EFF was launched in August 2013 and less than a year later won over a million votes in the 2014 general election. It has become the expression of a new political phenomenon, rooted in young black people's anger at exclusion and continued marginalisation from the economy. On another level, it is also an expression of infighting in the ANC, shifting coalitions and fights over the spoils of economic power and easy-to-grab riches. However, even if the EFF seems thin on policy, its antics in and out of parliament have caught the public attention and imagination. It is the new punk on the block.

The idea of 'economic freedom' is a powerful one. It is being used to mobilise many young black people who are justifiably angry that they remain marginalised, excluded and disadvantaged. Economic 'unfreedom' contrasts with political freedom, which loses its shine if it does nothing to change the social and economic conditions that were the legacy of apartheid.

Calling for measures such as nationalisation of the mines or banks to ensure economic freedom thus sounds radical and revolutionary. But for the purposes of my argument it is important to note that it has a totally different meaning to social justice. In our current context it refers to black people being able to achieve economic equality with white people, something that is necessary to self-advance and to acquire status and riches. This is fair and reasonable but once achieved it also includes the freedom to exploit others. Ironically, it is the economic freedom of the white minority in South Africa, or the one per cent in the world, that deprives the vast majority of real economic and social opportunity. Though it might seem heretical to suggest it, economic freedom is thus at heart a neoliberal concept.

Contiguous with the rise of the EFF has been the political rupture of the Congress of South African Trade Unions (Cosatu), accelerated by the refusal of its largest affiliate, Numsa, to participate any longer in the masquerade of the ANC/SACP/Cosatu 'Alliance', leading to its expulsion in November 2014. In the Declaration of its Special National Congress, held in December 2013, Numsa resolved to explore establishing a movement for socialism 'as the working class needs a political organisation committed in its policies and actions to the establishment of a socialist South Africa' (Numsa 2013). In keeping with this resolution, at a conference on socialism in April 2015, Numsa revived the call for 'socialist alternatives' to neoliberalism and capitalism. Then, in a meeting of the Central Committee in April 2015, Numsa resolved 'to forge ahead with the creation of a Marxist–Leninist revolutionary working class party' (Numsa 2015).

Given that it is only 20-odd years since capitalism 'triumphed' over socialism with the fall of the Berlin Wall, the collapse of the Soviet Union (USSR) and its client states in East Europe, it is remarkable how the scales have now shifted against neoliberalism. The pyrrhic victory of old capitalism was used to unleash neoliberalism which now stands accused by tens of millions of people of failing to meet their basic needs, creating gross inequality and jeopardising the future of the planet through environmental destruction (see, for example, Sassen 2014). In the context of what Satgar describes in chapter one of this book as 'an unprecedented civilisational crisis with multiple systemic dimensions: the systemic crises of capitalist civilisation,' there can be no question that alternative political and economic systems merit serious investigation and research.

As opposed to economic freedom, 'socialism' (however we understand it) is an idea that is much more palatable to, and in tune with, social justice because it is based on solidarity of the poor, the elimination of exploitation, and ultimately, equality.

Yet, as debates about 'socialist alternatives' recommence, it is crucial that the Left looks deeply into its own morally and politically compromised soul. It is also important to be objective and evidence-based, rather than to allow the wish to be mother to the thought. For example, capitalism, whilst still characterised by repeated crises, whilst still unable to disentangle itself from the 2008 financial crisis, is far from being on its last legs. With the eyes of vast multinational companies now on Africa and China, there remains ample opportunity for capital to exploit growing markets and new technologies in the years ahead.

The global one per cent leave in their wake ever greater inequality, war, waste and social and environmental degradation, but capitalism itself is nowhere near its last great crisis. Marx's argument that capitalism would ultimately collapse on its own internal economic contradictions at the same time as creating a more progressive class, the working class, that would usher in a more rational form of economic and social organisation no longer holds.

In addition, the proponents of a socialist alternative to neoliberalism still have a lot of explaining to do. They cannot overlook the history of 'socialism' in the twentieth century. Academics and historians may have found explanations for the degeneration of the world's first socialist government, the former USSR, and other forms of twentieth-century socialism (Williams and Satgar 2013). But for millions (if not billions) of poor and working-class people, socialism remains associated with dictatorship and failed economies. There is both scepticism and fear, and these fears about both its anti-democratic and economic form cannot just be dismissed.

Launching a new struggle for socialism without being clear about what this means and how that struggle must deepen democracy, rather than stifle it, has the potential to divide the poor from what left-pretenders (who have long made their peace with the capitalist class) call their 'class enemies' as well as from legions of middle-class people who now have a self-interest in a fairer society and a common interest with the poor. As Kumi Naidoo, the outgoing director of Greenpeace, and others have argued, it is essential that the struggle now be as inclusive as possible such 'that we break down the silos and centre the debate on a joined-up approach where human rights, human development and human security are seen as the interdependent tenets that they are' (Naidoo 2010: 20).

The research that Numsa proposes must take into account that many of the great economic and political theorists of socialism, particularly the famed quartet of Marx, Engels, Lenin and Trotsky, lived in a vastly different world, under a qualitatively different stage of capitalism and development. Programmes and plans that were put forward as solutions in the early and mid twentieth century, aiming for example to 'nationalise the commanding heights of the economy', need to be reconsidered in the globalised, financialised economy of the twenty-first century. Inviting new scorched-earth policies by those who can literally flick switches to prompt financial crises can help no one.

In addition, socialists must take cognisance of 'new' issues which were not at the forefront of nineteenth- and twentieth-century political theory, including the environment, gender equality, and equal employment of women and of people with disabilities. Finally, let's be honest, Marxism was a western-European notion, an idea that was developed largely without references to other great cultures and civilisations that, at that time, lived outside the boundaries of the world known by Marx and Engels.

Let me not be misunderstood: there is no doubt that there is a need for greater worker and citizen control over 'finance' and the conduct of multinational corporations. However, there needs to be a deeper examination of what instruments and organisations might exist to democratise both the production and the distribution of the wealth that the working class creates. Amongst other things, we need a far more sophisticated trade unionism than exists at present.

Finally, in a fashion much less choate than Numsa or EFF, recent years have seen the revival of campaigns led by social movements and NGOs. Social movements like the TAC, Equal Education (EE) and the Social Justice Coalition have tied their demands to realising the human rights in the constitution and to the notion of social justice in particular. They have been criticised from the Left for 'reformism' and particularly for using the law and the courts. Yet despite this criticism, many of these campaigns have been able to mobilise large numbers of people and, as I illustrate briefly below, win significant social reforms for the poor.

The Treatment Action Campaign is a case in point

The TAC was formed in late 1998. From the outset its campaign for access to anti-retrovirals (ARVs) for people living with HIV referred constantly to ensuring access to affordable medicines as being a duty on the state arising from section 27, the constitutional right of 'everyone to have access to health care services'. In the face of ANC-led AIDS denialism and pharmaceutical company profiteering (Loff and Heywood 2002), the TAC argued that section 27 created a duty on government to use its regulatory powers to take 'reasonable measures' to regulate the price of essential medicines so as to make them more affordable. TAC's methods simultaneously involved demonstration, political education in communities and mobilisation, building alliances with health workers and scientists, using the media and using the courts.

In post-apartheid South Africa, TAC reinvented the art of using the courtroom as a forum for political trials of both public and corporate power. For example, the announcement of TAC's arrival on the global stage took place in 2001 as a result of its successful attempt to enter the litigation brought by 39 multinational pharmaceutical companies challenging the South African government's amendment of the Medicines Act to allow generic competition, parallel importation of medicines and the setting up of a pricing committee. The admission of TAC as an *amicus curiae* (friend of the court) led the companies to withdraw their legal action in April 2001 (Heywood 2002), leading to rapid downward pressure on ARV prices that, in the subsequent decade, made it possible for about 10 million lives to be saved (Loff and Heywood 2002).

However, the political trial for which TAC is best known was the case against the South African government over access to the ARV Nevirapine. In the late 1990s, clinical trials had convincingly proven that this medicine could reduce the risk of HIV transmission between a pregnant woman and her child by up to fifty per cent. TAC's two-year political campaign for a policy and plan to use the drug to prevent mother-to-child HIV transmission (PMTCT) culminated in a judgment of the Constitutional Court in July 2002. This combination of law and mobilisation marked a turning point in the national response to the HIV epidemic. Commentators and academics who have subsequently analysed TAC's campaign often do so superficially, as if it all hung on the court case. They write as if the PMTCT campaign ended with the handing down of the judgment by the court, or as if it were the judgment that delivered the much-sought-after ARV programme. They betray ignorance of legal and non-legal strategies that have continued unrelentingly since then (Heywood 2005).[2] During all this time TAC was also painstakingly building a democratic social movement, working with the communities where its members lived. TAC's methods involved using personal stories to build empathy and solidarity; engaging in policy debates with the advantage of evidence, and, when necessary, using the courts to raise public awareness of an issue, thereby broadening support (Heywood 2015).

The results of this sustained campaign are indisputable. HIV is almost the only area of public policy where there has been a continual roll-out and improvement of public services (see Heywood 2009). In fact, in the sphere of HIV, TAC has been able to achieve social justice/substantive equality: people with HIV have equal access to ARVs regardless of class or gender. So far, this is the only post-apartheid campaign for rights that has achieved this. According to official statistics, 3 million people receive ARV medicines through public health facilities; life expectancy has increased again to over 60 years; the risk of HIV transmission of a mother to her infant has decreased to fewer than three per cent of pregnancies.

After TAC's victory in the Constitutional Court in 2002 several other social movements have also linked their campaigns directly to rights in the constitution, although not every campaign has involved a concurrent political mobilisation. This has included issues about housing rights, particularly the right not to be evicted, access to sufficient water and the right to basic education. Significant victories have been won in the courts and on the streets.

In relation to access to housing, a succession of judgments changed the balance of power between property owners and their tenants or people who occupy or live on the property. Legal action brought by organisations like Socio-Economic Rights Institute of South Africa (SERI) has made it more difficult to arbitrarily evict people, thereby rendering them homeless.

In relation to the right to basic education, campaigns that have either used or threatened to use the courts have brought millions of textbooks as well as furniture to schools and seen the finalisation of binding Minimum Norms and Standards for School Infrastructure. They have also contributed to the eradication of schools built from mud.

These campaigns vindicate the idea of combining social mobilisation and constitutional law as a means to advance social justice (Budlender, Marcus and Ferreira 2014). Could such an approach, broadened to tackle other issues of inequality and injustice linked to public and private accountability, emphasizing the importance of democratic participation in all policies, perhaps be the basis for Suttner's unifying vision?

Social justice and the transformation of property relations

Many on the Left would argue not. They caricature social justice as a liberal idea, relatively benign and incapable of challenging property relations, and thus the roots of inequality. Its association with law, its enforcement through the courts as well as the streets, becomes another negative. How well does this argument hold up?

Admittedly, the term 'social justice' is often used loosely and imprecisely. It is a political concept that dates back centuries but has come back into vogue in the twenty-first century.[3] Undoubtedly, work needs to be done to agree on what exactly we mean by it. However, groups such as TAC source the power of social justice in the fact that it is referred to as a guiding principle of the constitution. They point out how, according to the constitution's Preamble, social justice is one of the three pillars upon which we must 'establish a society' that can heal the divisions of the past. The other two pillars are 'democratic values' and 'fundamental human rights'.

Unfortunately though, the constitution does not explain what it means by social justice. And, up to this point, neither has the Constitutional Court. That is our job. Nonetheless, in its judgments the Constitutional Court has repeatedly affirmed the centrality of social justice to the duties of government and explored its implications for property relations. For example, in an important 2002 judgment analysing property rights,[4] the Court expressly referred to the fact that individual property rights must be qualified by the mandate that falls on government to realise social justice. How the government does this is for it to decide, but one thing can be said with certainty: where nationalisation of land, property or industry can be justified for 'a public purpose or in the public interest' it is permissible by law as long as it is not done in an arbitrary fashion.

In keeping with this, whenever the Court evokes social justice it is always linked directly to statements about the duty on the state to take concrete measures to realise socio-economic rights, such as access to health care, housing and basic education. In the words of former political prisoner and current Deputy Chief Justice Dikgang Moseneke:

> Of course, democratic values and fundamental human rights espoused by our Constitution are foundational. *But just as crucial is the commitment to strive for a society based on social justice.* In this way, our Constitution heralds not only equal protection of the law and non-discrimination but also the start of a credible and abiding process of reparation for past exclusion, dispossession, and indignity within the discipline of our constitutional framework.[5] (my emphasis)

Part of the Left's fear of being tainted by using the constitution to fight for real transformation appears to be a mistakenly held view that the 'property clause' creates an unbreakable right to private property, and thereby negates the value of the constitution as a whole. The feeling is that the property clause diminishes all other rights because it leaves the greatest cause of inequality and exploitation intact and beyond the reach of transformation.

But in answer, listen to the argument of ANC activist, lawyer and later Constitutional Court judge Zak Yacoob. In the 2013 Helen Suzman Memorial Lecture, Yacoob (2013) was at pains to explain how individual freedom and political equality relate to each another. He stressed that substantive equality may require the government 'to cut back the freedom of some very privileged people to achieve equality in the marginalised sectors of our society'. In his words:

> The law of the jungle, which is about the strong conquering the weak, which is about the rich riding roughshod over the poor, and about the strong taking advantage of the weak, is no longer for us. (Yacoob 2013)

Thus the constitution itself pre-empts criticism that it creates liberal individual freedoms rather than collective rights by tying all the rights in the bill of rights directly to social justice. The problem, however, as Karl Von Holdt (2013: 593) correctly points out, is:

> It is unclear how far the Constitution and the institutions it establishes are adequate to facilitate redistribution [because] the ANC in government has hardly tested the possibilities. It has precluded such innovation through conservative policy choices ... shaped by internal developments, the pressures and inducements from business, international development institutions and 'expertise', and the constraints of global capitalism.

The bottom line is that up to this point, as with land reform, the duties and obligations on private power and how it is exercised in the new democracy have not been properly tested. This is a problem for the Left and not the constitution. Indeed, on the rare occasion when the Constitutional Court has been called upon to unpack the meaning of section 25, it has made its bent clear, stating in the First National Bank case that 'the protection of property as an individual right is not absolute but subject to societal considerations.[6] Similarly, in 2013 in a test case brought by the conservative farmers association Agri South Africa, supported by the right-wing NGO AfriForum who were admitted as an *amicus curiae*, the Constitutional Court pointed out that it is important

> not to over-emphasise private property rights at the expense of the state's social responsibilities. It must always be remembered that our history does not permit a near-absolute status to be given to individual property rights to the detriment of the equally important duty of the state to ensure that all South Africans partake of the benefits flowing from our mineral and petroleum resources.[7]

The fact that there are not more judgments regulating the exercise of private power has more to do with the fact that activists on the Left have not seen the constitution as being of any assistance to struggles. In the words of academic Sandra Liebenberg (2014: 86) 'if socio-economic rights are to fulfill their transformative potential, intensive research and advocacy is required into how various forms of private power and the rules of law that sanction the exercise of such power, affect people's social and economic rights'.

WHY DOES THE LEFT ESCHEW USE OF THE LAW AND COURTS AS INSTRUMENTS FOR TRANSFORMATION?

In September 2014 during a political discussion between Awethu![8] and Numsa, Dinga Sikwebu, Numsa's political education officer, admitted that Numsa had never properly discussed how to use the constitution to advance workers' demands and rights. 'It had been on the agenda two years ago,' he said, 'but had been superseded by other issues.' In the second part of this chapter, I point to the transformative power that is latent in the constitution and argue that the South African Left is making an enormous error by not tapping into this power in its quest for equality.

Perhaps the largest cloud that blocks a view of the transformative potential of the constitution remains an ideological one. Many left-wing activists, trade unionists and academics remain suspicious of the law and the courts, seeing them as part of the apparatus of a hostile capitalist state, controlled and manipulated by 'the class enemy', and inherently unsympathetic to the poor. For the most part, therefore, the constitution is steered around, and social movements like TAC that use it are sometimes frowned upon or regarded as misguided 'reformist' liberals.

Such a quasi-anarchist approach fails to consider that thousands of years have passed since human beings lived entirely outside of legal systems and codified restraints on public and private conduct. Law of some form will necessarily govern human relations for the rest of time. In a capitalist system, where the poor are without power, legal relations are stacked against the poor. But that should not be the end of the story.

Built into the DNA of law is a gene that makes it susceptible to a constant process of evolution. Law as a system of rules and the means for their enforcement is subject to daily, ongoing contestation over its meaning. For 300 years in South Africa, systems of law were imported by the colonisers, both Dutch and British, primarily from Roman Dutch legal traditions. The law was used largely to govern white civilisation and to exploit black labour and land. But today, the evolution of the law is being rapidly propelled forward: centuries of anti-poor law suddenly have to accommodate the pro-poor dictates of the Constitution, particularly the bill of rights. To ignore the law, or to not consciously contest it, is to vacate the field of battle, allowing its use and meaning to become the propriety of those classes and individuals that are antagonistic to and resist social justice.

We need to grow up. It is understandable how after centuries of oppression under law an anti-law attitude, or a variation on it, prevailed amongst the majority of members of the liberation Alliance, and still does. Black people had been dispossessed by law and for the most part prevented from practising the law as a result of the inferior system of 'bantu education' and segregation. With rare exceptions, they were also excluded from protection by the law. Admittedly, the liberation struggle took advantage of a small number of great lawyers and on occasions the enemies' courtroom was utilised as an advocacy platform for the freedom struggle in trials such as the Rivonia trial. Yet, in a movement that until the early 1990s was focused on the seizure of power, very few activists in exile or at home were schooled to see the potential of law as an instrument that could also curtail undemocratic power and advance human rights.

Compounding this were the political traditions that ANC leaders were exposed to and endorsed during their years in exile. A close ideological affiliation via the SACP with the Stalinist states of the USSR and East Europe did not facilitate consideration of democratic constitutionalism as a vehicle for emancipation. When in 1989 the political logjam in South Africa began to break up, aided by the break-up of the Soviet Union, the liberation movement's donning of the clothes of the rule of law and democracy was done somewhat opportunistically, in a hurry, and was certainly not widely internalised. This helps explain why, to this day, there remains a scepticism and distrust of the judiciary, which is frequently caricatured by senior leaders of the ANC as a last redoubt of resistance to democracy, when in reality it has the potential to be one of its most potent instruments.[9]

An alternative tradition? Realising law's transformative possibility
During the 1980s amongst the ANC's allies internally (the United Democratic Front [UDF], Cosatu, the End Conscription Campaign [ECC], Black Sash and others) a different view of law began to develop. This was one which took advantage of law to both catalyse political struggle and to cement some of its victories. This process began as efforts were made at deepening the reforms in labour law that followed the 1979 Wiehahn Commission. The UDF and others also began to work with progressive human rights lawyers to use the

law against the law and knock chinks in the armour of apartheid (Davis and Le Roux 2009). As the trade union movement developed ever-greater momentum in the 1980s labour developed its own approach to law. This led to the rise of a dynamic labour law practice amongst unions, progressive labour law firms like Cheadle Thompson and Haysom, the rise of the annual labour law conference and so on. In 1988 the strike by Cosatu against amendments to the Labour Relations Act also developed a powerful consciousness amongst workers about labour rights.

But despite what Satgar describes as Cosatu's 'sensibility around labour rights' and its efforts to use the constitution to deepen these after apartheid, there seems to have been little analysis within Cosatu about the broader possibilities South Africa's supreme law offered for transformation.[10] Fortunately there was, however, another tradition and approach to the law in existence, although one by no means strong enough to counter the mainstream suspicions of law and the constitution.

As I have already mentioned briefly, throughout the history of apartheid and colonialism there were sporadic instances of *the law being used against the law* to try to remedy some of the evils inflicted by legalised racism. During the 1950s, the use of law for justice began to assume a more organised, theorised and ongoing shape, partly under the tutelage of leaders such as Nelson Mandela, OR Tambo, Bram Fischer and Joe Slovo. In the 1960s and 1970s the suppression of the ANC and imprisonment of its leaders made this approach redundant. Hence the decision was taken to commence the armed struggle and use the law mainly for defensive purposes in political trials.

However, during the 1970s, on the back of the rising trade union movement and the youth revolt, political law was brought back to life to serve the struggle for liberation (Cameron 2014). Pioneering activists like John Dugard and Arthur Chaskalson established organisations like the Centre for Applied Legal Studies (CALS) at the University of the Witwatersrand and the Legal Resources Centre (LRC) and Lawyers for Human Rights. Their aim was to use the law in order to advance the struggle for freedom, particularly through the labour movement and the UDF. During the political negotiations around the constitution, the ANC entrusted individuals from these organisations with significant responsibility and power to guide and advise it on the new shape of law (Spitz and Chaskalson 2000).

By the early 2000s this tradition of human rights law, and the organisations and individual lawyers associated with it, would become the greenhouse for training social justice movements in the use of constitutional law. Organisations like CALS helped seed new NGOs like the AIDS Law Project (Moyle 2015), TAC and later SERI. Latterly, this approach to law and social mobilisation has also catalysed further social movements such as EE.

At the heart of campaigns led by these organisations is the firm conviction that the constitution provides power to South Africa's poor. It is a power that is largely overlooked.

The constitution and its critics: Right and Left

On 10 December 1996 when then-president Nelson Mandela signed the new constitution into law, he effected a revolution of sorts. A supreme rights-based constitution marked a complete departure from the form of the rule of law that had existed under the 1961 and 1983 constitutions. Now the constitution rather than parliament or the Executive was supreme.

However, on another level, Mandela's signature heralded continuity rather than a rupture in the existing power relations. The fierce political uprising against apartheid of the 1980s led to a political and economic crisis that the ruling class sought to head off through a negotiated political settlement. Yet, whilst the constitution fixed in place an entirely new system of government, there was no revolution on the streets. The apartheid regime surrendered political power but the capitalist economic relations – and privilege – that had shored it up remained unchallenged. In the words of Zak Yacoob (2013), the constitution was 'a negotiated compact … a document of compromise'. It averted a racial civil war.

In recent years, as inequality has deepened and economic transformation been blocked, arguments have been made that this compromise, and particularly the constitution that embodies it, has become *the* barrier to far-reaching transformation. Ngoako Ramathlodi, minister of minerals and one-time premier of the province of Limpopo, has described it as 'reactionary' and as the means by which 'power was taken out of the legislature and executive to curtail efforts and initiatives aimed at inducing fundamental changes'.[11] Gwede Mantashe, ANC secretary-general, has echoed his sentiments. Similar anti-constitutional rumblings have also been heard from Julius Malema and the EFF.

Critics from within the government and the ANC attack the framework of governance that the constitution entrenches, particularly the role that may be played by the courts, especially the Constitutional Court, in either curtailing or directing executive action that is found to contradict the fundamental precepts of the bill of rights. They lament that the courts overstep the boundaries of their powers or that jurists who have an anti-transformation or anti-ANC agenda are abusing their powers. In 2013/14 this resentment was especially focused on some of the state institutions supporting constitutional democracy created by chapter nine of the constitution, and thus sometimes known as the 'Chapter Nine bodies'. For example, in the run-up to the 2014 elections and beyond, the public protector, Advocate Thuli Madonsela, came under sustained assault from the ANC and SACP for her investigation into and report on the corruption at President Zuma's private homestead in Nkandla, KwaZulu-Natal (Madonsela 2013/14). In a milder fashion, the South African Human Rights Commission (SAHRC) was criticised for its 2014 report on sanitation.[12]

However, these opinions are predictable. They emanate primarily from people in the ruling ANC who have a vested interest in having their own power unchecked, those who need a scapegoat onto which to transfer their responsibilities for governmental failure or who merely want to remain unaccountable for their actions. But they are not to be dismissed because they are also linked to a growing authoritarianism and measures such as the Protection of State Security Act, that aim to blunt the constitution's powers.

In the face of enemies like this it is all the more difficult to understand the failure of the Left to appreciate or exploit the power that resides within the constitution. These views range from denunciatory tirades from intellectuals such as Patrick Bond (2014)[13] from the University of KwaZulu-Natal's Centre for Civil Society to the scepticism of Rhodes University-based academic Richard Pithouse (2014).[14] Generally, these academics in the Left warn activists against what they call 'bourgeois legalism' and their 'co-option' into a system that, because we all live under the rule of law, we are all already squarely within. In particular, they hold up the constitution's 'property clause' as evidence that the constitutional compromise has left the spoils of centuries of land theft with the descendants of the thieves.

I have already discussed the 'property clause', but it is important to restate here that it does *not* create a positive 'right' to property for existing property holders. Instead, it protects against arbitrary deprivation of property by the state or private powers (something that the history of apartheid and colonialism demonstrates the poor also require) whilst stating plainly that property *may* be 'expropriated for a public purpose or in the public interest'.[15]

For Bond and others, the constitution-making process was nothing more than a neoliberal ploy to derail revolutionary transformation and control shifts in power so as to keep the poor in thrall. But such arguments overlook the historical facts of the constitution's messy gestation between 1993 and 1996. Undoubtedly, a variety of conservative agendas, agents and elites were closely at work in the making of the constitution. But these agendas had to take account of the huge public expectation that the new legal order would break symbolically and substantively with the past and would speak to the expectations of a free people (see Klug 2000).[16]

My argument is therefore diametrically opposed to the views of both Left and Right. I argue that none of the provisions of the constitution inhibit deep social transformation, not even the 'property clause'. Instead, as I hope to show below, *in theory* the constitution provides the poor with a significant degree of power over both government and the private sector. It is a legal instrument that permits South Africans to continue the political/democratic revolution so as to achieve social and economic equality, rather than simply stop with the formal political equality the constitution ushered in on 7 February 1996.

Thus the problem of powerlessness lies not in constitutional restraints but in the fact that, due to its capture by conservative interests, the ANC government has not taken advantage of the power the constitution bestows upon it and any elected government to advance social justice. Finally, compounding this problem is the fact that South Africa's citizens have, for the most part, been left ignorant of the power the constitution offers and the duties it imposes on the governing party (Fish Hodgson 2015) to pursue economic and political policies that advance human rights and narrow inequality.[17]

On the contrary, therefore, I argue that the constitution has enormous potential to contribute to efforts that aim at social justice, if it is used effectively. Let me now explain why this is so in greater detail.

The power we neglect at our peril

The constitution is South Africa's supreme law. Put simply, this means that the rights in and obligations created by the constitution trump the powers of the president, parliament, any political party, any religion or custom and the Executive. Where there are disputes about law *or conduct* that is considered inconsistent with these rights, the Constitutional Court is empowered to make the final determination about the legality of these acts.

If the constitution were narrowly constructed and did not contain an expansive bill of rights, this fact might not be of great importance. However, as Constitutional Court justice Edwin Cameron (2014) points out in his book

Justice: A Personal Account, many aspects of the constitution's structure and content go far further than constitutions in all other countries of the world. Most significantly, the 'positive duty on all organs of state to protect and promote the achievement of equality' and the rights of 'everyone ... to the full and equal enjoyment of all rights and freedoms', ought to have profound consequences for the transformation of political and economic structures in South Africa.

To try to illustrate my argument, I draw attention now to four particular aspects that make South Africa's constitution revolutionary. These are:

- its applicability to all private, as well as governmental conduct;
- the justiciability of socio-economic rights and social justice, meaning that disputes between people and the government about issues such as access to health, housing and basic education can be taken to, and decided by, a court of law;
- the power given to the Chapter Nine institutions to ensure accountability and
- the injunctions that it makes regarding good governance.

The constitution governs the conduct of private power and mandates economic transformation

If people in South Africa are to be freed from poverty and inequality and if social justice is to be achieved, then all the historical causes of inequality must be confronted. Or, in the words of Chief Justice Mogoeng Mogoeng in a 2013 judgment examining the meaning and purpose of the Mineral and Petroleum Resources Development Act, there is:

> *a constitutional imperative* to transform our economy with a view to opening up access to land and natural resources to previously disadvantaged people ...[18] (emphasis added)

Apartheid was not just a legal system for white people's political domination but also a form of capitalism that accrued wealth and assisted economic exploitation in a thousand and one painful ways though the migrant labour system, the creation of landlessness, its support to the gold-mining industry and so on. Consequently, class inequality almost exactly correlates with racial inequality: apartheid gave economic freedom to the white minority and left the majority exploited by or else completely outside the economy.

Yet 21 years after the ANC was elected to government under a new demo-cratic dispensation in 1994, disproportionate economic power still resides with property owners, landowners and those who accumulated wealth in the past. Economic power, largely maintained through private ownership of capital, is frequently and illicitly used as the basis for maintaining political influence, unregulated party political funding being one of the most egregious examples of this. In turn, political influence is used to sustain unequal conditions and permit the continued transfer of wealth or resources created by labour into the hands of a few. Gold and platinum mining are a fine exemplar of this.

However, in respect of economic power the constitution makes it clear that its rules do not only apply to the government. The bill of rights also binds 'natural and juristic persons if, and to the extent that it is applicable, taking into account the nature of the right and the nature of any duty imposed by the right'. If we decipher the legalese it means simply that companies too are bound by duties to respect and protect fundamental rights. Laws that have already been passed by parliament to give effect to these principles include the Promotion of Equality and Prevention of Unfair Discrimination Act as well as the Prevention of Illegal Evictions Act. More recently, and of course controversially from the perspective of business, is the Promotion and Protection of Investment Bill.

My argument is that had civil society used these and other laws effectively, the constitution could have been an instrument to try to ensure that private conduct aids the constitution's vision of a society where there is equality, dignity and a progressive move towards social justice. But it has not.

Consequently, whilst we have made much sound and fury about inequality in the last two decades, the concentration of ownership and wealth has enor-mously intensified.[19] Matters that seek to regulate or restrict corporate power, except when it relates to contractual disputes between companies, have rarely been brought to the courts. Activists have largely failed to monitor corporate lawlessness and profiteering at the expense of fundamental rights. Challenges to the mining, banking, food or financial sector have rarely been heard or evaluated by the courts. However, where they have, the courts have usually supported reasonable measures the government is entitled to – indeed, which it is under a positive duty to take – to narrow inequality. Almost the only area where this has happened has been in relation to access to affordable medicines including, but not limited to, ARVs needed by people living with HIV.

Finally, it is also important to remember that economic power is not the only power requiring transformation. Inequality also exists in gender relations, particularly with men's disproportionate power; in discrimination on the grounds of ethnicity, of religion and in relation to certain customary and religious practices. Such discrimination also underlies economic inequality. Overcoming inequality must therefore be understood as a larger, more multi-dimensional task than was imagined.

In this regard there has been some limited progress. For example, there have been a number of successful judgments in cases brought by civil society asserting women's and spousal rights in relation to property inheritance, including under customary law. As a result of litigation brought mainly by SERI, there is now an extensive body of new law that limits the power that private property owners previously held to evict tenants or occupiers and which requires alternative housing or negotiations to govern final decisions on eviction (Liebenberg 2014).

These tidbits are pointers to a power we could command to far greater effect in the quest for economic transformation.

The constitution requires the government to respect, protect, promote and fulfill a range of socio-economic rights

One of the distinguishing aspects of the constitution is the bill of rights, (contained in its Chapter Two), and the inclusion within it of socio-economic rights, specified as the rights to 'adequate housing', 'health care services', 'social security and appropriate social assistance', 'sufficient food and water' and 'a basic education'.[20]

At the time of the writing of the constitution there were debates within legal academia as to whether the inclusion of such an extensive set of instructions relating to socio-economic rights was fundamentally undemocratic. Legal activists and academics, such as Dennis Davis, argued that doing so would rob a democratically elected government of its own power to decide between different policy choices, priorities and the allocation of public resources (see Davis 1992; Mureinik 1992).

However, the counter to that argument, then and now, is that the constitution does not prescribe *how* policy must be made or resources utilised, only that there *must* be progressive improvement in people's access to a list of public goods that are non-negotiables in so far as they are now declared to be 'rights'. Were this constitutional prescript to be obeyed there would be a continuous narrowing of inequality. The economic freedom expected by the sixty-six per cent majority who voted for the ANC in 1994 was precisely in access to health care, housing, food, education and so on. The inclusion of such economic rights in the constitution, therefore, was actually a means to bind every future government to meeting this expectation and to prevent their non-delivery. It thus crystallised the will of the people into an inviolable legal contract.

Contrary to what some have argued, these rights are more than just a wishlist or set of symbols because each of these rights is justiciable, meaning that if there is a dispute between people and the government about their meaning or the measures government should take to achieve them, this can be resolved by a court.

Further, socio-economic rights are not just set out as a constitutionally recognised list but they are linked to an injunction – a legal instruction – that they should be 'progressively realised' by 'legislative and other measures' taken by the government 'within its available resources'. Section 237 of the constitution adds further that '*all* constitutional obligations *must* be performed diligently and without delay' (emphasis added).

Consequently, in the words of Zak Yacoob (2013):

> it can never be said that any government in this country, whichever political party it is motivated by, if it is to be constitutionally compliant, can ever say that they have the option whether to take the measures to ensure that people who were disadvantaged in the past are taken forward, protected and advanced. Government MUST do so.

In essence, although obviously not framed in this language, the bill of rights should be regarded as a compulsory mandate on any government to implement policies and budgets that advance social justice. I would argue that the National Development Plan (NDP), which was endorsed by the Cabinet in 2013, waters this duty down. It should be carefully assessed as to whether it goes as far as the constitution requires in its plan to transform South Africa, as well as whether the NDP envisages using the full legal armoury of powers to regulate the economy that are provided for in the constitution.[21]

The constitution is often criticised from the Left for linking rights to 'available resources'. But it is important to note the existence of a small number of rights which are not qualified in any way, including quality basic education and children's rights. The Constitutional Court has already stated that the government has a duty to find the resources to make these rights immediately available to all who need them.

Let's look at education. In recent years there has been *exposé* after *exposé* regarding the poor quality of basic education, as well as mounting evidence of very poor learning and teaching. In the 2014 Annual National Assessments of Grade nine learners, for example, the average result in a mathematics test was ten per cent.[22] However, it has only been in the last few years that social movements like EE as well as human rights organisations like SECTION27 and the LRC have begun to mobilise to create awareness that the government is under a duty to do everything possible to achieve the right to basic education immediately. This is different from rights such as health or housing, which the government is permitted to realise progressively and 'within its available resources'. Organisations like EE and SECTION27 are trying to catalyse a mass movement for radical and immediate investment in and improvements to school infrastructure so as to improve the quality of schooling.[23]

Shockingly, despite the extremely poor quality of paediatric health-care services, there has been no campaign to demand that there be a definition of the 'basic health care and social services' that all children in South Africa are immediately entitled to.

As a starting point at least, the rights listed in the constitution make it clear on which issues citizens can expect the government to take measures to achieve equality. It is incumbent on social justice activists to monitor and challenge the sufficiency of these measures, and to expose and challenge conduct by the private sector that undermines these rights. To a very limited degree, we have seen this happen in relation to housing, basic education and most effectively in relation to access to medicines for HIV. However, there remain huge issues – such as the right to sufficient food and water – on which there has been no progress at all and where campaigns have been weakened by the fact that they do not take advantage of the constitution.[24]

The constitution demands accountability of public officials

I have already made several references to the Chapter Nine institutions: the public protector, Human Rights Commission, Commission on Gender Equality and the auditor general. My argument here is simply that their wide-ranging powers add another string to the people's bow and can assist in promoting accountability.

But for most of the short life of our democracy these institutions have been ineffective, hamstrung either by timid leadership and/or insufficient budgets. Research has shown that amongst ordinary people there is little awareness of their existence, never mind their powers. The vital information on issues such as spending by government departments or local municipalities that is gathered and published by the auditor general, is seen as not related to people's lives.

However, under the tenure of Advocate Thuli Madonsela the potential power of these bodies has been very publicly demonstrated. Before Madonsela's tenure there was little public awareness of the public protector's office. Its previous incumbent, Lourence Mushwana, kept the institution obscure and largely irrelevant and, when called upon, it is alleged that he used it to cover-up wrongdoings by the ruling party, rather than to unravel them. However, the current public protector's investigation and recommendations into public spending on the private presidential homestead in Nkandla have considerably raised its profile and so provoked the ire of the ruling faction in the ANC (Madonsela 2013/14).

The problem once again, though, is that these institutions are not understood by the Left as part of the schema for ensuring social justice and transformation that has been created by the constitution. Thus resort to them is generally infrequent, ad hoc and marginal. There has been little critical engagement to test their powers, defend their independence or to demand that parliament provide them with budgets sufficient to carry out their mandates.

Yet another sword has been left in its scabbard.

The constitution describes the 'basic values and principles' of lawful government

Finally, in its chapter on Public Administration, the supreme law of South Africa set out the 'Basic values and principles governing public administration', values which it says must apply 'to every sphere of government; organs of state; and public enterprises'. It is relevant to quote these in full:

- 'A high standard of professional ethics must be promoted and maintained
- Efficient, economic and effective use of resources must be promoted
- Public administration must be development-oriented
- Services must be provided impartially, fairly, equitably and without bias
- People's needs must be responded to, and the public must be encouraged to participate in policy-making
- Public administration must be accountable
- Transparency must be fostered by providing the public with timely, accessible and accurate information

- Good human-resource management and career-development practices, to maximise human potential, must be cultivated
- Public administration must be broadly representative of the South African people, with employment and personnel management practices based on ability, objectivity, fairness, and the need to redress the imbalances of the past to achieve broad representation.' (Constitution s 195)[25]

I hope that in the sections above I have been able to illustrate the latent power that resides in the constitution. But ultimately, the achievement of social justice will depend on whether the citizenry test this new power or not. For this to happen, two things are necessary.

The first is that there must be popular knowledge of the bill of rights and the power that it places in people's hands. The second is that there must be a much greater degree of access to legal services. At this point, change is stymied by the fact that neither exists.[26]

So, despite the constitution's guarantee to 'everyone' of a right 'to have any dispute that can be resolved by the application of law decided in a fair public hearing before a court or, where appropriate, another independent and impartial tribunal or forum' (Constitution s 34), access to legal services is as blighted by inequality as access to other human rights. Although Legal Aid South Africa has grown into an impressive network of lawyers and justice centres, employing the largest number of attorneys of any organisation in South Africa, it provides legal services primarily in criminal matters.[27] When it comes to civil or human rights issues, poor and middle-class people are largely unrepresented, dependent on the Chapter Nine bodies (if they are aware of them) or NGOs providing legal services.

If common purpose could be found to address these two deficits in the democratic project, of a general lack of knowledge of the bill of rights and lack of access to legal services, the results would have a multiplier effect on empowering citizens to have greater control over their lives.

CONCLUSION: TOWARDS A NEW POLITICS OF STRUGGLE FOR RIGHTS AND SOCIAL JUSTICE

In order to conclude this chapter, let me make the following points. The effectiveness of the constitution in bringing about far-reaching economic and political transformation depends primarily on civil society and political organisation, not on lawyers or even the highest judges. Yet one would have thought that a supreme law that makes such sweeping commitments and binds government so tightly to a duty to fulfil human rights would be regarded as a gift by every stripe of social justice activist. A rich body of social justice law has come into being in the last 19 years and continues to develop rapidly. The text of this jurisprudence, and the opportunities it creates (or doesn't), requires much deeper consideration by the Left.

My argument is not that all campaigns should be channelled through the courts. Neither am I seeking to encourage an illusion that this powerful piece of paper is self-enacting, self-sufficient or wipes away social contradictions. The courts are but one part of democracy, not democracy itself. They are still peopled mainly by white men, who are as corruptible as politicians and equally capable of making wrong and unjust decisions. The judiciary is susceptible to both threat and favour. As a result, the success of the constitution's vision of social justice depends entirely on whether people take advantage of it at every level: through exercising rights to freedom of expression and association; through advocacy campaigns for rights via engagements with national, provincial and local government; in the processes of policy formulation; and in order to identify and answer research questions.

South Africa is at a crossroads. The year 2015 finds the ANC in disarray and the vast majority of South Africa's people still mired in grinding poverty. Whilst the rich consolidate their wealth the poor remain blighted by corruption and failures of service delivery.

Against this backdrop there appear to be promising harbingers of a different future. In December 2014 in Johannesburg, a Preparatory Assembly of the United Front (2014) was organised and hosted by Numsa, and a formal launch is planned for late 2015. But regrettably, the United Front has so far failed to recognise the constitution as an instrument for achieving transformation. It has not yet offered up the type of unifying vision called for by Suttner.

In this chapter I have argued that the vision Suttner and many others call for should be constructed around a deeper understanding of social justice and that the most potent instrument that exists to advance this vision is the constitution. Reluctantly, I predict that without it, deepening inequality and authoritarianism, of one form or another, risks overwhelming the struggle for democracy and equality.

Let us accept that the term 'social justice', therefore, refers to *a society that is just in the way it distributes resources.* It refers to *achieving substantive equality* between people, regardless of class, race, gender or ethnicity. This is different from the more limited concept of justice which relates to the right of individuals and which forms the basis of much of criminal and civil law. Thus, whilst the bill of rights lists as *individual* socio-economic rights goods such as health services, housing, sufficient food and water and basic education, they are goods that 'everyone' or 'every citizen' is entitled to. They are therefore collective rights and the existence of social justice as a lodestar in the constitutional firmament requires of government the just prioritisation and allocation of societal resources, including finances, to ensure that there is equity in access to these rights.

This makes human rights a common good. It also brings the practical meaning of social justice very close to the equalities many people associate with socialism.

The struggle for social justice is therefore a struggle for equality. Without equality in access to health-care services, housing or basic education it is nigh impossible for people to live with dignity and to have autonomy. Inequality also negates their ability to participate as active and informed citizens in our participatory democracy. Thus the wheel comes full circle. Participatory democracy requires an active citizenry, which in turn necessitates social justice because only people whose fundamental rights are respected and fulfilled, who have dignity, can be fully free to participate as informed and empowered citizens in democratic process. Democracy, human rights and social justice thus come to depend upon one another.

It is on this basis that I now argue that the focus of the Left should be on a struggle for social justice, that is, for the full gamut of constitutionally enshrined human rights which, as they are realised, will create a more socially just and politically empowered society. Seizing hold of the power already provided to people by the constitution could and should constitute the 'unifying vision' called for by Suttner and many others.

ACKNOWLEDGEMENT

The author would like to acknowledge the following persons for helpful comments on drafts of this chapter: Edwin Cameron, Heinz Klug, Gilbert Marcus and Vishwas Satgar.

NOTES

1   Suttner, R. 2014. 'Building unity to restore democratic rule'. Accessed 31 March 2014, http://www.dailymaverick.co.za/article/2014-03-31-op-ed-building-unity-to-restore-democratic-rule/.

2   This included serving papers for contempt of court in late 2002 after certain of the provinces, Mpumalanga in particular, only grudgingly implemented the order; going to court to gain access to the implementation plan for the provision of ARVs in late 2003; setting up a new network to monitor implementation, known as the Joint Civil Society Monitoring Forum in 2004; replacing this forum with another one, the Budget Expenditure and Monitoring Forum at the point in 2009 when it became clear that corruption combined with poor budgeting was the main threat to medicines provision; mobilising and bringing legal action around prisoners' rights of access to medicines in 2006; working with the government to re-establish the South Africa National AIDS Council and to develop the 2007–2011 and then 2012–2016 National Strategic Plans on HIV, tuberculosis and sexually transmitted infections.

3   For a description on the occurrence and evolution of ideas about social justice, see http://en.wikipedia.org/wiki/Social_justice.

4   *First National Bank of SA Ltd v Commissioner for the South African Revenue Services (SARS) 2002 (7) BCLR 702* (16 May 2002). Available at http://www.safli.org/za/cases/ZACC/2002/5.pdf.

5   *Minister of Finance and Other v Van Heerden (CCT 63/03) [2004] ZACC 3; 2004 (6) SA 121 (CC); 2004 (11) BCLR 1125 (CC); [2004] 12 BLLR 1181 (CC)* (29 July 2004). Available at http://www.saflii.org/za/cases/ZACC/2004/3.html.
More recently, in a speech given to mark 20 years of democracy, Moseneke (2011) said: 'Let's slaughter a few shibboleths. The Constitution does not protect property it merely protects an owner against arbitrary deprivation. Deprivation that is not arbitrary is permissible. The property clause does not carry the phrase: "willing buyer: willing seller" which is often blamed for an inadequate resolution of the land question. The state's power to expropriate does not depend on the willingness of the land owner. The compensation may be agreed but if not, a court must fix it. The compensation must be just and equitable and not necessarily the market value of the land. Market price is but one of five criteria the Constitution lists for a court to set fair compensation. The property clause is emphatic that the state must take reasonable measures, within available resources, to enable citizens to gain access to land on an equitable basis.'

6   *First National Bank of SA Ltd v Commissioner of SARS; 2002 (7) BCLR 702.*

7   *Agri South Africa v Minister for Minerals and Energy, 2013 (4) SA 1 (CC); 2013 (7) BCLR 727 (CC).* Available at http://www.saflii.org/za/cases/ZACC/2013/9.html.

8   See https://www.facebook.com/AwethuSocialJustice.

9   For example, in a revealing interview with the *Sowetan* newspaper, ANC Secretary-General Gwede Mantashe claimed: 'There are many things happening in the judiciary that will only be seen in 10 years' time. One of the things that is dangerous: The independence of judiciary and separation of powers must never be translated into hostility, where one of those arms becomes hostile to the other. My view is that there is a great deal of hostility that comes through from the judiciary towards the executive and Parliament, towards the positions taken by the latter two institutions.' Accessed 8 August 2015, http://www.sowetanlive.co.za/news/2011/08/18/full-interview-ancs-mantashe-lambasts-judges.

10   Vishwas Satgar, comment on first draft of this chapter, December 2014.

11   Ramathlodi, N. 2011. ANC's fatal concessions, *The Times*. Accessed 1 September 2011, http://www.timeslive.co.za/opinion/commentary/2011/09/01/the-big-read-anc-s-fatal-concessions.

12   Within days of its release, the SAHRC (2014) report on the right to access sufficient water and decent sanitation in South Africa was attacked by the minister of water and environmental affairs as 'outdated, baseless and misleading'.

13   In Bond's (2014: 462) article he variously describes the constitution as a law that 'facilitates inequality because it serves as a mythmaking, deradicalising meme, its grounding in property rights typically trumps activist claims to human (socio-economic) rights.' After a factually inaccurate 'analysis' of the use that has been made of the constitution in a small minority of the campaigns that have been brought by progressive civil society, Bond concludes that, 'The exception of AIDS activists' victory in 2002 proves the rule that only in the rarest case – one crafted so creatively around child rights to healthcare, with a very specific micro-intervention (supply of a two-dose life-saving medicine) – can the South African Constitution accompany a broader repertoire of strategies and tactics.'

Bond's ideological antagonism to the constitution leads him to make claims that cannot be supported by facts. For example, he explains the genesis of the profoundly important bill of rights as being 'seen as permissible by capital and leading politicians for the constitution to also include empty rhetoric about not only civil and political rights, but also socio-economic rights' after what he quotes ANC leader Ronnie Kasrils as calling a 'Faustian pact' had been concluded by the ANC leaders and capital to simultaneously protect property rights (Bond 2014: 463).

However, it is important to distinguish between a phantasmal polemic, based on romantic notions of people's power, and a reasoned and evidenced-based analysis. Peculiarly for an academic, Bond does not appear to have actually studied (or possibly even read) the judgments of the Constitutional Court or the constitution itself; neither has he analysed the actual methods of those social movements that have successfully or unsuccessfully invoked the constitution to achieve change. This would be fine if Bond's mission was purely to sword-play with straw men, but its tragedy is that it not only overlooks but delegitimises a source of power for the poor.

Strangely, he projects blame for growing inequalities and 'concessions to capital' onto individuals like current ANC Deputy President Cyril Ramaphosa, ignoring what were in reality extremely powerful class and economic forces, which succeeded precisely because there was no strategy from 'the Left' to recognise or counter them.

Interestingly, in the concluding paragraph of his article, Bond (2014: 480) does recognise the need for a constitution, 'a law of the land that ensures systemic oppression is truly a thing of the past'. But what he overlooks is that the current constitution does regulate power, and whilst it does give 'capital' some rights, it also creates a framework for ongoing contestation and challenging of economic policy, and forms of land and property ownership that can achieve social justice.

14   Pithouse (2014) adopts a more nuanced attitude to the constitution, which he admits he has not studied, mainly criticising an over-reliance on the courts which he tellingly says are 'not democratic institutions', overlooking the fact that they are not meant to be.

15   For the full text of section 25 (the property clause), see http://www.gov.za/documents/constitution/chapter-2-bill-rights#25.

16   In the remaking of a country's legal system it is impossible for either all the benefits or risks of a political and law-making process to be envisaged in advance. However, one enormous benefit of the certification process undertaken by the newly appointed judges of the Constitutional Court, including progressive and activist judges like Arthur Chaskalson, Kate O'Regan, Albie Sachs and Pius Langa, was that it allowed South Africa to import into its new constitution the most modern thinking and understandings of human rights and governance to be had on the planet at that point.

17   Fish Hodgson's 2015 article cites a study revealing 'only 46% of people in South Africa have heard of the existence of either the bill of rights or the constitution. Only 10% of people have ever read the Constitution or had it read to them'.

18   *Agri South Africa v Minister for Minerals and Energy, 2013 (4) SA 1 (CC); 2013 (7) BCLR 727 (CC)*. Available at http://www.saflii.org/za/cases/ZACC/2013/9.html.

19   A 2015 report by New World Wealth reveals that South Africa has 46 800 millionaires with a net worth of over US$1million. Their combined wealth amounts to US$184 billion. In the years of the global financial crisis, between 2007 and 2014, the number of millionaires rose from 526 to 639, and the number of billionaires increased by fifty per cent. See S Govender, Rise of the ultra rich reveals a tale of two nations, *Sunday Times*, 17 May 2015.

20   Socio-economic rights are distinguished from civil and political rights, such as the right to vote, to demonstrate, to form unions, to freedom of expression, which are also contained in the bill of rights. In reality, however, they are inseparable. The ability to enforce socio-economic rights depends heavily on respect for civil and political rights.

21   I believe the NDP falls short of meeting constitutional requirements for far-reaching transformation towards equality (see Heywood 2013).

22   See http://www.education.gov.za/Newsroom/MediaReleases/tabid/347/ctl/Details/mid/2929/ItemID/4115/Default.aspx.

23   For a description of EE's campaign, see https://www.equaleducation.org.za/campaigns/minimum-norms-and-standards. See also SECTION27 submission on Minimum Norms and Standards for School Infrastructure, 2014, available at http://www.Section27.org.za.

24   Heywood, M. 2013. 'Food glorious food!' *Daily Maverick*. Accessed 12 August 2013, http://www.dailymaverick.co.za/article/2013-08-12-food-glorious-food/#.VI60PlaKhlI.

25　It is important to note that in an appeal concerning an alleged unfair dismissal where the applicant tried to rely on s 195 of the constitution (the Chirwa case, available at http://www.saflii.org/cgi-bin/disp.pl?file=za/cases/ZACC/2007/23.html& query=Chirwa) the Constitutional Court decided that these principles could not be directly enforced through the courts. Nonetheless, the Court stated that their existence in the constitution means that they create 'valuable interpretive assistance' against which courts can assess government conduct.

26　In 2013 the Foundation for Human Rights interviewed 4 200 people and found only forty-six per cent of respondents were aware of the existence of *either* the constitution or the bill of rights. This figure decreases to thirty-seven per cent in rural areas, forty per cent of farm workers and only twenty-six per cent of refugees/migrants. When interviewees were asked what they did the last time that they felt their rights were violated, sixty-five per cent of people said 'they did nothing' (Foundation for Human Rights 2015). Research published in 2014 revealed that in South Africa there is one lawyer per 2 176 people, compared to Brazil where there is one lawyer per 326 people (Klaaren 2014).

27　Legal Aid South Africa is an independent statutory body established by the Legal Aid Act. According to its website (www.legal-aid.co.za), its mission is to 'provide legal representation at state expense … to those who cannot afford their own legal representation. It does this in an independent and unbiased manner with the intention of enhancing justice and public confidence in the law and administration of justice'.

REFERENCES

Bond P. 2014. 'Constitutionalism as a barrier to the resolution of widespread community rebellions in South Africa'. *Politikon: South African Journal of Political Studies*, 41:3, 461–482. Accessed 8 August 2015, http://dx.doi.org/10.1080/02589346.2014.975931.

Budlender, S., Marcus, G. and Ferreira, N. 2014. 'Public interest litigation and social change in South Africa: strategies, tactics and lessons'. Accessed 21 October 2014, http://www.atlanticphilanthropies.org/learning/book-public-interest-litigation-and-social-change-south-africa-strategies-tactics-and-lesso.

Cameron, E. 2014. *Justice: A Personal Account*. Cape Town: Tafelberg.

Davis, D. 1992. 'The case against the inclusion of socio-economic demands in a bill of rights except as directive principles', *South African Journal on Human Rights*, 8 (4): 475–491.

Davis, D. and Le Roux, M. 2009. *Precedent and Possibility: The (Ab)use of Law in South Africa*. Cape Town: Double Storey Books.

Fish Hodgson, T. 2015. 'Bridging the gap between people and the law: transformative constitutionalism and the right to constitutional literacy'. In *Acta Juridica*, edited by M. Bishop and A. Price. Cape Town: University of Cape Town.

Foundation for Human Rights. 2015. Report of the baseline survey on awareness of, attitude and access to, constitutional rights.

Heywood, M. 2002. 'Debunking "conglomo-talk": a case study of the *Amicus Curiae* as an instrument for advocacy, investigation and mobilization'. *Law, Democracy and Development*, 5 (2): 133–162.

Heywood, M. 2005. 'Shaping, making and breaking the law in TAC's campaign for a national treatment plan'. In *Democratizing Development: The Politics of Socio-economic Rights in South Africa*, edited by P. Jones and K. Stokke. Oslo: Martinus Nijhoff Publishers.

Heywood, M. 2009. 'South Africa's Treatment Action Campaign: combining law and social mobilization to realize the rights to health', *Journal of Human Rights Practice*, 1 (1): 14–36.

Heywood, M. 2013. 'The missing link – using the constitution to demand equitable development and distribution: do we need a development plan at all?' Presentation to SWOP breakfast seminar, September 2013. Accessed 8 August 2015, http://www.wits.ac.za/academic/humanities/events/breakfastseminars/21070/breakfast_seminars_second_semester_2013.html.

Heywood, M. 2015. 'The Treatment Action Campaign's quest for equality in HIV and health: learning from and lessons for the trade union movement', *Global Labour Journal*, 6: 3.

Klaaren, J. 2014. 'The cost of justice'. Briefing paper for Public Positions Seminar. Accessed 8 August 2015, http://wiser.wits.ac.za/event/public-positions-history-and-politics-cost-justice.

Klug, H. 2000. *Constituting Democracy: Law, Globalism and South Africa's Political Reconstruction*. New York and Cambridge: Cambridge University Press.

Liebenberg, S. 2014. 'Socio-economic rights beyond the public-private law divide'. In *Socio-Economic Rights in South Africa: Symbols or Substance?* edited by M. Langford, B. Cousins, J. Dugard and T. Madlingozi. Cambridge: Cambridge University Press.

Loff, B. and Heywood, M. 2002. 'Patents on drugs: manufacturing scarcity or advancing health?' *American Journal of Law, Medicine and Ethics*, 20: 4: 621–631.

Madonsela, T. 2013/14. 'Secure in comfort: Report of an investigation into allegations of impropriety and unethical conduct relating to the installation and implementation of security measures by the Department of Public Works at and in respect of the private residence of President Jacob Zuma at Nkandla in the KwaZulu-Natal Province'. Report of the Public Protector. Report No. 25 of 2013/14. Accessed 20 March 2014, http://www.publicprotector.org/library%5Cinvestigation_report%5C2013-14%5CFinal%20Report%2019%20March%202014%20.pdf.

Moseneke, D. 2014. 'Reflections on South African constitutional democracy, transition and transformation'. Accessed 12 November 2014, http://www.mistra.org.za/Library/ConferencePaper/Documents/Moseneke%20Keynote%20Address%20at%20the%2020%20Years%20of%20Democracy%20Conference%2012%20-%20 13%20November%202014.pdf.

Moyle, D. 2015. *Speaking Truth to Power: The Story of the AIDS Law Project*. Johannesburg: Jacana.

Mureinik, E. 1992. 'Beyond a charter of luxuries: economic rights in the constitution', *South African Journal on Human Rights*, 8 (4): 464–474.

Naidoo, K. 2010. 'Boiling point: can citizen action save the world?' *Development Dialogue*, 54. Accessed 12 April 2014, http://www.daghammarskjold.se/wp-content/uploads/2010/07/dd54_high.pdf.

Numsa. 2013. 'Special National Congress Declaration' 17–20 December 2013. Accessed 8 January 2015, http://www.numsa.org.za/wp-content/uploads/2013/12/SNC-Declaration-final-copy.pdf.

Numsa. 2015. 'Central Committee Statement'. Accessed 8 June 2015, http://www.numsa.org.za/article/numsa-central-committee-statement-2/.

Pithouse, R. 2014. 'South Africa: after the end of our innocence'. Accessed 10 January 2015, http://www.sacsis.org.za/site/article/2146.

Preparatory Assembly of the United Front. 2014. 'Declaration of the Preparatory Assembly of the United Front'. Accessed 15 December 2014, http://www.numsa. org.za/article/declaration-preparatory-assembly-united-front/.

SAHRC. 2014. 'Report on the right to access sufficient water and decent sanitation in South Africa: 2014'. Accessed 8 August 2015, http://www.sahrc.org.za/ home/21/files/FINAL%204th%20Proof%204%20March%20-%20Water%20%20 Sanitation%20low%20res%20(2).pdf.

Sassen, S. 2014. *Expulsions: Brutality and Complexity in the Global Economy*. Cambridge, MA: Harvard University Press.

Spitz, R. and Chaskalson, M. 2000. *The Politics of Transition: A Hidden History of South Africa's Negotiated Settlement*. Johannesburg: Wits University Press.

Vavi, Z. 2014. 'Zwelenzima Vavi's open letter to the SACP'. Accessed 17 December 2014, http://www.numsa.org.za/article/response-comrade-jeremy-cronin-open-letter-leaders-members-south-african-communist-party-sacp-zwelinzima-vavi-general-secretary-congress-south-african-trade/.

Von Holdt, K. 2013. 'South Africa: the transition to violent democracy', *Review of African Political Economy* 40 (138): 589–604.

Williams, M. and Satgar, V. (eds). 2013. *Marxisms in the 21st Century: Crisis, Critique and Struggle*. Johannesburg: Wits University Press.

Yacoob, Z. 2013. 'The Constitution: A liberal democracy and patriotic criticism'. Helen Suzman Memorial Lecture. Accessed 10 January 2015, http://hsf.org.za/ resource-centre/lectures/hsf-memorial-lecture-2013.

CONCLUSION

Vishwas Satgar

Dogmatic Marxism reduces the contemporary capitalist crisis to an economic one. Reducing this crisis simply to economic factors is not very different from the ideological discourses emanating from mainstream economic commentators and analysts. This volume does not reject the importance of economic mechanisms and processes in contributing to the crisis of capitalism, but argues that it is not sufficient to merely hold up declining profit rates, output levels, or the presence of financialised practices to explain it. This volume breaks new ground in understanding the complexity, totality and spatial spread of the contemporary capitalist crisis. Many of its features are unprecedented, such as the climate crisis and peak oil. For many activists as well as movements and progressive scholars, this historical specificity is crucial for a compelling analysis. The contributors to this volume rise to this challenge to show what is new and distinctive in contemporary capitalism's crises and how these crises are understood among global left forces.

Beyond thinking about capitalism's crises, a number of chapters in the volume highlight the emergence of new forms of resistance, which challenge neoliberal capitalism with a new politics and new institutional political forms. This takes us beyond twentieth-century vanguardist politics. Social movements that have emerged over the past few decades are driving struggles from below in relationships with left think tanks, parties, alliances and trade unions. The chapters in this volume highlight a post-vanguardist politics, practice and imagination in the making among the new global Left and as part of the new cycle of resistance. At the same time, some of the cases in the volume also demonstrate that where the mass democratic impulse from below is curtailed by left parties, like Brazil's Workers' Party, contestation through the streets and mass symbolic actions, including voting for the opposition to challenge technocratic class pacting at the top, are all possibilities. In places such as India, where the Left has demonstrated a dogmatic and formulaic vanguardist politics in its approach to national politics, this has ended in disaster. The unwillingness to rally and unite an array of progressive social forces from below has opened the way for right-wing fundamentalist forces to capture mass discontent while continuing neoliberalisation, despite its limits in economic terms and its negative social impacts.

In South Africa, the African National Congress (ANC)-led Alliance, in its vanguardist orientation, has consistently managed and eviscerated mass, working-class aspirations, as it has neoliberalised and globalised accumulation. The state-capital-labour relationship underpinning this process was ruptured by the Marikana massacre of mineworkers by the ANC state. This conjunctural development has inaugurated significant working-class political realignment.

The telling lesson in all these experiences is simple: a left project wanting to shift the relations of force today has to be consistent about democratically aligning mass social forces from below while ensuring that the logic of state power strengthens mass-led transformation. Anything short of this deepens co-option by capital's 'passive revolution'. At the same time, the democratic alignment of mass forces from below contains the prospect of utilising the crisis to open up the space for systemic alternatives and trajectories beyond neoliberal capitalism. These are crucial insights contained in the chapters in this volume.

RETHINKING CAPITALISM'S CRISES

For most dogmatic Marxists, the conception of capitalism's crises and the various political economy analyses shared in this volume about the spatial dynamics of the capitalist crises are easily dismissed as anachronistic. Put differently, the analyses in this volume do not speak in the abstract categories of crisis associated with classical Marxism. Moreover, for many in society it is either denialism or catastrophic thinking that frames the responses to capitalism's contemporary logic of marketisation and the destruction of life, both human and non-human. These are responses that undermine the role of human beings and, ultimately, a strategic class agency in the present. This volume demonstrates that it is necessary to analyse contemporary capitalism's crises from the standpoint of recognising that these crises are the result of capitalism's class and imperial practices, in the context of transnational techno-financial accumulation (1973 until the present). These crises are socially constructed and can be overcome through class struggle. By suggesting class struggle, this does not mean evoking jaded and outmoded ways of advancing transformation of the capitalist system. Resistance today is conjoined to capitalism's crises and is also shaped by the contradictions, limits and crises of contemporary global capitalism. An effective resistance is able to use these crises to find exits and solutions that build a new, popular and working-class hegemony to sustain life.

At the same time, the perspectives in this volume appreciate that capitalism is not in a singular economic crisis or what is popularly referred to as the 'global financial crisis'. Global capitalism is not experiencing a narrow economic crisis which can merely be fixed by cranking up the growth machine and allowing the market to continue on its path of business as usual. While the financialised chaos of contemporary capitalism might be its most visible expression of crisis, capitalism's crises today are multiple and exist at different levels of the global system. These crises have their roots in how production, trade and finance are organised around short-term profit horizons but they cannot be adequately explained by these dynamics. To appreciate the specificity of the crises, however, it is important to be less abstract and to look at concrete tendencies and dynamics. In this volume, we look at the multiple dimensions of capitalism's crises by focusing on how crises register at the systemic level of capitalist civilisation, in multiple spatial locales (US, Europe, Brazil, India and South Africa) and at a conjunctural level in terms of the neoliberal class project. The volume shows how many activists, movements and left think tanks around the world are also thinking in these terms.

TRANSFORMATIVE ALTERNATIVES AND CLASS STRUGGLE

Dogmatic Marxism does not appreciate the new contradictions of capitalism's crises that have to be harnessed to class struggle. Instead, dogmatic Marxists purport a narrow, abstract and productivist 'reform versus revolution' politics as part of responding to the capitalist crisis in which the working class is limited to fighting for reformist concessions within the system or fighting to overthrow capitalism in a revolutionary moment. For many movements today, this bifurcated formulation of struggle does not capture the dynamism and range of struggles that are happening across the world. Today's global and national struggles have given rise to a transformative politics that appreciates the weaknesses, contradictions and limits inherent in capitalism's crises. Transformative politics uses capitalism's crises against it to create space and to engender the conditions for systemic transformation. Moreover, such a transformative politics seeks to rebuild popular and working class-capacities from below to advance a new political economy analysis or critique, to advance systemic alternatives, to deepen democracy and to invent democratic political instruments.

The chapters in this volume contribute to this new debate through highlighting a range of issues: a new conception of the systemic crises of capitalist civilisation; a critique of methodological nationalism and varieties of capitalism; a critique of the global South as the dynamo for global accumulation, particularly Brazil and India; a critique of neoliberalism's narrative of high labour costs and labour aristocracy, such as in South Africa; and a critique of left orientations that eschew democratic instruments found in progressive constitutionalism. Moreover, a number of chapters identify various systemic alternatives that are driven by class struggle, such as the solidarity economy, democratic public-sector reform, decentralised participatory budgeting and structural reform. All of this is tied to deepening democracy through contesting ideological discourses through left think tanks, promoting trade union capacities for worker-controlled politics, advancing a rights-based conception of social justice, and constructing systemic alternatives through a mass-driven democratic politics.

With regards to inventing political instruments, there is clearly a shift to new political forms that are neither social democratic nor communist. A postvanguardist imagination is shaping and developing new ways of organising mass collective will and creating multiple political forms capable of advancing class struggle on different terrains and fronts. In the US the emergence of Occupy Wall Street demonstrated how mass popular discontent can be galvanised through a process of mass-based participatory democratic politics. This provided spaces for prefiguration and experimentation to ensure the alternative was lived as part of struggling. Moreover, such a politics demonstrated the use of symbolic power, the meme of the 99 per cent versus the 1 per cent, as a means to rupture hegemonic discourses legitimating elite notions of the 'American Dream'. At the same time, such a political form also displayed its own particular limitations in terms of how mass popular struggle should be institutionalised and threw up challenges of interpretation. It raised a number of questions. Was a shift required in Occupy toward a more goal-oriented mass politics? Can the results achieved be construed as success given the conservative class and power structure prevailing over American society? Did Occupy play the historical role it needed to play given the limits it faced?

On the other hand, in the European context left political parties like Syriza in Greece and Podemos in Spain are consciously trying to ensure that power-as-domination is subordinated to power-as-transformative-capacity from below. Many challenges and questions plague these political initiatives, including the recent setback faced by Syriza when the Troika (European Central Bank, European Commission and International Monetery Fund) refused to soften the terms of debt restructuring. However, it is clear that inventing a political instrument capable of constituting power from below and wielding state power at the same time cannot be in the strategic frame of electoralism or state-centric vanguardism. A new mutation and frontier of political invention is being achieved with these initiatives. There are no guarantees of success but valuable lessons, whether of success or failure, are being learnt that take the global Left beyond dogmatic formulas of what constitutes a left political instrument.

This volume and the terrain of transformative politics it identifies poses serious challenges to working-class-led politics. Both the empirical cases studied and the current cycle of global resistance suggest three important issues to be considered for a renewed democratic Marxist politics. In the first instance, the volume as a whole suggests that the working class has to be willing to consider and embrace new analyses of capitalism's crises. This means that the everyday lived experiences of poverty wages, hunger, environmental degradation and democratic narrowing have to be connected and challenged as part of a broader approach to working-class struggles rather than simply understanding working-class struggles in narrow silos. In practice, this would entail fighting the struggle on different fronts and building allies on all these fronts.

Second, organisation together with capacity building for grassroots struggles and organising are key. All the chapters dealing with trade union politics affirm the need to renew traditions of worker control and working-class collective leadership as crucial. This also means valorising not only political parties as political instruments, but appreciating that every institutional form expressing class and popular agency, from movements, unions, left think tanks, to networks, fronts and alliances are as important as political parties. The left political party today should not embody the monopoly of truth, knowledge and understanding of how to advance the struggle. Instead, a thoroughly democratic left party has to learn, negotiate, work with and even be led by other political forms with which it chooses to align. Its function in such a configuration might be very limited in a democratically agreed approach to the political division of labour. This is the 'modern prince' of a new type, not the party, but the sum total of all the political forms united around a common vision, political project and strategy.

Third, systemic alternatives have to be grasped and understood. This requires rethinking debates and learning from various social forces that are championing such alternatives, from the unemployed, the homeless, small-scale farmers and the landless, to solidarity economy movements, food sovereignty movements and climate justice movements, amongst others. Moreover, it means looking to international experiences to critically learn lessons about contemporary struggles and to extract relevant insights. This is not about merely copying but about translating left experiences in a context-specific way. All of this does not mean the state is unimportant, but in a conjuncture in which states are failing to address the systemic crises of capitalism and in which various constraints face internationalised states, a new mass politics from below is important alongside and on the terrain of the state. It is this transformative politics that could overcome capital's passive revolution and create the conditions for a fundamental response to the crises of capitalism. Without a new transformative politics confronting capital, it will triumph but in the process it will destroy human and non-human life. The logic of marketisation and destruction will prevail.

THE CLIMATE CRISIS AND JUST TRANSITION

The conjuncture of systemic crises and transformative resistance is going to define the terrain on which class and popular struggles unfold. With climate change and its attendant climate shocks, capital can prevail in this conjuncture, through co-opting, dividing, rolling back and even ensuring states' discipline any expression of militant resistance. Capital's passive revolution will prevail as the logic of marketisation and destruction continues until all life falls victim to ecocide. This is the business-as-usual scenario with green capitalism asserted as the solution to the crises of capitalist civilisation. At the same time, another imminent possibility exists given that green capitalism is a false solution and will not address the systemic roots of the crisis. This possibility would be driven by the ecocidal logic of global capitalism and US-led imperialism such that a fascist solution prevails. This simply means the global passive revolution is also likely to give way to an outright and naked supremacy to ensure capital prevails as a geological force and the system is maintained, despite its destructive logic. These possibilities in the conjuncture of systemic crises and transformative resistance require further analysis. This volume has broken the ground analytically for this to happen and has demonstrated that it is not only climate change that changes everything but, instead, the multiple crises of capitalist civilisation and the various levels through which it is expressed. At the same time, the climate crisis and the just transition it requires have to be more deeply interrogated from a democratic Marxist perspective. Does Marxism have an adequate conception of nature or is it anthropocentric? Is Marxism inherently productivist and hence part of the problem? Or, is Marxism capable of going beyond productivism to provide intellectual resources and strength to transformative politics to confront the climate crisis dimension of capitalism's crises? These are questions to be explored in the next volume in the democratic Marxism series.

CONTRIBUTORS

Andreas Bieler is professor of Political Economy and fellow of the Centre for the Study of Social and Global Justice in the School of Politics and International Relations, University of Nottingham, UK. He is author of *The Struggle for a Social Europe* and a co-editor of *Free Trade and Transnational Labour*. He maintains the blog *Trade unions and global restructuring* at http://andreasbieler.blogspot.co.uk/.

William K Carroll is a member of the Sociology Department at the University of Victoria. He established the Interdisciplinary Program in Social Justice Studies in 2008, serving as its director to 2012. He has written extensively on the political economy of corporate capitalism, social movements and social change, and critical social theory and method. His books include *The Making of a Transnational Capitalist Class* and *Corporate Power in a Globalizing World*.

Isham Christie is currently a labour organiser with the Writers Guild of America East. He was intimately involved very early on in Occupy Wall Street. Before this he was an anti-war and environmental activist with the New Students for a Democratic Society. Isham has studied philosophy, social theory, and cinema at the City University of New York – Graduate Center.

Sumangala Damodaran is an economist in the School of Development Studies at Ambedkar University Delhi. She has taught at the University of Delhi, worked as a researcher at the Institute for Studies in Industrial Development and as a consultant with the National Commission for Enterprises in the Unorganised Sector of the government of India. Her research has been in the area of industrial and labour studies.

Leah Hunt-Hendrix is an associate fellow at the Institute for Policy Studies. She is also a co-founder of Solidaire, a movement support organisation, and she is on the board of directors of three organisations, including the New Economy Coalition. Her work is focused on political economy, corporate power, and movement strategy.

Mark Heywood is the director of SECTION27, a human rights and public interest law organisation that campaigns to advance the rights to health-care services and basic education in particular. He is also a founder and leader of the Treatment Action Campaign. He has edited several books on health and human rights and published over 250 articles on politics, law, human rights, health, HIV and culture.

Jamie Jordan is a PhD candidate and fellow of the Centre for the Study of Social and Global Justice in the School of Politics and International Relations, University of Nottingham, UK. His research interests are in the areas of International Relations and International Political Economy, focusing particularly on the regional political economy of Europe.

Niall Reddy is a research affiliate of the Alternative Information Development Centre and a post-graduate researcher at the Centre for Civil Society at the University of KwaZulu-Natal, South Africa. His work focuses on distribution and inequality, precariousness, wage-led growth and organising strategies.

Alfredo Saad-Filho is professor of Political Economy at the School of Oriental and African Studies, University of London, and was a senior economic affairs officer at the United Nations Conference on Trade and Development. He has published extensively on the political economy of development, industrial policy, neoliberalism, democracy, alternative economic policies, Latin American political and economic development, inflation and stabilisation, and the labour theory of value and its applications.

Vishwas Satgar is a senior lecturer in International Relations at the University of the Witwatersrand, South Africa, and has been involved in grassroots activism for over three decades. He is the editor of the Democratic Marxism series and has published widely on Africa, South Africa, transnational alternatives and Marxism. In 2015, he received the Distinguished Achievement Award of World Political Economy of the Twenty-first Century for initiating and editing the Democratic Marxism series.

Hilary Wainwright is a fellow of the Transnational Institute in Amsterdam which supports her work on democracy-driven, public service reform; the development and spread of the solidarity economy and new, more deeply democratic and participatory forms of political organisation. She is a director and co-editor of *Red Pepper* magazine and website. She has written several books contributing to new radical thinking on the state, political organisation and political economy.

INDEX

Page numbers in italics refer to information in illustrations.
Page numbers with 'n' refer to information in notes.

A

accountability 93, 266–267
activist intellectuals 50–51
   and alternative thinking 60
   a dual crisis 51–53
   and knowledge and praxis 55–57
   opportunities and openings 66–70
   passive revolution and anti-passive
      revolution 53–55
   prognoses and challenges 59–66
   understandings of the crisis 58–70
   see also transnational alternative
      policy groups
African National Congress
   as critical of the constitution 260
   and democratic constitutionalism 257
   discontent with 246
   distrust of the judiciary 257, 272n9
   labour and liberation 214–215
   and National Democratic Revolution
      235
   and National Development Plan
      237–238, 239
   and neoliberalism 215, 231, 237
   vanguardist orientation 278
agency 6–10, 42–45
agriculture
   food-system crisis 36–39
   India 195, 196, 202, 204, 209n5
   industrial 37–38
   and oil 39
   peasant farming 38
   and transnational corporations 37–39
   United States 36–37
Alinsky, Saul 89–90

Alternatives International 60, 67
Alter Summit movement 113
Amin, Samir 58–59
anarchism 88, 92, 93
ANC *see* African National Congress
anti-passive revolution 53–55, 65, 71
anti-war movement, US 82
Arab Spring 8, 83, 85
austerity
   and Occupy Wall Street 83–84
   and structural adjustments 59
   and Syriza 148
   see also Eurozone, austerity in
authority, rebellions against 126
autonomy of social movements 137, 155,
      157

B

Back of the Yard organising 89–90
bailout packages 78, 104
banks 31
   bailout of, US 78
   Eurozone 97, 99, 113
   India 190, 199–200, 203
   see also financial institutions
Barchiesi, Franco 214–215, 229
bargaining council system, SA 230–231
basic education, SA 253, 266
'Battle of Seattle' 140
Benn, Tony 133, 136
Berlusconi, Silvo 142, 143, 144
bill of rights, SA 255, 263, 264–266, 268,
      270, 272n13, 274n26
Black Economic Empowerment 236
Blair, Tony 130, 137

Bond, Patrick 60, 260, 272n13
Brangsch, Lutz 65, 68
Brazil 166–167
   Cardoso administration 166, 169,
     173, 177
   confluence of frustrations 183
   Dilma Rousseff's administration
     177–179
   distribution under Lula and Dilma
     179–183
   economic growth rates 171, 175–177,
     177–178, 179–180
   financial sector 171
   first Lula administration 172–175
   fiscal deficit 176
   foreign capital flows 170, 178
   import substitution industrialisation
     167–168, 169
   inflation 168, 170–171, 177, 178, 183
   jobs created 179–180
   Left, challenges to 182–185
   mass protests 182, 183–184
   mensalão corruption scandal 174
   Movimento dos Trabalhadores Rurais
     Sem Terra 173, 179, 186n5
   neo-developmentalism 175, 177, 183,
     186n4
   neoliberalism 168–172, 173, 175
   poverty in 177, 179–180, 181–182,
     186n8
   private investment 176, 177, 178
   procedural democracy 172
   Real Plan 170–171
   second Lula administration 175–177
   social spending 173, 177, 180–181
   state-led investment 175–176
   transitions to democracy, neoliberal-
     ism 169–172
   wages 170, 180, 181
   weakening of working class 171–172
   Workers' Party (PT) 173–175, 179,
     182, 183, 184
BRICS 59
Butler, Judith 85–86

C

Candeias, Mario 64, 69–70
capital
   and democracy 41
   fictitious 51–52
   as a geological force 25–26
   mobility of 136
   valorising money into 22–23
capitalism 3
   apartheid as form of 262

crisis dependence of 51
crisis 'of ' and crisis 'in' 64, 74n5
expansion of 100–101
future opportunities for 249
green capitalism 73, 68, 283
reforming of 4–6, 44
separation of 'political', 'economic'
   40
capitalism, crisis of 1
   aberration to self-regulating market
     20
   catastrophism or transformative mo-
     ment? 42–45
   as civilisational in scope 72
   and class struggle 5–10
   current crisis 3–6, 20
   cyclical or systemic crisis 3–6, 20–21
   democratic Marxist perspectives on
     11–16
   as economic crisis 277
   and financialisation of the global
     economy 4
   general or systemic 3
   and global financial crisis 279
   in the global South 4
   the Great Depression 1, 3, 5
   political-economic and political-
     ecological 53
   and profitability 51
   propagandising of 2
   psycho-cultural aspects of 73
   rethinking 278–279
   'stagflation' crisis, 1970s 3
   as subjective 60
   and weaknesses of Marxist theory 2
   see also activist intellectuals, under-
     standings of the crisis
capitalist civilisation
   accumulation 28–30
   crucial dimensions of 30
   periodising the making of 27–30
capitalist civilisation, crises of 4–5, 21,
    30–31
   analysis of and transformative resis-
     tance 43–44
   climate crisis 32–34
   financialised chaos 31–32
   food-system crisis 36–39
   peak oil 34–36
   securitisation of democracy 39–42
Caracazo 7
carbon trading 33
Centre for Applied Legal Studies 258
Chartist tradition 151–152
   and a common enemy 151–152

and equivalential and differential demands 151–152
and the Left today 153
and Podemos 153–155
and Syriza 153, 155
Chávez, Hugo 7, 8
China, contrast with India 189, 202–203
Chomtongdi, Jacques Chai 60–61
civil society 88, 90–91, 126, 135, 269
class
and race, SA 214
restructuring of 9
and right-wing government, India 204–206
see also working class
class struggle
and crisis of capitalism 5–10
and labour in Eurozone 113–116
and localism 71–72
and movements and government 135–136
climate change 32–34, 282–283
catastrophic 66
and passive revolution 282–283
US 32–33
as weapon of progressives 73
Climate Justice Movement 8
cognitive praxis networks 56–57, 57
collective bargaining 83, 105, 108–109, 229, 230
colonialism 27, 28, 29
common good 270
communist parties, Europe 129
Communist Party of India (Marxist) 207
communist traditions, exhaustion of 124
Congress of South African Trade Unions 258
and labour crisis 211, 212, 227, 229, 236
consensus and horizontalism 92–93
conservatising impact of fear 60–61
consumerism 54
Co-operative and Policy Alternative Center (COPAC) 72
core and peripheral development 100–101, 102–104
corporate capture 93, 130, 134, 135 see also transnational corporations
corruption
Brazil 174, 183
Greece 148–149
Italy 142
Cosatu see Congress of South African Trade Unions
counter-hegemony 43–44

courts see law and courts, South Africa
crises 52, 66–67, 80–81
crisis of imagination 60–61

D
debate 158–160
debt 52, 79, 101
decentralisation 207
decoupling 189, 199–200, 206–208, 209n1
Demirovic, Alex 65–66
democracy 62
and law and courts, South Africa 269
market democracy 40, 41
narrowing of, Europe 123
and national security 40–42
procedural democracy 172
representative democracy 88, 91–92
securitisation of 40–42
social democracy 7, 124, 126, 129
see also liberal democracy; participatory democracy
democratic constitutionalism 257
democratic Marxism 11–16
democratic political forms, building new 10
democratic political pedagogy 45
democratising knowledge 126–127
deregulation 78, 105, 130, 190, 197, 201, 225
development, core and peripheral 100–101, 102–104
devolution 207
Dove, Fiona 68

E
ecocide 36, 39, 282-283
economic freedom and social justice 248
Economic Freedom Fighters (EFF) 212, 248
economic growth 73, 74n1
Brazil 171, 175–177, 178, 179–180
India 190–200, 201, 209n3
economic reductionism 21, 24–25
Egypt, Tahir Square movement 8
elites 63, 69, 145, 149–150, 168, 169
'elite capture' 62
elite formation 236–237
equivalential and differential demands 151
European Parliament 126, 149
Europe, Left organisations in transition in 123–124
see also movements engaging with government; Podemos; revolts of 60s, 70s, legacy of; under Syriza

Eurozone, austerity in 97
    and bailout packages 104
    and banks 97, 99
    core and peripheral development
        100–101, 102–104
    dynamics of the crisis 101–104
    and financial institutions 101–102
    and financialisation 103–104
    and Fiscal Compact 107
    fiscal cuts 104–105
    and foreign direct investment
        103–104
    initiatives against austerity 112–116
    liberalisation and globalisation 98–99
    and methodological nationalism
        99–100
    and privatisation 106
    and productivity levels 102–104
    Stability and Growth Pact 106–107
    state, form of 104–108
    and surveillance 107
    uneven and combined development
        98–104
    and Varieties of Capitalism literature
        98–99
    and wage cuts 106–107
    and wage formation institutions
        99–100
Eurozone, labour in 100, 105
    and broader class struggle 113–116
    and collective bargaining 108–109
    Confederation of German Trade
        Unions (DGB) 112
    European Citizens' Initiative (ECI)
        111, 113–114
    European Federation of Public Ser-
        vice Unions (EPSU) 113, 114
    European Metalworkers' Federation
        (EMF) 108–109
    European Trade Union Confederation
        (ETUC) 109, 112
    indignados movements 114–115
    initiatives against austerity 111–116
    losing ground 108–110
    new Marshall Plan 113
    resisting restructuring 110–116
    socialisation of banks 113
    support for internal market 108
    and trade union autonomy 116
    trade unions and labour parties 111
    and transnationalisation 108–109

F
feminism 126
financial institutions

    and Eurozone austerity 101–102
    United States 78, 81
    see also banks
financialisation 29, 31, 65, 197
    and Eurozone austerity 101–104
    financialised chaos 31-32, 43
    and South Africa 224–227
financial regulation 171, 190,191
financial overaccumulation 24, 32
fiscal stimulus, India 203
Focus on the Global South (Focus) 60,
        63–64, 69
food-system crisis 36–39 see also agricul-
        ture
Fordism 29, 30, 36, 128
foreign investment 38, 170
    and Greece 103–104
    India 194, 197, 200–201

G
gender 126, 264
George, Susan 62–63
Germany 70
    cut in welfare system 110–111
    Left in 67–68
    productivity and wage levels
        102–104, 110
globalisation
    and liberalisation, Eurozone 98–99
    and workplace struggles 136, 213
globalised industrial agriculture 37–38
global warming see climate change
Golden Dawn 62
government see movements engaging with
        government; state, the
Gramsci, Antonio
    and crises 52
    and transformative resistance 44
    war of position 44
grassroots struggles 56, 71–72
Great Depression 1, 3, 5, 80
Greater London Council 134, 137
Greece 62, 100
    bailout packages 104
    fiscal cuts 104–105
    and foreign direct investment
        103–104
    Indignados 114–115
    privatisation 104–106, 114, 117, 147,
        149
    productivity levels 103
    Social Solidarity Clinics 115
    see also Syriza
greenhouse-gas emissions 32–33, 39

H

hacking political institutions 137–138, 162n7
hegemonic politics that sustains life 44–45
high and low value-added industries 102–103
historical conjuncture 42–43
HIV/AIDS *see* Treatment Action Campaign
horizontalism and consensus 92–93
Hubbert Curve 34–35
human rights
    bill of rights, SA 255, 263, 264–266, 268, 270, 272n13, 274n26
    as a common good 270
    and obligations 262
    and social justice 254–256
    socio-economic rights 256, 264–266, 270, 273n20
    and water 113–114
hunger by design 38
hydrocarbons boom 35–36

I

ideology 9, 94
    rejection of 89-90
import substitution industrialisation 167–168, 169, 193
India
    agrarian sector 195, 196, 202, 204, 209n5
    banking sector 190, 199–200, 203
    Bharatiya Janata Party (BJP) 205
    break in growth trajectory 192–193
    burgeoning middle class 193
    capital account 200–201
    class and the right-wing government 204–206
    consumption 196, 206
    contrast to China 189, 202–203
    current account 201–202
    decentralisation 207
    decoupling 189, 199–200, 206–208, 209n1
    devolution 207
    economic growth 190–200, 201, 209n3
    economic reforms 192–199
    employment 198–199, 202
    financial liberalisation 194–199, 201
    financial response to the crisis 203
    fiscal stimulus 203
    foreign investment 200–201
    impact of the crisis 199–202
    import substitution industrialisation 193
    industrial growth 193
    inequity in growth 192
    land reform 206, 207
    market-oriented economic reforms 194–199
    metropolitan capital 193, 194, 195
    monopoly 193, 194
    New Economic Policies 192–194
    poverty 195–196
    pro-poor policy 193, 194
    public investment 193
    and purchasing power 192–193
    and Reserve Bank of India 190
    response to the crisis 202–203
    rising capital intensity 198–199
    short-term capital 197–198, 201
    stagnant real wages 199
    structural features of growth 192–199
    sub-prime lending 199–200
    'success' in withstanding the crisis 190–191
    'sunrise' industries 193
    trade openness 193, 196–197
    urban-rural divide 204
indigenous knowledge systems 38
indignados movements 114–115
individualism 61, 90, 158
inequality
    India 204
    and marketisation 26
    and social justice 270
    South Africa 221–223, 262–264
    Spain 159
informalisation 228–229, *229*
intellectuals *see* activist intellectuals
Ireland 100, 102, 104
Italy 105, 107, 163n16
    Rifondazione Comunista 140, 142–143

J

job creation 79, 179-180, 181–182, 226–227

K

Klein, Naomi 73
knowledge
    and authority 126
    democratising 126–127
    indigenous systems 38
    and praxis 55–57
Kuehn, Steffen 64
Kyoto Protocol 33

L

labour
defeat of SA 223–235
and methodological nationalism
99–100
and restructuring 110–116
weakening of 25–26, 105, 108–110,
128–130
see also Europe, Left organisations in
transition in; Eurozone, labour
in; South Africa, labour crisis;
trade unions; working class
labour aristocracy 212, 212–215
labour broking 230, 233–234
labour flexibility 105, 213
labour law, SA 258
labour markets
Brazil 174, 176, 180–181
flexible 105, 145
South Africa 214, 215, 216–223,
227–228, 230–232
Labour Party, Norway 141
Labour Party, UK 132–134, 137
Laclau, Ernesto 151
Lambert, Michel 60, 67
land reform 184, 206, 207, 255
law and courts, South Africa
constitution and its critics 259–261
and democracy 269
and evolution of the law 256–257
and failure of the law 256–257
Left eschewing use of 256–269
and progressive labour law practitio-
ners 258
transformative possibility of the law
257–259
Treatment Action Campaign and the
251–253
see also South Africa, Constitutional
Court
Left, the
agency of 6–10, 43–45
analysis and transformative resistance
43–44
and Chartist tradition 153
eschewing use of law and courts, SA
256–268
in Germany 67–68
response to crisis, US 82–84
and SA Constitutional Court 253–254,
255
state of, United States 82
transformative resistance and hegemonic politics 43–45

see also political parties, radical Left
left populism
and basic security 150
and debate 158–160
defensive action and transformative
capacity 150
importance of 151
and political organisation 158–160
see also Chartist tradition; Podemos;
Syriza
Lenin, Vladimir 27–28
liberal democracy
as global standard 40
origins of 152
problems with 159
and security in US 40–42
liberalisation 98–99, 228–235
India 194–199, 201
liberalism 40
Livingstone, Ken 134, 137
localism and class struggle 71–72
Lucas Aerospace 133
Lula see under Brazil

M

Madonsela, Thuli 260, 267
Malema, Julius 212
Mandela, Nelson 259
Mantashe, Gwede 231, 260, 272n9
manufacturing expansion 167
Marikana massacre 211, 235–238
market democracy 40, 41
marketisation 26, 282–283
Marxism
democratic and crisis 11–16
dogmatic 277, 278, 279
and Occupy Wall Street 89
reduction of crisis to economics 279
reform versus revolution 279–280
relevance of 250
structural determinism 2
and transformative politics 279–282
voluntarism 2
Marx on capitalist crisis 20–21
and abstractions 21, 22–24
Capital 24–26
and capital today 25–26
and destruction and progress 26
and disproportional production, consumption 23
and economic reductionism 21, 24–25
and forces of production 22
limits and challenges to 24–26
and nature 25–26

and new historical tendencies 25
and stages of capitalism 27–28
and technological determinism 22
and underconsumption, overproduction 23
and value of labour power 222–223
Maura, Eduardo 149, 153, 154, 155, 157
McCarthyism 89
media 41, 56, 84–85, 213
mercantile accumulation 28
metabolic rift 25
methodological nationalism 99–100
middle class 60–61, 182, 193
minerals–energy complex, SA 223–228, 236, 237
minimum wage 173, 174–175, 180–181, 228
model thinking 10
Modi, Narendra 205
monopoly 193, 194
monopoly industrial accumulation 28–29
movements engaging with government 131–132
    autonomy of 137, 155, 157
    British Labour Party, trade unions 132–136
    extent of corporate capture 135
    and hacking political institutions 137–138
    and importance of autonomy 137
    intensity of class war 135–136
    internationalisation of the terrain of conflict 136
    mechanisms of marginalisation 136–137
    narrowing space in political institutions 144
    networked political organisation 160
    and new organisational forms 144–145
    and party realities 138–144
    shifting of balance of power 135
    United Kingdom 132–138
    see also under political parties, radical Left

N
National Democratic Revolution, SA 235
National Development Plan, SA 237–238, 239
    and bill of rights 265–266
nationalism, revolutionary 7
national security and democracy 40–41
National Union of Metalworkers of South
Africa
    and Cosatu 211, 212
    strikes 211
    and Tripartite Alliance 212
    and United Front 269–270
nature and Marx 25–26
neighbourhood as locus of power 90
neo-developmentalism 175, 177, 183, 186n4
neoliberalism
    and ANC 215, 231, 237
    appropriation of left rhetoric 63
    Brazil 169–172, 173, 175
    crisis-management strategies 65
    failure of 42–43, 249
    triumph of 6–7
New Labour, UK 137, 138
Norwegian SV 140–142
Numsa see National Union of Metalworkers of South Africa

O
Obama, Barack 91
obesity 39
Occupy movement 79–80, 83
Occupy Wall Street 79, 80
    and Adbusters Magazine 84–85
    and alternative labour movement 94
    and anarchism 88, 92, 93
    and benefits for communities 93–94
    consensus and horizontalism in 92–93
    demand for justice 86–87
    demands of 84–85, 86–87
    and ecological awareness 95
    and encampment 85–86
    and Marxism 89
    and McCarthyism 89
    new advocacy and organising 89–91
    and 'new economy' movement 95
    and New York City General Assembly 84, 85
    and New Yorkers Against Budget Cuts 83–84
    and non-profit sector 90–91
    and the Old Left 88, 89
    and participatory democracy 92–93
    the path ahead 94–96
    and prefiguration 85
    and prefigurative practices 93–94
    and protest against austerity 83–84
    and the Red Scare 89
    and representative democracy 88, 91–92
    and social media 84–85

and solidarity 87–88
three antagonisms of 88
oil
and agriculture 39
peak oil 34–36
organic crises 52–53
and revolution 53–55
and transnational alternative policy
groups 58–59
Organization of Petroleum Exporting
Countries (OPEC) 34
overaccumulation 24, 32
overproduction/underconsumption 23,
196, 206
overregulation, myth of 228–235

P
participatory democracy 207, 270
and Occupy Wall Street 87, 88, 92–93
Participatory Research in Asia (PRIA)
61–62, 68
passive revolution 6, 60, 69, 73
and anti-passive revolution 53–55
and climate 73, 282–283
Patnaik, P 193–194
Pere-Marzano, Nathalie 61, 67
Pithouse, Richard 260, 273n14
pledge-and-review and climate change 33
plutocracy 67, 73, 93
Podemos
anti-elitism of 149–150
and Chartist tradition 153–155
and individualism 159
and language of Left and Right 149
and populism 157
and social movement activism 150
and Syriza 149
political parties, radical Left 138–140
and anti-neoliberal constituency
139–140
debilitating legacy of 140
Norwegian SV 140–142
number of functions in 160
Rifondazione Comunista 140,
142–143
see also left populism; movements
engaging with government;
Podemos; Syriza
populism 151–152
claimed positively and subverted
155–156
and Podemos 157
and Syriza 156–157
see also left populism
Portugal 100, 102–103

bailout packages 104
labour 105
privatisation 106
productivity 102–103
poverty
Brazil 177, 179–180, 181–182, 186n8
India 195–196
South Africa 212, 223, 262
power
and gender 264
neighbourhood as locus of 90
positive 262–268
private 255–256, 262–264
understandings of 124–126
power-as-domination 125–126, 160–162
and globalisation, crisis 130
for power-as-transformative-capacity
126–128
and Syriza 156
power-as-transformative-capacity
125–126, 160–162
and autonomy of social movements
157
and populism 156–157
and Syriza 156–157
and weakening of nationally organised labour 128–130
praxis and knowledge 55–57
precariat 65, 66, 214, 234
precariousness of labour 214–215, 224,
229, 233–234
prefiguration 85
prefigurative practices 93–94
privatisation
and Eurozone, austerity in 106
Greece 104–106, 114, 117, 147, 149
of pensions 65
of water 114, 117
procedural democracy 172
productivity 102–104, 110
property relations 22
and social justice 253–256
South Africa 254–256, 261, 264,
271n5, 272n13
Public Protector 260, 267

R
race 78–79, 214
Ramaphosa, Cyril 235–236, 237
rebellions against authority 126
recession 20, 54, 108, 130
redistribution, SA 255
reform versus revolution 44, 279–280
regulation 129
Brazil 171, 178

Europe 107
and globalised markets 31
India and US 190, 197, 199
South Africa 211, 213, 214, 228
representative democracy 88, 91–92
revolts of 60s, 70s, legacy of 124–131 *see also under* power
revolution
    and organic crises 53–55
    versus reform 44, 279–280
revolutionary nationalism 7
RosaLux 64–65, 70
Russia 100–101

S
SECTION27 266
sectoral determinations 230–231
Seierstad, Dag 141, 142
September 11, 2001 58, 82
shareholder value revolution 225–226
shop stewards 133, 232
skills-biased technological change 221–222
social democratic parties 124, 126, 129
social grants, SA 227–228, 247
socialism
    failures, relevance of 249–250
    and social justice 249
    South Africa 248–249
    Soviet 7
social justice
    and economic freedom 248
    and human rights 254–256
    and inequality 270
    and property relations 253–256
    quest for, South Africa 247
    and socialism 251
    and South African Constitutional Court 253–255
    and Treatment Action Campaign 251
social media 84–85
social movements and NGOs 251–253 *see also* movements engaging with government
social spending, Brazil 173, 177, 180–181
socio-economic rights 256, 264–266, 270, 273n20
Socio-Economic Rights Institute of South Africa 253, 259
solidarity economy 72, 148–149, 156
Solon, Pablo 63–64, 66
South Africa
    competing visions for 246–250
    economic freedom 248
    Economic Freedom Fighters (EFF)
        212, 248
    failure of democratic reforms 247
    and inclusive struggle 246, 250
    levels of protests 246
    Movement for Socialism 248–249
    National Union of Metalworkers of South Africa 248–249
    and promoting democracy 246
    quest for social justice 247
    socialism 248–249
    social movements and NGOs 251–253
    see also Treatment Action Campaign
South Africa, Constitutional Court
    and basic education 253
    and housing 253
    individual freedoms and collective rights 254–256
    and the Left 253–254, 255
    and private power 255–256
    and property relations 253–256
    and redistribution 255
    and social justice 253–255
    social justice and human rights 254–256
    and Treatment Action Campaign 252
    see also law and courts, South Africa
South Africa, Constitution of, 1996 247
    and accountability of public officials 267
    and basic education 253, 266
    and 'basic values and principles' of government 267–268
    bill of rights 255, 263, 264–266, 268, 270, 272n13, 274n26
    Chapter Nine institutions 260, 266–267
    criticisms of 256, 259–261, 272n13
    critics: Right and Left 259–261
    as ideologically unsound 256
    positive power of 262–268
    private power and economic transformation 262–264
    and property relations 254–256, 261, 271n5
    as revolutionary 262
    rights in and obligations created by 262
    and section 25 255
    and section 27 251
    and social justice 245–253, 262, 263, 266, 269–270
    and socio-economic rights 264–266
South Africa, labour crisis 211–212
    anti-labour attitudes 213

and bargaining council system
230–231
and black capitalist class 237
and Black Economic Empowerment
236
and capital flows 224–225
and centralised bargaining 230
and Cosatu 211, 212, 227, 229, 236
and Cyril Ramaphosa 235–236, 237
debates on wage inequality 221–223
defeat of labour 223–235
and downwards adjustment of wages
214–215
Economic Freedom Fighters (EFF)
212
and economic liberalisation 228–235
and employer groups 211
eroded trade union abilities 229–233
and financialisation of economy
225–227
formal-sector workers 212
Global Competitiveness Index 213
and government 211–212
and illegal capital flight 225
and investment 227
and job creation 226–227
Julius Malema 212
labour aristocracy thesis 212–215
and labour broking 230
and labour law 228
levels of strike action 233
and mainstream economic theory
213–214
Marikana massacre 211, 235–238
and media 213
and minerals–energy complex
223–228, 236, 237
and minimum wage legislation 228
myth of overregulation 228–235
and National Democratic Revolution
235
and National Development Plan
237–238
and the National Treasury 238
and neoliberalism 221, 231, 222,
237–238
and a new distributional regime 214
and patriotic bourgeoisie 235–238
and precarious labour 214–215
precariousness of labour 215, 224,
229, 233–234
and race and class 214
and rand instability 225
real wages, post-apartheid *216–220,*
216–221

and SACP 227
and sectoral determinations 230–231
and shareholder value revolution
225–226
and shifts to informalisation 228–229,
229
and shop stewards 232
and skills-biased technological
change 221–222
and social grants 227–228
and state-bourgeoisie 237
Tripartite Alliance 212, 235
and unemployment 226–228
and union co-option 231–232
unionisation 232–233, *232*
United Front 212
wages and unemployment 227
the way forward 239–240
and white monopoly capital 235
South African Communist Party 227 *see
also* tripartite alliance
Soviet socialism 7
Spain 100, 102
Indignados 114–115
Mortgage Victims Platform (PAH)
114–116, 127
unions and social movements 116
see also Podemos
Spivak, Gayatri 92
'stagflation' crisis, 1970s 3
state, the
and capital 31–32, 40, 52, 54, 278,
282
corporate capture 93, 130, 134, 135
form of, Eurozone 104–108
in and against 137–138
see also movements engaging with
government; *specific states*
state-bourgeoisie, SA 237
Stiglitz, Joseph 84, 190
strikes 114, 211, 232–233
structural adjustments 37, 54, 59, 194
structural determinism 2
struggle, current cycle of 7–10 *see also*
class struggle
sub-prime lending 31, 199–200
surveillance 58, 107
Suttner, Raymond 246, 269, 271n1
Synaspismos 145, 146
Syriza 62, 115–116, 126–128, 145–147
and austerity 148
Centre for Public Administration and
Local Government 148
and Chartist tradition 153, 155
and convergence on Syntagma Square

146
    and corruption and clientelism
        148–149
    and Parliament 146–147
    and Podemos 149
    and populism 156–157
    and social roots 147–149
    and young activists 145–146
Syriza, Podemos and left populism
    145–149

T

Tandon, Rajesh 61
technological determinism 22
Thatcher, Margaret 130, 134
trade unions
    autonomy of, Eurozone 116
    and British Labour Party 132–136
    co-option, South Africa 231–232
    eroded abilities, South Africa
        229–233
    internationalisation of 136
    and labour parties, Eurozone 111
    unionisation, South Africa 232–233,
        232
    see also movements engaging with
        government
transformative capacity see power-as-
    transformative-capacity
transformative human agency 42–45
transformative politics
    and Marxism 279–282
    and working class 281–282
transformative possibility of the law
    257–259
transformative resistance 43–44
transnational alternative policy groups
    55–58, 72–74
    beyond crisis, towards a global Left
        70–74
    ideas and beliefs 55–56
    new forms of knowledge and praxis
        55
    and think tanks 55–56
    understandings of the crisis 58–70
transnational corporations 108
    as ecologically destructive 36, 39
    global domination of agriculture
        37–39
    and government 40, 41, 83, 91, 130
    and labour 108, 133, 136
    see also corporate capture
Transnational Institute (Amsterdam) (TNI)
    62–63, 68
transnational techno-financial accumula-

tion 29–30
Treatment Action Campaign 251, 271n2
    and the ARV Nevirapine 252
    building a democratic social move-
        ment 252
    and the Constitutional Court 252
    and the courts 251–253
    methods of broadening support 252
    and pharmaceutical companies 251
    and social justice 251
Treaty of Maastricht 106
triangular employment 230
tripartite alliance
    and National Democratic Revolution
        235
    and National Union of Metalworkers
        of South Africa 212
    and South African labour crisis 212,
        235
    vanguardist orientation 278
Troika and Greece 148, 153
    and privatisation 105–106, 147–148,
        149
Trotsky, Leon 100–101
Tsipras, Alexis 145, 146, 163n25

U

unconventional hydrocarbons 35–36
underconsumption, overproduction 23,
    196, 206
unemployment 79, 223–228
uneven and combined development
    99–104, 111, 117
United Democratic Front 257–258
United Front 269–270
United States
    agricultural system 36–37
    anti-war movement 82
    bailout of banks 78
    banking in 78
    burden of debt 79
    and the climate crisis 32–33
    concentration of wealth 78
    and crises 80–81
    crisis and race 78–79
    crisis and social mobilisation 80
    crisis and students 78–79
    decline of as hegemonic power 31
    deregulation of financial sector 78
    and financial institutions 78, 81
    Left response to crisis 82–84
    liberal democracy and security in
        40–42
    Madison protests 2011 83
    May 12 Coalition 83–84

New Yorkers Against Budget Cuts 83
and peak oil 34–35
and resolving systemic crises 43–44
Seattle protests 1999 82
state of the Left 82
Tea Party 81
youth unemployment 79
see also Occupy Wall Street
Upper Clyde Shipbuilders 133

V
'vanguardist' dyad 2
vanguards 277–278
tripartite alliance SA 278
twentieth century and current 9–10
Varieties of Capitalism literature 98–99
Vavi, Zwelinzima 211
Venezuela 7
voluntarism 2

W
wages
Brazil 170, 180, 181
Eurozone 99–100, 106–107
South Africa 214–215, *216–220,*
216–223, 227
Wallerstein, Immanuel 31
War on Terror 40–41, 58
water

as a human right 113–114
pollution of 39
privatisation of, Greece 106, 114, 149
privatisation of, Portugal 106
referendum on, Italy 106, 114, 144
remunicipalisations of 117
wealth, concentration of
South Africa 262–264, 273n19
United States 78, 79, 94
welfare state 113, 115, 130
worker occupations of factories 133
working class 248–249
current resistance 8–9, 279–282
South Africa 248–249, 278
and systemic alternatives 282
and transformative politics 281–282
weakening of 6–8, 25–26, 171–172
see also labour; trade unions
work ins 133
World Social Forum 7–8

Y
Yacoob, Zak 254, 265
young people 68, 79, 139–140, 248
in Syriza 145–146, 153

Z
Zuma, Jacob 237, 238, 239

www.ingramcontent.com/pod-product-compliance
Lightning Source LLC
Chambersburg PA
CBHW022139020426
42334CB00015B/968